"Nothing but Blood and Slaughter"

The Revolutionary War in the Carolinas

Volume Two
1780

"Nothing but Blood and Slaughter"

The Revolutionary War in the Carolinas

Volume Two
1780

Patrick O'Kelley

Reviews for "Nothing but Blood and Slaughter, Volume One"

"This collection is a chronological listing of everything from small skirmish raids that really aren't much more than bandit attacks, through the major actions of the war in that theater. Mr. O'Kelley includes a very comprehensive Order of Battle of units and leaders for each action with extensive and thorough endnotes. This is the, I say again, T H E best compilation of information on the Southern campaigns that I've seen in decades of reading. He's got it all - literally everything that can be found regarding any action in this theater of war. If you have any interest in the American War of Independence, you really must have this book. Buy it. You'll like it."
  -Jay Callaham
  Brigade of the American Revolution Newsletter

This is not a book that you take home for a good read, but a well-documented reference you keep as a handy tool. If you had ancestors that participated in the battles in Georgia or South Carolina you will find this a useful book. This is an excellent tool for compatriots who are doing history programs for local schools.
  -Brett W. Osborn
  Marquis de Lafayette Chapter, Georgia SAR

The book is written in a terse military style, which only adds to the book. It lists every land, naval, battle or skirmish. I could never make any sense of the fuss about the savage fighting in the Carolinas, until I read this book. I can hardly wait to see what happens to Lord Cornwallis's army when he invades the Carolinas in the following volumes. It is a gold mine of Militia unit information
  - Dwayne Meyer
  Amazon.com Review

MAJ James O'Kelley
ODA 323, 5th Special Forces Group (Airborne), and 1st Infantry
Division, and 1st Cavalry Division, and 2nd Infantry Division
Vietnam 1965 and 1969

SGT Sean O'Kelley
H+S Company, 1st Battalion, 2nd Marines
and
3rd Battalion, 75th Ranger Regiment
Killed 1987

1SG Isaac Ragusa III
4th Battalion, 6th Infantry Regiment, 5th Mechanized Infantry
Panama
and
Long Range Surveillance, 4th Ranger Training Battalion
Bosnia
and
504th Parachute Infantry Regiment, 82nd Airborne Division
Kosovo, Afghanistan and *Iraq*

1SG Herbert Puckett
2nd Battalion, 75th Ranger Regiment
Panama
and
504th Parachute Infantry Regiment, 82nd Airborne Division
Afghanistan and *Iraq*

And gentlemen in England, now abed,
Shall think themselves accursed they were not here;
And hold their manhoods cheap while any speaks
That fought with us upon Saint Crispin's day

We few, we happy few…

"Nothing but blood and slaughter has prevailed among the Whigs and tories, and their inveteracy against each other must, if it continues, depopulate this part of the country"

General Nathanael Greene

PREFACE

In the first volume I covered the Revolutionary War in the Carolinas from 1771 to 1779. I ended that book with the siege of Savannah, a terrible defeat and is considered the *Pickett's charge* of the Revolutionary War. It was the worst defeat for French and American forces in the war.

This volume is written just about the year of 1780. In that year the war in the north had become a stalemate and the British held onto New York. When Savannah fell it opened a back door for the British to mount a major invasion and conquer South Carolina. However conquering a country and keeping it are two different things.

For those who have read Volume One the following will be a repeat of the preface in that book, but it needs to be explained again.

I had to change my way of thinking on what is a battle and what is a skirmish. *The Annual Register or a View of the History, Politics, and Literature for the Year 1781* wrote that "Most of these actions would in other wars be considered as skirmishes of little account, and scarcely worthy of a detailed narrative. But these small actions are as capable as any of displaying conduct. The operations of war being spread over that vast continent…it is by such skirmishes that the fate of America must be necessarily decided. They are therefore as important as battles in which a hundred thousand men are drawn up on each side."

So a major battle in the Revolutionary War would only be a footnote in the War Between the States, but so much more was decided because of it. If an incident is listed as a "battle" then it is a fight between two commanders that have brought all they can to the fight. If an incident is listed as a "skirmish" then it is smaller units that are not with their main command. It is very hard to determine exactly what happened in most of the battles. The accounts were written many years later and from old memories. Newspapers wrote some accounts and the more bloodier details were fabricated for use in propaganda. In many of the accounts, that were written right after the battle, the authors wrote what they saw, but the numbers of casualties or dates may be wrong. This is not a new phenomenon, reading accounts of the communist dead in the Viet Nam War makes anyone wonder if there were any Viet Cong were left alive in the entire country. The numbers of dead and wounded that I list for each battle may vary, depending on which account you read. I have tried to give the most realistic numbers, but in time these may be found out to be wrong. It is the best "guess" I made with the available information. We may never know the true story of the war, but having been in a couple of wars myself, I doubt if anyone will ever really know the truth. All we can do is get close enough and hope that the future shines more light on the subject.

I have tried not to describe the two sides as British and American. To do so would not be correct. There were many battles that were fought entirely by Americans. Some were for the King; some were for the United States. It was said that during the war 1/3 of the people were for the King, 1/3 were for Independence and 1/3 didn't care either way. If you look at the recent Presidential elections you will notice that not much has changed. The nation is still divided into thirds. In the South a better description would be that 40% were for the King and 50% were for the Patriots. For the undecided 10% it was very dangerous not to choose sides.

The different types of troops in the United States forces were Continentals, State Troops and Militia. The Continentals were fighting for the United States and were the regular standing army. Those who joined the Continental army would join for about three years, or the duration of the war. They would be issued an actual uniform and weapon. They would be better trained and disciplined, mainly due to the time spent on drill in camp, and the punishment that could be inflicted if they did not obey the commands. The State Troops fought for the United States and are more like the modern day National Guard. They also enlisted for a specific time period and many had uniforms issued by their State. The Militia were civilians and would show up with whatever weapons they had at home. They would wear civilian clothes and would have officers who might have been in the Continentals at one time. The militia would only show up when called upon to do their duty, and then they would go home. At the start of the war most thought it would be over very quickly, an attitude that is reflected in most wars. The enlistments were for 6 months, and many joined the Continentals. However as the war dragged on for years, the enthusiasm dwindled, and the States had to resort to a type of draft. By the time of this book, 1780, the war had been going on for almost 5 years, longer than the War Between the States, or World War II.

The forces fighting for Royal Government were the Regulars, Provincials, Militia, German Auxiliaries and Indians. The Regulars were the British equivalent of the Continentals. They were the standing army and at the time of the war they were the best-armed and trained army on the face of the earth. Provincials were Americans fighting for the British cause. They were similar to the State Troops of the United States army. They were armed and equipped by the British army and many of their officers were British Regular officers. Loyalist Militia was the same as the Patriot militia. They were Americans fighting for the King.

Many historians commonly call the German Auxiliaries, Hessians, or Mercenaries. However they did not all come from Hesse and they were not mercenaries. Each German soldier went where his Generals told him to, and they did not get any extra money for their time. The only one who profited by their service was their ruler.

The Indians tended to side with the British. To do so would only benefit them because the King had promised that no settler would move west of the modern day Blue Ridge Mountains. If they lost, the United States would take their land. If they won they would be able to keep it.

When the France, Spain and the Netherlands declared war on England, it became a world war. They could no longer devote their entire military might to fight the rebels in America. In something that was similar to the Viet Nam war, public support in England for war dwindled as it went on. Many people and politicians were sympathetic to the American cause.

The main infantry weapon of the war was the musket and bayonet. The musket was smoothbore, meaning that it was not rifled. It had the same range and accuracy, and about the same caliber, as a modern shotgun. Major George Hanger wrote that "A soldier's musket, if not exceedingly ill bored...will strike the figure of a man at eighty yards; it may even at 100; but a soldier must be very fortunate indeed who shall be wounded...at 150 yards, provided his antagonist aims at him...I do maintain...that no man was ever killed at 200 yards, by a common soldier's musket, by the person who aimed at him."

The picture battles being fought in regular lines, and the soldiers firing nice crisp volleys, is not what really happened. A regiment may fire a solid volley with the first shots, but as the battle rages, and the fear, noise and fatigue take over, the men fired in a more ragged manner. A British officer commented on the 1st Foot Guards at Dettingen in 1743, "They were under no command by way of Hyde Park firing, but the whole three ranks made a running fire of their own accord.... The French fired in the same manner, without waiting for words of command and Lord Stair (the allied commander) did often say he had seen many a battle, and never saw the infantry engage in any other manner."

H. Berenhorst described Frederick the Great's army, "You began by firing by platoons, and perhaps two or three would get off volleys. But then would follow a general blazing away - the usual rolling fire when everybody blasted off as soon as he had loaded, when ranks and files became intermingled, when the first rank was incapable of kneeling, even if it wanted to."

During a battle the range would close until it came time to charge with the bayonet. Inspector General of Army Hospitals Robert Jackson wrote that the bullets did not decide the battles. He reflected that when a unit fired "Such explosions may intimidate by their noise: it is mere chance if they destroy by their impression... History furnishes proof that the battle is rarely gained by the scientific use of the musket: noise intimidates; platoon firing strikes only at random; the charge with the bayonet decides the question."

In America both sides had men that used the rifle. There were some Regular rifle regiments, but most of the riflemen were in the militia. Owning a rifle did not make them a sharpshooter, and a myth of the Revolutionary War is that the Americans hid behind rocks and trees to shoot from cover, while the British stood in line, in the open, to be slaughtered. In this war both sides took cover when they could, and both sides had their riflemen. Many times the Americans had to fight in the open, using linear tactics of the day, to defeat the British army. The rifle took longer to load, and it could not hold a bayonet. However the advantage of the rifle is the longer range and the better accuracy. A rifleman, if he was an excellent shot, might be able to hit a target 400 yards away. However a more practical range for the rifle would be 150 to 200 yards.

In this book the spellings of all the towns are done in the same manner as they were spelled in the 18th Century. I have decided to not footnote the source of every single sentence, because to do so would interrupt the description of the battles. I have included footnotes at the end of the book to let the reader know where the information came from. Unfortunately, due to the publisher's format, the endnotes will be all the way at the end, even after the bibliography and the index. This book will contain the bibliography for all three books. I only put the bibliography in a single book, to reduce the number of pages, and to reduce the cost.

Finally I have placed the order of battles in a format that needs to be explained if one is not used to it. If the main commander is General One and his unit is Division Number One, it will look like this:

General One
  Division Number One

Regimental commanders, company commanders and lesser commands would be indented to the right of them, such as this:

General One
  Division Number One
    Colonel One
      Regiment Number One
      Captain One

Patrick O'Kelley

Company Number One

A listing of just an officer's name means it is his command.

Regiment Number One
    Captain One
    Captain Two

Organization for a military unit at the time of the Revolutionary War was the same for both sides. A British regiment would consist of about 500 men. These men would be broken down into twelve companies of about 70 men each. Three of these companies would be the Colonel's Company, the Lieutenant Colonel's Company and the Major's Company. Two of these companies would be the Light Infantry and the Grenadier companies.

The Grenadiers were supposed to be the tallest and bravest of the regiment, and were allowed to wear special clothing, such as the bearskin cap, to identify their elite status. Originally Grenadiers were the shock troops to attack fortified positions, lobbing grenades into the works and chopping their way into the defensive position with axes. By the Revolutionary War they had lost the grenades and the axes.

The Light Infantry was first used in the French and Indian War, but was disbanded afterwards. They made their come back in 1770 and were used extensively in the Revolutionary War. The officers and sergeants of the flank companies carried fusils, a shorter, lighter musket. The other company officers and sergeants carried spontoons, a type of spear, and halberds, a polearm that looked like an axe on the end of a long pole. These were their symbols of rank. By the time the British army returned to the Southern colonies in 1780 the polearms were discarded.

The remaining seven companies would be "hat" companies and would be commanded by a captain. This was a textbook regiment that would not have been seen very much on the battlefield due to losses, and men detailed out to other assignments. Regiments would be placed under the command of a higher officer and would then become Brigades or Divisions. The Patriot army was very similar to the British army, but only a few units, such as the South Carolina Continentals, had grenadier companies. In some battles, such as King's Mountain, some of the "companies" only had six men. Many battles have more than one name. This is because each person who wrote about the incident would give it a different name. Each alternative listing will be in the footnotes. Many of the battles have different dates; some might even be in a different year. For those that do not have a specific date I have listed only the month. Reverend McCalla described this problem of finding a true history, when he wrote, "You never can get a true reliable account of it. Men, even officers, in the same battle, differ greatly in their statements."

FOREWARD

This book is a never-ending quest to attempt to put everything that happened in the Carolinas into print. It is never ending because even as I started publishing Volume One, I found more information to include. Something is always turning up, and there are papers and manuscripts that have not ever been published.

Like Volume One, I have tried to use all primary accounts in this book. It is like being a detective, trying to determine from the evidence what is true, and what is not. In many situations I included all the different versions in the endnotes. For those who have not read Volume One, I highly recommend it, since many of the terms, and tactics are explained. Many of the key players who were Regular soldiers in Volume One, become irregular "partisans" or guerillas, in Volume Two.

While researching this book I had continued help from historians, Park Rangers, Reenactors and other authors. I would like to again thank Larry Babits (author of "A Devil of a Whipping"), John T. Hayes (publisher of the Saddlebag Almanac), John K. Robertson, John Rees, Dan Elliot, and Charles B. Baxley of the Kershaw County Historical Society.

I would also like to thank the reenactors, those who carry the torch. Dave McKissick, Todd Braisted, Jay Callaham, Linea Bass, John White, Robert Sulentic, Brad and Denise Spear, Walt McIntyre, Stephen Gilbert, Brett Osborn, Mark Hubbs, Alex Loggins, and Todd Post.

Finally I would like to again like to thank my wife Alice and my daughters, Cailín, Katy and Adee. I am glad that they continue to put up with my immersion into 225-year-old documents, for several hours each night.

Patrick O'Kelley
Barbecue Township, Harnett County, North Carolina 2004

Contents

1780
"Shout like hell and fight like devils!"

Tybee Lighthouse, South Carolina
21-24 January 1780

To aid in the defense of Charlestown four Continental ships were ordered south from Massachusetts, under the command of Commodore Abraham Whipple. The ships were the frigates *Queen of France* and *Boston*, and the sloops *Providence* and *Ranger*. It took twenty-seven days to reach Charlestown, and the Continental fleet had to pass through a heavy gale northeast of Bermuda. Commodore Whipple arrived with his fleet on the 23rd of December, however the gale had damaged the *Queen of France* so much that a "jury of carpenters" condemned her.

On January 17th Lincoln dispatched two ships patrol between Cape Romain and St. Augustine to give an early warning when any British troopships might approach Charlestown. The two ships, the *Ranger* and the *Providence*, were becalmed outside the harbor for three days. Finally on the 23rd a brig was spotted in the fog outside the bar to Charlestown harbor.

The captain of the Royal Navy brig was decoyed into thinking that the Tybee River was the entrance to the Savannah River. The British brig followed the Continental ships into the harbor and was captured. On board were seventeen reinforcements for the New York Volunteers. The Royal Navy brig was given to Captain Hoysteed Hacker and renamed the *General Lincoln*. Three days after this incident a British ship captured the tender of the *Ranger*, the *Eagle*, right outside the harbor.

At sunrise on January 24th Whipple and Captain Simpson put out to sea and headed south looking for any sign of the British navy. They spotted two Royal Navy sloops and a brig off of the Tybee Lighthouse. The British ships were quickly overtaken and captured.

On board the ships were a few infantrymen, forty light dragoons of the British Legion and the Bucks County Light Dragoons, seven or eight officers, and as many passengers. The ships had been blown off course by a gale off of Cape Hatteras. Two horses were on board, along with the gear for forty more horses, which was all thrown overboard.

Once Whipple saw the approaching British fleet he quickly returned to Charlestown and alerted General Lincoln. The Charlestown Bar was a shallow sand bar from where the rivers emptied into the ocean. It was only four feet deep at points. To navigate around the Bar ships would have to go through narrow channels in the Bar and then sail up another channel, while being under the guns of Fort Moultrie. The Bar was the first line of defense for Charlestown against any naval attacks. Lincoln wanted Whipple to defend the Bar, but Whipple said that it couldn't be done because it was too shallow to allow maneuver room.

Three days later, during another reconnaissance, the Royal Navy chased both of the American ships back into Charlestown harbor. This was the last time the Continental ships left Charlestown harbor.[1]

Fort Johnson, South Carolina
Charlestown Campaign
14 – 16 February 1780

The British were not having much success in the northern theater. After Burgoyne had his entire army captured at Saratoga, General Henry Clinton assumed control of all the British forces in the colonies. When he withdrew from Philadelphia to New York he marched his Regulars overland and encountered Washington's army. The ensuing battle was the longest of the war, the battle of Monmouth Courthouse. The battle was long, but not decisive. The British went into New York, and further operations by them made very little success against Washington's forces.

In the South the British under Archibald Campbell had retaken Georgia, and Prévost had made the French and American forces suffer the worst defeat of the war so far. The successes in Georgia encouraged the British, and Henry Clinton turned his eyes to the South.

Prior to the siege of Savannah Lord Germaine had wanted Clinton to mount an expedition into the South. Clinton did not do it because he needed to have a larger army. He needed to be able to hold New York, Rhode Island and Canada, while he was attempting to conquer the South. An even bigger reason was that Clinton did not know where the French fleets were. Since the French had entered the war the possibility of attack from the sea was very real.

In August and September of 1779 Clinton's first concern was alleviated when 3,800 reinforcements arrived from England. Clinton was worried about an attack by the French and had his troops abandon Rhode Island, bringing 4,000 more men into the New York City.

The French fleet finally materialized in Savannah in September 1779. Admiral D'Estaing united with the Patriot army, and after a bloody defeat at Savannah, the French left American shores. When Clinton learned of the one-sided defeat he immediately put the campaign for South Carolina into motion.

The voyage to the South was not a trip any wanted to repeat. One of the worst winters in the 18th century hit the American coast. The fleet was supposed to have departed on the 19th, but "cold weather and rough water" stopped any ships from leaving. The transport ship *Pan* was destroyed by ice floes pushing into the harbor. Six other transports were damaged by the ice and had to have their cargoes removed to other ships. This took even more time. Finally on December 26th, 1779 ninety British troopships, escorted by fourteen warships, sailed out of New York Harbor bound for Charlestown.

The fleet barely escaped being caught by the ice floes in New York Harbor, when they were caught in a gale that lasted for four days. The British fleet was scattered across the Atlantic Ocean. One ship, the *Anna*, with thirty Hessians, Ansbach Jägers and artillery, was dismasted and then drifted for eleven weeks until landing at St. Ives on the coast of Cornwall, England.

The British fleet rendezvoused in Savannah in the early part of February. Eleven ships had come up missing in the gale. In addition to the *Anna,* the transports *Judith,* and *Russia Merchant,* and a one-masted artillery transport were lost. The *Russia Merchant* had carried most of the heavy siege artillery and ammunition needed to conquer a fortified town.

The gale had pushed other ships far southeastward and the men were dangerously low on food and water. A voyage that would normally take 10 days took the British fleet 5 weeks to make.

Clinton held a council of war and stated that he wanted to proceed to Charlestown by the inland waterways. Most of his officers were strongly opposed to this maneuver and Clinton deferred to the opinion of his officers. They would not be able to get very good intelligence, since the cavalry had no horses. They had been thrown overboard during the gale to save the ships. The horses would have also been used to move the heavy equipment, artillery and supplies.

Clinton put Brigadier General James Patterson ashore, with 1,400 infantry, to mount a diversion by the way of Augusta. He was also sent into Georgia to keep the backcountry militia tied down so they couldn't reinforce Charlestown. With Patterson were Major Patrick Ferguson and Lieutenant Colonel Banastre Tarleton. Clinton sent orders to New York, West Indies and the Bahamas for artillery and ordnance stores to replace those lost on the passage with the sinking of the *Russia Merchant.*

Clinton also asked Arbuthnot for artillery from his own ships to replace those lost by the *Russia Merchant.* Arbuthnot agreed. One of the British ships of the line, the *Defiance,* foundered off the coast of Tybee Island during the winter storms. The ship sank, and took with it a large portion of entrenching tools. Arbuthnot promised Clinton that he would be able to get the cannon that his sailors had taken off the 64-gun *Defiance,* but they were never delivered.

Lincoln ordered Colonel Daniel Horry and his South Carolina State Dragoons to patrol near the Savannah to act as an early warning for the British invasion fleet. Lincoln also began to prepare his troops for a land engagement. Every soldier was supposed to be issued 50 rounds of ammunition and a bayonet for his musket. In the 18th century the bayonet was critical to winning the battles. The bayonet killed very few, but the weapon did decide the outcome of battles by pushing the enemy off of an objective, or making him surrender.

The British needed cavalry to be effective and to gain information on what the Patriots were doing, so Colonel Banastre Tarleton was sent to the plantations and farms around Port Royal to seize any horses that were suitable for his cavalry. These horses were not equal to the ones he had lost at sea, but they would have to do.

The British fleet left Savannah on February 9th and anchored off of Trench Island.[2] The command of the invasion was shared by both Clinton and Admiral Arbuthnot, and neither one had to take orders from the other. Luckily Clinton was assigned Captain George Keith Elphinstone as naval officer overseeing the landing. Elphinstone proved himself invaluable during the campaign, since he had been in the same waters the year before with Prévost.

Elphinstone was able to guide the fleet into the North Edisto and then anchor the entire fleet in a circular basin off Simmons Island.

On the evening of February 11th Major General Alexander Leslie landed unopposed on Simmons Island with the Light Infantry and the Grenadiers.[3] Throughout the night the weather did not cooperate and it rained heavily. General Clinton came ashore with the first wave and spent the night under a tree in the rain.

On February 12th the rest of invasion force was issued three days rations and disembarked. The artillery had to remain on board because there were no horses to pull them. The Hessian troops slept on the ground, since they had brought no tents from New York. On the morning of February 14th the Jägers and the 33rd Regiment set out in search of Stono Ferry.

Captain Johann Ewald of the Jägers wrote that the march was "through a wilderness of deep sand, marshland, and impenetrable woods where human feet had never trod." They did not see any of the Americans, but they did hear firing in the swamps. When the Hessians went to investigate the shooting they found the British

Grenadiers, firing their muskets to attract attention since they were lost.

Captain Ewald found a "Negro boy" who guided them, but was very hard to understand the boy due to the Gullah dialect of the area. At one point as they marched to the Stono Ferry the entire British column discovered that they were exposed to the American's cannons on the high ground on the other side of the river. The British quickly turned around out of the fire of the artillery. Amazingly the Americans simply watched and did not fire a single shot.[4]

When it became evident that Clinton's objective was Charlestown, Lincoln began to consolidate his forces. He recalled the 1st Virginia Detachment and the dragoons from Augusta. South Carolina troops were recalled from Sheldon, north of Savannah. The 1st and 3rd Continental Dragoons, Horry's South Carolina horse and the remnants of Pulaski's Legion were placed at Bacon's Bridge, twenty-eight miles from Charlestown.

Once Clinton found out that reinforcements were on the march to Charlestown he ordered Patterson to march overland to join his force.

Francis Marion was ordered by Moultrie to form a light infantry unit from the best men of the 2nd South Carolina Regiment. Marion's unit had been decimated during the assault on the Spring Hill redoubt in Savannah, but he had been reinforced with remnants of the 6th South Carolina Regiment. Lincoln ordered that the five South Carolina Continental regiments be consolidated into three on February 11th, due to the losses suffered at Savannah.

Out of the 246 men in Marion's regiment his "best" consisted of 227. Marion's force was moved to Bacon's Bridge at Monck's Corner to delay General Patterson's force that was then marching up from Savannah. The normal load of the Continental soldier was 40 rounds per man, but Marion's men only had 25 rounds per man to hold back any British forces.

The 1st South Carolina Regiment continued to garrison Fort Moultrie and improve the defenses, with the labor of "a number of Negroes." The rest of the Continental infantry and the Charlestown

Battalion of Artillery manned the trenches on Charlestown Neck. The Charlestown Militia would man the batteries in the city facing the harbor.

Every man who was left was utilized, improving the defenses. Lincoln himself was "on horseback from 5 in the morning until 8 or 9 at night pushing on the Works." He even worked on the trenches with the men when they needed assistance.

Almost four thousand American troops were stationed around Charlestown, of which 2,000 were the militiamen from the Carolinas. When Lincoln began bringing the troops into the city, the militiamen from the outlying areas refused to enter. They feared an outbreak of smallpox. An outbreak had happened right after the failed first British invasion in 1776, and the militiamen still remembered that time. Even after Rutledge threatened to confiscate any property the militiamen owned in Charlestown, only a little over 200 responded and came into the city. On February 10th 1,248 North Carolina militiamen under General Alexander Lillington, did finally come into town.

Moultrie was ordered to keep a watch on the British, and remove any horses, cattle, wagons, boats or anything else that might be of use. The highest point in Charlestown was St. Michael's Church. The white steeple was so tall that it was used as a landmark to guide ships into the harbor. Peter Timothy volunteered to observe from the steeple and report on any British movements. From there he could see the Royal Navy off the Charlestown Bar and he could see the campfires of the British army on Johns Island.

Clinton and Cornwallis arrived early on the morning of the 15th at James Island. That night the Americans silently abandoned their position. As the British moved across the Stono, the defenders of Charlestown had still not fired a shot.

To remove any aids to British navigation the Americans had St. Michael's church blackened and all the buoys in the channels were removed. Governor Rutledge ordered Whipple to destroy the beacon and the lighthouse near the present day Morris Island lighthouse.

On February 14th Continental Marines blew up the lighthouse. Two days later the Marines were landed on James Island and they planted explosives inside Fort Johnson. When the charges went off the fort was leveled and the Marines withdrew across the harbor. Since Prévost's attack a year earlier Fort Johnson had been burned and blown up and was no longer considered a defendable position.[5]

Stono Ferry, South Carolina
Charlestown Campaign
18- 22 February 1780

One of the big disadvantages of the British during the approach to Charlestown was that they did not have any cavalry. Lieutenant Colonel Banastre Tarleton had gone to Beaufort to seize all the horses he could to outfit his men, but until the British cavalry could be refitted, the army was unable to counter the American dragoons.

On February 18th Major John Jameson with the 1st Continental Light Dragoons captured three British soldiers of the 23rd Regiment when they drifted too far from their lines.

On the night of the 19th one of the British row galleys blew up in the Stono River. It was blamed on two drunken sailors who had a "nymph" with them. Clinton wanted to get the transports into the protection of mouth of the Stono. Elphinstone arrived from the fleet with two schooners carrying a 24-pound cannon and a flatboat armed with a 12-pounder to cover the movement of the transports. The British light infantry was ordered to march down the river to Mathew's Ferry to reduce the distance that the ships would have to move. On the 20th Elphinstone was able to get the transports up the river and to Mathew's Ferry, where they began unloading supplies to the army.

On February 22nd Major Maham, of Colonel Daniel Horry's South Carolina State Dragoons, and Captain William Sanders, of the Round O Company, conducted a reconnaissance of the British lines near Stono Ferry. The American cavalry captured Captain McDonald and eight men on a British picket.[6] This was the first offensive action of the siege.

The weather continued to be miserable. On the 23rd it snowed, leaving ice on ground, but the next day the sun came out and the temperature rose to a "beautiful May day." The fortifications at Stono Ferry were finished on February 24th, and the next day Lord Cornwallis brought his men across onto James Island.[7]

Oohey River, Wallace's Road, James Island, South Carolina
Charlestown Campaign
26 February 1780

Major Chevalier Pierre-François Vernier commanded the remnants Pulaski's Legion, posted on the Stono River to monitor the British movements. Every day each British brigade sent out one hundred men to drive in livestock, and to forage for food. The local people informed Vernier that a British foraging party had moved out of the British lines near the Oohey River. This was several officers of the 7th and 23rd Regiments and fifty of their men who went out to collect "Negroes and livestock."

Vernier followed alongside them on their return march until they were inside the narrow approaches between two ponds. He set up an ambush at this chokepoint.

The British foragers marched back in raised spirits, and without any formation. The soldiers were intermingled with the livestock. When they entered the kill zone Vernier attacked them on all sides, and killed or wounded nearly half of the British. The inexperienced British soldiers fired their muskets too soon, and before they could reload Vernier's lancers killed three Fusiliers.

The Jägers on duty in the camp rushed to rescue their British comrades. An intense firefight developed, and Vernier withdrew, leaving a sergeant, four soldiers, two lancers and three horses were captured. The British lost ten men killed and nine wounded.[8]

Though the British did not have any force to match the American cavalry, they did have sheer numbers. The cavalry could hit, but they could not stay and fight, they had to leave quickly to avoid being captured. The cavalry also did not have enough equipment and ammunition to carry on a prolonged fight. They needed swords, saddles and clothes. Vernier's force only had four rounds per man during this fight.[9]

Fort Johnson, South Carolina　　　　　　**Naval Skirmish**
Charlestown Campaign
26 February – 2 March 1780

American Forces
Commanding Officer　　　　　Commodore Abraham Whipple
Continental Navy
　　Commodore Abraham Whipple
　　　Sloop *Providence*
　　　　18 and 12-pounders　　　　　　　　　32
　　　　Lieutenant Robert Davis
　　　　Continental Marines　　　　　　　　　16
　　Captain Thomas Simpson
　　　Sloop *Ranger*
　　　　6-pounders　　　　　　　　　　　　　20
　　　　Lieutenant William Morris
　　　　　Continental Marines　　　　　　　　35
　　Captain Samuel Tucker
　　　Frigate *Boston*
　　　　12-pounders　　　　　　　　　　　　　5
　　　　9-pounders　　　　　　　　　　　　　19
　　　　6-pounders　　　　　　　　　　　　　2
　　　　4-pounders　　　　　　　　　　　　　4
　　　　Swivel guns　　　　　　　　　　　　　16
　　　　Captain Richard Palmes
　　　　　Continental Marines　　　　　　　　50
South Carolina State Navy
　　Captain Thomas Curling
　　　Frigate *Bricole*
　　　　24 and 18-pounders　　　　　　　　　44

British Forces
Commanding Officer   Major General von Kospoth
    Captain John Peebles
      42nd Regiment of Foot (Royal Highland Regiment) [10]
        Grenadier Company   Unknown number
      Royal Regiment of Artillery
        24-pounder   1
        12-pounder   1
        8-inch howitzer   1
        24-pounders "en barbette" [11]   2
      German Auxiliaries
       Major Wilhelm Graff
        4th Battalion   450
         Hesse-Kassel Grenadier Battalion von Graff
    Artillery   2 fieldpieces
Casualties   6 killed

Clinton did not make the same mistake he had made in 1776 when he attacked Sullivan's Island. For this second invasion of Charleston he took the destroyed Fort Johnson on James Island, by approaching it from the landward side to the rear. The Hessians that occupied the fort found that there was not any cover left.

After the fort was occupied on February 26th the Continental Navy ships *Providence* and *Ranger* fired into the fort with little or no effect.

The next day the Continental Navy ships *Boston* and *Ranger* and the South Carolina frigate *Bricole* moved from Sullivan's Island and fired on Fort Johnson. Three British were killed in the bombardment. To counter the naval firepower the British moved in a 24-pounder, 12-pounder and an 8 inch howitzer.

On February 27th some transport ships arrived from Savannah with the grenadier companies of the 63rd and 64th Regiments, and one battalion of the 71st Highlanders. There was also "two companies of Negroes from Savannah. The remainder were supply and horse ships." The horses would be used to haul cannons to the newly constructed positions, but the horses were not put to work for a few more days, so the soldiers had to drag the artillery to their camps.

On February 28th, while work was being done on a redoubt in Fort Johnson, the *Boston* and *Ranger* both fired into the fort from an unprotected side.[12] A Hessian captain brought up some of the Hessian Grenadiers, and two artillery pieces, and returned fire. One shot by the *Boston* killed a gunner, and two grenadiers of the Grenadier Battalion von Graff.[13]

The 42nd Highlanders moved a fieldpiece into the road leading to Fort Johnson and also fired upon the ship. General von Kospoth recalled the grenadiers and the fieldpieces, and the frigates moved away from the fort. The British moved two 24-pounders, "en barbette", into the unprotected side of the fort.

Clinton rode out to the fort and ordered General von Kospoth to "retire into the woods with his Brigade, so that he should not be exposed to the cannonading."

Carl Bauer described Fort Johnson as the fort that "General Prévost destroyed last year and of which one can still see the ruins... consist of tabby bricks and the trunks of palmetto trees...Behind Fort Johnston a redoubt was built on an old cemetery, to which heavy cannons and ammunition were brought. A great number of dead corpses were dug up, which struck us as all the more curious since this island was not thickly inhabited. Therefore we asked about the cause and learned that these were all soldiers from two English regiments, who had been quartered in a nearby and now destroyed barracks. Both regiments had died out almost completely in one year after their arrival from Europe. This news caused us to wish that we would not remain here very long."

On March 2nd the *Providence, Boston, Ranger, Bricole, Notre Dame* and several other galleys, fired into Fort Johnson again, with no effect. When the first British schooners appeared off the bar the American fleet ceased the shelling of Fort Johnson.

The capture of Fort Johnson allowed the British to protect their ships when they crossed the bar, and send occasional harassment fire into Charlestown.[14]

Stono River, Mathew's Ferry, South Carolina   **Skirmish**
Charlestown Campaign
5 March 1780

Late in the afternoon of March 4th elements of Pulaski's Legion scouted the British redoubt at Mathew's Ferry. At 11 o'clock the next day they returned to test the defenses of the works. The British fired upon the reconnaissance patrol, and Vernier's men suffered the loss of several men and horses.

Captain Ewald commanded the position that Vernier had tested, and he expected the Americans to return.[15] Ewald placed six Highlanders and six Jägers in two ambush positions along the main road. Two other Jägers were placed in a sentry position in the open, as a decoy, in front of the works. Around 7 o'clock that night Pulaski's Legion horse appeared and circled the sentries to cut them off from the works. When Vernier's men got in the kill zone of the ambush, the sentries fired, signaling the hidden soldiers to fire on the cavalry. Nearly all of the Vernier's cavalry was shot or bayoneted. A few were able to escape into the night.

The next day Captain Ewald was ordered to abandon the Mathew's Ferry works. He pulled down the earthworks, set the abatis on fire and crossed the Stono River. After crossing he destroyed the boats he had used. Clinton's entire army, except for a small detachment, had moved over from Johns Island to James Island.[16]

Ferguson's Plantation, South Carolina
Charlestown Campaign
6 – 7 March 1780

On the night of March 6th the two British light infantry battalions tried to surprise the American cavalry near Ferguson's plantation, by crossing the Wappoo River and marching throughout the night. Unfortunately for the British an officer's servant had deserted and warned the American cavalry.

When the British arrived they found that the Americans had fled. The Light Infantry was worn out from the fourteen-mile march over clay paths, and on the return eight of the men had to be left behind, too fatigued to make it back. Major Maham, of the South Carolina State Cavalry, sent word to the Continental Light Dragoons, that the British were on the mainland.[17] The Light Dragoons had spent an enjoyable time at their plantation by playing cards, hunting and dancing at night with the local beauties, but within the hour they headed towards the retreating British. The Dragoons captured seven of the eight stragglers. The eighth man had overcome his exertion, and rejoined his unit.[18]

Charlestown, South Carolina [19]   **Siege**
Charlestown Campaign
7 March – 12 May 1780 [20]

American Forces
Commanding Officer   Major General Benjamin Lincoln[21]
 Continentals
  Brigadier General William Moultrie [22]
   South Carolina Continental Brigade
    Colonel Charles Cotesworth Pinckney
     1st South Carolina Regiment [23]   231
      Lieutenant Colonel William Scott
      Colonel's Company
      Captain George Turner
      2nd Company [24]   18
      Captain Simeon Theus
      3rd Company   18
      Captain Joseph Elliott
      4th Company   23
      Captain Charles Lining
      5th Company   25
      Lieutenant Alexander Fraser
     6th South Carolina Regiment

Captain Thomas Gadsden
  6th Company
Captain John Williamson
  7th Company
Captain Levalier de Sainte-Marie [25]
  8th Company
Captain William Jackson
  9th Company
Captain Charles Skirving
  10th Company
Pulaski's Legion Infantry
  Captain James de Segon
  Captain Frederick Paschke
  Captain Monsieur O'Neil
  Captain Joseph Baldesqui
Lieutenant Colonel Francis Marion
  2nd South Carolina Regiment [26]   266
  Sergeant Major Alexander McDonald
    Colonel's Company [27]   29
  Unknown Captain
    Light Infantry Company [28]   43
  Captain Thomas Moultrie
    1st Company   22
  Captain Daniel Mazyck
    2nd Company   26
  Captain Richard Bohun Baker
    5th Company   30
  Captain Adrien Proveaux
    6th Company   20
  Captain Richard Mason
    7th Company   23
  Captain Peter Gray
    8th Company   22
  Captain Albert Roux
    9th Company   22

Captain George Warley	
6th South Carolina Regiment	26
Captain Thomas Shubrick	
5th South Carolina Regiment	21
Lieutenant Colonel William Henderson [29]	
3rd South Carolina (Ranger) Regiment [30]	302
Major Edmund Hyrne	
Light Infantry Company [31]	34
Captain Felix Warley	
1st Company [32]	24
Captain Joseph Warley	
2nd Company	16
Captain Uriah Goodwyn	
3rd Company	19
Captain John Buchanan	
6th South Carolina Regiment	17
Captain Jesse Baker	
5th Company	15
Captain Field Farrer	
6th Company	15
Captain George Liddell	
7th Company	17
Captain Richard Pollard	
8th Company	9
Captain John Carraway Smith	
9th Company	
Captain Oliver Towles	
10th Company	
Brigadier General James Hogun [33]	
North Carolina Continental Brigade [34]	
Colonel Thomas Clark [35]	
1st North Carolina Regiment	260
Captain-Lieutenant James King	
Colonel Clark's Company	50
Captain-Lieutenant Thomas Callender	
Lieutenant Colonel's Company [36]	35

Major John Nelson	44
Captain Joshua Bowman	
Light Infantry Company	64
Captain Tilghman Dixon [37]	44
Captain Griffith John McRee	46
Lieutenant George Cook	
Captain James Read's Company	46
Captain John Sumner	40
Captain Howell Tatum	45
Colonel John Patten [38]	
2nd North Carolina Regiment	244
Captain-Lieutenant Charles Stewart	
Colonel Patten's Company	26
Lieutenant Thomas Evans	
LTC Selbey Harney's Company	27
Lieutenant John Daves	
Major Hardy Murfree's Company	26
Captain John Ingles	28
Captain Benjamin Andrew Coleman	29
Lieutenant Jesse Read	
Capt Clement Hall's Company	27
1st Lieutenant Thomas Finney [39]	
Thomas Armstrong's Company	22
Captain Robert Fenner [40]	22
Lieutenant Colonel-Commandant Robert Mebane [41]	
3rd North Carolina Regiment[42]	
Captain-Lieutenant William Fawn	
James Campbell's Company	34
Captain Kedar Ballard	25
Captain George "Gee" Bradley	35
Lieutenant Colonel John Laurens	
Corps of Light Infantry [43]	175
Captain Joseph Montford [44]	
Major Thomas Hogg [45]	
Major Hardy Murfree [46]	

Colonel Richard Parker [47]
  2nd Virginia Brigade [48]
    Lieutenant Colonel Samuel Hopkins [49]
      1st Virginia Detachment [50]   258
        Captain Alexander Parker [51]   72
        Captain Benjamin Taliaferro [52]   69
        Captain Tarleton Payne [53]   68
        Captain Beverly Stubblefield [54]   48
    Colonel William Heth
      2nd Virginia Detachment [55]   323
        Lieutenant Colonel Gustavus Wallace
        Captain Thomas Buckner [56]   84
        Captain Lawrence Butler [57]   77
        Captain Thomas Holt [58]   76
        Captain Robert Beale [59]   83
    Unknown Captain
      Hicks' South Carolina Militia Regiment 23
    Lieutenant Colonel Archibald Lytle [60]
      Battalion of North Carolina Volunteers [61] 202
        Captain Pulliam [62]   50
        Captain Johnson [63]   73
        Captain Hervey [64]   46
        Captain Lowman [65]   46
Captain Robert Yancey
  1st and 3rd Continental Light Dragoons   31
Unknown Captain
  Armand's Legion of Horse and Foot [66]   4
Colonel Leonard Marbury
  Georgia Regiment of Horse Rangers   41
Colonel John White
  Georgia Continental Officers [67]   6
North Carolina State Troops
  Colonel Marquis Francis de Malmedy, Marquis of Bretagne
    North Carolina Dragoons   41
      Major Cosmo de Medici
      Captain Samuel Ashe

Captain Robert Council
Captain George Lowman
Anson County Militia
Colonel Bernard Beeckman
  Brigade of Artillery [68]   391 guns
    Lieutenant Colonel John Faucheraud Grimkè
      4th South Carolina Regiment (Artillery) [69]   93
      Captain James Wilson
        Number 1 Battery   10 guns
      Captain James Fields
        Number 2 Battery   6 guns
        Captain Harman Davis
      Captain John Francis de Treville
        Number 3 Battery [70]   3 guns
      Captain James Mitchell
        Number 3 Battery   3 guns
        Captain Daniel Mazyck [71]
        Captain Richard Bohun Baker
        Captain Adrien Proveaux
      Captain Barnard Elliot
        Number 4 Battery   2 guns
        Captain Peter Gray
        1st Lieutenant Josiah Kolb
      Captain John Wickly
        Number 5 Battery [72]   6 guns
      Captain Richard Brooke Roberts [73]
        Number 6 Battery   4 guns
      Captain William Mitchell
        Number 6 Battery [74]   4 guns
      Captain Andrew Templeton [75]
        Number 7 Battery [76]   4 guns
      Major Ephraim Mitchell
        Number 8 Battery   4 guns
        Number 9 Battery   4 guns
        Number 15 Battery [77]

Unknown commander
    Number 10 Battery   2 guns
Unknown commander
    Number 11 Battery   2 guns
Unknown commander
    Number 12 Battery   9 guns
Unknown commander
    Number 13 Battery   7 guns
Unknown commander
    Number 14 Battery   3 guns
Captain Thomas Heyward, Jr.
    Charlestown Battalion of Artillery
    Hornwork Battery   26
Captain John Kingsbury
    Kingsbury's Company of North Carolina Artillery
    North Carolina Battery [78]   64
Colonel Thomas Marshall
    Virginia State Artillery Regiment   100
    Half Moon Battery
Lieutenant Colonel Louis Jean Baptiste Cambray [79]
    Cambray's battery   2 guns
Major Thomas Grimball
    Charlestown Battalion of Artillery [80]   168
    Major John Gilbank
    Captain Edward Rutledge
    2nd Independent SC Artillery Company
    Captain-Lieutenant William Hassell Gibbes
    6th Independent SC Artillery Company
      Gibbe's Wharf Battery   7 guns
      Captain Edmund Arrowsmith
      Continental Marines [81]
    Captain Francois Trovin
    Charleston Bombardiers
    Mortar battery [82]

Captain Samuel Tucker
Continental Frigate *Boston*'s Sailors
Broughton's Battery [83]
 26-pounders   20
Unknown commander
Continental Sloop *Providence*'s Sailors [84]
Exchange Battery
 18-pounders   12
 26-pounders   2
Berkeley County Regiment
James Island Companies [85]
Captain Benjamin Stiles
Lieutenant John Garden
Hornwork Battery [86]
Major Joseph Darrell
Company of Cannoneers   167
Unknown commander
Liberty Battery   6 guns
Unknown commander
Lauren's Wharf   10 guns
Unknown commander
Craven's Governor-bridge   7 guns
Unknown commander
Lyttleton's Battery   12 guns
Unknown commander
Britigney Battery [87]   4 guns
Unknown commander
Sugar House Battery   7 guns
Captain Richard Palmes
Continental Marines [88]
Grenville's Battery [89]
 18-pounders   5
 26-pounders   3
Brigadier General Louis le Bégue de Presle Duportail [90]
American Engineer Corps [91]   7
Colonel Jean Baptiste Joseph de Laumoy

Lieutenant Colonel Chevalier Luigi de Cambray-Digny[92]
Major Ferdinand de Brahm [93]
Slaves used in digging earthworks   600
Brigadier General Alexander Lillington
    Brigade of Militia   1,231
    Brigadier General Lachlan McIntosh
        Brigade of South Carolina Militia [94]   About 300
            Colonel Robert Barnwell
                St. Helena Volunteer Militia Company
            Colonel James Dillard
                Laurens District Militia
            Colonel Robert Herriot
                Georgetown Militia
            Colonel George Hicks
            Colonel Benjamin Garden
                Granville County Regiment of Foot
                    Major John Barnwell
                    Captain Lewis Bona
            Colonel William Skirving
                Colleton County Regiment of Foot
            Colonel Hugh Giles
            Major Philip Love
                Duplin County, North Carolina Militia   90
            Colonel John McDonald   87
            Lieutenant Colonel Eli Kershaw
                Camden District Militia
Brigadier General Henry William Harrington [95]
    Brigade of North Carolina Militia
        Lieutenant Colonel John Hinton
            1st North Carolina Regiment of Militia
                Unknown Captain
                    Wilmington District Militia   112
                    Captain Cray
                        Onslow County Militia   41
                    Captain Samuel Wood
                        Bladen County Militia   30

Captain Joseph Grimes
    Duplin County Militia   23
Major Jonathan Dunbibin
    New Hanover County Militia   4
Unknown Captain
    Light Horse   20
Unknown Captain
    Edenton District Militia   52
Ensign Eule
    Gates County Militia   23
Colonel James Read
2nd North Carolina Regiment of Militia
Lieutenant Colonel Stephen Moore
    New Berne District Militia   187
    Captain Pierce
        Craven County Militia   34
    Captain McCullers
        Johnston County Militia   28
    Lieutenant Boyd
        Beaufort County Militia   18
    Lieutenant Colonel John Shepard
        Dobbs County Regiment   36
        Captain Thomas Shute
    Captain Faulkner
        Pitt County Militia   36
    Unknown Sergeant
        Hyde County Militia   16
Unknown Captain
    Halifax District Militia   165
    Captain Bill
        Edgecombe Militia   33
    Captain Jacob Turner
        Halifax Militia   27
    Captain Arent
        Nash County Militia   27

Unknown commander
   3rd North Carolina Regiment of Militia
      Salisbury District Militia   426
         Colonel Andrew Hampton
         Lieutenant Colonel Frederick Hambright
         Ensign McDonald
         Jones County Militia   20
         Unknown Captain
         Light Horse   30
   Unknown Colonel
   4th North Carolina Regiment of Militia
      Unknown Lieutenant Colonel
         Hillsborough District Militia   256
         Captain Ranson
         Franklin County Militia   35
Unknown commander
   Virginia Militia   Unknown number
      Amelia County Militia
         Captain William Worsham
         Captain Robert
         Captain William Fitzgerald
         Captain Jones
Colonel Maurice Simons
   Charlestown Militia Brigade
      Lieutenant Colonel Roger Smith
      1st Battalion [96]   302
         Lieutenant William Graham
         Grenadier Company   46
         Captain John McQueen
         Charles Town Forresters   42
         Captain John Baddeley
         Light Infantry   43
         Captain William Livingston
         German Fusileers   78
         Captain John Raven Mathews
         True Blue Company

Captain James Bentham
    Charles Town Volunteers   42
Colonel Agers
    2nd Battalion   485
    Lieutenant Colonel John Huger
    Lieutenant Colonel Abel Kolb
    Captain Francis Kinlock
    Unknown commander
        Cannon's Company of Volunteers
Colonel Marquis de Britigney
    Britigney's Volunteer Corps of Frenchmen [97] 40
    Captain Louis-Antoine Magallon de la Morlière [98]
        French Company [99]   43
        Spanish Company [100]   42
Commodore Abraham Whipple
Continental Navy
Captain Thomas Simpson
    Sloop *Ranger*
        6-pounders   20
        Lieutenant William Morris
            Continental Marines   35
Captain John Peck Rathbun
    Frigate *Queen of France* [101]
        9-pounders   28
        Captain Edmund Arrowsmith
            Continental Marines   50
Captain Hoysteed Hacker
    Sloop *Providence*
        18 and 12-pounders   32
        Lieutenant Robert Davis
            Continental Marines   16
Captain Samuel Tucker
    Frigate *Boston*
        12-pounders   5
        9-pounders   19
        6-pounders   2

4-pounders	4
Swivel guns	16
Captain Richard Palmes	
Continental Marines	50
French Navy ships [102]	
Captain J. Courannat [103]	
Sloop *L'Aventure*	
9 and 6-pounders	26
Captain James Pyne [104]	
Sloop *Truite* [105]	
12-pounders	26
Lieutenant de Vaisseau	
Polacre *Zephyr* [106]	36
6-pounders	18
South Carolina State Navy [107]	1,000
Captain Thomas Curling	
Frigate *Bricole* [108]	
24 and 18-pounders[109]	44
Charlestown Militia [110]	Unknown number
Captain George Melvin	
Schooner *General Moultrie*	
6-pounders	20
Captain William Sisk [111]	
Brig *Notre Dame*	
6-pounders	16
Captain Charles Crawley	
Galley *Marquis de Britigney* [112]	7 guns
Captain Marshall Boetis [113]	
Galley *Lee*	36
12-pounder	1
9-pounder	1
4-pounder	2
Swivel guns	8
Captain George Farragut	
Galley *Revenge*	7 guns

American Reinforcements that arrived on 8 April 1780 [114]
Commanding Officer   Brigadier General William Woodford
  1st Virginia Brigade [115]
    Colonel William Russell [116]
      1st Virginia Regiment [117]   336
        Lieutenant Colonel Burgess Ball
        Captain Callohill Minnis
        Captain Custis Kendall
        Captain Holman Minnis [118]
        Captain Mayo Carrington
        Captain William Moseley
        Captain William Bentley [119]
        Captain William Johnston
        Captain James Wright [120]
        Captain Thomas Hunt [121]
    Colonel John Neville
      2nd Virginia Regiment [122]   306
        Lieutenant Colonel Nicholas Cabell
      Major David Stephenson
        Major William Croghan [123]
        Captain John Blackwell
        Captain LeRoy Edwards [124]
        Captain James Curry
        Captain John Stith [125]
    Colonel Nathaniel Gist
      3rd Virginia Regiment [126]   252
        Captain Joseph Blackwell
        Captain John Gillison
        Captain Clough Shelton [127]
        Captain Abraham Hite [128]
        Captain Alexander Breckinridge
        Captain Francis Muir [129]
Total American Forces engaged   6,577
Casualties   92 killed, 146 wounded, 5,500 captured,
        21 civilians killed [130]

British Forces   6,839
Commanding Officer   Major General Sir Henry Clinton
    British Regulars
      Major General Alexander Leslie[131]
        Light Infantry and Grenadiers
          Lieutenant Colonel Robert Abercromby
           1st Battalion of Light Infantry   640
             Captain James W. Baille
               7th (Royal Fusilier) Regiment of Foot
               Light Infantry Company
             Captain William Raymond
               22nd Regiment of Foot
               Light Infantry Company
             Captain William Gore
               33rd Regiment of Foot
               Light Infantry Company
             Captain Eyre Coote
               37th Regiment of Foot
               Light Infantry Company
             Captain George Dalrymple
               42nd Regiment of Foot (Royal Highland)
               Light Infantry Company
             Captain Eyre Power Trench
               54th Regiment of Foot
               Light Infantry Company
             Captain Bent Ball
               63rd Regiment of Foot
               Light Infantry Company
             Unknown commander
               70th Regiment of Foot
               Light Infantry Company
             Captain Campbell of Balnabie
               74th (Argyll Highlanders) Regiment
               Light Infantry Company
     Amusettes [132]   4

Lieutenant Colonel Thomas Dundas
2nd Battalion of Light Infantry　　　637
Captain The Honorable Lionel Smythe
23rd Regiment of Foot
Light Infantry Company
Captain St. Lawrence Boyd
38th Regiment of Foot
Light Infantry Company
Captain Charles MacLean
43rd Regiment of Foot
Light Infantry Company
Captain James Graham
57th Regiment of Foot
Light Infantry Company
Captain William Snow
64th Regiment of Foot
Light Infantry Company
Captain James Fraser
76th Regiment of Foot
Light Infantry Company
Captain John Hathorne
80th Regiment of Foot
Light Infantry Company
Captain Ronald MacKinnon
84th Regiment of Foot (Royal Highland)
2nd Battalion
Light Infantry Company
Lieutenant Colonel Henry Hope
1st Battalion of Grenadiers　　　611
Captain Walter Home
7th (Royal Fusilier) Regiment
Grenadier Company
Captain George Phillip Hooke
17th Regiment of Foot
Grenadier Company

Captain Thomas Peter
23rd Regiment of Foot
Grenadier Company
Captain Hildebrand Oakes
33rd Regiment of Foot
Grenadier Company
Captain Kenneth McKenzie
37th Regiment of Foot
Grenadier Company
Captain Mathew Millet
38th Regiment of Foot
Grenadier Company
Captain John Peebles
42nd Regiment of Foot (Royal Highland)
Grenadier Company
Captain John Hatfield
43rd Regiment of Foot
Grenadier Company
Lieutenant Colonel John Yorke
2nd Battalion of Grenadiers   526
Captain Henry Elwes
22nd Regiment of Foot
Grenadier Company
Captain Stephen Broomfield
54th Regiment of Foot
Grenadier Company
Captain James Dalrymple
57th Regiment of Foot
Grenadier Company
Unknown commander
63rd Regiment of Foot
Grenadier Company
Lieutenant Thomas Freeman
64th Regiment of Foot
Grenadier Company

Captain Thomas Dunbar
   70th Regiment of Foot
      Grenadier Company
Captain Ludovick Colquhoun
   74th (Argyll Highlanders) Regiment
      Grenadier Company
Major Peter Traille
   Royal Regiment of Artillery   200
   3rd Battalion
      Captain Thomas Johnson
         Number 1 Company
      Major Peter Traille
         Number 6 Company
   4th Battalion
      Captain Robert Collins
         Number 1, 2, 3, 4, 5 and 8 Company
   Unknown commander
      Hesse-Kassel Artillery
      "Negroes employed by the Artillery"[133] 154
Captain George Keith Elphinstone
   Royal Navy Artillery
      Fort Johnson Battery
         24-pounder   2
         Howitzer   1
      Fenwick Point Battery
         32-pounder   6
         24-pounder   3
         Howitzer   1
   Captain Evans
      Number 2 Battery
         12-pounder   1
         24-pounder   11
         9-inch howitzer   1
   Captain Lawson
      Number 6 Battery (hot shot)

Ensign Abbot
Number 7 Battery
24-pounder   6
12-pounder   1
7-inch howitzer   1
Royal Mortars   12
18-inch mortar   1
Colonel Beverly Robinson
Corps of Guides and Pioneers
Captain John Aldington   20
Lieutenant John Stark
Captain Francis Fraser's Company 7
Lieutenant Benedict Eli
Captain McAlpine's Company   27
Captain Peter McPherson   18
Major James Moncrieff
Brigade of Engineers   Unknown number
Lieutenant Wilson
Captain Allan Stewart
Black Pioneers [134]
Lieutenant Colonel Alured Clarke [135]
Clarke's Brigade
Lieutenant Colonel Alured Clarke
7th (Royal Fusilier) Regiment of Foot   463
Lieutenant Colonel Nisbit Balfour [136]
23rd Regiment (Royal Welch Fusiliers) 400
Major Thomas Mecan
Lieutenant Colonel James Webster [137]
Webster's Corps
Major William Dansey
33rd Regiment of Foot [138]   450
Lieutenant Colonel Ludwig Johann Adolph von Wurmb
Hesse-Kassel Feld Jäger Korps   224
Major Phillip von Wurmb
Captain von Rau

Captain Johann Ewald
2nd Company 80
Captain Moritz von Donop
Captain Johann Hinrichs
"Lawson" swivel guns 2
Captain Friedrich Wilhelm von Röder
III Feld Jäger Regiment Anspach-Beyreuth 46
Major General Johann Christoph von Huyn
Huyn's Brigade
Major James Wemyss
63rd Regiment of Foot [139] 400
Major Robert McLeroth [140]
64th Regiment of Foot [141] 350
Captain Peter Russell
Colonel Friedrich von Benning
Hesse-Kassel Garrison Regiment von Benning [142]
Lieutenant Colonel Franz Kurtz
Major Johann Philip Hillebrand
Captain Heinrich Sonneborn
Captain Reinhard Heilmann
Captain Dietrich Reinhard
Captain Benjamin Wickham
60th (Royal American) Regiment of Foot
2nd Battalion 45
German Auxiliaries
Lieutenant Colonel Fredrich von Porbeck
Hesse-Kassel Garrison Regiment von Wissenbach [143]
Major General Henrich Julius von Kospoth
Hessian Grenadiers [144]
Lieutenant Colonel Otto Wilhelm von Linsingen
1st Battalion [145] 350
Lieutenant Colonel von Lengercke
2nd Battalion [146] 360
Lieutenant Colonel Friedrich Heinrich von Schuter
3rd Battalion [147] 365

Major Wilhelm Graff
4th Battalion [148]   450
Provincials
Colonel Edmund Fanning
King's American Regiment   100
Lieutenant Colonel George Campbell
Lieutenant Colonel's Company
Major James Grant
Captain Isaac Atwood
Captain Thomas Chapman
Captain Abraham DePeyster
Grenadier Company
Captain Robert Gray
Captain John William Livingston

British Reinforcements from Georgia   1,750
Commanding Officer   Brigadier General James Patterson
British Regulars
Lieutenant Colonel Alexander McDonald
71st Regiment of Foot (Fraser's Highlanders) [149]
Unknown commander
1st Battalion   378
Captain Norman McLeod
Major Archibald McArthur
2nd Battalion   491
Major Colin Graham
Light Infantry [150]   243
Major Colin Graham
16th Regiment of Foot
Light Company   126
Captain Hutchinson
71st Regiment of Foot (Fraser's Highlanders)
Light Company

Captain Peter Campbell
New Jersey Volunteers
3rd Battalion
Light Company
Captain William Henry Talbot
17th Regiment of Light Dragoons 73
Brigade of Engineers Unknown number
Captain Angus Campbell
Black Pioneers [151] 20 white, 186 black
Provincials
Lieutenant Colonel Banastre Tarleton
British Legion [152]
Major Charles Cochrane [153]
Legion Infantry [154] 287
Lieutenant Colonel Banastre Tarleton
Legion Cavalry [155] 211
Major Patrick Ferguson
American Volunteers [156] 335
Captain Abraham DePeyster [157]
Captain Charles McNeill [158]
Captain James Dunlap [159]
Captain Samuel Ryerson [160]
Captain-Lieutenant Frederick DePeyster [161]
Colonel Alexander Innes
South Carolina Royalists [162]
Lieutenant Colonel Joseph Robinson
1st Battalion
Captain-Lieutenant Charles Lindsay
Colonel's Company Unknown number
Lieutenant Colonel Joseph Robinson 36
Captain Faight Risinger 39
Lieutenant Francis Fralis
Captain John York's Company 43
Captain Robert Pearis 38
Captain Martin Livingston 49
Captain Levi Youman 52

Lieutenant Colonel Evan McLauren
2nd Battalion
Lieutenant David Black
Colonel McLauren's company   55
Captain John Murphey   60
Lieutenant Colonel John Hamilton
Royal North Carolina Regiment[163]   Unknown number
Lieutenant John Martin
1st Company
Major Nicholas Welsh
2nd Company
Captain Daniel Manson [164]
3rd Company
Major James Wright
Georgia Loyalists   32
Captain Archibald Campbell
Georgia Dragoons   40
Lieutenant Colonel George Turnbull
New York Volunteers [165]   Unknown number
Major Henry Sheridan
Lieutenant Colonel George Turnbull's Company
Captain William Johnston
Captain Bernard Kane
British Reinforcements from New York on 18 April 1780   2,566
Commanding Officer   Colonel Max von Westerhagen
British Regulars
Lieutenant Colonel Duncan McPherson [166]
42nd Regiment of Foot (Royal Highland Regiment) 783
Major Charles Graham
1st Battalion
Lieutenant Colonel Duncan McPherson
2nd Battalion
German Auxiliaries
Colonel Max von Westerhagen
Hesse-Kassel Fusilier Regiment von Dittfurth [167]
Major Ernst von Bork

Captain Wilhelm von Malsburg
Captain Heinrich Hugo Scheffer
Provincials
Lieutenant Colonel Thomas Pattinson [168]
   Prince of Wales American Regiment [169]   334
Lieutenant Colonel John Graves Simcoe
   Queen's Rangers [170]   200
    Captain Stair Agnew
    Captain James Kerr
    Captain John McKay
     Highland Company
    Captain Robert McCrea
    Captain John McGill
     Grenadier Company
    Captain William Moncrief
    Captain James Murray
    Captain John Saunders
    Captain David Shank
     Captain Alexander Wickham's Hussars   7
    Captain Francis Stephenson
     Light Infantry Company
Colonel Francis Lord Rawdon
   Volunteers of Ireland [171]
    Captain-Lieutenant David Dalton
     Lord Rawdon's Company   39
    Lieutenant Colonel Wellbore Ellis Doyle   43
    Captain William Barry   51
    Captain William Blacker   45
    Captain John Campbell
     Grenadier Company   55
    Ensign Marcus Ransford
     Captain John Doyle's Company   50
    Ensign Edward Gilborne
     Captain Charles Hasting's Company   45
    Captain James King   50
    Captain John McMahon   45

Unknown commander
King's Orange Rangers   detachment
Total British Ground Forces engaged   12,847
Casualties   76 killed, 189 wounded [172]

British Naval Forces
Commanding Officer   Admiral Mariot Arbuthnot
    Captain William Sweeney
       His Majesty's Ship of the Line *Europe* [173]   64 guns
       Royal Navy Seamen   500
    Commodore Francis Samuel Drake
       His Majesty's Ship of the Line Russell [174]   74 guns
    Captain Phillips Cosby
       His Majesty's Ship of the Line Robuste   74 guns
       Royal Navy Seamen   600
    Captain T. Fitzherbert
       His Majesty's Ship of the Line *Raisonable*   64 guns
    Captain George Dawson
       His Majesty's Ship of the Line *Renown*   50 guns
    Captain George Gayton
       His Majesty's Ship of the Line *Romulus*   44 guns
    Captain Sir Andrew Snape Hammond
       His Majesty's Frigate Roebuck   44 guns
    Captain Barkley
       His Majesty's Frigate *Blonde*   32 guns
       Royal Navy Seamen   220
    Captain George Keith Elphinstone
       His Majesty's Frigate Perseus   32 guns
    Captain Charles Phipps
       His Majesty's Frigate *Camilla*   20 guns
    Captain Gambier
       His Majesty's Frigate *Raleigh* [175]   28 guns
    Captain Hudson
       His Majesty's Frigate *Redmond*   32 guns
    Captain John Orde
       His Majesty's Frigate *Virginia* [176]   28 guns

Captain Charles Hudson
 His Majesty's Armed Transport Richmond [177] 16 guns
 Royal Navy Seamen 220
Unknown Captain
 His Majesty's Armed Transport Polly
Captain John Anderson
 His Majesty's Armed Transport Apollo [178]
Unknown Captain
 His Majesty's Armed Transport *Diana*
Unknown Captain
 His Majesty's Armed Transport *Silver Eel*
Unknown Commander
 His Majesty's Supply Ship *Aeolus* No guns
Unknown Captain
 His Majesty's Armed Schooner *New Vigilant*
  18-pounders 18
Captain Jackson
 His Majesty's Row Galley *Comet* 45 seamen
  18-pounders 2
Armed Schooner
  24-pound cannon 1
Armed Schooner
  24-pound cannon 1
Armed Flatboat
  12-pound cannon 1
Provincial Navy
Lieutenant John Mowbray
 Armed Sloop *Lord George Germaine*
  2 and 3-pounders 20 guns
Unknown Captain
 Armed Sloop of War *Sandwich* Unknown guns
Lieutenant James Duncan
 Row Galley *Scourge* Unknown guns
Unknown commander
 Row Galley Unknown guns
Total British Naval Forces Engaged 4,500

Royal Navy Casualties   23 killed, 28 wounded, *Richmond* dismasted, *Comet* and *Aeolus* run aground and burned

By March 1st the British controlled James Island. Their Light Infantry had crossed the Wappo Cut to establish itself on the mainland. The bridge across the cut had been repaired and the bloody skirmishing with the Patriot cavalry continued. Lincoln ordered the sentries in the trenches to be relieved every half hour. He did not want any man to sleep and allow the British to go undetected. He also ordered St. Michael's church bell to ring every 15 minutes, so that the sentries would know when to call out to each other. When the bell rang each sentry would cry out "All's Well" to the next one, until the cry had gone around the entire cities defenses.

To make sure that no one wasted any ammunition by shooting at shadows Lincoln ordered that the "firing in the Vicinity of the Camp or lines is strictly forbid." He sent a detail to "patrol the several streets & alleys in the town, & kill all the dogs they shall find...destroy them in any way whatever, saving that of shooting." He did this because he did not want the garrison to be alarmed by a barking dog and think that the British were attacking.

On the 3rd of March the Charlestown garrison was increased by the arrival of 600 North Carolina Continentals under Brigadier General James Hogun. The North Carolinians had marched south from Washington's army and had been in the hottest fighting there was in the north. Slowly Clinton brought his army forward, in well-planned stages. He did not want a repeat of the defeat in 1776. Clinton sent a message to General Knyphausen in New York that he would need more troops. One of the drawbacks to Clinton's plan was that he had to work with an admiral he disliked and distrusted, who had not yet brought the fleet across the bar to complete the naval blockade of the city.

Captain de la Morlière, of Britigney's Corps, wrote that on the night of March 4th "The enemy had fired several rockets at nightfall that were believed to be a prearranged signal to attack." There was no attack, but the rockets did set part of the town on fire. "The militia was sent to the fire and the rest of the troops were transported to the bank of the Stono River facing the enemy. They extinguished the fire and the rest of the night was considerably quieter than they had expected."

On the 8th of March a Lieutenant, with eight sailors from the ship *Queen of France,* stole a guard boat and deserted to the British army. They said that they didn't think themselves safe in the city.

Several Americans had deserted to the British because they thought that any resistance was futile against the superior British forces. Lincoln made an example of one soldier, Hamilton Ballendine, when he attempted to desert to the British. He was hanged just outside the trenches. The British were able to watch the hanging from James Island.

The British made a battery on Lighthouse Island, which prevented the Americans from firing on the British ships trying to get over the bar. The British were also able to raise a 32-pounder that had been sunk in a creek, so it wouldn't be captured.

On March 10th American ships fired grapeshot on the Hessian batteries being constructed at Fort Johnson, but it had no effect. At the point where Wappoo Creek flows into the Ashley the British used slaves to build triangular fortifications, opposite the southern fortifications of Charlestown.[179] To clear their field of fire the British burned down a house on Fenwick's Point.

On March 12th two 32-pounders, two 24-pounders and a howitzer was mounted on the platforms built at Fenwick's Point. These cannons fired on the city for the first time, but the citizens of the city didn't know it until they found two 32-pound balls at Cumming's Point and the Sugar House.

The galleys *Lee* and the *Britigney* fired upon the British battery, but did not cause any damage. The American ships that were located at Sullivan's Island moved up the Cooper River for better protection. Later that afternoon the *Notre Dame* anchored beside Fenwick Point by mistake. The British "fired several well directed shot at her" and the balls ripped apart the ship's rigging. The ship quickly sailed down the river and out of harm's way.

On March 13th the British mounted another howitzer, three 32-pounders and two 24-pounders in a second battery built near the Fenwick battery. This artillery was mounted to shell American ships and the fortifications on the opposite shore. A redoubt was built between the two batteries so that they would not be assaulted by troops on the land.

The British fleet was still outside the Bar, waiting for the conditions to improve so they could run for the harbor. Admiral Whipple had decided not to stand and fight at Five Fathom hole because he said that there would be no room to maneuver, and his ships would be shot full of holes. Lincoln personally sounded the channels to determine if a defense could be fought there. He was in command of the land and naval forces and he could have ordered Whipple to fight, or relieve him of his command, but he did neither.

Lincoln ordered Whipple's fleet to construct a barrier in Rebellion Road that would slow the British ships. It was decided to let the British pass over the Bar and then take a stand near Fort Moultrie, where the guns of the ships and the guns of the fort would be able to rake the British fleet. This obstruction would consist of sunken ship hulks lashed together with chains and cables. If the British tried to remove these obstacles, they would do so under the guns of Fort Moultrie. Another line of defense would be fireships, which could be set ablaze and launched towards the British fleet. Unfortunately by March 16th none of the defenses had been constructed because "the wind blows so hard." The fireships had not been prepared because they were not able to collect the materials for them.[180]

Lincoln ordered Lieutenant Colonel William Washington to harass the movement of Patterson's army towards Charlestown. Washington was the cousin of George Washington and had only recently arrived with his dragoons. Patterson's force mainly consisted of Provincial units. These included the New York Volunteers, the American Volunteers, the South Carolina Royalists and the Royal North Carolina Volunteers.

Patterson's force moved across the countryside taking livestock and plundering the property of the citizens of South Carolina. The men destroyed furniture, tore down fence lines and broke windows. Many of the men in Patterson's army were Loyalists who had been abused by the Patriots over the years, and now was their chance to get revenge. Anthony Allaire wrote that they were living "on the fat of the land, the soldiers every side of us roasting turkeys, fowls, pigs, etc., every night in great plenty."

With Patterson were hundreds of slaves that had been confiscated or had left their master's and joined the British army. In March the British commissary said that there were 317 Negroes in their service, however Major John Andrè requested "500 blankets and 500 hats for Clothing negroes." So many slaves came in that Clinton ordered Cornwallis to come up with a way to "discourage them from joining us."

Not all the runaway slaves stayed with the British. They soon discovered that they worked just as hard as they had on the plantation. Many ran off from the British to return to a less dangerous life they knew.

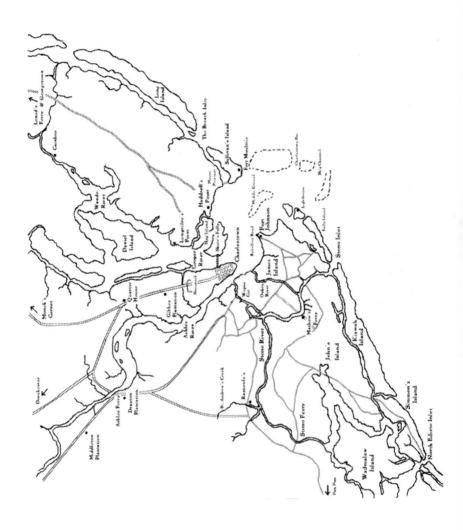

Banastre Tarleton and his British Legion had been outfitted with horses seized from citizens of Beaufort and they rode towards Patterson's army. The horses he confiscated were no match for the Patriot cavalry. Tarleton wrote that they were "inferior to those embarked at New York."

On the 17th of March the morale of the Charlestown defenders took a blow. Lillington's North Carolina militia's term of service expired. Rutledge offered a $300 bounty and new clothes to those who would stay on an additional three months, but even with that incentive 700 of the militia headed home. Only 150 stayed in Charlestown. On a rainy March 18th British morale got a boost when Captain Saunders of the Queen's Rangers had found Patterson and his Savannah column. Patterson told Saunders to expect him at Stono Ferry on March 25th. Some help arrived for the defenders of Charlestown when Colonel Garden and 100 South Carolina militiamen overcame their fear of smallpox and entered the city.

The British fleet had been stalled outside the Bar for sixteen days, waiting for the weather to cooperate. A hard rain had hit the low country on the 18th and 19th, and the wind blew against the British fleet. Finally on March 20th the wind changed its course and Admiral Arbuthnot was able to cross the Bar with his smaller warships. He had to leave the large ships of the line behind, since they would not have been able to make it over the shallow sandbar. Even with the smaller ships it would be hard to cross over. Most of the heavy guns and ammunition were removed so that they would be light enough to make it.

Arbuthnot transferred his flag to the *Roebuck* and crossed over with the *Richmond*, *Romulus*, *Blonde*, *Perseus*, *Raleigh*, two transports and several smaller vessels. The British fleet sailed unopposed into Five Fathom Hole.

If Admiral Whipple had decided to make a stand there then he would have been outnumbered, but every British ship would have to attack by using just their bow guns, while Whipple could annihilate them with broadsides. Whipple had been given almost 1/3 of the entire Continental Navy to protect Charlestown, and he did not want to lose any of the ships to British gunfire. He also did not think that a ship as large as the *Renown* could even get over the Bar. His lack of an aggressive attack would cost the Patriots dearly.

A South Carolina Galley Captain, Charles Crawley, suggested that Whipple order the galleys to the Bar to attack the British before they could remount their guns. These smaller, faster ships could make quick work of the British fleet. Whipple held a council of war with his other ship captains, and they voted no. The only galley captain there, Crawley, voted yes. So Whipple let another chance to stop the British slip through his fingers. The British now had nothing standing between them and Fort Moultrie.

Lincoln finally realized that his naval commander was not a fighter, and he ordered the ships to return to Charlestown and anchor in the Cooper River. The citizens of Charlestown did not realize that their situation just became more desperate. They still had hope that the British would be easily defeated, just like they had been in 1776 at Fort Sullivan, and when Prévost tried to take the city in 1779.

On March 27th the British anchored ninety flatboats and longboats at Wappoo Neck. These boats would be used to ferry the British across the Ashley River. The next day the American frigate *Boston* fired upon Fort Johnson, killing a British gunner and shooting the leg off of a Hessian grenadier. The Hessian died later. One grenadier was severely wounded in the arm, and several muskets were shot to pieces.

On March 28th Clinton made all the necessary preparations to cross the Ashley River. A redoubt had been built five days earlier to cover the movement across the river. Seventy-five flatboats were moved by the Patriot batteries, at three in the morning, using muffled oars.

The British and Hessian Grenadiers, the British cavalry, and the 7th, 23rd, and 71st Regiments rendezvoused with the flatboats at Drayton's Plantation. The Light Infantry, 33rd Regiment and the Jägers were camped there awaiting them. The 63rd and 64th Regiments, along with the rest of Paterson's army stayed west of the

Ashley River to keep the lines of communication open between Clinton's army and the Royal Navy.

A few hours after arriving the Royal Navy seamen had to conduct a river crossing into enemy territory. At 8 o'clock in the morning on 29th the troops at Drayton Hall entered the Ashley River, while the 23rd Regiment and the British Legion covered the crossing.

The first wave consisted of the Light Infantry, the 1st Battalion of British Grenadiers, and the Jägers. As they began some Patriot riflemen fired at them from long range, but with no effect. They sailed up the Ashley River under the escort of an armed row galley, looking for a landing location.

After four miles a slightly raised bank was located at the house of Benjamin Fuller. At the plantation was a Patriot double cavalry post. The row galley approached the house and fired on it to determine if there were any cannon there. The Patriot cavalry returned fire, but did not have any artillery. The Light Infantry and Jägers quickly disembarked on the shore, and secured a half-moon perimeter around the house.

The second wave of troops consisted of the British and Hessian Grenadiers, and then the third wave with the 7th, 33rd, and 71st Regiments came ashore onto the Charlestown peninsula.

Captain Ewald moved ahead to establish a forward post, and skirmished with some of the Patriot cavalry. The British Row Galley fired artillery at the cavalry and drove them off.

The British troops at the perimeter remained there until the rest of the soldiers had crossed the Ashley River. The only opposition to the landings was a picket of "Negroes" that they saw at a distance that were "observing rather than hindering".

Lincoln could not oppose the landing because he did not have enough men and were denied the "advantages of opposing them with any considerable force in crossing this river."

Captain Peebles described the area they marched through, "The country as far as we went has the same uniform appearance, a dead flat intersected with swamps, marshes & creeks. The wood mostly pine & only clear'd about the Houses, several of which we saw that look'd very well, but all deserted." By 9:00 that night the British had reached the Quarter House Tavern located six miles from Charlestown.

On the evening of the 29th the British army moved into camp near the Quarter House. The Ashley River protected their right flank, and the army formed a front facing three sides. The entire British army, with General Patterson's reinforcements, consisted of ten thousand men.

Lieutenant Colonel Laurens with a detachment of light infantry exchanged fire with the British advance elements at Gibbe's Plantation. The British artillery returned fire, killing Captain Bowman of the North Carolina Continentals. On that same afternoon a patrol of light infantry found five Jägers who had been missing. All were dead, killed by bayonets, and the eyes of one had been cut out. Captain Ewald thought that this might have meant the Patriots were angry at losing heavily in the previous day's action at Gibbe's Plantation.

Commodore Whipple had 9 armed vessels to oppose the British, but he decided that he could not take on the Royal Navy. Whipple pulled back to the Cooper River when Arbuthnot moved his vessels across the bar. This was the last practical defensive use for Whipple's fleet. They no longer had any maneuver room to take on the British ships, and were reduced to guarding the Cooper River supply line to Bacon's Bridge.

Lincoln ordered Whipple to block the channel between the city of Charlestown and Shutes Folly. This was a large sandbar beside Mount Pleasant. Though Lincoln wanted to sink ships in the narrow channel between Sullivan's Island and James Island, he couldn't because the current was too swift.

Ships that could have stopped the British were now useless. Four frigates, the *Queen of France, Bricole, Boston, Truite* and several merchant vessels, had chevaux de frise constructed on their decks and were sunk in the mouth of the Cooper River.

A boom, or chain, from the Exchange building, to Shutes Folly, linked the ships to the shore and would stop any other ships from crossing the Cooper River. The guns and crews of all but two vessels were brought ashore to strengthen the Patriot defenses.

The Hog Island channel between Shutes Folly and Mount Pleasant remained open. Behind the boom were Whipple's remaining warships, the *Providence*, *Boston*, *Ranger* and *L'aventure* to protect the river.

When Whipple decided to abandon the Bar he ended the Continental Navy's chance to stop the British. George Washington commented that his failure had amounted "to the loss of the town and garrison…it really appears to me that the propriety of attempting to defend the town depended on the probability of defending the bar."

On March 30th the British began moving artillery, ammunition, tools, siege materials and provisions across the Ashley, to the peninsula, and stockpiling them at Gibbe's Plantation. Towards evening the Jägers on the picket line stood about a mile from the city. Before them lay a flat, sandy plain, unbroken by a house, tree, or bush. The only shelter consisted in a few ditches. [181]

The American defensive line was an unbroken wall of defenses that stretched from the Ashley to the Cooper Rivers. In front of the defensive line Lincoln had ordered that all trees and underbrush be destroyed, and any houses were removed. Captain Hinrichs wrote that the Americans had "every house razed and every tree and shrub chopped down."

In the center of the Patriot works was an eighteen-gun fortress known as the "old royal work", or the Hornwork, constructed of lime and seashells that had the strength of reinforced concrete. Over that tough exterior were laid palmetto logs to absorb any cannonballs.

The Hornwork was three tiers of artillery, and there was a ditch that would slow any attackers. It was flanked on both sides by bastions that allowed the defenders to fire on any attackers trying to go over the walls of the Hornwork. It guarded the gate to city on King Street. The gate also had a lunette right in front of it. A Lunette was a small half moon fortification.

In front of the Hornwork, stretching from river to river was a series of redoubts and batteries that were connected by a wall, or parapet. Two main redoubts were built on the Ashley and Cooper Rivers to anchor the parapet. The Cooper redoubt was in front of the line, so that the defenders could fire upon any troops trying to assault the main works.

Both these redoubts were constructed in the same way that Fort Sullivan was in 1776. Palmetto logs were laid one upon the other in two parallel rows that were sixteen feet apart. The space between the logs was filled with sand. The walls were fifteen feet high to protect the batteries, and longer planks were set up along the walls to stop any musket fire from the marines located in ship's tops.

In front of the parapet there was a ditch that was six feet deep and twelve feet wide. This raised the height of the parapet and it would slow down any assaulting force. The soldiers on the parapet, and the soldiers in the redoubts would fire upon any attackers caught in the ditch.

To make it even harder to assault, the ditch had a double palisade. These were two rows of sharpened wooden stakes set close together at the bottom of the ditch. In front of the ditch were two lines of abatis. Just just cutting down trees could make these naturally, and then placing them on the ground with their sharpened branches facing outwards, or an abatis could be made by constructing a chevaux de frise. A chevaux de frise was a portable obstacle used to stop cavalry or to form roadblocks. It was formed by large beams traversed with long pointed spikes, forming an "x" if observed from the side. The chevaux de frise was the 18th century version of barbed wire.\

In front of the abatis was the canal, or wet ditch. This was an eight-foot deep, sixteen-foot wide canal that had been dug to connect the Ashley to the Cooper Rivers. Sluices on the side of the Cooper River could control the depth of the water. An advanced work, known as the Half Moon Battery, was constructed on the Ashley River side of the ditch to fire upon any attackers trying to cross the ditch.

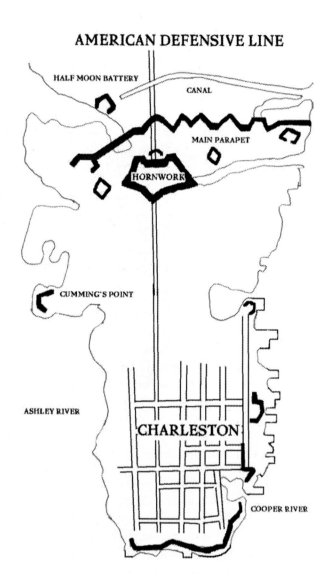

In between the canal and the main defensive line parapet was dug several "wolf pits" that would break up any linear formation approaching the parapets. It would seem that the assault upon Charlestown would annihilate the British army.

Lincoln had put the Virginia continentals and the 2nd and 3rd South Carolina Regiments in camp on the left of the lines. They were under Colonel Richard Parker. The North Carolina Brigade was on the right of the line. Colonel Laurens and his light infantry were in reserve, near the Hornwork. The 1st South Carolina Regiment was in Fort Moultrie, while most of the militia was along the waterfront batteries in town, under the command of General Lachlan McIntosh. The Artillery brigade under Colonel Beekman was posted on the batteries along the trench lines.

At sunset on April 1st 3,000 soldiers and laborers marched from Gibbe's Plantation to the place chosen by Clinton's chief engineer, Major Moncrief, to begin the siege. They were within 800 yards of the Patriot works at Hempstead Hill near the Cooper River. Half of the men began digging the trenches while the light infantry and grenadiers guarded against attack.

Moncrief had all the wooden buildings in the area torn down, and used the wood to erect a wall of mantelets, six feet high and sixteen feet long in which to work behind. Since the soil was sandy they were able to work quickly. In a single night they built redoubts number 3, 4, and 5, and a communication trench to each of the redoubts, without having a single shot fired at them. The communication trench was the easiest to make, since it had been a trench that the Americans had failed to fill in. In the morning the Americans were surprised to find three redoubts facing the Hornwork. A single 24-pounder fired shots against the British works.

The approach to Charlestown was done in a style of fighting that was similar to the trench fighting of World War I. The day was occupied with digging approach trenches in the sandy soil, while at night the British waited for an assault by the Patriots.

The first step in siege warfare was to gather men and materials out of range of gunfire and observation. The British had done this at Gibbe's Plantation. The approach trenches were dug to within 600 to 800 yards of the defenses, then a trench twelve to fifteen feet wide, and three feet deep, was dug at right angles to the approach trenches.

The dirt removed from the trenches was used to make a parapet four feet high in front of the trench. The first trench was called the first parallel. The digging on the first parallel went quickly due to the soft sand. Walls made of planks were constructed at Gibbe's Plantation and then brought up to the trenches. The wall was placed in the appropriate place and sand was piled up on either side. Along the first parallel the three redoubts that would contain artillery were built, 600 paces between each other.

All day long on April 2nd the British watched boats going up the Cooper River, moving civilians and their property out of the city and into the backcountry. On the night of April 2nd The British strengthened the first three redoubts, and then began building a fourth one, Redoubt Number 1, that would be on the Ashley River.

On April 3rd the Americans had finally brought up some artillery to deal with the British work parties. Field guns and howitzers ploughed up the ground, but did little damage. British Captain Russell wrote, "The Rebels fired near 300 shot and 30 small Shells, but did no manner of Injury."

This may have been true where Russell was, but the thirty 6-inch mortar bombs that were thrown into the trenches wounded two Hessian Grenadiers and killed four English Grenadiers.

The British could not return fire yet, because they had not brought up any cannon. Since the British had thrown their horses overboard during the gale, they had to use men to haul the guns to the trenches. Sometimes it would take up to one hundred men to move a 24-pound cannon on a naval carriage. These men would then have to haul and drag all of the ammunition and artillery stores needed to fire the guns to the batteries.

Due to the lack of roads the British engineers would "corduroy" a road. Trees were cut down and placed on the sand to make a solid roadway. The British laid hundreds of hurdles, made by the light infantry, across the marshes so they would be passable by the troops.[182]

Once an artillery parapet was constructed they would haul a wooden platform into place. This was needed so that the artillery would not sink into the sand with the recoil of each shot. Mortar batteries had to have heavy frames built, which would absorb the shock of the mortars as they fired. Without them the mortars would bury themselves in the ground after a few shots.

The Patriot artillery fire stopped after the sun went down on April 3rd, and the British resumed the building of the trenches, mainly focusing their efforts on building a battery on Hempstead Hill, 350 yards away from the Patriot lines.

By morning the Hempstead Hill battery had become Redoubt Number 6. It was only partially completed though, with a one wall towards the Patriot batteries, and one wall towards the Cooper River. The battery would hold nine cannons with masked embrasures, as soon as the artillery could be dragged up there.

Every redoubt required sixteen mantlets, which were carried by 400 workmen, and accompanied by 100 more workmen with tools. The men would pack twelve feet of earth against the mantlets as protection against the large cannons of the Patriots. The back of the redoubt was left wide open, inviting a sortie by the Americans. To insure that this did not happen Clinton posted 100 Jägers, under the command of Ewald, at the redoubt.

When the Americans noticed the new battery they began to direct their fire towards it. Initially only two cannon could fire upon the newly constructed battery, but the Patriots were able to drag up three more and fired over 600 shots from the 12, 18 and 24-pounders into the redoubt.

The Continental ships *Ranger* and *Providence* sailed up the Cooper River added their firepower to the barrage against the battery. The *Providence* and two galleys sailed closer to the battery, and fired broadsides into the small fort, however the fort was so low to the ground that most of the shots sailed past it.

The *Providence* moved away and then fired plunging fire into the fort, dropping the balls into the center of it. The Jägers inside the fort was protected by a trench that had been built, and no one was wounded.

The *Ranger* sailed up Town Creek and was able to fire into the unprotected side of the fort. Ewald wrote that for "over an hour we had to endure heavy cannon fire." Lieutenant Wilson wrote that there was "no Loss from the Enemy's fire", but he had been inside the battery. Outside the battery the men trying to get to the redoubt did not have it so easy. One British soldier was killed and another was wounded.

Lieutenant MacLeod, of the Royal Artillery, had eighty sailors move a 24-pound cannon and a howitzer close to Town Creek, and fired two shots at the *Providence*, forcing her to withdraw. Another shot hit the *Ranger* in the bow and lodged in the ship's hull. Captain Simpson of the *Ranger* ordered the ship to return back down the river. During the bombardment the British had managed to close up the back of the redoubt.

On board the *Ranger* was Lincoln's aide-de-camp, Major Matthew Clarkson. He had been sent with the *Ranger* to determine if an assault could be made upon the works. Once Clarkson saw that the British had finished the fort he advised Lincoln against an assault.

After the sun went down the British started constructing Redoubt Number 2. Both redoubts were 200 paces in front of the first parallel, so they could cover any attack made by the Americans. The Americans did not let them build in peace. Quartermaster John Lewis Gervais wrote that they "Fired a great deal all night, & threw Several Shells at the Enemys Works."

When the Patriots discovered the new redoubt on the morning of the 5th, they directed all of their artillery on it and the Hempstead battery, killing three soldiers of the 33rd Regiment, and wounding three more. Two Hessian Grenadiers were also wounded. The constant thud of large iron cannon balls smashing into the redoubts, and the hissing fuses of the bombs thrown about the trenches did not allow the British to get any rest.

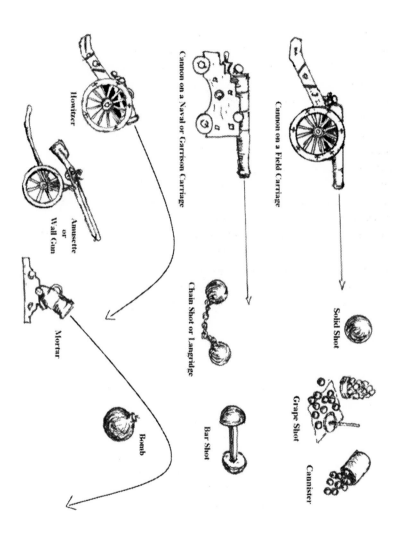

Howitzer

Cannon on a Naval or Garrison Carriage

Cannon on a Field Carriage

Amusette
or
Wall Gun

Chain Shot or Langridge

Solid Shot

Mortar

Bomb

Bar Shot

Grape Shot

Cannister

One of the Patriot bombs fell into Redoubt Number 6, between two powder kegs that were just in front of the position occupied by General Clinton and Lord Cornwallis. Neither man was hurt.

For the next 24 hours the Patriots threw 573 shells into the British trenches. The *Boston* and the *Providence* came up and supported the Patriot artillery barrage. Moncrieff placed two 12-pounders and a howitzer, on a promontory on the Cooper River and drove off the frigates.

Toward evening an American brigantine, whose deck was "crowded with men and women", sailed towards the British works and fired twenty-three shots, then sailed back.

Women were a constant sight in the Patriot lines, observing the one-sided fight. They were safe since the British had not been able to mount any large cannon and return the American's fire. General Moultrie wrote "The women walk out from town to the lines, with all the composure imaginable, to see us cannonade the enemy."

Toward the evening the Patriots redoubled their fire. Lieutenant Alexander Grant of the 42nd Highlanders was hit in the shoulder by a cannonball, but he survived with only a minor wound. One of the grenadiers of the 23rd Fusiliers lost an arm, and a fusilier of the 7th Regiment deserted to the American side. One of the British batteries randomly fired onto the Cooper River to prevent any more frigates from gaining the flanks of the redoubts.

At 9 p.m. Clinton ordered the Fenwick batteries across the Ashley River to fire upon the city. Two of the British Row Galleys also fired red-hot shot into the town. Over two hundred 24 and 32-pound balls smashed into the homes, tearing out the other side.

A cannonball killed "Morrow, a Carpenter…just as he was going out of his house." One soldier of the 3rd South Carolina was wounded at the battery on Cumming's Point. Five cannonballs hit one house and the outbuildings. Two balls tore through General McIntosh's quarters and killed two of his horses.

Clinton specifically ordered the town to be fired upon, and not the Patriot defenses. The British galley *Scourge* fired 85 times, and "every shot of them went into the town." This firing angered the inhabitants of the city since it was totally unexpected. Ewald took some of his Jägers on a reconnaissance, and he heard the "loud wailing of female voices" coming from the city. The next day the Americans were "pretty quiet".

The quiet may have been because the Americans had run low on ammunition, and not because of the shelling of the town. Throughout the daylight hours of April 6th the American batteries replenished their ammunition and supplies. Each battery was to have 100 rounds per gun, and an equivalent amount of powder.

During the lull in fire the British placed a battery of nine 24-pounders, manned by two hundred sailors, in the first parallel. All the artillery pieces and the ammunition had to be brought up from the landing place at Gibbe's Plantation, and carried across the swamps by the "sailors and Negroes."

Clinton was pleased with the progress of his men and wrote that they had constructed "a parallel of 2 miles in 3 days." He was not pleased with the Royal Navy and wrote that Admiral Arbuthnot had slowed down the progress of the campaign. To make matters worse the Royal Navy manned their own battery during the siege, because Arbuthnot demanded that only naval officers would command them.

The Hessians felt that the British covering parties were not protecting them adequately and they voiced their displeasure, or showed it by deserting to the American lines. On April 5th three British and two Hessians came into the American lines, while another paddled over from James Island on a plank.

Clinton and his second in command, Charles Cornwallis had an intense dislike of each other. If Clinton was killed, captured or resigned, then Cornwallis would become the new British commander in North America. Cornwallis feared that Charlestown would be a disaster and attempted to distance himself from command decisions. During a reconnaissance of the Ashley River Cornwallis told Clinton that he did not want to be "consulted as he was afraid of responsibility." Clinton wrote that he could "never be cordial with such a man."

Approach trenches were dug from the first parallel towards the Patriot works. Normally these would be dug in zigzag lines, so the enemy would not be able to fire down into the trenches, but

Moncrieff had his men dig the trenches in straight line. He did not feel threatened by the American firepower.

As Clinton closed in, artillery was moved forward into the redoubts to begin the work of blasting an opening in the defenses and to keep the Americans occupied while the British work parties dug the lines. Very few of the artillery was in place.

The British had built a machine to transport boats from the Cooper River overland to the Ashley River. The machine had "two wheels in front and a sledge in back. The machine was pulled by a hundred and thirty-four Negroes." This was to stop the flow of supplies coming down the Cooper and Ashley rivers to the defenders of Charlestown.

Even with these protective measures, at 1 o'clock on the afternoon of April 8th, eleven American schooners and sloops, loaded with troops, sailed down the Cooper River, right past the British lines and into the city. Ewald wrote that the sailed "right before our eyes."

The reinforcements were 750 Virginia Continentals under General Woodford. They had forced-marched 500 miles in twenty-eight days to reach Charlestown. The Virginians had come by way of the crossroads at Monck's Corner, and then down the Cooper River. With Woodford were 120 North Carolina militiamen under Lieutenant Colonel Harrington. Shortly after arriving in Charlestown, Harrington was promoted to Brigadier General of the Salisbury District Militia.

Upon the arrival of the Continentals the people of Charlestown celebrated, and continuous church bells sounded. The reinforcements landed at Gadsden's Wharf and marched to the lines. The men defending the lines gave three cheers and the cannons fired a feu-de-joie thirteen times, one for each of the States.[183]

The morale in the city rose as high as it would be during the siege. These men weren't country militia, but were veterans of Washington's army. John Wells wrote that they "wear the appearance of, what they are in reality, Hardy Veterans." Combined with the veteran Continentals of the North Carolina line it seemed that the fight for Charlestown would be too much for the British to stomach.

The Virginians took their place in the line, to the left and right of the Hornwork. Though the city seemed elated that the Continentals had arrived, for many it was a chance to leave the city. When the ships that brought the Virginians sailed back in the afternoon, it was loaded with civilians evacuating the city.

The church bells continued to ring into the night and cannon and mortar fire fell on the British trenches and redoubts in celebration. The celebration would only last for 24 hours.

On April 8th Admiral Arbuthnot sailed the British fleet past intense gunfire from Fort Moultrie, so that they would be able to fire on the city defenses. British losses were minimal. During the naval battle in the harbor, the fighting on land ceased for the time to watch the spectacle.

When the British ships anchored near Fort Johnson it reversed the mood of the city. This was the first time that British ships had forced their way into the harbor since 1775. One Hessian soldier wrote that they now had "revenge for yesterday's cheering."

Captain Heinrichs of the Jägers wrote that right after the British ships sailed past the fort he watched a crowd of small boats on the Cooper River carry off even more of the citizens. Clinton wrote, "They sent off many of their women."

Now that Arbuthnot had succeeded in forcing his way into the harbor the relations between him and Clinton became more cordial. The two commanders were able to meet and make final plans for the siege. Arbuthnot said that his ships would ensure that the lines of communication would remain open to James Island. This freed up soldiers that Clinton needed to seal off the Cooper River and tighten the noose. Clinton sent Banastre Tarleton to cease the flow of movement at Monck's Corner.

Clinton wanted Arbuthnot to send ships into the Hog Island Channel, in between Shutes Folly and Mount Pleasant. On April 9th the British transported four gunboats and two flatboats from the Ashley, to the Cooper by the use of the two wheeled sledge.

Patrick O'Kelley

The British received a reinforcement of Captain Collins and his 80 Royal artillerymen. The artillerymen had been separated from the fleet during the big storm, and had been saved by an English privateer. They had been taken to Bermuda and then brought to Charlestown.

The British did lose the heavy siege guns and ammunition that were on their ship. To take the place of the needed siege guns, the British had to take the heavy cannon off the warships, and drag them across land, to place them in the batteries.

The Patriots constructed a battery at Hobcaw to check the British ships now in range of the town. On the night of April 9th the Hessians built embrasures that would mount six 12-pounders 150 yards in front of the Redoubt Number 5. This was connected to the first parallel by a trench. Unfortunately for the British they had only been able to mount artillery in two fortifications by April 10th, and they could not return fire effectively.

As was the custom in siege warfare once the first parallel was finished Clinton called on Lincoln to surrender the city. Lincoln replied that he felt it his duty to continue to resist "to the last extremity", but he also urged Governor Rutledge to leave the town and form a government in exile in the backcountry.

When Prévost had attempted to capture Charlestown the year before, Lincoln had been away from the city, trying to get the British to attack in the countryside. Because Lincoln was not there Charlestown was almost lost. The citizens of Charlestown criticized Lincoln for not protecting the largest port in the South. Lincoln asked to resign, but Congress would not let him. Now that Charlestown was threatened again Lincoln would not leave the city defenseless a second time.

At ten o'clock that night the British soldiers in their trenches knew of the decision to fight on by the Americans, because the Patriots began to fire artillery at them that lasted until morning.

On the morning of the 11th the Patriots discovered the new Hessian works, and bombarded the positions with 300 cannon shots and 41 shells. Pieces of the breastworks were seen flying in the air during the bombardment. One Jäger and five Hessian grenadiers were killed. One of the Hessians had his head shot off by a cannonball.

General Clinton had been inspecting the trenches during the bombardment and wrote, "The rebels fired some shells too well. ONE BURST CLOSE TO ME. Their fire from cannon trifling."

That night a trench had been dug from the first parallel to the advanced Hessian battery. The Patriots brought up two heavy mortars and four howitzers to the right of the parallel. Every time they fired, the British battery at Fenwick's Point silenced them. One of the Patriot mortars burst when the charge was too much for the barrel.

During this period in the siege Clinton was worried about not having enough shot for the cannon. He blamed Admiral Arbuthnot for not bringing a sufficient supply.

On the night of April 11th three British armed boats were transported overland by wheels, and rowed out to the French Polacre *Zephyr,* located in the Cooper River. The *Zephyr* had a number of prisoners and Loyalist civilians on board. When the boats approached to within musket range, a sentry challenged them from the deck of the *Zephyr.* The British tried to deceive the sentry by telling him that they were from the city, and they were only trying to row to the other side. While they were talking the British tried to move closer to the brig, but they discovered that the decks were full of armed men. As they quickly rowed back the Patriots demanded to know who was on board. The British sailors replied, "Our cargo consists of sabers and pistols!" They then began laughing, and clapping loudly, firing grapeshot and muskets at the *Zephyr*, but to no effect.

On April 12th Major John Gilbank of the Charlestown Battalion of Artillery was killed by accident when a shell exploded. During the siege the American gunners were not as effective as the British. They would fire thousands of rounds, and do very little damage. Some historians suspect that this may have been in part due to the death of Major Gilbank. He specialized in the making of fuses, and with his death there was no one with his experience to take his place.

Lincoln knew that the key to fighting the British was to keep the Cooper River open. He had ensured that the British would not be able to sail up the river, because of the boom that stretched to Folly's Island. However he needed to keep the northern end of the river open so that supplies and reinforcements could come in. Colonel Marquis Francis de Malmedy and 200 North Carolina militia were ordered to "secure the several passes on the Cooper River." They were also supposed to build defenses on the north side of the Wando River, at Cainhoy and Lempriére's Point.[184]

Six 18-pound cannon were sent to Lempriére's from Fort Moultrie, along with slaves to build the redoubt. Since the Royal Navy had passed by Fort Moultrie, the cannon weren't needed there anymore. The polacre *Zephyr* was ordered to guard the mouth of the Wando River. Malmedy was also ordered to find every armed boat he could and use them on the Cooper and Wando River, to cover all the different crossing points.

To ensure the security of the two posts at Mount Pleasant and Lempriére's Point Lincoln sent 300 additional troops from Charlestown to Colonel Malmedy. The men included Lieutenant Colonel Laurens and his Light Infantry. The slaves had built a strong redoubt and the British described it as "tolerable" with a "good ditch" surrounding it. Cornwallis said that any attempt to storm the fort would be done so with "considerable loss".

Any enemy ship trying to sail up the Cooper River would be hit by two sides, from the Charlestown batteries, and from the guns at Lempriére's Point. If the Royal Navy tried to run through the Hog Island Channel the Mount Pleasant battery would fire them upon.

To guard the upper reaches of the Cooper River Lincoln sent Brigadier General Isaac Huger and all of the Patriot cavalry to guard Biggin's Bridge, near Monck's Corner. This consisted of the 1st and 3rd Continental Dragoons, the remains of Pulaski's Legion cavalry and Horry's South Carolina dragoons.

On April 12th an English frigate and two schooners sailed past the heavy gunfire of Fort Moultrie, increasing the fleet in Charlestown harbor.

By April 13th the British had been able to mount seventeen 24-pounders, two 12-pounders, three 8-inch howitzers, and nine mortars in three of the seven batteries. About 750 feet from canal a second parallel was begun.

Between the parallels short parallel trenches were dug on the flanks of the approach trenches. The infantry were gathered in all these to protect against possible sorties from the Patriots aimed at destroying work parties, trenches, and artillery positions.

At the head of the approach trenches a squad of soldiers would begin digging a narrow, shallow trench called a sap. The lead man would excavate a small trench only a foot and a half wide, and deep. He would push ahead of him a two-wheeled device called a mantalet, used to protect him from enemy fire. As he went along he would place gabions along the route.[185] The men behind him would widen and deepen the sap and put fascines on the parapets.[186] Working parties from infantry units later dug the sap to regular size.

The chance of a midnight raid by the Patriots could catch these "sappers" without any protection, and they would be in danger of being bayoneted, before their infantry could reach them. Mysteriously this midnight sortie by the Patriots only happened once, much later into the siege.

Lincoln called a council of war of his senior officers and told them the situation did not look very good. They were wanting in troops, clothing, provisions, artillery and ammunition. He also told them that there would be no more reinforcements, and his engineers told him that the defensive lines could only hold out for a few days. He wanted opinions from the officers on whether they should stay or evacuate the garrison. General McIntosh wanted to leave the city and at least get the Continental troops out. He believed that "the Salvation not only of this State but some other" depended on it. Lincoln said that all the officers needed to consider the idea of evacuation by the next meeting.

At 10:00 in the morning a giant roar of cannon fire interrupted the meeting. The British guns had finally opened fire. Prior to this there had only been sporadic cannon fire from some small batteries or the Fenwick batteries. Now the British fired cannons and mortars at the town from morning until midnight. The first thirty shots fired by the British dismounted three Patriot pieces on their right. A 26-pounder was destroyed and an 18-pounder dismounted. Major William Croghan wrote that "the balls flew thro' the streets, & spent their fury on the houses; & those who were walking or visiting in the town, as was usual during the former quiet, now flew to their cellars, & others to the works, as the places of greatest safety."

The Americans returned fire, adding to the noise of the bombardment. A British grenadier was killed and two infantrymen were wounded in the trenches. Toward midday an incident occurred that enraged Clinton, when the Hessian batteries on Hempstead Hill bombarded the city with carcasses. Carcasses were iron shells pierced with holes and filled with incendiary materials for use against buildings and ships. They had the desired effect of igniting several houses in the Ansonborough district of the city.

Captain de la Morlière wrote "The houses being separated one from another, the fire extinguished itself after having consumed seven or eight. There were several persons killed in the town." A child, its nurse, a sergeant and a private of Hogun's North Carolina Brigade were killed.

The Royal Navy seaman aboard the ships shouted their encouragement when they saw the town in flames. Clinton wrote that it was "Absurd, impolitic, and inhuman to burn a town you mean to occupy," and ordered his artillery to stop such bombardments against the town.

Arbuthnot disagreed with Clinton about shelling the city, and sent the following message ashore to Elphinstone: "The Admiral and Sir A.S.H. begs their compliments to you and begs you will burn the Town as soon as possible and send 24 pound shot into the stomacks of the women to see how they will deliver them."

The British remembered how the French guns shelled the town of Savannah, killing women and children as they hid in their cellars. Fortunately for Charlestown Arbuthnot was not in command of the land artillery.

Three British soldiers became casualties when their artillery piece exploded while loading it. Peebles wrote, "an artillery man lost an arm & an assistant kill'd by one of our own Guns hanging fire & going off when they put in the spunge, a man of the 37th. Light Infantry had his backside shot away looking for balls."

On the American side there were accidents too. Two men in the South Carolina artillery were killed when their 12-pounder went off accidentally as they were loading the cannon. Another man was killed for the same reason in the militia artillery.

The artillery stopped at midnight, to the relief of the city. The British were more accurate with their artillery, but this was due to having actual Royal Artillerymen on the guns. Up until April 13th the Americans had done most of the firing. Captain Russell of the British wrote that they had fired "above 4,000 Shot and Shells" with very little effect. The British guns had destroyed two American guns and an embrasure in just one day.

Lincoln convinced Rutledge that he needed to leave the city so that he could "keep alive the Civil authority, give confidence to the people, and throw in the necessary… supplies to the garrison." Rutledge agreed, and he crossed the Cooper River around noon. As he rode into exile he looked back at his city in flames, and could hear the rolling thunder of the bombardment.

Christopher Gadsden would remain behind as lieutenant governor. Lincoln hoped that Rutledge would be able to convince the country militia to come to the relief of the city. When Rutledge left the city so did a number of invalids and wounded men.

One of these men was Francis Marion. On March 19th Marion had attended a dinner party at a house on the corner of Orange and Tradd, hosted by Moultrie's adjutant general, Captain Alexander McQueen. In a custom of the time, McQueen locked all the doors and first floor windows so his guests could not escape.

Marion was not a drinking man. He was descended from French Huguenots, and the hardest thing he drank was vinegar. Marion decided to go to the second floor and jump out the window. Upon landing he badly fractured his ankle, which put him in the category of an officer unfit for duty. By April his injury had still not healed and he was evacuated. His injury saved him from capture and would create a South Carolina legend.

For the next three days there was heavy cannonading and bombarding by both sides. Lieutenant Colonel Grimkè moved mortars to the right of the line so that they could fire all night on the British work parties. General Moultrie ordered that the advanced battery on the left fire solid shot, "en recochet", down the British trenches.[187] Moultrie also directed that a 12-pounder and three 4-pounders in the Cooper River redoubt keep up a continuous fire of grapeshot at the ground between the two parallels.

During this intense bombardment Captain Jackson of the row galley *Comet* had his leg shot off, and another sailor was wounded. Captain Peebles of the 42nd Highlanders wrote, "The Rebels throw their shells better than we do." The American firepower was so effective that the British work parties had to "retire for a while." Their cannonballs continuously tore down through the middle of a communication trench. Captain Hinrichs wrote that nineteen 18-pound balls, and thirteen mortar shells had fallen into the second parallel.

The British must have thrown their own cannon balls rather well, because on the 14th Clinton wrote, "Not a gun appears in rebel right work." A British bomb battery was created that consisted of twenty royal and coehorn mortars. They bombarded Charlestown and its defenses. General McIntosh wrote that they kept up "an Incessant fire from their small Arms, Cannon, and Mortars."

Six 24-pounders were moved to Stiles Point, on James Island, and became known as the Admiral's Battery. They also fired on the city. Grimkè wrote that during the bombardment "an Inhabitant of the Town was killed & a Woman wounded in bed together." One of the cannonballs fired from James Island struck a statue of William Pitt, on the corner of Broad and Meeting Street, and broke off the right arm.

The American firepower was still intense, because on the night of the 14th Clinton thought that the Americans were assaulting the second parallel. A British grenadier was killed in the exchange of fire. One North Carolina sergeant was killed by a cannon ball, and one of the Charlestown Artillery was killed, while another was wounded. Two matrosses of the 4th South Carolina Regiment were killed. During the bombardment the British soldiers would train all their muskets on the embrasures of the Patriot cannons. Whenever the crew appeared to reload the cannon they would come under a hail of fire. Very accurate sniper fire was recorded on both sides as the Jäger and Patriot riflemen exchanged fire throughout the day. One of the British light infantry of the 16th Regiment was shot through the eye, and four of the Regulars were killed.

The Jägers would post their sharpshooters before the sun would came up, ready to take a shot at anyone they could see at the American lines, 300 yards away. The sun would be to the Patriot's back, and silhouette them for the Jägers. All the other men in the trench, light infantry and grenadiers, would stand by ready to repulse any sorties until the sun came up.

The Americans built an advanced work in front of the Cooper River redoubt, "for Riflemen, to annoy the Enemy in their Approach." On April 15th they were able to wound two British soldiers working on the new parallel, and the next day a rifleman shot a light infantryman through the eye as he looked over the wall of the trench.

To bring about the end to the siege Clinton wanted Arbuthnot to send frigates up the Cooper River, but the admiral did not want to sail near the Patriot's in Lempriére's Point and have his ships destroyed.

One problem with trying to take measurements in the channel was that the entrance of Hog Island channel was within musket shot of the Lempriére redoubt. If any British ships tried to cover the reconnaissance, they were fired upon by Fort Moultrie. Clinton wrote that it would take at least 1,000 troops to secure the point, and any troops landing to attack the fortifications would have to do so without naval support.

Clinton had sent Colonel Webster with his brigade to attack the American's on the east side of the Cooper River, but he had not heard from Webster in days. He hoped that if Webster were successful the Americans would abandon the fortifications.

An 18-inch mortar arrived for the British from St. Augustine on April 16th. With the mortar were several French field pieces that had been captured at Savannah. Toward the evening a Patriot Row Galley moved towards the Cooper River and fired on the British hospital, wounding one man. It was forced to withdraw when the Hessians brought up two French and one English 24-pounder.

Clinton determined that the firepower on the work parties trying to construct the second parallel was too intense. On the night of April 16th the British started a new approach trench between Redoubts Number 2 and 3. They created a 300 yard sap before the sun came up, and the new section of the second parallel was begun.

On the 17th the British constructed demi-parallels, under intense grapeshot and musket fire. They connected the two parts of the second parallel, to complete it. The price to finish the works had cost them. Five Hessian grenadiers and three British infantry were killed, and fourteen others were wounded. The Patriots fired scrap iron and broken glass, which wounded nine of the British in the legs.

The Patriots received their share of wounded from British and Jäger snipers, and from artillery fire. Thirty of the Patriots were wounded on the 17th. In the Wappoo battery a man and woman, who were spectators from Charlestown, were wounded.

During the siege Clinton constantly worried about the ammunition for the artillery, and did not want any indiscriminate firing from the batteries. Because of the loss of the *Russia Merchant* the artillery did not have enough 24-pound shot. Unfortunately for Clinton, half of the guns used in the siege were 24-pounders.

On the night of the 17th the British army batteries were tired of listening to the constant firing of the Royal Navy battery, and told them to cease firing on order of General Clinton. Arbuthnot complained and Clinton denied that he had done this. He suspected the order came from the commissary of artillery.

On April 18th almost 3,000 men from New York arrived and reinforced Clinton. Though relieved, Clinton still worried about Webster's corps. He had not heard from him at all, and he sent Lieutenant Colonel Nisbet Balfour and the 23rd Regiment to find Webster.

That same day Moultrie's aide, Philip Neyle, was killed when a cannonball took off part of his head. The Patriots built another rifle breastwork to the left of the hornwork to harass the British on their approach.

That night the British had one light infantryman killed, and two others wounded. Ten men of the British artillery were killed or wounded. The Patriots had five men killed by rifle fire from the Jägers, and a shell wounded three others. Friendly fire was common in the intense storm of shot and shell. An American "Sentinel at the abatis near the advanced redoubt, had his arm shot off" by one of his own cannons.

During the shelling a Patriot 12-pounder in the Hornwork burst and wounded two men. One of the men had his arm blown off. Moultrie wrote, "This was one of the guns belonging to the *Acteon* frigate, that got on shore while engaged with Fort Moultrie, in 1776, and was burnt. It is remarkable that eight or ten of those guns which we weighed, and mounted on our lines, were every one of them bursted, after two or three rounds: which makes me suppose that their being heated by the fire of the ship, and suddenly plunging into the water while red-hot, destroyed their metallic parts, and left only the dross behind."

On April 19th the British brought up coehorn mortars to the second parallel, 450 yards from the Hornwork. They fired bombs and grenades into the Hornwork, but most of the shells fell in the North Carolina camp. They killed one man and wounded two others. One highlander of the 71st Regiment was killed, while two Hessian and two British grenadiers were wounded in the bombardment. The British discovered that the second parallel could not be connected to the first parallel due to a swamp.

It had taken two days under intense fire, but the British had been able to dig two saps leading to third, and final, parallels. There would be two third parallels, but they would not be connected in the middle. The third parallel was within 800 feet of the main American lines. During the bombardment the chief of the Lower Creek Indians came and inspected the British works. The chief's name was Ravening Wolf and he "wore a shirt of coarse linen and over this a blue coat with red lapels and collar, but had neither breeches nor stockings. His feet were clad in sandals. His head was shaved except for the crown and pendants of silver pistols and swords hung from his ears. His face was daubed with red paint in several places, and in his nose he wore a double silver ring. With great skill, he had wound around his head a silk scarf, which was fastened with silver clasps. On his chest he wore a ring-shaped silver collar and around both arms silver shields fastened with red ribbons, which were gifts from England and on which the monogram "George Rex" was engraved." This was the only Indian presence during the siege. No Indians fought for the British during the siege.

Throughout the night of the 19th the batteries on James Island continued to fire into the Patriot lines. The next day the lines were so close together that a cannonball killed an Ansbach Jäger as he rested behind the sandbags. The rest of the Jägers replied by firing into the artillery embrasures every time they opened, keeping the guns silent for the rest of the day.

The Jägers quickly adapted to the tactics used in the Southern campaign. They had copied the Patriot riflemen, by constructing sandbagged positions. Moultrie wrote "The sand bags were about two feet long and one foot thick, we laid down first two of them, three or four inches one from the other, and a third laid upon the top of the two, which made a small loop hole for the riflemen to fire through, the British immediately followed our example: many men were killed and wounded through these holes."

The British built a mortar battery that night, and erected a battery in the middle of the main road. They paid for their efforts when the Patriots shelled their lines, killing three and wounding five. Two Patriot powder magazines, in Captain Sisk's battery, took direct hits from mortar shells and exploded. At times as many as sixteen shells were hitting the city at the same time. Three people were killed in the town.

The British light infantry had two killed and seven wounded by grapeshot. Clinton was inspecting a redoubt within seventy yards of the Patriot lines, which was only partially built. In his journal he wrote "I RUN TOO MUCH RISK FOR MY STATION."

By April 20th the situation in the city began to look hopeless. Lincoln would not be getting any more reinforcements from Virginia, and he was disappointed that Scott's Virginia Brigade had not been able to leave Virginia. The South Carolina militia proved to be little help, and when he asked for 2,500 troops from North Carolina, only 300 militia arrived. He had 4,200 men to counter Clinton's 8,300. The strong currents had swept away some of his defensive line in the Cooper River, so it seemed that the Royal Navy would make a move to occupy it soon. Admiral Whipple did not seem to want to defend the river either, and only offered marginal support for any plans. Lincoln's commissaries told him that there were only provisions for eight to ten more days. His engineers told him that the British would be in the American works in another seven days.

Lincoln had tried to hold a council of war after the meeting on April 13th, but they were constantly interrupted. General McIntosh wrote that they were "often interrupted so much, that we could come to no determination, or do any business."

On April 20th another Council of War met to determine the options of the army. There were only two options open for Lincoln. Evacuate Charlestown, or surrender the city to the British. The Cooper River was still open and if they needed to evacuate they would be able to go that route. General Huger had brought all the boats he could find to Charlestown for just this purpose. The militia would stay in the city as a diversion, while the Continentals would withdraw to the countryside. In the end Colonel Laumoy argued that it would be better to surrender, since Clinton would most likely grant favorable terms due to their heroic defense.

Lieutenant Governor Gadsden arrived and was invited to "Sit as on of the Council." Gadsden was shocked that the Patriots were about to abandon the city to the British, and to the plunder and destruction that would follow. Gadsden told them that he would have to consult with the members of the Privy Council before any action could be taken. The officers adjourned until that night, when Gadsden brought the Privy Council with him.

The Council tried to embarrass the officers, and treated them "very Rudely." Gadsden said "the Militia were willing to Live upon Rice alone rather than give up the Town upon any Terms." Gadsden also said "even the old Women were accustomed to the Enemys Shot now that they traveled the Streets without fear or dread." However Gadsden also said that if Lincoln decided to surrender he would assist the officers on the articles of capitulation.

One of the Council members, Thomas Ferguson, told them that if they chose to evacuate the army, the citizens would know, and "he would be among the first who would open the Gates for the Enemy and assist them in attacking" the Continentals before they got on the boats.

After the Council members left the commander of the 1st South Carolina Regiment, Colonel Charles Cotesworth Pinckney, barged into the meeting and repeated the same opinion as the Privy Council. This was an insult to Lincoln, and bordered on insubordination. McIntosh was angered by Pinckney's outburst and told the officers that they should not do any of the options, and instead hold out "to the last extremity."

A third council of war met the next day, and Colonel Laumoy again argued that they should attempt to get honorable terms from the British while they still could. Since evacuation was no longer possible the officers unanimously agreed to ask for terms from Clinton.

The terms they proposed seemed generous, to the point of being absurd. The city and forts would be surrendered to the British. All the Continentals and militia, to include all the naval vessels, would keep their arms, artillery and ammunition, and have thirty-six hours to evacuate the city. Once Lincoln's army arrived at Lempriére's Point, the British would give them a ten day head start "to march wherever General Lincoln may think proper...without any movement being made by the British troops."

That day drums beat on the Patriot defenses, and a parley was requested. Lincoln sent the proposals to Clinton, along with a request for a six-hour cease-fire. Clinton did grant the cease-fire, while he consulted with Admiral Arbuthnot. Once Clinton and Arbuthnot read the terms they immediately rejected them as being preposterous. The British commanders told Lincoln that he had until ten o'clock to surrender.

When Clinton received word that the Patriots would not accept the terms offered by the British, he ordered the batteries to fire towards the Cooper River. He suspected that the American's would try to evacuate in the night. At 10:30 that night the British began firing, "with greater violence & fury than ever." The British fired 850 rounds into the American works. Of these, 489 were 24-pound iron shot.

Early in the morning of the 21st the British advanced a battery of four 6-pounders to demolish the gate and barrier in front of the Hornwork. The Patriots returned fire by loading anything they could into their mortars. Some of the British artillerymen were injured.

The killing went on. One soldier was killed, and two wounded in the North Carolina camp. On the 22nd a Patriot rifleman killed one of the Jägers of Captain Bodungen's command. A grenadier was killed in the trenches by cannon fire, while three Patriots were wounded. A servant of a British officer was "blown all to pieces with a shell."

Clinton finally received word that on April 14th Banastre Tarleton and Colonel Webster were able to attack the American cavalry at Monck's Corner. The assault was swift and bloody and the Patriots fled from the area. This threatened the Cooper River and left the northern supply route wide open to the British. Lincoln ordered all of the infantry east of the Cooper River to withdraw to the redoubt at Lempriére's Point. With the capture of Monck's Corner, the British began to seal the Patriots into the city.

Arbuthnot would not let Clinton use his ships for naval support for an assault on Lempriére's Pint, because he feared the loss of the ships. He wrote that the fortification at Mount Pleasant "prevents me from sending the armed Vessels I intended through the Hog Island Channel."

Clinton was frustrated that he could not get any support from the Royal Navy, and he knew that he would have to weaken his defensive line and send men across the Cooper to deal with the threat of an American evacuation. He ordered the 42nd Regiment, the Queen's Rangers, Prince of Wales American Regiment, Volunteers of Ireland, Hessian Regiment von Dittfurth, New York Volunteers and the South Carolina Royalists to join the 23rd Regiment on the east side of the Cooper.

Clinton also decided to rid himself of the presence of Lord Cornwallis by forming an independent command for him. He placed him in charge of the forces east of the Cooper, to insure that the Patriots did not get any supplies or reinforcements.

The British had dug a third parallel near the ten-foot deep ditch, located in front of the Patriot lines. It was so close that "one could easily throw a stone" into the canal. This was all they could do until they could drain this canal. Eighteen carronades were placed at the edge of the ditch to cover the work parties of the British.[188]

During April 23rd the British had one man killed, and six others wounded by grapeshot. Another man was wounded by long-range rifle fire. That night the defenders expected an attack by the British so they could drain the canal. "The troops remained under arms until daylight."

The British were confused on why the Americans had not sent out any sorties to try to kill the work parties and spike the cannons. Lincoln did plan to attack the Hempstead Hill battery as it was being constructed, but his lack of troops prevented him from doing so. The British believed that the Americans would never attack, and it lulled them into a false sense of security.

Around five o'clock in the morning Lincoln finally sent out a sortie of Continentals led by Lieutenant Colonel Henderson. The sallying party was made up of 300 soldiers of Hogun's North

Carolinians, Scott and Woodford's Virginians and twenty-one South Carolina Continentals. Their objective was the third parallel in front of the water-filled trench. As a diversion Moultrie told the batteries to "keep up the fire on the Enemy's Works as usual this night." At 3:30 in the morning they were told to cease fire and load all cannon with grapeshot. The Continentals assembled in the advanced work on the left of the line. Henderson had them fix bayonets. The assault would be with unloaded muskets. Henderson "made the men march up to these works, with their priming thrown out, and gun cocks let down." Many of these men had been at the storming of Stony Point in New York, and were familiar with this tactic.

The men charged across a temporary bridge built over the canal, and into the British third parallel. The British work parties had finished their night's work and noticed the Americans pouring over the side. They cried out, "Damn me the rebels are here!" The British fled in panic to the second parallel, leaving the Jägers to fend for themselves.

Lieutenant von Winzingerode led thirty of his Jägers, and an officer with fifty men of the Light Infantry, and counterattacked. In the desperate fight two Jägers were killed, four wounded, and two Germans and eight Englishmen were made prisoners. Two grenadiers of the 38th Regiment deserted in the confusion. The fighting was so close that the Jägers could not shoot, and had to defend themselves with their hunting swords.

Captain Hinrichs "heard a loud yelling" in the other sections and realized that the Americans had got behind the trenches. When the second parallel began firing volleys at the third parallel, Henderson ordered the men to retreat back to their lines.

Moultrie wrote in his memoirs "they brought in twelve prisoners, and bayoneted fifteen or twenty more." Seven of the prisoners were wounded. The Patriot artillery covered the withdrawal of the raiding party by firing canister made up of "old burst shells, broken shovels, pickaxes, hatchets, flatirons, pistol barrels and broken locks." Henderson's men left behind sixteen muskets in their hasty departure.

Captain Hinrichs had borrowed two modified brass coehorn mortars from Captain Lawson of the Royal Navy. These "Lawsons" "threw a hand grenade 1,800 feet." Hinrichs fired 130 shots at the retreating Patriots. The Patriots only had one killed and two wounded. The single death was Captain Tom Moultrie of the 2nd South Carolina Regiment, who was General Moultrie's brother. He was killed, and two other men were wounded, on the return into the lines.

Hinrichs continued firing the next day, and had to constantly move his "Lawsons", due to the counter-battery fire being directed against his "trench mortar." Hinrichs would wait until a Patriot firing port would open, and then fire 100-bullet canisters into them.

At eight o'clock that morning Colonel Parker, of the 1st Virginia Detachment, was killed while he was looking over a parapet. A sniper's ball hit him in the forehead. That same morning two privates were killed and seven wounded.

Anticipating a British assault on the works Lincoln recalled most of Colonel Pinckney's 1st South Carolina Regiment from Fort Moultrie, and Laurens' Light Infantry from Lempriére's Point, adding two hundred men to the lines. Fort Moultrie had lost its strategic importance once the British fleet had entered Charlestown harbor. The 1st South Carolina was initiated into the trench warfare when Captain Thomas Gadsden was killed.

The next night both sides anticipated an attack. Men manned the trenches and searched the darkness for any movement, or listened for the sound of an attack. At 1:00 in the morning some nervous American sentries thought they heard noises coming from the canal and they believed the British were attacking in force. They fired their muskets, and the men in the main American trenches thought that this was a signal that the British were assaulting the works. All across the line muskets, rifles and artillery fired at the British trenches.

Panic swept the ranks of the British in the trenches, and for over an hour the British fired muskets into the night. They abandoned the third parallel and fled to the rear. The first and second parallels saw the surge of men running towards them and fired into the men of the third parallel.

Some of the 71st Highlanders ran into their trenches without their coats on, and they were mistaken as attacking Americans. Ensign Duncan McGregor of the 71st Regiment was killed, and Captain Norman McLeod and Lieutenant John Wilson were wounded. Most of the casualties came from the Highlanders, but the Hessian grenadiers had two killed and eleven wounded. A lieutenant of the British engineers was severely bayoneted.

That night at least twenty British were killed or wounded.[189] There wasn't a single Patriot had moved forward from his trenches. That night at least twenty British were killed or wounded.[190] There had been no American casualties at all, and up till then only ten Americans had been killed and forty wounded during the whole siege.

The one-sided attack must have sounded like an assault on the works by those who did not know what was happening. Captain de la Morlière wrote, "The English attacked our lines in three columns…we then made such an artillery and musket fire that they retired into their trenches. Having been rallied there they charged again but with no more success that the 1st time."

The next day Captain de la Morlière "found some English soldiers who had been killed at the foot of a redoubt that we held on our left and in front of our lines that they had tried to penetrate." This may have been British soldiers trying to escape their own cannons.

After the friendly fire incident Clinton issued orders that no firing would happen unless the men could answer for it. Some of the officers in the 42nd Regiment did not want their men to have loaded muskets, but Clinton said he had no objection to the troops having loaded muskets. They compromised by allowing the third parallel to remain loaded.

Lincoln also worried about a night attack from the British. He ordered barrels of turpentine to be burned in front of the defenses to illuminate the no-man's land between the two armies.

The British continued to dig and move forward, while the Patriots continued to defend, and slowly withdraw. On the 25th the Patriots abandoned the trenches at the abatis because it had filled with water. The British occupied the position, which included the barrier and a demolished bridge. Captain de la Morlière wrote "they had water up to the waist in their trench, and… they lost men there every day from sickness or because of their wounds."

That same night the British dug a sap from the left of the third parallel, toward the dam, to destroy the lock. This would let water out of the canal that protected the front of the Patriot fortifications on the right.

The soldiers of both sides suffered the heat, lack of good water, and the annoyance of sand flies and mosquitoes. Since all the approaches were built in white, sandy soil they could barely open their eyes when the wind blew from the south, because of the thick dust. The soldiers could not put a bite of bread in their mouths that was not covered with sand. The few wells dug in the trenches for water were mixed with sand, and was as white as milk.

The Patriots kept three barrels of pitch and turpentine burning in front of their works, since they expected to be taken at night, and this lent an added amount of oily smoke to the humid air.

The North Carolina battery of Captain Kingsbury had run low on artillery ammunition and was firing broken glass and scrap iron at the work parties.

The artillery fire tore apart embrasures and collapsed the trenches. These had to constantly be repaired and strengthened. The Jägers and light infantry continued working in the shot up batteries. They filled sandbags and fixed embrasures. While they worked, the threat of a Patriot raid was ever present in their minds.

Captain Hinrichs ordered his company sentries to "stand at all times with cocked and leveled arms, so that upon the slightest movement about the enemy's guns they would get our bullets."

The Patriots were able to fire each cannon only once in the daylight. To reload meant becoming a casualty to the Jäger's rifles. The Patriots tried to mask their movements by placing cowhides over the firing ports of the cannons. However whenever any of the cowhides moved, the Jägers would fire into them. Moultrie had his men fire through slits in sandbags that were only three to four inches wide. Many men were shot even through this small opening. Charles Stedman wrote that "numbers of the besieged were killed at their guns, and scarcely any escaped who ventured to show themselves over the lines."

The Americans also had to repair their damaged fortifications, but they "pressed Negroes" into service to perform the labor. Detachments of the militia roamed the city looking for any slaves who they could seize for the artillery corps. These men had to "be pressed daily, & kept under guard, as the masters as well as the Slaves, were unwilling that they should work." After the sun set the slaves would work, in the dim glow of the burning turpentine barrels, to make the repairs. Many were killed or wounded doing the labor while iron cannonballs smashed into the parapets, showering them with sand, and mortar shells bounced across the ground spitting out sparks from fuses.

General Moultrie was almost killed by Jägers when he tried to get into the advance battery. As he ran towards the fortification he looked up to the British parapet, and saw the "heads of twelve to fifteen men firing upon me." He wrote that as he ran "an uncommon number of bullets whistled about me." When he reached the battery the officer there said that it was "a thousand to one" that he had not been shot.

On the 26th the British erected a battery of six pieces to fire on the Hornwork. While they did this they were fired upon by accurate sniper fire. Two Hessian Jägers, two light infantrymen and two gunners were killed by the Patriot rifles. Lieutenant Arthur Beaver of the 33rd Regiment, and eight grenadiers were wounded. Not all casualties were caused by long-range fire. A double-barreled blunderbuss killed a soldier from the 42nd Regiment when he got too close to a house.

During the night of the 26th the British contemplated an assault upon the trenches. Arbuthnot had a favorable wind to attack from the water, and the British trenches were filled with the Light

Infantry ready to assault. Unfortunately when Arbuthnot could not get around the sunken ships in the channel, the attack was called off. The Patriots kept the three fires burning between the abatis every night.

Outside of the defensive line Cornwallis arrived with his forces at Hobcaw Ferry. The Patriot forces evacuated the fort there, leaving behind four artillery pieces. Three British row galleys and two schooners fired upon the Patriot battery at Mount Pleasant.

Brigadier General Louis Duportail had arrived in Charlestown on the 25th, after having been sent by Congress to "put himself under General Lincoln." Duportail did not give Lincoln any good news. So far the other Engineer officers, Colonels Laumoy and Cambray, had told Lincoln that the British would break through the defenses soon. Duportail made the same prediction and he reported to Lincoln that protracted resistance was impracticable. He suggested that Lincoln evacuate the troops across the Cooper River, but Duportail did not know that an evacuation was out of the question.

Lincoln did convene another council of war and asked his officers if an evacuation was possible. They all agreed that it was impossible, since the British were too close, and the citizens of Charlestown would "cut up their boats and open the gates to the enemy."

Duportail asked Lincoln if he could leave the city and cross the Cooper, but Lincoln refused. He said that if his chief engineer left the city it would dispirit the garrison.

During the night of April 27th the British lost one killed and four wounded due to the shelling. A 12-pounder took a direct hit and was disabled. Redoubt Number 7 was "shot to pieces." The Patriots lost one private killed and five wounded. Five militiamen from the James Island Company deserted from the city in a boat.

Clinton was still not ready for an assault, because the ten-foot water-filled trench in front of the Patriot defenses first had to be drained. This meant that the British sappers had to dig to that point, and the infantry had to stand by to protect them in case the Patriots sallied.

To further light up the trenches the deputy quartermaster general brought seventeen burn barrels to the trenches. This lit up the area in front of the American works, and put them at ease, but it also let the British know that there would be no more American sorties. Clinton warned Cornwallis of the batteries on Mount Pleasant, thinking that they were heavily defended. He told him to not conduct an attack if there was "any Considerable risk." Cornwallis's forces, along with Royal marines and sailors, easily took the two Patriot positions on the left bank of the Cooper when Colonel Malmedy's men abandoned the redoubts, without putting up a fight. These actions sealed off Lincoln's army.

On the 28th the British brought up four 9-inch mortars and twelve coehorn mortars to the first parallel so that they could fire on the Patriot works. The artillery pieces in the second and third parallel could no longer fire on the Patriot lines without hitting their own forward defenses. Two American privates were killed in the bombardment. Captain James Campbell of the North Carolina Continentals and two privates were wounded.[191]

Duportail suggested that Lincoln completely enclose the Hornwork, creating a Citadel, and build two redoubts to the sides. This would be used when the British stormed the works. Fatigue parties went into the city to collect boards and wood to build the new Citadel. Laurens and his Light Infantry were assigned the honor of defending the entrance to the Citadel.

The British work crews had opened the sap into the dam, and the water began to drain off. The Patriots knew what danger they would be in if the canal drained, and resisted fiercely by firing small shells and stones. Artillery and small arms fire continued against the British work parties the entire night. Six English grenadiers were killed and fourteen English and Hessian grenadiers were slightly wounded.

Hinrichs had his Jägers only aim at the firing ports of the Patriot line, while 300 light infantry were told to fire upon the infantry in the trenches. The light infantry also had some Royal mortars, and the "Lawsons" that fired hand grenades into the trenches.

When the British returned fire the Patriots could not take shelter in the casemates, because the trenches had filled with water. Thirteen of the Patriots were killed that night, including Captain Templeton of the 4th Georgia Regiment.

The conditions of trench warfare began to take a toll on the soldiers. Similar circumstances would reduce the British army 135 years later on the fields of the Somme and Verdun. Every day scores of men were unable to work due to diarrhea. Three men of the 63rd Regiment, and two Hessians, deserted because they could no longer stand the trenches.

Desertion continued to plague Lincoln too. A Patriot militiaman, who had been a former surveyor, deserted to the British and gave them full details on the defenses and the supplies of the defenders. Two American deserters were convinced by Major Traille to "point out certain marks on the Enemys works for the direction of the fire to the most advantage." One of the soldiers coming into the British lines was a soldier of the 7th Regiment, who had deserted three days earlier. He thought that life in the American trenches was worse.

Clinton knew that he did not have enough men to work on the trenches and conduct security too. Shifts of men were at reduced strength, and there were not "a sufficient number of Artillery soldiers for a single relief."

To bring the trenches some relief Clinton ordered Lieutenant Colonel Alured Clarke, at Monck's Corner, to send a detachment of the 23rd Regiment to serve as artillerymen. Cornwallis was ordered to send the 64th Regiment back to Charlestown Neck to work on draining the canal.

The ship of the line *Renown* and the galley *Comet* tried to attack the bridge connecting Sullivan's Island to Mount Pleasant, but they both ran aground. The *Renown* was able to free herself, but the *Comet* was stuck. The Americans moved an artillery piece from Fort Moultrie to Haddrell's Point and sank the *Comet*.

Water from the dam started to drain off on the 30th, but it had cost the British. Two were killed and eight wounded. Lieutenant Hall of the North Carolinians had his leg broken by grapeshot from his own artillery when they fired at the approaching British.

Lieutenant Phillips of the Virginia Continentals was wounded in the thigh by a shell. During the night a violent wind made life in the trenches unbearable, and very few were able to get any rest. On the first of May, while the British worked at cutting through the dam, the cannon and small arms fire remained constant. Over 300 rounds were fired that night, killing four English and three Hessian grenadiers, and wounding just as many others. After the sun came up a Jäger and a light infantryman were killed, while another Jäger had his right arm shot off. Captain Joseph Montford of the 3rd North Carolina Light Infantry was wounded.

Disposition of Patriot forces by the end of April
Brigadier General William Moultrie
Charlestown Neck
   Woodford's 1st Virginia Brigade
      1st Virginia Regiment
      2nd Virginia Regiment
      3rd Virginia Regiment
   Scott's 2nd Virginia Brigade
      Parker's 1st Virginia Detachment
      Heth's 2nd Virginia Detachment
      2nd South Carolina Regiment
      3rd South Carolina (Ranger) Regiment
   Hogun's North Carolina Brigade
      1st North Carolina Regiment
      2nd North Carolina Regiment
      3rd North Carolina Regiment
   Brigade of Artillery
      1st South Carolina Regiment
      4th South Carolina Regiment (Artillery)
      Kingsbury's Company of North Carolina Artillery
      Charlestown Battalion of Artillery

Brigadier General Lachlan McIntosh
Charlestown city batteries
    Charlestown Militia Brigade
        1st Battalion of Charlestown Militia
        2nd Battalion of Charlestown Militia
        Britigney's Volunteer Corps of Frenchmen
        Spanish Company
    Brigade of Country Militia
        South Carolina Militia
        North Carolina Militia

Lieutenant Colonel William Scott
Fort Moultrie
        1st South Carolina Regiment
        South Carolina Militia
Colonel Marquis Francis de Malmedy, Marquis of Bretagne
Mount Pleasant batteries
    Laurens' Corps of Light Infantry
    1st South Carolina Regiment
    North Carolina Dragoons
    North Carolina Militia

Brigadier General Isaac Huger
East of the Cooper River
        3rd Regiment of Continental Light Dragoons
        1st Regiment of Continental Light Dragoons
        Pulaski's Legion of Horse and Foot
        South Carolina Dragoons
        North Carolina Militia

Disposition of British forces by the end of April
Major General Alexander Leslie
Charlestown Neck
    Light Infantry and Grenadiers
    7th (Royal Fusilier) Regiment of Foot
    42nd Regiment of Foot (Royal Highland Regiment)

63rd Regiment of Foot
71st Regiment of Foot (Fraser's Highlanders)
Royal Regiment of Artillery
Hesse-Kassel Feld Jäger Korps
Hessian Grenadiers

Major General Johann Christoph von Huyn
West of the Ashley River
   Hesse-Kassel Garrison Regiment von Benning
   Hesse-Kassel Fusilier Regiment von Dittfurth
   Prince of Wales American Regiment

Lieutenant General Charles Earl Lord Cornwallis
East of the Cooper River
   23rd Regiment (Royal Welch Fusiliers)
   33rd Regiment of Foot
   64th Regiment of Foot
   American Volunteers
   British Legion
   New York Volunteers
   Royal North Carolina Regiment
   Queen's Rangers
   South Carolina Royalists
   Volunteers of Ireland

During the siege several citizens volunteered for duty in the trenches. Two of them, Mr. Lord and Mr. Basquin, were in the advanced redoubt commanded by Major Mitchell. Both men had been sleeping on the same mattress when a shell fell upon them. Mr. Lord was killed instantly, but Basquin was so fatigued that he continued to sleep. His hair had been singed off by the blast.

Moultrie wrote, "the fatigue in that advance redoubt, was so great, for want of sleep, that many faces were so swelled they could scarcely see out of their eyes." When Moultrie visited this redoubt he "stayed in this battery about a quarter of an hour, to give the necessary orders, in which time we were constantly skipping about to get out of the way of the shells thrown from their howitzers, they were not more than one hundred yards from our works, and throwing their shells in bushels on our front and left flanks."

Ammunition was very low and many of the Patriot guns fired whatever they could fit in the barrels. Grimkè directed that "pebbles or stones... be fired from the 10 Inch Mortar on the left of the Lines."

On May 2nd Patriot fire was so effective that it destroyed the lodgment at the advanced ditch. This held up the work opposite the dam so much that little was accomplished. One Jäger, one artillery corporal, and eight men were wounded.

Just as in every war, there were casualties caused by accidents. A Patriot 9-pounder burst in battery number 12, and a large quantity of ammunition was blown up by accident in batteries 10 and 12.

The Patriots learned from deserters when the Jägers changed their shifts. They posted four cannon to fire on the Jägers as they were entering, and exiting the trenches. The information from the deserters proved effective. A cannon ball hit a tree near seven Jägers, beside Redoubt number 3. One of the Jägers lost a leg; a second was wounded in the thigh. Splinters from the tree hit the other five men. In the trenches one Jäger and one British soldier were killed, and one Jäger and two British wounded.

The British answered all Patriot artillery and musket attacks with the firing of mortar bombs. Several shells filled with rice and sugar landed in the Patriot trenches, and the Americans had a laugh at this. The British must have thought that the defenders were hungry, but the one thing they had plenty of was rice, coffee and sugar. At times the soldiers would pursue the hot shot fired by the British and throw sugar on it to make candy.

Meat was a different matter. Since the Cooper River route had been cut off there was no more meat coming into the city. At first the soldier's rations were cut in half, and then in a third. Lincoln's officers were allowed to search the houses in Charlestown, but there was hardly enough food for "the supply of private families." By May 8th Grimkè recorded that there was "no more Meat served out."

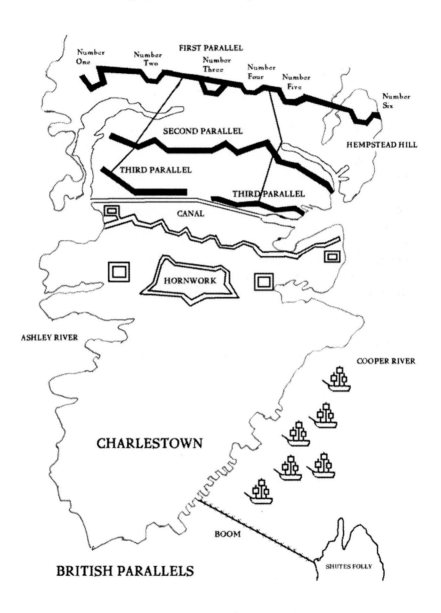

On May 3rd Captain Peebles wrote that "Above 300 militia have deliver'd up their arms & return'd to their house on parole. A great number of women there who retir'd from the town." It rained heavily for the next two days. Anthony Allaire wrote "This night took their hospital ship that lay opposite the town."

Lincoln sent Captain Edward Rutledge to his brother, the Governor, to urge the militia and whatever regulars were left in the state, to raise the siege. With Rutledge were a few other officers, including Colonel Malmedy. He had been warned to leave the city, since many of the citizens resented his abandoning Lempriére's Point. All of the officers were captured attempting to pass through the British lines.[192]

The British built a main battery in the third parallel, opposite the Citadel. All of the American guns in that sector of the line focused on this close and inviting target. Every night the battery was destroyed, and every day the British rebuilt it. This continued every night until the end of the siege.

Since firing during the day was extremely dangerous, Moultrie ordered that the artillery should begin firing "immediately after dark, to be continued every Night till Countermanded." A British officer wrote that seven or eight men had been wounded by the constant artillery fire "every 24 hours for 8 or 10 Days past."

On May 4th four Jägers of Captain Bodungen's command were wounded, and one had his foot blown off. Another Jäger was killed later in the day. Angered by the constant loss of life of those working on the siege lines, Cornwallis sent twenty Patriot prisoners into the trenches, including Captain Rutledge, forcing them to work on the approaches. That night it rained, filling the trenches with mud and wet sand, and refilling the canal. No work could be done, except on the main battery facing the Citadel.

Even though the British army had captured the redoubts at Lempriére's Point, the Royal Navy still would not move up the river. Arbuthnot told Clinton that he would "push a Force into the Cooper river", but he never did. Clinton would have to end the siege by himself, with no help from the navy. Clinton set up a camp on the forks of the Wando that would cut off any attempt by the Americans to evacuate the city. A ship that Cornwallis had captured earlier, the *New Vigilant*, captured a three-masted schooner in the Cooper River. The ship turned out to be a former prison ship that was now a hospital ship with "sick Negroes on board" that all had small pox.

On May 4th the fire of the Patriots was violent, but the water ran off the dam noticeably quicker. This brought a sense of urgency to the front-line American troops. 1st Lieutenant Charles Gerrard of the 2nd North Carolina light infantry was wounded during the fighting.

At ten o'clock on the evening of the 5th the cannon and musketry fire of the Patriots was so violent and accurate that the workers could do very little. One Jäger was killed, and two British wounded. A shell wounded Captain William Mitchell of the South Carolina Artillery.

Lincoln sent Thomas Pinckney to the Governor to again urge the militia to raise the siege. After moving two days through the swamps, Pinckney arrived in Georgetown and met with the Governor, but it was too late for the defenders of Charlestown.

There was a small group of reinforcements marching to Charlestown from Virginia. This was Virginia Continentals under the command of Colonel Abraham Buford. However this unit was only 350 men and was not a threat to the British.

On May 6th the sap leading to the dam had drained all the water out of the canal, and a house that was lying between the two abatis was burned by red-hot shot. This house had been covering the Patriot snipers that fired against the British workers. With the absence of accurate fire Hinrichs had his men fill 300 sandbags, and make rifle embrasures.

Around 5 o'clock in the afternoon thirteen Patriot guns opened up on the Jägers. Their shots struck beneath the sandbags and blew them into the air, refilling the trench. The Jägers were all knocked to the ground and many of their rifles were destroyed.

Clinton did not think the Americans would surrender at all. He wrote Cornwallis, "I begin to think these people will be Blockheads enough to wait for the assault." The British began to prepare for the impending final, and murderous assault on the Patriot lines. Some of the British had been at Savannah during the American's futile assault on the Spring Hill Redoubt, and they knew the amount of casualties that would be taken in such an attack.

Cornwallis wrote back to Clinton and asked if he could be in the attack with "my old friends the grenadiers & Light Infantry". Clinton knew that any officer leading the assault would most likely be killed. He had been at Bunker Hill, and knew of the cost against attacking a fortified position. Bunker Hill had been hastily constructed, and it had cost the British more casualties than any other battle of the war. Now, five years later he wrote, "the success of a Storm is uncertain."

One reason that Clinton feared the assault would fail was because of the lack of support from the Royal Navy. The ships could fire from the Ashley and Cooper Rivers and prevent soldiers from manning guns or rushing to the trenches. However Arbuthnot told Clinton that he would still not send any ships up the Cooper River. He wrote, "I confess it would be against my judgment to place the Ships against the Enemy's Batteries circumstanced as they are merely for a diversion."

Arbuthnot did support Clinton's army in the capture of a key point in the harbor. On May 7th Fort Moultrie surrendered to the British without putting up a fight. This was a major psychological victory for the British, since this was the scene of their defeat in 1776. When Royal Navy ships sailed between Sullivan's Island and the city it was a psychological victory against the citizens as well. They could see the British Union Jack in plain sight, flying over the fort. They now looked at themselves as being completely cut off, and there was no hope on the horizon.

Back in the trenches the killing continued when a Patriot 13-inch mortar killed another Jäger, and two Patriot 24-pounders at the bastion on Ashley River fired on the flank of the third parallel, killing one Jäger and two Highlanders.

The primary Patriot magazine behind St. Philip's Church was destroyed when a 13-inch shell hit within ten yards of it. Luckily the powder in the magazine did not explode. Moultrie took the 10,000 pounds of powder and removed them to the northeast corner, under the exchange. He had the doors and windows bricked up. After the British took possession of the town they never found the gunpowder.[193]

On May 8th Clinton called for unconditional surrender. He thought that the fall of Fort Moultrie would have been the last stand of the Patriots. He reminded Lincoln that if he had to storm the works, he would not be able to control the actions of his men as they plundered the town. Lincoln still thought he could negotiate, and he tried to gain the honors of war. Clinton was losing patience and refused. He did allow a cease-fire until midnight, while Lincoln gathered the military and civilian authorities, and considered the terms of surrender.

Lincoln had a council of war in the Citadel that included the "General and field Officers in Garrison, and Captains of the Continental Ships." Lincoln asked the British commander for more time, and Clinton allowed the cease-fire to continue until 8 o'clock the next morning.

Clinton did not trust the Americans and had Cornwallis keep an eye on the Cooper River, so that there would be no attempted evacuation.

During the cease fire the peace and quiet seemed unnatural. Many men were exhausted and fell asleep where they were. They did not have to worry about fixing the damaged fortifications, because part of the agreement was that there could be no repairs on the works.

The militia used the cease-fire to their advantage. Gabriel Manigault wrote "the militia looked upon all the business as settled, and without orders, took up their baggage and walked into town, leaving the lines quite defenceless."

Most of Lincoln's officers wanted to surrender. Only twelve out of sixty-one officers believed that they should continue to fight. Most of the officers who wanted to fight were from South Carolina, and did not want to see their homeland defeated. The Patriots drafted their articles of surrender.

Lincoln submitted the terms of surrender to Clinton before the sun came up. The Patriots wanted a cease-fire until the two sides agreed to terms. They also wanted the militia to be allowed to return to their homes, and the officers to keep their horses, side arms and servants. The army would be allowed to march out with the "honors of war." This was a time-honored custom by which the defenders would be allowed to leave the city with colors flying, bands playing, bayonets fixed, in possession of arms and equipment. The town and fortifications would be surrendered, while the ship and shipping would be allowed to leave. The citizens would be allowed to retain all their property and would be allowed to leave.

Clinton agreed to most of the articles, but he wanted the surrender of all, to include the ships and shipping. He also wanted the militia to return home, as prisoners on parole, and the officers would not be allowed to retain their horses. He also did not agree to the "honors of war." He wrote that the Americans would have to march out with colors cased, and they could not beat a British march. He also did not agree to let the citizens go unmolested.

Negotiations would be broken off at 9 p.m. Moultrie wrote that at 8:00 the men in the batteries "remained near an hour silent, all calm and ready, each waiting for the other to begin." At 9:00 the Patriots cheered "Hurrah" three times, bells rang in Charlestown, and the batteries opened fire "seemingly at Random as if in a drunken Frensy."

The British violently returned fire at the town and trenches. Orders were given to the British in the forward trenches to constantly fire upon the Patriot lines. Peebles wrote that double-barreled guns were distributed to the men, and cartridges were placed along the parapets so that the firing could be sustained continuously. Carl Bauer wrote, "whole Barrels of musket cartridges were set in the trenches so that the people might fire as much as they wished or could."

At 8 o'clock on May 9th the final cannonade began. Moultrie wrote "About 180 or 200 pieces of heavy cannon fired off at the same moment." The mortars from both sides threw out an enormous number of shells. General von Kospoth was injured in his headquarters, an hour's ride from the city, when the concussion from a cannonball caused a pot over his head to fall on him. Twenty British soldiers, three Hessian Grenadiers and one Jäger was wounded in this intense fire.

The fire was continuous throughout the night. Moultrie wrote that there were "cannonballs whizzing, and shells hissing, continually amongst us; ammunition chests and temporary magazines blowing up; great guns bursting, and wounded men groaning along the lines." The men in the trenches threw grenades at the enemy throughout the night. At times nineteen shells could be seen in the air at the same time and it looked as if they were "meteors crossing each other".

The British guns were lower than the Patriot defenses, so each shell that missed the trenches passed overhead and smashed into the city. The artillery in the Citadel was thirty feet higher than the British lines and was able to destroy any British battery underneath it.

On May 10th the British dismounted two Patriot guns in the center of the line. The Americans in turn fired on a 12-pounder, striking it and killing or wounding twelve men. Lieutenant Frisch of the Hessian Grenadiers was wounded "dangerously in the head." Major Traille wrote that one of the shots split the muzzle of a British 12-pounder, while a 6-pounder was hit and disabled.

Clinton knew that the final assault had to begin and he ordered the third parallel on the right to be extended across the drained canal, and into the abatis behind it. By morning they had dug to within 25 yards of the American parapet.

Toward nine o'clock in the morning orders were given to the British to fire on the city with red-hot shot. This set fire to twenty houses. Afterwards Patriot fire weakened somewhat. Clinton did not want the city being reduced to ashes, and issued orders around ten o'clock to stop the firing of red-hot shot.

The Patriot artillery fire did not stop, but increased with scrap iron and stones. The Jägers return fired 2,000 rounds in two hours. The British continued their bombardment until two o'clock in the afternoon.

The Royal Navy ships were positioned to be able to fire up the streets of the town, and cannonballs rolled down the street as if they were careening down a giant bowling alley. In one part of city a soldier had been relieved from his post and returned to his house. He entered his home and embraced his wife just as a cannonball tore through the house, killing them both.

Many of the citizens had evacuated the city, but a few thousand remained. During the siege the artillery fire killed about twenty citizens and burned down thirty houses. Their homes were searched by soldiers looking for food, wood for the defenses, or slaves to work on the fortifications. They wanted to siege to end. The citizens were luckier than they could have been. Since the beginning of the siege Clinton did not have enough 24-pound shot, and the damage to the city would have been much greater if he had. The British guns had fired 469 rounds of solid shot and 345 shells since the cease-fire ended.

After a night like that one the Patriot's no longer had the will to resist. They were exhausted. Lincoln wrote "the Troops on the line were worn down by fatigue having for a number of days been obliged to lay upon" the firing step inside the parapet. Many of the militia refused to fight anymore and abandoned the lines. Some just threw down their arms and walked away.

William Lewis wrote that he and several other militiamen cut their way through the British lines. "Every fifth man had a pole with a large knife or hatchet or something of the kind attached to it. When the British charged, they cut right and left, and by that means escaped being captured."

At 2:00 a.m. on the morning of May 11th Christopher Gadsden and the Governor's Council came to Lincoln and asked him to surrender the city under the best terms he could get. Petitions were also presented from a great majority of the inhabitants and of the country militia, begging general Lincoln to accede to the terms offered by Clinton.

Lincoln had been holding out, trying to get better conditions for the citizens and the militia, and now the citizens and militia told him that they didn't mind the conditions that Clinton had offered.

Lincoln had risked his Continentals to defend the city, and now the city did not want to be defended. In the middle of the bombardment an officer appeared on the parapet, waving a white flag. A drummer beat the cease-fire beside him. Captain Ewald escorted the officer in. He had a letter from Lincoln, addressed to Clinton, agreeing to the terms. After a siege of 42 days the city of Charlestown surrendered.

In the silence that followed the citizens of Charlestown came to the trenches to look at the British army, while the officers of both sides met in the middle to talk about what they had been through.

Clinton could have demanded unconditional surrender, but he did not, since showing some clemency would let the Patriots accept the terms more peacefully.

On May 12th the junior and non-commissioned officers had their companies form, with their regimental colors cased. They formed into a column at the gate of the city, in front of the Citadel. At 2:00 two companies of Hessian and British Grenadiers passed through the gate and occupied the Citadel. The rest of the British army was lined along the canal, and on top of the second parallel, to observe the surrender.

The two American commanders, General Lincoln on horseback, and Colonel Moultrie on foot, came out of the gate and moved forward to offer the surrender. Behind them came the Brigade of Artillery, followed by the South Carolina, North Carolina and Virginia Continentals. Behind them came the Marquis de Britigney, and his small force of French and Spanish volunteers.

According to the surrender terms the Patriots were not allowed to play an English march upon their surrender, but instead played the "Turk's March" and the "Janissary March". Forty British Light Infantry and Jägers led the Patriot column midway between the Citadel and the Canal, in between the two lines of abatis. Here they piled their arms. The Grenadiers in the Citadel raised the British Union Jack while the Royal Artillery fired a 21-gun salute.

Lieutenant Bartholomai of the Jägers wrote that "chagrin and anger" was seen on the Patriot's faces. Benjamin Lincoln, his officers, and his men would march off as prisoners. Tears coursed down the cheeks of Moultrie. Lincoln limped out of the city at the head of his ragged army. Peebles wrote "they are ragged and dirty looking set of people, as usual, but more appearance of discipline than what we have seen formerly & some of their officers decent looking men."

Hessian Ensign Hartung wrote, "the rebels were in the most miserable condition, very few of them wore shoes, and the coats that most of them were wearing were all torn." Ewald wrote that their "apparel was extremely ragged, and on the whole the people looked greatly starved." British officers asked where the second division was, and were shocked to realize that that only this ragged group had held back their army for a month and a half.

The militia was not allowed to march out with the regulars. Their arms were taken from them and placed in the Citadel. There were 500 of the militia that showed up at the surrender. The British could not believe that there were not more, and ordered that a second muster would be held on May 15th. The militia would "bring all their arms with them, guns, swords and pistols." If they did not turn in all their arms they would set loose the Grenadiers on the city.

Moultrie wrote, "this threat brought out the aged, the timid, the disaffected, and the infirm, many of them who had never appeared during the whole siege, which swelled the number of the militia prisoners to, at least, three times the number of men we ever had upon duty."

At 10 a.m. on the 13th the gates of the city opened, and General Leslie marched in at the head of the British Grenadiers, the 7th Fusiliers, the 63rd Regiment, the 64th Regiment and the Hessian Grenadiers.

Lincoln and his senior officers were sent to relatively comfortable quarters and had the hope of being exchanged for British prisoners. Prison ships awaited the other ranks and junior officers. Many of these men would never see their homes again. Some could not take the hell of the prison ships, and joined the British army to serve in the Caribbean.

The militia and civilians who had taken up arms and manned the fortifications were released on parole on the 13th and 14th. The

British most likely did this because they could not feed that many men. Ewald thought it was a mistake and wrote "I am convinced that most of these people will have guns in their hands again within a short time."

During the siege the Patriots lost 89 killed and 138 wounded. Far more serious to the cause were the 3,371 men captured, of whom 2,571 were Continentals. There was no more Patriot army in the South. The British had 99 killed and 217 wounded. They captured 311 artillery pieces, 5,916 muskets, 9,178 artillery round shot, 15 Regimental colors, 33,000 rounds of small arms ammunition, 212 hand grenades, and 376 barrels of flour.[194] The best muskets and flints had been thrown in the harbor. Forty-nine ships and 120 boats were taken, including large magazines of rum, rice and indigo.

The captured Patriot muskets were brought to the powder magazine inside the city. A Hessian officer warned the British that some of the muskets might be loaded, but they ignored him. One of the muskets went off, and 180 barrels of powder exploded. To add to the blast an estimated 5,000 muskets in the magazine discharged simultaneously. About 200 people were killed and six houses were destroyed, including a poorhouse and a brothel. Thirty British soldiers, along with Captain Collins and Lieutenant Gordon of the Royal Artillery, and Lieutenant Alexander McLeod of the 42nd Regiment, were killed in the blast. A Hessian artillery officer was also killed.

This destruction of muskets would hurt the British in the upcoming campaign to conquer the Carolinas. With the destruction of the 5,000 muskets, and the loss of a shipment of 4,000 rifles at sea, the British were unable to arm the backcountry Loyalist militias. This left Charlestown isolated in its defense against the country militia.

A French fleet off the South Carolina coast, under the command of Admiral Ternay, had been sailing to relieve the siege of Charlestown. This relief force consisted of seven ships of the line, five frigates and 5,000 French troops. When they captured a ship carrying Clinton's account of the surrender Charlestown they turned back.

Some South Carolina militia had been on the march to relieve Charlestown also. Colonel John Thomas, Jr. had been marching towards the city with his Spartan Regiment. When they reached Granby they were told the news of the surrender, and turned back. Colonel Edward Lacey and his Chester District militia were at Nelson's Ferry when they received the news and returned. Captain William Smith had marched towards Charlestown with his company, but he too turned back upon learning of the surrender.

Slaves from the plantations had been accumulating in the British camp. Two companies of them had been brought from Savannah at the end of February, and the slaves of Whigs had also been confiscated. According to the journal of the Hessian Battalion von Platte, the field hands usually "received a quart of rice or Indian corn a day. This they ate half-cooked, finding it more nourishing in that condition than if fully boiled. Many of them had hardly a rag to cover their nakedness. Few could understand English." On May 31st ten slaves were given to each Hessian regiment starting for New York. These slaves formed a part of the booty of the campaign. Thousands of other slaves were shipped to the West Indies to be sold back into slavery.

Loyalists who had been waiting for a victory began to arrive in Charlestown, offering their services. Two hundred Loyalists were there to greet the British as they marched into the city. Peebles wrote "a Party of 25 men with arms & horses arrived at Hd.Qrs....to acquaint the Gen. that they and a great many more friends to government are ready to shew their loyalty by their services against the Rebels by who they have been persecuted & wish to take revenge -- they are in a hunting dress mostly riffle shirts, arm'd with riffles & travel on horseback, & are call'd Carolina Crackers."

Sir Henry Clinton did two things before turning over command in the field to Lord Cornwallis, and leaving for New York. Clinton gave Cornwallis specific instructions that his primary responsibility was to safeguard Charlestown and South Carolina. He told Cornwallis that he was not to take the army into North Carolina, if such a move would jeopardize his main task. Clinton's second decision was a very serious error of judgment.

On June 3rd 1780 he issued a proclamation declaring that all men who had been given parole were released from the state, and now they were required to swear allegiance to the crown. Afterwards they would be expected to serve, when called on by the British, to maintain His Majesty's government in South Carolina.

Anger swept the ranks of the paroled. It was one thing to give up the fight against seemingly hopeless odds, but it was quite another to pledge active support to the British against their comrades still in the field. Some of the men fled to the Patriot ranks, while others took the pledge but had no intention of honoring it.

Even though over 1,500 Loyalists had volunteered their service, Clinton angered others when he "required every man having but three children, and every single man to do six months duty out of their province when required." Clinton appointed Major Patrick Ferguson as the Inspector of Militia for Georgia and the Carolinas, and his assignment was to organize the newly created militia.

Alexander Chesney wrote, "This appeared like compulsion, instead of acting voluntarily as they conceived they were doing." The Loyalists "were in consequence ready to give up the cause." Quite unaware of the trouble he had created the Clinton returned to his headquarters in New York.[195]

Two Sisters, Savannah River, South Carolina [196]   **Skirmish**
Charlestown Campaign
12 March 1780

After Captain Tawse was killed at Savannah, the command of the Georgia Dragoons fell to Lieutenant Archibald Campbell. On March 5th Patterson left Savannah with a column of 1,500 men and marched for the siege of Charlestown. On March 11th the column crossed the Savannah River at Two Sisters and encamped a quarter mile from the river. The next day a foraging party led by Captain

Campbell dispersed a party of Patriot light horse. Campbell was slightly wounded in the skirmish.[197]

Hammond's Plantation, South Carolina [198]   **Skirmish**
Charlestown Campaign
12-15 March 1780

At dawn on March 12th Colonel Abercromby and the Light Infantry marched to Hammond's Plantation. The lights carried two huge wall guns known as an amusette. These wall guns were giant muskets and were more like a cannon. They fired a 1-inch ball that Charles Lee wrote, was able to hit a piece of paper at 800 yards. Abercromby had been ordered to march to Hammond's Plantation to find forage for the artillery horses. Colonel Webster marched up the road along the left bank of the Stono River, with the 33rd Regiment and a detachment of Jägers, to cover Abercromby's flank.

Webster's covering party ran into a patrol of fifty cavalry and about one hundred infantry, at Savage's Plantation. Webster skirmished with these men for over two hours, during which time two Jägers were wounded. The Patriot force withdrew from Webster's force and attacked Abercromby and his light infantry. As soon as Webster heard the amusettes firing, he sent the Jägers to support the Light Infantry. The Jägers quickly set up an ambush, but the Patriots detected the ambush site and stayed clear of it.

At daybreak on March 15th Lieutenant Colonel Dundas was sent with his 2nd Battalion of Light Infantry, to the right side of St. Andrews Creek to forage the plantations located there. At the same time Webster moved with his force to Lowndes Plantation, to cover Dundas's left. The Patriots had placed a number of riflemen near a bridge that had been demolished at St. Andrew's Church. The Jägers skirmished with the riflemen until the foraging was done. Neither side suffered any casualties. [199]

McPherson's Plantation, South Carolina
Charlestown Campaign
14 March 1780

General Patterson continued his march towards Charlestown, crossing the Coosawhatchie and Tullyfinny Rivers. On March 13th several horses, a quantity of furniture stores and ammunition was found, that had been hidden in a swamp by American commissary John Stafford. At 4 o'clock in the afternoon Major Patrick Ferguson took a part of his American Volunteers along with twenty men of the British Legion and proceeded nine miles to McPherson's Plantation. Ferguson's force arrived at 9 o'clock, just after fifty mounted Patriots had left. He sent a party to pursue them, but they weren't able to overtake them.

Major Cochrane, with the Legion infantry, pursued another party of Patriot militia, but his guide led them the wrong way. At daybreak Cochrane arrived in front of his own pickets and mistook them for the Patriot militia they had pursued all night. As he was moving in position to attack the pickets, his force was detected and fired upon. Cochrane rushed the pickets and drove them from the house they were near.

Inside the house was a detachment of the American Volunteers, who fired on the British Legion. They thought a Patriot force was attacking them. During the fighting Major Ferguson was wounded by a bayonet stab in his arm that left him reduced to riding with the reins in his teeth. Lieutenant Donald McPherson was also wounded in the arm and hand. In the intense fighting Cochrane and Ferguson recognized each other's voices, and stopped the melee. After the fratricidal incident Captain DePeyster secured Coosawhatchie Bridge with sixty American Volunteers and twenty British Legion.[200]

Jacksonborough, South Carolina [201]   **Skirmish**
Charlestown Campaign
17 March 1780

After Tarleton had confiscated horses from Port Royal he passed through Jacksonborough and met a body of South Carolina Militia on horseback. The militia soon learned of the folly of trying to defeat well-trained cavalry. Three were killed, one wounded and one was captured. Several good horses were also taken.[202]

Salkehatchie River, South Carolina [203]   **Skirmish**
Charlestown Campaign
17 – 18 March 1780

Patterson's army arrived on March 17th, and rested at the plantation of prominent Whig Isaac McPherson for three days. Captain Abraham DePeyster's force detected a Patriot reconnaissance patrol six miles to the front of their position.

This was the Colleton County militia who had been busy felling trees across the roads leading to the Saltketcher Ferry. Colonel James Ladson had his men destroying all the boats along the river so that the British couldn't use them to cross. DePeyster ordered a pursuit of the militia and captured three of the men. Several horses were also taken.

On Saturday, March 18th, the column moved to the Salkehatchie River crossing, and encountered Colonel Ladson and eighty militiamen. They had destroyed the bridge and occupied a tavern on the north side of river to oppose any crossing by Patterson's army.

They fired upon lead elements of the British, the British Legion under the command of Banastre Tarleton. Tarleton had one of his companies return fire on the South Carolina militia, while the remainder of the Legion and the Light Infantry crossed the river below the site, and encircled Ladson.

After maneuvering into position they charged with bayonets and drove off the militia. Four Americans were wounded, three by bayonets and one by gunshot.[204] Major Graham and Major Wright, of the British forces, were both slightly wounded.[205]

Salkehatchie River, South Carolina   **Skirmish**
Charlestown Campaign
20 March 1780

It took Patterson's army two days to cross the Salkehatchie River, using boats brought with the army. A detachment of New York Volunteers was assigned to place the boats back onto the carriages after their use. As the Provincials were doing this, snipers on the far shore, from Captain William Sanders' Round O Company, fired upon them. Three of the detail was killed. After the Loyalists secured the boats they moved on to Godfrey's Savannah.[206]

Wappoo Cut, South Carolina   **Skirmish**
Charlestown Campaign
21 March 1780

On the 18th of March two grenadier battalions left Fort Johnson and joined the forces at Hudson's House on James Island. The British had constructed a fort there that was occupied by Major Thomas Mecan of the 23rd Regiment, and 120 men of the Hessian Regiment von Benning. By the next day Hudson's house had been surrounded by a breastwork twelve feet thick. Two redoubts were constructed 300 feet away from the fort, and had an abatis of sharpened apple and peach tree limbs. The left redoubt was on the Stono River, and the right redoubt was on the Wappoo Canal. The fort was built to protect the fleet and transport vessels on the approach to Charlestown.

On the 21st Captain Ewald conducted a reconnaissance of the Patriot lines, and found the place where the main guard stayed. He also discovered the different paths of the individual guard posts. He placed a corporal and five men on one of these paths, and gave them each "a guinea, a bottle of water, and some bread." The men were to stay there until they were able to ambush one of the returning guards. About midnight a party of dragoons rode up to the redoubt on the Wappoo Canal and fired their pistols. When the dragoons returned to their lines the Jägers ambushed them. One sergeant major and his horse was wounded and captured. [207]

St. Andrews Creek, South Carolina   **Skirmish**
Charlestown Campaign
22 March 1780

As Clinton tightened the noose on Charlestown, General Alexander Leslie led the Jägers, the 33rd Foot and the Light Infantry, on the road toward Drayton Hall and Middleton Place. At the bridge crossing at St. Andrew's Creek the British were greeted by Patriot artillery fire. Leslie asked Captain Ewald if it was possible to cross the creek farther up the river, and drive the Patriots away from the bridge. If Ewald were unable to conduct the mission, Leslie would have to bring up artillery. For heavy firepower Ewald's force had four amussettes.

Ewald took fifty Jägers, and was supported by Captain St. Lawrence Boyd and three companies of light infantry. Ewald crossed the creek at seven o'clock in the evening, and then found a swamp that took a half an hour to cross. The swamp was so deep that many of Ewald's men sank up to their chests. When they emerged from the swamp they found that the Patriots had abandoned their position. There was a short skirmish with the retreating Patriots, which wounded two of Ewald's men. Ewald quickly positioned his men in the churchyard and began work on the bridge immediately.

At eight o'clock the next morning Ewald and Boyd received orders to try and get to Drayton's Plantation, the home of Vice Governor Henry Drayton. After marching for half an hour a detachment of Patriot cavalry discovered Ewald and his light infantry. Ewald immediately attacked with his riflemen, and kept the cavalry at a distance. The Patriot cavalry continued to observe but did not attack. At noon Ewald reached Drayton's plantation and posted his men in the zoological gardens. Ewald asked Mrs. Drayton for some food, and she gave them bread and wine. In the afternoon Leslie arrived and took up quarters in Drayton's Plantation.[208]

Pon Pon River, Bee's Plantation, South Carolina[209] Skirmish
Charlestown Campaign
23 March 1780

The day after the skirmish at the Salkehatchie River, Patterson's column marched seven miles. During the entire march snipers were continually harassing the British. The Patriots also destroyed bridges and causeways, which further slowed the column. On March 23rd Tarleton's dragoons surprised a party of mounted Catawba Indians and drove them off at Governor Bee's Plantation. The Patriots had ten men killed and four captured. Tarleton seized the much needed horses for his troopers.[210]

Dorchester Road, South Carolina   Skirmish
Charlestown Campaign
25 March 1780

General Leslie received information that 600 of Colonel Washington's dragoons and Vernier's Legion had occupied the pass to Bacon's Bridge. At daybreak on March 25th Heinrichs and his Jägers detected a party of cavalry approaching their post on the Dorchester Road. Heinrichs sent several men to the woods on the right of his position so that they could fire on the flanks of the cavalrymen. When the Jägers fired their rifles they only hit one man, a sergeant of the 3rd Regiment of Continental Light Dragoons. The sergeant had rode far in front of the other cavalry, and had been wounded in the stomach.

Ewald asked the dying sergeant why he acted so rashly. The sergeant said, "Sir, Colonel Washington promised me that I would become an officer right away if I could discover whether the jägers were supported by infantry and had cannon with them, because if not, he would try to harass the jägers." The surgeon told the sergeant that his wound was mortal. The sergeant replied, "Well then, I die for my country and for its just cause." Heinrichs gave the sergeant a glass of wine, "which he drank with relish, and then died." [211]

Savannah, Georgia   **Skirmish**
25 March 1780

After the British laid siege to Charlestown, the garrison at Savannah felt a sense of false security. The daily patrols would go out into the countryside and would return with no incidents at all. This routine would cost them.

On March 25th a detachment of New York Volunteers rode out of Savannah, and was ambushed by a party of militia under Colonel Andrew Pickens.[212] Pickens' men were armed with rifles, and a small portion acted as saber-wielding cavalry. Their primary tactic was to approach the enemy, dismount, and fire on the British. Whether they were victorious or were beaten, they returned to the horses and retreated.

The King's Rangers sallied forth and rescued the New York Volunteers, pinned down by the riflemen. Pickens' men retreated, but not before plundering and burning Royal Governor Wright's rice plantations. General Prévost deployed the Light Horse of Daniel McGirth into the countryside to reconnoiter for the rebels. McGirth's men were worse than the raiders and caused much resentment among the civilian population.[213]

Rantowle's Bridge, South Carolina [214]   **Skirmish**
Charlestown Campaign
26 March 1780

On March 26th William Washington conducted a twelve-mile ride towards the British lines. With him were Major Vernier, with the remnants of Pulaski's Legion, and Major John Jameson, with the 1st Continental Light Dragoons.[215] Washington put his men in an ambush position by an old rice field, along a main road, twelve miles from the British lines. A few South Carolina militia "wearing bright clothes" attempted to draw the British out, but this produced no result.

Washington shifted his men half mile to the east, and then took an advance party to Governor Bull's house. Along the way he captured Inspector General Ludwig Schmidt of the British hospital, and then they captured Lieutenant Colonel John Hamilton of the Royal North Carolina Regiment, along with seven cavalrymen.

Hamilton and Schmidt had crossed the river at Rantowle's with Paterson's army, and were captured in front of the main body. The Pennsylvania Packet reported "This action happened within one hundred yards of the British flying army, consisting of light infantry and grenadiers, whose marching across the field to get in the rear of the Americans obliged Colonel Washington to order a retreat; otherwise their whole party would have been cut to pieces."

As Washington returned back to Bacon's Bridge he received word that Tarleton's British Legion was approaching from the rear. Tarleton had been able to refit his cavalry with mounts procured from the local plantations, and from his skirmish at Pon Pon. He had been covering the left flank of Patterson's column as they crossed the river, when he encountered Washington's dragoons at Rantowle's Bridge.

When Washington saw the British cavalry, he turned in their direction and charged with his dragoons. One of Tarleton's inexperienced officers charged his troop down a causeway that was too narrow for two to ride abreast. The officer ran into Washington, waiting at the end of the causeway with superior numbers and superior horses. Tarleton knew that this would be a disaster, and had his men retreat back across the causeway. During the melee Tarleton and Washington personally fought each other. When Tarleton's men were behind him he put the spurs to his horse and sped to his lines. He left behind many wounded and had eight of his dragoons captured. Washington had a man wounded through the knee, and Major Jameson had his sergeant major killed. This would not be the last time that Tarleton and Washington would fight.

Earlier in the day Clinton, Cornwallis, Ewald and a very small escort had gone to Rantowle's Bridge to meet Patterson. If Washington had arrived earlier he could have captured them all, and altered history.[216]

Sunbury, Georgia   **Skirmish**
28 March 1780

A party of Georgia Militia routed some Loyalists and Indians, killing ten of them.[217]

Gibbes Plantation, South Carolina [218]   **Skirmish**
Charlestown Campaign
29-30 March 1780

American Forces
Commanding Officer   Lieutenant Colonel John Laurens
    Continentals
        Lieutenant Colonel John Laurens
           Corps of Light Infantry   200
        Continental Artillery   6 fieldpieces

North Carolina Militia
    Major Jean-Baptiste Ternant
        Duplin County Militia   90
            Major Philip Love
            Major Robert Barnwell
Casualties   1 killed, 8 wounded

British Forces
Commanding Officer   Lieutenant General Lord Cornwallis
    British Regulars
        Brigade of Light Infantry   Unknown number
            Lieutenant Colonel Robert Abercromby
            1st Battalion of Light Infantry
            Lieutenant Colonel Thomas Dundas
            2nd Battalion of Light Infantry
            Amusettes [219]   2
    Captain Johann Ewald
        Hesse-Kassel Feld Jäger Korps   Unknown number
    Unknown commander
        Royal Regiment of Artillery
            12-pounders   2
            6-pounders   2
Casualties   9 killed, 11 wounded, 5 missing

After Clinton had his army across the Ashley River he encountered no resistance until he approached Gibbes Farm, two miles from Charlestown. The British had brought ashore two light 12-pound cannons, and two 6-pounders. At 9:00 in the morning on March 30th they moved down the King Street Road, the main route to the city.

Lincoln did not have enough men to oppose the British landings, but he did order the creation of a light infantry battalion, consisting of the light infantry companies of the North Carolina Brigade and the 2nd and 3rd South Carolina Regiment. He placed this Corps of Light Infantry under Colonel Laurens and ordered him "to watch the motions of the Enemy and prevent too sudden an approach."

Laurens posted his troops in an advanced redoubt on the King Street Road, about a mile from the city. Another mile and a half from them he placed a detachment of riflemen who set up an ambush in a wooded area along the road. An officer in the Jägers described the force as "three hundred Rebels, consisting of Light Infantry and Negroes who had lain in ambush along both sides of the road, in the woods, and had a small defensive position behind them to cover their retreat."

Around noon the riflemen fired upon the British as they entered the ambush area. In the lead of the British column were Clinton, Cornwallis, General Leslie and the Jägers. The Earl of Caithness was standing beside Clinton when he was shot through the stomach.[220]

The Jägers returned fire while the Light Infantry began to flank the riflemen. The riflemen knew they were outnumbered and began to withdraw. They "fell back but kept up a considerable fire from behind the Trees." The running gun battle continued until the riflemen reached the redoubt and took cover inside.

Laurens decided to make a reconnaissance of the advancing enemy force, and took with him Major Edmund Hyrne, deputy adjutant general of the Southern Department, and commander of the 3rd South Carolina Light Infantry. The officers ventured too close to the Jägers moving through the trees, and Major Hyrne was knocked from his saddle, wounded in the cheek by a Jäger's bullet. Laurens "had barely time to cover his Retreat and drive off his horse" so that the Jägers wouldn't capture it. Laurens then helped Hyrne to safety, while rifle balls whistled around him.

After returning to the redoubt Laurens waited to see what the Jägers would do. Ewald brought up an amusette and sent the Light Infantry around to outflank Laurens's position.

The British slowed their advance against the redoubt, because they did not know how many cannon they had. All the British had in the advanced party was the two amusettes that the Light Infantry was carrying. They continued to fire the amusettes against the redoubt until Clinton ordered them to stop.

Lincoln sent Jean-Baptiste Ternant, a French officer in service with the American army, with reinforcements. Ternant told Laurens that he was ordered to fall back, one platoon at a time, because Lincoln did not desire a battle at this time. Laurens understood that he was outnumbered and "the advantages of a serious affair were all on the side of the Enemy."

During the fighting a Hessian captain noted that the Carolinians "were very good marksmen." After Laurens's Light Infantry withdrew, a small detachment of Jägers occupied their breastwork.

When the fighting had first started Laurens had requested two cannons, and by late afternoon six fieldpieces arrived. Laurens did not know why they were there, since Lincoln had insisted that Laurens avoid a major encounter. It was most likely a mistake of orders.

Laurens decided that "in order to gratify my young officers" he would attack the position he had previously held. Laurens' men came yelling at the Jägers, with bayonets fixed and attacked "with considerable violence."

The small Jäger force fled, leaving behind one dead, one slightly wounded and another missing. The British did not find the dead Jäger until two days later, with three bullets in his body. That same Jäger had grabbed Major Hyrne's hat as a souvenir earlier, and it was found clutched in his hands.

The British Light Infantry did a counterattack and forced the Carolinians to retreat back to the American lines. Clinton ordered his men to return to the redoubt, because he suspected it was a trick to lure his men into a larger ambush.

The British brought up artillery pieces and the two sides exchanged artillery fire. One cannon ball killed Captain Joshua Bowman, commander of the 1st North Carolina Light Infantry. Laurens stated that he was "a valuable captain of Infantry." During the artillery duel several women from Charlestown viewed the action from the safety of the fortifications.

Laurens skirmished with the British advance guard and Jägers until nightfall, and then fell back to the Patriot lines. He wrote "Upon the whole it was a frolicking skirmish for our young soldiers." It was also a great confidence builder, since his men were able to hold back the British elite.

Lachlan McIntosh called the skirmish "a mere point of honor without advantage." Major Hyrne's facial wound proved to be minor, but it kept him out of action for the rest of the siege.

Laurens' light infantry moved back and occupied a position in the Hornwork. In Clinton's "Journal of the Siege of Charleston", he criticized Cornwallis for not sending in the Light Infantry or artillery for some time, after the beginning of the skirmish.

Elizabeth Ellet wrote "When the conflict was over, Mrs. Gibbes sent her servants to search among the slain left upon the battle-ground, for Robert Barnwell, her nephew, who had not returned. They discovered him by part of his dress, which one of the blacks remembered having seen his mother making. His face was so covered with wounds, dust and blood, that he could not be recognised. Yet life was not extinct; and under the unremitting care of his aunt and her young daughter, he recovered."

After the skirmish Clinton rode down to the left of the battlefield and saw rising ground near the town. This was Hempstead Hill near the Cooper River, and was 800 yards from the city. Clinton wrote, "It may cost to get it, but when in possession of it we take the town. I showed it to Moncrief who agreed." Gibbes Farm became the location of the British Artillery Park, powder magazine and laboratories during the siege of Charlestown.[221]

South Carolina coast
1 April 1780

American Forces
   South Carolina State Navy
      Captain Charles Morgan
         Snow *Fair American*   14 guns
   South Carolina Privateer
      Unknown Captain
         Sloop *Argo*   10 guns

Loyalist Forces
  New York Privateers
    Captain Lawrence
      Brig *Elphinstone*

Iron cannon	4
Brass cannon	8

    Unknown Captain

Brig *Arbuthnot*	14 guns
Casualties	Both ships captured

The South Carolina ship the *Fair American* teamed up with the Privateer *Argo* and was able to capture the two privateers, *Elphinstone* and *Arbuthnot*. The British ships were from New York and had been bound for St. Kitts. The American team sailed the ships through the British fleet and into Charlestown on the 2nd of April.[222]

**Wright's Plantation, Ogeechee River Ferry, Georgia
5 April 1780** [223]

American Forces

Commanding Officer	Colonel Andrew Pickens
South Carolina Militia	
Upper Ninety-Six Militia	300
Captain Robert Anderson	
Captain Tarleton Brown	
Cracker's Neck Rangers	

Loyalist Forces

Commanding Officer	Captain Thomas Conkling
Provincials	
DeLancey's Brigade	
1st Battalion	
Light Company	64
Armed Plantation slaves	Unknown number
Casualties	3 killed, 5 wounded

During the siege of Charlestown Colonel Andrew Pickens conducted operations around Savannah. On April 5th his militia raided the rice plantations of Royal Governor Wright. Captain Conkling and a reinforced company of DeLancey's Brigade were ordered to find and engage Pickens. The slaves on Wright's plantation had been armed, and were commanded by the overseers of the plantation.

A story in the Pennsylvania Gazette stated that sixty "Negroes in arms and two overseers" were killed. A different report listed the casualties as three men from DeLancey's Brigade being killed and five wounded. Captain Conkling was killed in this action.[224]

Fort Moultrie, South Carolina   **Naval skirmish**
Charlestown Campaign
8 April 1780

After Admiral Whipple decided to withdraw from the entrance of Charlestown harbor, the men in Fort Moultrie were on their own and had to fend for themselves. There had not been any moves towards the fort because the British fleet had been occupied in removing the artillery from the ships because of their weight, and then moving the lighter ships over the bar, afterwards replacing the artillery. Arbuthnot had been waiting since March 20th for the tides and weather to cooperate, so that he could make a run past Fort Moultrie, and on to safety at Fort Johnson.

Inside Fort Moultrie was the 1st South Carolina Regiment, under the command of Colonel Charles Cotesworth Pinckney, and a battalion of South Carolina country militia. The people of Charlestown had faith that the fort would stop the British fleet, like it did in 1776. Things were different this time. The British in 1776 were attacking the fort, thinking that it could not stand against the might of the Royal Navy. The British had learned a lot about fighting in America since then, and now they were not going to attack the fort, but sail by it as quickly as possible.

On the morning of April 8th the weather was rainy, dark and cloudy, and had a slight breeze. The conditions were still not good enough to make the run by Fort Moultrie, but by that afternoon the wind had become stronger and was blowing from the southeast. This was what Arbuthnot had waited for. At 3:30 he weighed anchor. Nine warships and three transports bore down the channel to Fort Moultrie.

Arbuthnot was in the lead ship, the *Roebuck*, and was followed by several small boats that sounded the bar. "One of these boats was sent with a blue flag to the point of the shoal opposite the fort."[225]

The British ships were told to pass as close as possible to the cutter with the blue flag, so that they would be less vulnerable to the artillery in Fort Moultrie.

The second battle of Fort Moultrie began when the fort fired upon Arbuthnot's ship. This time the fort was not limited in powder, like it was in 1776, and it soon became veiled in smoke and fire. The roar of forty-three heavy guns resembled a terrible thunderstorm.

The *Roebuck* had passed by the fort without any damage. Behind the *Roebuck* came the transport *Richmond*. Fort Moultrie's gunners now had the range, and the transport was hammered by shot. Her foretopmast was torn away and several cannonballs tore into her hull, dismounting a gun. Lieutenant Oben on the *Richmond* wrote that they lost "2 Men & 1 Boy killed & 3 wounded."

Despite the firepower threatening the fleet, the British sailed slowly past the fort with colors flying proudly. The ships were one behind the other, and passed by without firing a shot. As soon as it had passed the fort, each ship made a sudden turn and fired a broadside, then sailed to its designated anchoring place. Each ship took about fifteen minutes to pass by the fort.

One of the transports, the *Aeolus*, had her rudder shot away, and ran aground within range of the fort. She was cut up by concentrated artillery fire. The crew abandoned the ship.

By 5:30 fourteen ships had safely sailed into the harbor, to add their guns to those mounted in the British siege works. British losses were minimal, with only seven men killed and fifteen wounded. Though considered minimal, this was the largest loss of life in a single day for the British forces. There was some damage to masts, rigging and hulls, but nothing that would stop the ship's combat abilities. Arbuthnot said that the "damage was so trifling that 'twas not worth mentioning."

During the fight at the mouth of the harbor the fighting in the trenches ceased. Some of the soldiers even stood on the parapets, in direct view of the enemy, but no fire was directed towards them. All attention was directed towards the naval battle.

They couldn't see much after the first few shots. Hessian Ensign Hartung wrote "neither the ships nor Sullivan's Island could be seen for some time owing to the smoke." Captain Ewald wrote that the noise from the battle "resembled a terrible thunderstorm."

Hessian officer Carl Bauer wrote, "Some six thousand people were on the ramparts, who had wished the pleasure of seeing the ships blown into the sky. But as soon as the second one was out of the fire of the fort, everyone disappeared from the ramparts; and soon thereafter we saw a quantity of small vessels sailing up the Cooper River into the country... The city was now completely cut off from Fort Moultrie."

The next day Admiral Arbuthnot dispatched twenty sailors to set the *Aeolus* on fire. Under an intense fire from the fort the sailors were able to set the vessel on fire. After the sailors had left, the Patriots salvaged two 18-pounder cannon and a quantity of provisions from the transport before it was completely destroyed.[226]

Monck's Corner, South Carolina [227]   **Skirmish**
Charlestown Campaign
14 April 1780

American Forces   Unknown number
Commanding Officer   Brigadier General Isaac Huger
   Continentals
      Lieutenant Colonel William Washington
         3rd Regiment of Continental Light Dragoons
            Major Richard Call
            Captain Walker Baylor
            Captain John Stith
      Major John Jameson
         1st Regiment of Continental Light Dragoons
            Captain Thomas Pemberton
            Captain John Watts
            Captain Baylor Hill
            Captain John Belfield
      Major Chevalier Pierre-François Vernier
         Pulaski's Legion of Horse and Foot
            Cavalry
               Captain Charles Baron de Frey
                  1st Troop Lancers
               Lieutenant Louis de Beaulieu I
                  1st Troop Dragoons
               Captain Jerome Le Brun de Bellecour
                  2nd Troop Dragoons
   South Carolina State Troops
      Colonel Daniel Horry
         South Carolina Dragoons
   North Carolina Militia
      Brigadier General Richard Caswell's Brigade [228]
         Colonel James Branyen's Regiment
             Captain William Bethel
Total American forces engaged [229]   400
Casualties   15 killed, 18 wounded, 63 captured [230]

British Forces   Unknown number
Commanding Officer   Lieutenant Colonel Banastre Tarleton
   British Regulars
     Captain William Henry Talbot
      17th Regiment of Light Dragoons
   Provincials
     Lieutenant Colonel Banastre Tarleton
      British Legion
       Major Charles Cochrane
        Legion Infantry
       Lieutenant Colonel Banastre Tarleton
        Legion Cavalry
         Captain David Kinlock [231]
     Major Patrick Ferguson
      American Volunteers
       Captain Abraham DePeyster
       Captain Charles McNeill
       Captain James Dunlap
       Captain Samuel Ryerson
Casualties   3 wounded

During the siege of Charlestown General Huger's militia and all the American dragoons occupied the crossroads at Monck's Corner. Just north of the crossroads was Biggin's Bridge that crossed the Santee River. Huger's mission was to keep open Charlestown's line of communications along the Cooper River. This location proved its importance on April 5th, when the Virginia Brigade marched through on their way to join the forces in Charlestown. The Virginians boarded vessels near Monck's Corner, and sailed down the Cooper River, past the amazed British forces.

Huger had about 400 dragoons and militia with him at Monck's Corner. The militia had just arrived and they were not ready to fight anyone. One company had muskets but no ammunition. Two other companies had no muskets at all. Huger put the militiamen on the eastern end of Biggin's Bridge as an early warning. The cavalry would guard the western side of the bridge. Huger was not pleased with the cavalry, because they would "never move without a large detachment of infantry."

Clinton knew that he had to close off his hole in his siege and he sent Lieutenant Colonel Webster with 1,500 men to attack Huger's force and destroy the supply base located there. At seven in the evening on April 12th Major Patrick Ferguson and his American Volunteers left Linning's Plantation, and proceeded north to Goose Creek. The North Carolina Royalists had joined the American Volunteers that morning.

The Loyalists arrived at Bacon's Bridge at five o'clock the next morning, after marching twenty-two miles. They rested there that day, and then proceeded an additional eighteen miles through Dorchester, to the Middleton Plantation. At 1 o'clock they met Tarleton's Legion, along with the 33rd and 64th Regiments under Colonel James Webster.

Tarleton's mission was to take the British Legion and the American Volunteers, then proceed swiftly and silently during night to attempt to take the Patriots at Monck's Corner by surprise. Webster was the commander of the expedition, and would be with the main body that would follow to provide support.

At seven o'clock in the evening of April 13th Tarleton's men began their march. Complete silence was observed on the march. Along the march Tarleton captured a "Negro bearing a letter for Charlestown" from General Huger. He learned from the letter how the post at Monck's Corner was arranged.

During the march the British ran into no scouts, and encountered no patrols. Tarleton had covered the 18 miles in five hours in pitch-black darkness.

At three o'clock in the morning the advanced guard of dragoons and mounted infantry of the British Legion, charged the militia on the eastern end of the bridge. Tarleton's men did not slow at the militia "grand guard", but continued on into the main camp. The Patriots were stunned but the reacted quickly. Huger and Jameson fled with other officers and men, into the swamp, without their horses.

Some of the Continental dragoons, led by Captain Baylor Hill, followed behind the British Legion, and made their escape by blending in with them in the darkness. Washington had been captured, but was able to escape before the sun came up.

Major Cochrane and the British Legion infantry charged the remaining militia at the Meetinghouse with fixed bayonets, dispersing them into the swamps.

The Loyalists captured thirty wagons loaded with arms, clothing and ammunition. They also captured 98 horses belonging to the Patriot officers and cavalry. The horses were needed, since Tarleton's cavalry was still mounted on poor quality horses from the Beaufort farms. Tarleton's men were now better equipped than they had ever been.

The raid on Monck's Corner established a pattern Tarleton would continue. This was a swift approach march, followed by an immediate assault with sabers and bayonets. A second pattern of Tarleton's tactic also developed at Monck's Corner, one of brutality.

Chevalier Pierre-François Vernier, had been wounded while commanding the remnants of Pulaski's Horse. He asked for quarter from the Legion, but instead was slashed and hacked with sabers. Vernier lingered for hours, cursing the Americans as cowards, and insulting the privates of the Legion. Another French officer, Lieutenant Louis Beaulieu, was wounded twice.[232]

A second incident took place at a plantation owned by a prominent Tory, Sir John Colleton. Inside the plantation were gathered some Loyalist women, including the Lady Colleton. Two Legion dragoons entered the house and abused Lady Colleton. One of the men, Henry McDonagh, accused her of hiding enemy soldiers, and cut on her hand with his broadsword. He tried to force her to have sex, but she screamed and wrestled free, stopping him "from accomplishing his Designs." The two men stole a jug of rum and left.

Ann Fayssoux, the wife of Patriot Surgeon Peter Fayssoux, encountered the two men. McDonagh struck her too and "almost strangled her." Miss Betsy Giles and Miss Jane Russell were with her. She begged McDonagh to just "take her Life & not violate her

Person." McDonagh ignored her, and raped her in front of the other two women.[233]

Tarleton sent a surgeon and a guard of men to protect the Loyalist women from further attack. He also had McDonagh and the other man arrested. Tarleton suggested to Lieutenant Colonel Webster that the two men should be hanged. Major Ferguson was so enraged that he wanted to line the two dragoons up and shoot them right then, but Webster decided that he did not have court-martial authority. Webster ordered the two men sent to Charlestown where they were afterwards tried and whipped.

The morning after the attack the Loyalists conducted mopping up operations around Monck's Corner. Two "Negroes" came in and informed Webster of a party of twenty Patriot dragoons that were in the swamp three miles from the camp. Webster ordered twenty American Volunteers to pursue the dragoons. The Volunteers found the dragoons where the slaves said they were, and killed two of them. The rest fled the area. The Volunteers took one prisoner and five "very fine" horses and saddles.

A quantity of goods, including three barrels of gunpowder, was found in a store. At 11 o'clock that night the storehouse holding the gunpowder was accidentally set on fire, destroying the building.

The prisoners from Monck's Corner arrived in Charlestown on April 16th, along with "twenty-four four-span wagons and three hundred and fifteen horses." When Tarleton captured Monck's Corner he had sealed off the west branch of the Cooper River.

On April 16th Webster moved to Strawberry Ferry and ordered Tarleton to seize all the boats at Bonneau's Ferry, sealing off the east branch of the Cooper River. The next day Webster took Miller's Bridge on the Wando River.

On April 18th about 3,000 men from New York reinforced Clinton. He formed an independent command for Cornwallis, and assigned him both Webster and Lord Francis Rawdon. Cornwallis's mission was to prevent supplies and reinforcements from getting into Charlestown. Tarleton proceeded to the northern end of the Wando on the 20th and took nine sloops with a large amount of stores, and twenty pieces of artillery.

Some historians have labeled this attack a total surprise and blamed Huger for not putting out appropriate security. The Americans had been probed by the British before, but were always able to retreat quickly and avoid being attacked. The week before the attack on Monck's Corner Tarleton had tried to surprise Huger at Goose Creek, but he "eluded the maneuvre by retiring."

William Washington did not believe the attack was a surprise and thought that Tarleton was lucky and had struck at the perfect time. Loyalist Anthony Allaire also adds evidence to this argument because he said that when Tarleton struck the Americans were breaking camp and getting ready to march. If Tarleton had tried to attack a few hours earlier, he would have encountered a stronger picket. If he had waited for a few hours later there would have been no one there.

No matter whether it was a surprise or not, Tarleton did get the credit for one-sided victory. He conducted a swift night movement, and then gathered valuable intelligence about the disposition of the enemy before he attacked. In the world of "behind the lines" operations, the glory goes to those who dare.[234]

Haddrell's Point, South Carolina   **Skirmish**
Charlestown Campaign
2 May 1780

When the British fleet sailed past Fort Moultrie on April 8th most of the garrison within the fort was withdrawn to the city defenses. This included most of the 1st South Carolina Regiment.

Arbuthnot could not sail up the Cooper River to close off the support line into Charlestown because of the redoubt at Lempriére's Point and Mount Pleasant. [235]

Initially this post was defended by the North Carolinians under Colonel Marquis Francis de Malmedy, and with the Light Infantry of Lieutenant Colonel Laurens. When the Light Infantry was recalled to defend Charlestown Neck, Lincoln sent Malmedy 75 North Carolina militia to replace them. Malmedy then had 100 1st South Carolina Continentals and 200 North Carolina militia under his command to hold off any British attempt to sail up the Cooper River.

At two o'clock in the morning on April 26th the American Volunteers, the 23rd Regiment and the Volunteers of Ireland, marched seventeen miles from Wappetaw Bridge to Mount Pleasant. The British arrived at Haddrell's Point in the afternoon. The defenders of Mount Pleasant had one 18-pounder there, but they deserted the position when they learned of the nearness of the Cornwallis's men. Cornwallis wrote that he found "no resistance" there.

On the 27th the British troops marched back from where they came, and stopped at the Waputa Meetinghouse. Malmedy heard of the movement of the British forces and thought they were about to attack. What Malmedy didn't know was that Cornwallis thought the Lempriére's was too strong to attack.

Malmedy panicked and had his men evacuate the fort and move into Fort Moultrie. The withdrawal was not an orderly one, and every man was for himself, and they left behind the artillery. Some of Malmedy's men tried to get to Fort Moultrie by boat, but it sailed into Hog Island Channel and was captured by the British. The boats had three officers and 80 men.

The next day the American Volunteers received word that Lempriére's Point had been abandoned. They marched with the New York Volunteers back to Mount Pleasant to investigate, while at the same time Arbuthnot had organized a brigade of 500 sailors from the fleet to capture Lempriére's Point. At daybreak on April 29th the sailors landed at Mount Pleasant and joined the American Volunteers and the New York Volunteers, then marched to Lempriére's Point.

The British captured four 18-pounders, two 4-pounders and five swivel guns. Captain Charles Hudson of the Royal Navy raised the British flag over the fort. The citizens of Charlestown could clearly see the flag, and they knew that the British now occupied the east side of the Cooper River, and had done so without firing a shot. Lieutenant Anthony Allaire described the fort as a "disagreeable post. You must always keep your eyes shut or they fill with sand due to the high winds."

Malmedy was not popular with the people of Charlestown after he had evacuated his post. He was advised to leave the town. Malmedy did leave, but soon afterwards he was captured.

On the 2nd of May Ferguson and sixty American Volunteers marched to Haddrell's Point to attack the small fort that stood on a causeway that led to Fort Moultrie. The fort was about 150 yards from the mainland, and when the tide was high it became an island on the causeway. Defending the fort was Captain John Williams and twenty soldiers of the 1st South Carolina Regiment. If the fort were taken it would sever communications between Fort Moultrie and the mainland.

Ferguson divided his force into two 30-man elements. One would attack from the right, and one from center. When Major Ferguson marched to the fort, the tide was so low that the thirty men who were with him on the right side of the fort marched on dry land. Captain Abraham DePeyster and his thirty men marched down the other side of the causeway in knee-deep water, and stormed the fort.

After the fort was taken the men were under constant fire until dark from four cannons in Fort Moultrie. After dark the Volunteers fortified their fort against a possible attack. The firepower from Fort Moultrie was not very accurate, and did not cause any casualties. The only real danger to the British was losing eyesight due to blowing sand. Anthony Allaire wrote that the fort was "nothing but a bank of sand, where, in a windy day, you must keep your eyes shut or have them filled with sand." [236]

Lenud's Ferry, South Carolina [237]   **Skirmish**
Charlestown Campaign
6 May 1780

American Forces
Commanding Officer   Colonel Anthony Walton White
    Continentals   350
        Colonel Anthony Walton White
            1st Regiment of Continental Light Dragoons
                Major John Jameson
                Captain Thomas Pemberton
                Captain John Watts
                Captain Baylor Hill
                Captain John Belfield
        Lieutenant Colonel William Washington
            3rd Regiment of Continental Light Dragoons
                Major Richard Call
                Captain Walker Baylor
Casualties   11 killed, 30 wounded, 67 captured

British Forces
Commanding Officer   Lieutenant Colonel Banastre Tarleton
    Regulars
        Captain William Henry Talbot
            17th Regiment of Light Dragoons   Unknown number
    Provincials
        British Legion
            Cavalry   150
                Captain David Kinlock
Casualties   2 killed

After the attack on Monck's Corner the Patriot cavalry moved north of the Santee River to regroup. Some had just arrived from the north, while others were survivors of Tarleton's attack on Monck's Corner.

On April 23rd Colonel Anthony White arrived from Virginia to assume command of the 1st Continental Light Dragoons. By April 27th orders were given to move the cavalry to Georgetown. Since he had been promoted to Colonel on 16 February 1780, White was the ranking Continental cavalry officer. He assumed command of the two Continental Dragoon regiments, which he considered as a brigade. He also appointed Cosmo de Medici, of the North Carolina Dragoons, as his Brigade Major and Judge Advocate.

Since the defeat at Monck's Corner the British were able to move unmolested through St. Thomas Parish, foraging and plundering at will. The soldiers who plundered "for the wanton pleasure of Spoil" were mainly the Loyalist militia and Provincials. These were Americans who had suffered at the hands of their own countrymen, and now it was time for revenge.

The Loyalists gave the wives of soldiers in Charlestown special attention. They took everything from Mary Motte, the wife of Colonel Isaac Motte, including her children's clothes. When she begged the men to leave something for the children, they said that they wished her husband were there, so "they would rip his damned rebel heart out."

Rawlins Lowndes's wife, Sarah, had a gang of soldier's enter her Crowfield Plantation, and told her that they had orders to plunder. She stood up to them, and only gave them breakfast. She had been lucky. In one case a couple of drunken British Legion soldiers had raped Ann Fayssoux, the wife of Loyalist Peter Fayssoux.

At the suggestion of Governor Rutledge, General Isaac Huger directed that a party be sent south of the Santee to disrupt British plundering. On May 3rd White called all the horsemen fit for duty to assemble in Georgetown at ten o'clock that night. In the group were remnants of Pulaski's Legion, and Daniel Horry's South Carolina Dragoons.

The plan had called for Colonel Abraham Buford to provide 300 men for support, but Buford could not supply the men at that time. He had a regiment of infantry and an artillery company that marched from Pittsylvania, Virginia to deliver reinforcements and two cannon to Charlestown.

Within an hour of leaving Georgetown the cavalry was entangled in "a strange woods." After much wandering they finally found a savannah that they recognized, where they stopped and rested. The cavalrymen stayed there in a continuous downpour, until the next night. William Washington took his regiment to the west, while White and the remaining troops moved down to Horry's Plantation, and crossed to the south bank of the Santee.[238]

White and Washington rendezvoused again at Lenud's Ferry, then moved two miles below St. James Church to set up camp. Baylor Hill wrote that in the morning "a negroe fellow with his Sword by his side" came into the camp and mistook the Continentals for a British patrol. He told White that if he gave him a captain's commission he could raise a company of Negro horsemen. He also told White that his master was a "great Rebell, and he would be the first man who would go and kill him." White ordered that the man receive fifty lashes, and then had him hanged. Before he died he was cut down and left in the swamp.

The cavalry moved on fourteen miles to the Loyalist plantation of Elias Ball, near Strawberry. When they arrived they spotted an officer and fourteen men of the British Legion infantry foraging on the plantation. The Loyalists were captured without incident. The only gunfire was when Captain Baylor Hill fired his pistol to stop the Patriot cavalry from hacking the captives to death. The Patriot cavalry still had the atrocity of Monck's Corner fresh in their minds, and only an alert officer stopped the same from happening at Ball's Plantation in retaliation.

White sent an officer to Buford requesting a strong party of infantry and boats be sent to Lenud's Ferry to support the crossing. Buford detached 150 men with an officer to take up a position between White's cavalry and the British.

On the return march Pulaski's and Horry's cavalry separated from White's column, and headed toward Horry's plantation. Washington wanted to cross over the river, but instead of looking for a safer location White insisted that they wait on the south bank. Unfortunately White's force arrived at Lenud's Ferry before Buford's infantry did.

Patrick O'Kelley

After the fall of Haddrell's point Tarleton's intelligence collecting grew in importance. He collected information that told him there were Rebels on the north side of the Santee River. Tarleton set out on the morning of the 6th with a patrol of 150 of his men, to gather more information on the force at Lenud's ferry. Along the way he met Elias Ball, who had witnessed the capture of Tarleton's men at his plantation. Tarleton didn't hesitate and started out for Lenud's Ferry right away. A force-march brought him to the south bank of the Santee by 3:00 p.m.

The Continental dragoons had been marching all night, and in the warm spring sunshine they dozed by the bank near Hell Hole Swamp. Their horses were unbridled, unsaddled and White had sent no patrols out to sound the alarm in time for the dragoons to deploy if something happened. The cavalry were not prepared for what happened next.

Captain Walker Baylor had just loaded the prisoners in the only boat, when an alarm pistol was fired. The Patriots were surprised by the sudden appearance of the Tarleton's cavalry. Buford's infantry on the other side of the river could offer no support.

Upon sighting the Continentals Tarleton immediately ordered a charge. They drove in the picket guards and then began hacking at the surprised cavalry. Captain Hill had just been relieved of the guarding of the prisoners, and tried to mount a horse, but the noise of the charge made the horse skittish. Hill tried to escape on foot, but was captured by a mounted Legion dragoon.

Baylor's load of prisoners escaped in the water when Lieutenant Lovet Ashe, the prisoner in the boat, threw the guards in the water. Baylor made it to the other side of the river.

Five officers and thirty-six men were killed and wounded in the fight. All the horses, arms and accoutrements of the Patriots were captured. Tarleton wrote that he had captured 67 officers and men. Hill and de Medici were both captured. White and Washington, with some officers and men, swam across the river and escaped. Many others tried to follow their example, but drowned in the river or in Hell Hole Swamp.[239]

The British dragoons lost two officers and four horses in the action. When Tarleton returned to Lord Cornwallis's camp that same evening, twenty of his horses died due to fatigue.

After this attack the Continental dragoons were rendered unfit for further service. The Virginians saw White as an intruding Northerner. William Washington never forgave White and when the Dragoons went to Halifax, North Carolina in the summer to remount and refit, Washington leveled charges on White, and had him arrested. A court martial later acquitted White.

When Nathanael Greene came into command that December, he wisely separated the two. White's Regiment was ordered back to Virginia to obtain new supplies, men and horses. [240]

Fort Moultrie, South Carolina   **Naval skirmish**
Charlestown Campaign
7 May 1780

American Forces
Commanding Officer   Lieutenant Colonel William Scott
    Continentals
       1st South Carolina Regiment   118
       1st & 2nd North Carolina Regiment [241]   4
       Fort Artillery   41 iron cannon
          24-pounders   9
          18-pounders   7
          12-pounders   10
          9-pounders   9
          6-pounders   2
          4-pounders   4
          10-inch mortar   1
    Unknown Captain
       Charlestown Militia   98
Casualties   All captured

British Forces

Commanding Officer	Captain Charles Hudson
Royal Navy	
Seaman and Marines	350
Provincials	
Major Patrick Ferguson	
American Volunteers	Unknown number

On April 27th Admiral Arbuthnot sent ashore 500 Royal Navy Seamen and Marines, under Captain Charles Hudson, to occupy Haddrell's Point. At Mount Pleasant Hudson learned from some deserters of the poor defenses at Fort Moultrie. He also learned that Lincoln had recalled Colonel Pinckney and most of the 1st South Carolina Regiment, so that they could occupy the trenches on Charlestown Neck. Commanding the fort was Lieutenant Colonel William Scott, with 118 Continentals and 100 militia.

When Arbuthnot learned of the situation at Fort Moultrie he ordered Captain Hudson to attack the fort from the northwest. During the night of May 4th Hudson took 150 sailors and marines, loaded up in small boats and rowed past the fort. They landed on the northeast end of Sullivan's Island before daybreak. Their target was a small redoubt on that end of the island. In 1776 this location proved critical when the British tried to cross the Breach Inlet and land on the island. The British found the redoubt deserted, and Hudson's men occupied the fortification.

After the north end of the island was secure an additional 200 men under the command of Captain John Orde reinforced Hudson. If Hudson needed support, Major Ferguson and his American Volunteers were poised to strike from Haddrell's Point.

When the Royal Navy moved into position on May 6th to begin a bombardment of the fort, Captain Hudson asked for the surrender of the fort. Lieutenant Colonel William Scott of the 1st South Carolina sent back the answer "Tol, lol, de rol, lol: Fort Moultrie will be defended to the last extremity."[242]

After a day of bombardment by the Royal Navy another message was sent. Scott was told that the offer for surrender would only last a half an hour, and that if the fort had not given up by that time, Hudson would storm the fort and put all to the sword. Scott assembled the captains of the garrison, half of which were militia. The regular officers opposed surrender, but the militia officers were intimidated by the threat of no quarter being given to the defenders. Scott knew that his position was hopeless, and asked for the "honors of war." His officers would be allowed to wear their side arms, and the militia would sign paroles and return to their homes until they were exchanged. After a period of haggling over terms of surrender Scott agreed to surrender.

At 8 o'clock in the morning of May 7th Scott marched his men out of the fort, and they stacked their arms. The Royal Navy sailors were not impressed by the poor defense of the Patriots, and held oars in their hands instead of weapons, to mock the Carolinians.

Inside the fort was "50 barrels of powder, 44 pieces of artillery, 1 brass 10 inch mortar, 3,000 cannon cartridges, 500 live 10 inch shells, 40,000 musket cartridges, along with a vast quantity of flint, 3 months of salt for 200 men, 18 tierces of rice, 40 head of black cattle, 60 sheep, 20 goats, 40 fat hogs, 6 wagons, 2 stands of colors and many other articles." [243]

Morris's Ford, South Carolina [244]
May 1780

Captain John Mumford had been in Colonel James Thompson's command early in the war. He was wounded in the knee at Hutson's Ferry, Georgia in 1777 and returned home. After the fall of Charlestown he was on his way to join the Patriot militia besieged at Charlestown, but he did not know that the city had surrendered. He was ambushed by a band of Tories under "Old Ben" John, at Morris's Ford, on the Salkehatchie River. Mumford was buried on the side of the road "at the foot of a large pine, on the left hand side of the main road to Barnwell Court House, a few rods south of the bridge, just at turn of the road from which you can see the bridge." [245]

Waxhaws, South Carolina [246]   **Skirmish**
29 May 1780

American Forces
Commanding Officer   Colonel Abraham Buford
   Continentals   350
      3rd Virginia Detachment of Scott's Virginia Brigade[247]
      Major Thomas Ridley
      Captain Andrew Wallace [248]
      Captain Claiborne W. Lawson [249]
      Captain Robert Woodson
      Captain John Stokes
      Captain Adam Wallace [250]
      Captain-Lieutenant Thomas Catlett [251]
   Unknown Sergeant
      3rd Regiment of Continental Light Dragoons
   South Carolina Militia   180
Casualties   113 killed, 203 captured [252]

British Forces
Commanding Officer   Lieutenant Colonel Banastre Tarleton
   British Regulars
      Captain William Henry Talbot
         17th Regiment of Light Dragoons   40
         Lieutenant Matthew Patteshall
   Provincials
      Lieutenant Colonel Banastre Tarleton
         British Legion
         Major Charles Cochrane
            Legion Infantry [253]   100
               Lieutenant Lochlan McDonald
               Lieutenant Peter Campbell
            Legion Cavalry   130
               Captain David Kinlock
               Captain Charles Campbell
Casualties   16 killed, 12 wounded [254]

After leaving the siege of Charlestown Governor Rutledge headed to the High Hills of the Santee, where the Wateree becomes the Santee River. Rutledge knew that the backcountry people would not respond to his rallying cry, so he asked General Washington for Continental troops. Washington was able to spare the Maryland Division, commanded by Baron De Kalb.

When Charlestown fell Rutledge withdrew northwest on the Camden Road, with General Huger, and a military escort consisting of a small party of 3rd Continental Dragoons. Huger had become the nominal commander of all the reinforcements from Virginia and the Carolinas. Rutledge had ordered William Washington and White to march by way of Wilmington, to Hillsborough, North Carolina.

After Monck's Corner Major Jameson had left the 1st Dragoons and joined Sheldon's 2nd Continental Dragoons in Westchester, New York. Colonel Daniel Horry had accepted parole from the British, possibly to preserve his estate. Upon arriving in Camden, Rutledge held a council of war, and decided to march on to North Carolina. On May 26th Rutledge and his entourage proceeded on to Clermont and stayed at the house of Loyalist, Henry Rugeley.

After Clinton gained control of Charlestown he sent troops into the interior to eliminate any pockets of resistance. One column went up the Savannah River to Augusta, another to Ninety-Six, and the third, under Lord Cornwallis, was ordered to take Camden. Cornwallis had 2,500 men and five pieces of artillery. Cornwallis directed Tarleton and his British Legion towards Georgetown, to find William Washington and his dragoons.

When Tarleton arrived there he found the district empty of any Patriot troops. As a result of Tarleton's sweep Francis Marion and Peter Horry moved northward, to find the Patriot army on its way to South Carolina. They had not been captured at Charlestown, and moved towards De Kalb to receive orders.

Colonel Abraham Buford was ordered by Huger to fall back to Hillsborough, North Carolina. Buford's force consisted of the 350 new recruits, or recalled veterans, intended for the various regiments of the Virginia Line. He also had with him some of the survivors of

Lenud's ferry, Governor Rutledge and a few members of his council.

Cornwallis's goal was Camden, and his army was on the same road taken as Buford, but Buford had a ten day lead. That lead was too much for the British infantry to catch him. Cornwallis decided that Tarleton and his Legion might have a chance to intercept Governor Rutledge, and the fleeing government in exile of South Carolina.

On May 27th Tarleton marched with his Legion, forty troopers of the 17th Dragoons, and a 3-pound field piece. The heat was oppressive and Tarleton pushed his horses until some died beneath their riders. He commandeered mounts wherever he could find them, and doubled up when necessary. He refused to give up the chase. Tarleton's force arrived in Camden the next day and stopped to rest.

Captain Charles Campbell, of Tarleton's Legion, rode to Thomas Sumter's plantation and had Sumter's wife, Mary, moved outside. She was paralytic and was taken out of the house while sitting on her chair. The British placed her under the shade of a tree and then "the house and meat house were plundered." Campbell asked her where her husband was but "she was firm and would give them no satisfaction." Incidents such as this would cause large numbers of recruits to support the Patriot cause.

When Campbell's men were done looting the house they set fire to the home. One of the dragoons had hidden a ham under his blanket, and as he passed by Mrs. Sumter he put it under her chair.

While they were resting Tarleton learned that Rutledge was at Henry Rugeley's mill, ten miles to the north of Camden. Buford and Caswell's 700 North Carolina militiamen lay fifteen miles south of Camden. When Caswell learned how close Tarleton was, he led his column to the Pee Dee River. Rugeley warned Rutledge of the approach of Tarleton's cavalry, and Rutledge left with General Huger. Huger turned over his military escort of Continental dragoons to Buford.

Buford's column was led by his artillery, two brass 6-pounders and two small mortars. Following this was an artillery forge on a cart, and two ammunition wagons with fifty-five barrels of powder. Behind them came twenty-six wagons with clothing, arms and camp equipage. An advance guard of 100 infantry guarded the artillery and baggage. Behind them came the main body of 200 to 250 infantry. The remaining troops were in the rear guard.

On the 29th Tarleton was moving swiftly to intercept the Patriot column when he learned that Buford was only twenty miles ahead. Tarleton wrote a letter to Buford to surrender, and sent it on by Captain David Kinlock. Kinlock's mission was meant to either trick Buford into surrendering, by greatly exaggerating British numbers, or at the very least delay him. Buford kept Kinlock by his side as he read the letter, never stopping the march.

Buford drew his officers together and presented them with proposals. They could surrender, or leave the wagons, but save the men by marching rapidly away from the area. The final proposal was to bring the wagons together as a makeshift fort and await the attack. The officers immediately rejected the first and second proposal, and they thought that Cornwallis's main force was close enough to provide support, so the third choice would be suicide. They chose to continue marching and hope that reinforcements would appear. Kinlock had been there for the entire meeting, and watched the column leave. He noted that the artillery was still in the vanguard.

Many of the British cavalry and mounted infantry were worn out, and dropped to the rear of Tarleton's column. The horses of Tarleton's artillery were unable to proceed. When Tarleton received Buford's response he decided to attack immediately, without taking the artillery.

Tarleton captured the Sergeant and four troopers of the 3rd Continental dragoons, at the rear of Buford's infantry at three o'clock in the afternoon. They were taken a few miles south of the North Carolina line, in a district then called the Waxhaws. In the Carolina heat Tarleton had come 105 miles, in fifty-four hours.

Buford witnessed the capture of the rearguard and had his men form for battle. Buford detached his supply wagons, and sent them on. He sent his artillery, under the command of Captain John

Champe Carter, on with the supply wagons. Buford would regret that he did not recall them. When he heard the sound of Tarleton's bugle he deployed his infantry into a single line, with a small reserve to the rear.

Tarleton's plan was simple. He assigned Major Cochrane with fifty cavalry, and about fifty dismounted infantry to harass Buford's left flank. Captains Talbot and Kinlock were to charge the center, with the forty men of the 17th Dragoons, and part of the Legion cavalry. Tarleton with thirty chosen horse and infantry would assault their right flank and reserve. Some British stragglers on their tired horses were beginning to arrive and were ordered to form a reserve, in the event of a counterattack.

Tarleton's small force formed on a low hill opposite Buford's center, and in full view of the Patriots. The high ground was a good spot to regroup in case the attack failed. The Legion cavalry was silhouetted against the hillside, making a considerable impression on the minds of the Buford's men.

After advancing 300 yards, the cavalry charged. When the British horses were within fifty paces, the Continental infantry aimed their muskets. The Virginia officers shouted to their men to hold their fire until the British were closer. The order to fire did not come until the charging horsemen were ten yards away from the single line of Continentals. The noise from the hundreds of charging horses was terrifying. There was time for only one volley, and it hit very few men and horses. As the cavalry smashed into the Continental line, they broke and ran.

Lieutenant Thomas Pearson, commanding the rear guard, was sabered and unhorsed. As he lay on the ground he was cut in the face across his nose, lips, tongue, and his jaw was split. Buford saw the bloody slaughter of Pearson's rear guard and decided to surrender. He sent Ensign John Crute with a white flag to Tarleton. As Crute approached Tarleton, the British commander's horse was hit in the head, bringing the horse down on top of him. Tarleton's troopers saw that the Patriots were violating their own flag of truce, and began to stab everything in sight. Crute was instantly cut down by the Legion. The demand for quarters from the Virginians was ignored and the Patriots were ridden down and slaughtered.

Captain Adam Wallace of the Virginia line saw that no quarter was being given and he ordered his men to sell their lives as dearly as possible. While Wallace stood his ground he "received a blow in the back of his neck, which nearly severed his head from his body." Buford and a few others escaped on horseback, along with the 100 men of the advance guard. Some of the Waggoners cut their horses from the wagons and galloped to safety.

The British Legion, mainly Americans from the northern colonies, began butchering the infantry. For fifteen minutes after the fight was over the Legion plunged their bayonets into any man that showed signs of life. Where several had fallen on top of each other, the Legion was seen to stab their bayonets into the top body, toss it aside, to stab at the bodies beneath.

Captain Stokes, an officer of the 2nd Virginia, was engaged in a fight with a dragoon, when another dragoon cut off his right hand. The two dragoons continued their attack on Stokes, cutting off his left forefinger and hacking his left arm in eight or ten places, from the wrist to the shoulder. His head was laid open almost the whole length of the crown to the eyebrows. After Stokes fell he received several cuts on the face and shoulders. A soldier passing by asked Stokes if he expected quarters. Stokes answered, "I have not, nor do I mean to ask quarters. Finish me as soon as possible." The soldier then stabbed Stokes twice with his bayonet. Another soldier asked the same question and received the same answer and he also thrust his bayonet twice through his body. Stokes had received twenty-three wounds, but he survived the war.[255]

After Tarleton was able to untangle himself from his dead horse he finally brought the fighting to a close, but his reputation in America would forever be infamous. He became known immediately as "Bloody Tarleton" and "Bloody Ban." The Patriot cry of "Tarleton's Quarter" and "Buford's Quarter" would be heard again and again on Southern battlefields.[256]

The Patriot losses are uncertain, but around 113 were killed, 150 wounded and 203 captured. Tarleton lost two officers killed, one wounded; three privates killed, eleven wounded; eleven horses killed, and nineteen horses wounded. Tarleton sent calls out to Camden and Charlotte for surgeons to come and look after the wounded Virginians. For the remainder of the day he collected the dead, wounded, and gathered arms and supplies of the defeated Patriots. The British captured three stands of colors, two brass 6-pounders, two Royal howitzers, two wagons with ammunition, one artillery forge wagon, fifty-five barrels of powder, and twenty-six wagons loaded with clothing, camp equipage, musket cartridges, cartridges boxes, flints and other supplies. On the evening of May 30th Tarleton marched back towards Camden with fifty-three prisoners to rejoin Cornwallis.

Reverend Jacob Carnes of the Waxhaw Church stated that he buried eighty-four men who were killed on that day, in one large grave. Twenty-five more died of their wounds the next day, and were buried 300 yards from the first grave.

The wounded were hauled in wagons to the Waxhaw Church that was being used as a hospital. More of the wounded died there, and were buried in the graveyard at the church. Susannah Smart told Lyman Draper that her mother helped feed the wounded, especially the men without any arms. One group that she fed was "six men with but two arms between them."

Buford was court-martialed for his conduct on the field, and was acquitted. Moultrie had written that, "On the approach of the enemy he ought to have formed them into a hollow square, with a small interval between each; in these intervals to have placed platoons; taking out the baggage and placed it a little in the front of each platoon, which would have served as a breastwork, and would have disconcerted the cavalry in their charge; his field pieces planted in the front angles of the square for the cavalry, who should face outward and be ready to sally when occasion should offer: six men in each waggon: with this disposition the enemy could have made no impression upon him: nay, Tarleton would never have attacked him."[257]

Near the Waxhaws, South Carolina   **Murder**
31 May 1780

Two days after the Waxhaws, Captain Christian Huck of Tarleton's Legion was ordered to patrol the region to find any resistance to the King.[258] Huck and his dragoons rode to the house of a young Quaker, named Samuel Wyly. Huck accused Wyly of having been in the militia during the siege of Charlestown. Wyly admitted that he had been there, but stated the authorities had paroled him. He then produced a copy of the parole. Huck refused to recognize the parole and held a trial. The jury consisted of three Loyalist militiamen and three of Huck's junior officers. Wyly was sentenced to be drawn and quartered. After they had finished the different parts of his body were set up on pikes by the roadside as a warning to others.

Wyly had not been the intended target of Huck's "justice". Huck had thought that Wyly was his brother, John, who was the sheriff in the Waxhaws. John Wyly had superintended the execution of a Loyalist for the crime of treason. This one small action would lead to the rising of partisan forces in the region. Soon this Presbyterian Rebellion would require larger and larger British units to secure their outposts. In the end, this one small murder, by a single careless British officer, would lead to the British defeat in Yorktown a year and a half later.[259]

Camden, South Carolina
31 May 1780

As the British army neared Camden on May 31st, two boys, Kit Gales and Samuel Dinkins, began sniping at the British column. The boys were quickly captured after they had fired several shots with no effect. Kit Gales was hanged on a tree. When Cornwallis marched into Camden on June 1st Samuel Dinkins was brought to Camden in chains.

Charles Stedman was the Commissary of Captures with Cornwallis, and he wrote in his book, *The History of the American*

War, "Upon the march to Camden, the British troops were supported from the country through which they passed. A number of negroes, mounted on horses, were employed under proper conductors in driving cattle for the support of the army, and, though they were in general very small, the army was plentifully supplied. The cattle were delivered alive to the regiments, who found their own butchers."

In Camden the British found "a store belonging to Joseph and Ely Kershaw" which had "21 rice tierces, 3 hogsheads and a half of indigo, some tea, sugar, coffee and linen, which were sent to the general hospital; a quantity of salt, 20 barrels of flour, 18 ditto Indian corn meal, one hogshead of rum, a quantity of bacon and hams, butter, brimstone, axes and wedges, sent to the Engineer department. Rhubarb in root, damaged, sent to the general hospital. A number of hats and some green cloth, distributed to the troops."

"In a barn near the river 90 hogsheads of tobacco – part of which was destroyed by the troops; the rest was ordered by Lord Cornwallis to be sent to Charlestown. Near 100 head of cattle were found in and near the town, together with some sheep. Lord Cornwallis ordered the commissaries to give no receipt to Colonel Kershaw for the property taken from him, as he was deemed a very violent man, and who was said to have persecuted the loyalists." After the capture of Camden the British began the construction of a well-fortified post.[260]

Cape Hatteras, North Carolina
7 June 1780

The *Adventure* was a Patriot ship that had been at sea for seventeen days. The ship was bound from St. Croix with a cargo of rum, sugar and fruit. Forty leagues east of Cape Hatteras the *Adventure* was spotted by the brig *Hammond* and the sloop *Randall*, two privateers from Bermuda.

Though it was merchant ship, the *Adventure* put up a strong fight. For three hours the ships maneuvered around each other, most of the time within "pistol shot". After suffering severe damage the *Hammond* struck her colors, indicating her surrender. However the *Adventure* could not get possession of the brig due to her own sails and rigging being disabled from the fight. The *Hammond* was able to escape when the *Randall* towed her off. The *Adventure* did not have a single man hurt in the engagement.

On her way to the James River the brig *General Wayne* and the schooner *Grand Tyger* joined the *Adventure*. The three ships saw eleven privateers in the distance, waiting for easy prey, but they left the small American convoy alone.[261]

Halifax, North Carolina
June 1780

After the surrender of Charlestown many of the American soldiers were held prisoner aboard prison ships in Charlestown Harbor. Lieutenant Edward Barnwell had been captured at St. John's Island and held on board the prison ship *Packhorse*. While the ship was on its way north Lieutenant Barnwell and 35 men took over the ship and ran it aground at Halifax, North Carolina.

When Lieutenant Barnwell returned home he was promoted to Lieutenant Colonel and given command of the Beaufort Regiment.[262]

Brandon's Defeat, South Carolina [263]   **Skirmish**
8 June 1780 [264]

Thomas Brandon had been a captain in the original Spartan Regiment in 1775, under Colonel John Thomas, Sr.[265] The Spartan Regiment divided in 1777, and became the 1st Spartan Regiment and the 2nd Spartan Regiment, with Brandon being chosen as the colonel of the 2nd Spartan Regiment.[266]

Ever since the British had been victorious in South Carolina Brandon had established a camp and gathered his forces. He met with Colonel John Thomas and Lieutenant Colonel James Liles and they agreed to concentrate their forces at a camp near Fair Forest Creek. Brandon's secondary mission for the camp was to keep the

Loyalists in check, so they could not join the approaching British.
[267]

Brandon had several Loyalist prisoners in his camp and during the night one of the prisoners, Adam Steedham, escaped and warned Captain William Cunningham of the location of the camp. William Cunningham had originally been in the 3rd South Carolina Rangers, but went to the Loyalist's side after Captain William Ritchie beat his brother to death. After Cunningham killed Ritchie he hid out until Campbell captured Savannah. Cunningham then gathered the Loyalists in the Ninety-Six District, and rendezvoused with 600 other Tories. They marched to Georgia, where they were "Attacked by the Rebels on the march, many of the men killed, or taken, & others declining the enterprise".

He arrived with 330 men and joined Archibald Campbell at Briar Creek in February 1779. Campbell appointed him as a lieutenant in the 2nd Battalion of the South Carolina Royalists.

When Prévost marched into South Carolina Cunningham was captured by the Patriots, and sent to the jail in Charlestown. After four months in the jail he was able to escape, and take shelter with other Loyalists in Ninety-Six. When Clinton captured Charlestown Cunningham rejoined the Loyalist Militia, as a captain.

Brandon had about 10 or 12 men in the camp that began making breakfast and feeding the horses, when Cunningham rushed into the camp, completely routing Brandon's men. Brandon had situated his men beside a steep ravine, and many were able to get away by jumping into it. Cunningham's horses could not pursue them.

Not everyone got away. Joseph McJunkin's brother, Daniel, "was ran through by a trooper with a bayonet entering between his shoulders and the point emerging through his heart, so he seized or clutched in agony with his hands. When the Tory trooper said, "Let go, my good fellow and I'll pull it out as carefully as possible" and putting one foot on McJ's back, pulled it out. When McJ fell upon the ground."[268] There were five of Brandon's men killed.[269]

Incidents like the killing of prisoners worked against the British objectives in South Carolina, and brought bitter feuds to the fighting. Thomas Young learned of his brother's death at Brandon's defeat, and joined Brandon's forces. He would later avenge his brother's murder by hanging Adam Steedham. Captain Joseph McJunkin wrote that after this "the rest of the whigs of Union District fled beyond the Broad River". They rendezvoused at the Bullock's Meetinghouse, where the Reverend Doctor Alexander was the pastor. Alexander's "zeal for liberty and activity in exhorting his people to join in the cause of their country had made him so obnoxious to the British and Tories that he had been compelled to leave the State." Refugees from Union, Spartanburg, Laurens and Newberry, with some others from Virginia, all gathered there.

When it was time to decide what course of action to take next, Colonel John Thomas, Jr. told them "shall we declare ourselves cowards and traitors, or shall we pursue the prize of liberty as long as we have life?" Thomas then quoted Patrick Henry, and said, "Give me Liberty, or give me death!"

McJunkin told the crowd of men, "All who were in favor of that course should throw up their hats and clap their hands. In an instant every hat was thrown up and the air resounded with unanimous clapping of hands and shouts of defiance."

The men disbanded to go home and visit their families one final time, and then they rendezvoused with Sumter at Tuckasegee Ford on the Catawba River in North Carolina.

Steedham expected retaliations against himself, since he had brought Cunningham to Brandon's camp. He rode to Georgia and stayed there for several months, until everything had calmed down. However Brandon had men looking out for the return of the Loyalist. On the night that he returned home Brandon's men, under the command of Thomas Young, captured him and hanged him from a tree. Young had avenged his brother, who was slain at Brandon's defeat. [270]

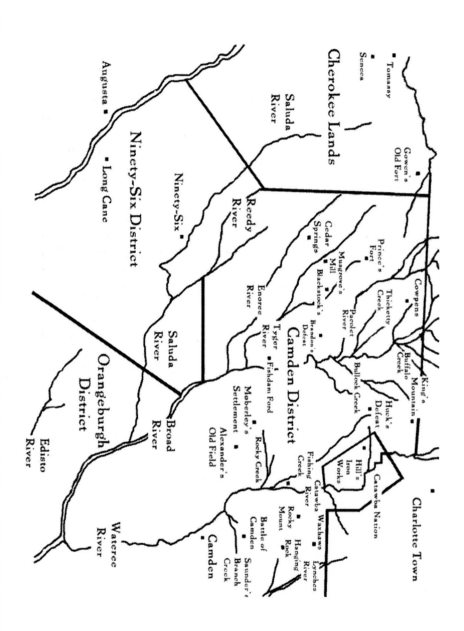

Alexander's Old Field, South Carolina [271]   Skirmish
Presbyterian Rebellion
8 June 1780 [272]

Before Clinton left for New York he appointed Major Patrick Ferguson to be the Inspector of Militia, under Lord Cornwallis. Ferguson immediately went about his assigned task, and a call went out to the people in the Rocky Mount area to assemble at Beckham's Old Field to take the oath of allegiance to the King. One of the Loyalist officers attempting to gather support for the British was Colonel Houseman. Lossing wrote that Houseman was the commander of a British post near Rocky Mount. Houseman rode to a large Patriot family, headed by Justice John Gaston. John Gaston, Jr. wrote that Houseman was "in a dress altogether plain, accompanied by about fifty of those plundering banditti, which the British policy had dignified with the name of *loyalists*."

Houseman begged, and then threatened the family to join the King's forces. Gaston told him "never." After Houseman rode on John Gaston sent out his seven sons to gather their neighbors to disperse the assembly of Loyalists.

John Gaston's nephew, Captain John McClure, had been at Monck's Corner when he learned of the surrender of Charleston. He returned home with his Chester District militia and learned of the defeat of Buford at the Waxhaws. He and his militia swore to continue fighting. John Gaston, Jr. wrote "On the reception of this news, he (Captain McClure), and three of said Gaston's sons, and Captain John Steele, I think arose upon their feet and made this united and solemn declaration, "that they would never submit nor surrender to the enemies of their country; that liberty or death, from that time forth, should be their motto!" Each of these young men had served three years in the company of Captain Eli Kershaw, of the Third Regiment of South Carolina, commanded by Wm. Thompson, with the above motto inscribed on the front of their military caps."[273]

McClure led thirty-two kinsmen and neighbors along an Indian path to Beckham's Old Field. The men "were clad in hunting-shirts and moccasins, wool hats and deer-skin caps, each armed with a butcher-knife and a rifle." With McClure was Reverend John Simpson, the pastor of Fishing Creek Church, Lieutenant Hugh McClure, his brother, and Lieutenant John Steele. John Gaston, Jr. wrote, "They were principally of the Knoxes, Walkers, Morrows, McClures, and Johnsons."

The militia met at Gaston's house and agreed to attack the Loyalists immediately. John Gaston brought out "a gallon of peach brandy and gave them all a dram, then addressing them said "Move off now brisk, and when you come in sight of the Tories rush right in among them and shoot as fast as you can and kill as many of them as you can and I'll warrant you'll gain the victory."

The thirty-two Patriots surrounded the 200 Loyalists and began firing and shouting to scare them off. The tactic worked, and the Loyalists fled.[274]

There are differing accounts to how many casualties there were. Some accounts state that there wasn't a man lost on either side. A different account states that four Loyalists were killed and two of McClure's men were wounded. Samuel Morrow told Draper that Hugh McClure was wounded in this action. Daniel Stinson also wrote that McClure was badly wounded in the right arm, making him a cripple for life and that Joseph Morrow was wounded in the arm. John Craig wrote that they took nine prisoners.

John Gaston, Jr. wrote that McClure and William McGarroty was wounded. He also wrote "it is most possible that McClure's men did not wish to kill, knowing that many good men might be there who knew of no relief, but to submit and take parole. Only one was killed, and he was known to be a real friend to his country."

Joseph Gaston wrote that he lost two brothers in the fighting. He was also badly wounded when he spotted "one of the enemy, both raised their pieces at once and both fired the same instant and both fell, his antagonist shot through the heart." Gaston was hit by the ball "striking the bridge of his nose and passing under the left eye, shattering the cheek bone and going out of the ear, partially impairing his sight and hearing."[275]

Houseman was "filled with rage," and sent some men to capture the 80-year-old John Gaston. "They found his dwelling deserted. His wife, concealed in some bushes near, saw them plunder the house of every thing, and carry off the stock from the plantation. Nothing was left but the family Bible."

After the fight McClure and his militia rode on to find Sumter and join his growing force.[276]

Gibson's Meeting House
Moberley's Settlement, South Carolina [277]　　　　**Skirmish**
Presbyterian Rebellion
10 June 1780

The militia of the New Acquisition lands met at Bullock's Creek Presbyterian Church, to talk about what to do about the approaching British forces. They learned that General Williamson had surrendered and gave his parole. Colonel Samuel Watson and Lieutenant Colonel William Bratton resigned their commands, and said that any further resistance was useless. They advised their men "to do the best they could for themselves."

Major Richard Winn had been in the 3rd South Carolina Regiment and had not given his parole. He learned that a group of Loyalists were going to meet at Gibson's Meeting House. Since the New Acquisition Militia had broken up, he was unable to get any men to put down the Loyalists, and he joined with Colonel Bratton to raise some men for the attack. After McClure ran the Loyalists out of Alexander's Old Fields he joined with Colonel William Bratton, and Major Winn, because the two commanders had collected one hundred militiamen in the New Acquisition area.[278]

The Loyalists that fled from Alexander's Old Field encountered Captain John Hampton and stole "thirty negroes, two or three wagons and teams and thirty valuable horses and a large quantity of household furniture."

"They also made prisoners of Captain John and Henry Hampton, which… they sent under a strong guard to Camden, the British headquarters."

Winn, Bratton and McClure rode to put down these Loyalists.[279] James Collins described the militiamen riding with Winn as "men acting entirely on our own footing, without the promise or expectation of any pay. There was nothing furnished us from the public; we furnished our own clothes, composed of course materials, and all home spun; our over dress was a hunting shirt, of what was called linsey woolsey, well belted around us. We furnished our own horses, saddles, bridles, guns, swords, butcher knives, and our own spurs."[280]

He continued, "We carried no camp equipage, no cooking utensils, nor any thing to encumber us; we depended on what chance or kind providence might cast in our way."

The Loyalists were under the command of Colonel Charles Coleman, and met in a house that they were using as a blockhouse. The Patriots rode until dark and then "were directed to keep our horses with the saddles, lie down on our arms, and be ready when called."

After a few hours of rest they continued their ride until right before sunrise. When they arrived at the Loyalist's meeting place Bratton sent out a reconnaissance. He learned that they were "in a large log building, having three guards placed out – one in the yard and the other two at no great distance from each end of a long lane, through which the main road passed by the house."

As soon as the sun came up Bratton's men moved slowly through the woods, then "formed into regular order." Before they could finish moving into their attack positions, the sentries fired on them, but Bratton's men were too close to be stopped. The Patriots rushed into the blockhouse yard and fired. Some of the Loyalist rushed out of the house, but were cut down. Others jumped out the windows and left their weapons, running "some distance on all fours before they could recover their legs."

Some accounts state that there were no casualties, however Winn wrote that the Loyalists were "totally defeated with a small loss of killed and wounded. The Whig party lost nothing." Daniel Stinson wrote, "Some Tories got killed in hastily descending the bluff."

Collins wrote that "We took possession of most of their guns, which were stacked in the yard, and also took several of them prisoners; likewise, most of their ammunition, swords, and pistols. When all was over, we found that we had killed three of their best officers, and five others; sixteen were badly wounded."

Samuel Walker wrote in his pension "We attacked them and took 30 prisoners and sent them to Hillsborough." William White, a militiaman who was there, told Lyman Draper that they "killed a number of them." They also were able to capture some stolen horses.

After this skirmish Bratton, Winn and McClure rode to Reverend John Simpson's house and made camp. They then joined other Patriots who had fled to North Carolina. Sumter arrived in North Carolina with "two to five hundred men, generally mounted and armed with rifles."

At the Catawba River they "succeeded in procuring some barley, put it in a crock, which was placed in the ground, covered with hot ashes and embers." Joseph McJunkin said that "it was unaided by salt, pork, bacon or beef" but it was "delicious."

On June 15th they held a convention at Tuckasegee Ford on the Catawba River west of Charlotte Town. The members of this assembly elected Thomas Sumter as their general, and agreed to serve under him until the end of the war.[281] They unanimously agreed that they should join Colonel Francis Locke to oppose "a body of 1000 Tories who had collected at Ramsower's Mill in No. Carolina under their leader Colo. Moore."

The successful attack upon Alexander's Old Field, and Gibson's Meeting House, doubled the Patriot ranks. When the local Loyalists learned that Winn had masterminded the raid on Gibson's Meeting House, they "had all his houses burnt to the ground, and every negro plundered, together with every property he possessed in the world. His wife was plundered of her clothes and she was drove off with two infant children." Winn wrote, "It is no more than I expected."

Cornwallis had positioned key posts throughout the South Carolina backcountry from which he intended to conquer the Carolinas. One of these posts was Rocky Mount, where Lieutenant

Colonel George Turnbull had command of the New York Volunteers. With Turnbull was Captain Christian Huck's troop of the British Legion, and a number of Loyalist militia units from the district. When Turnbull learned of the attacks on the Loyalists at Alexander's Old Fields, and Gibson's Meetinghouse he ordered Huck to disrupt Sumter's recruiting, and "to push the Rebels as far as you deem convenient." [282]

Caldwell's Place, South Carolina   Skirmish
June 1780

After the skirmish at Moberley's Meetinghouse, there was a skirmish at Caldwell's Place, on Lee's Creek. Thomas McDill wrote "There was a Colonel Phillips of the British Army who as up in York District, plundering for Cornwallace." Lieutenant Colonel James Hawthorne and some of his New Acquisition Militia pursued the Loyalists, and surrounded them at Caldwell's Place. The Tories did not fight, but fled at the first sign of the Patriot forces. [283] Their leader, "Colonel John Phillips, was found squatting in a briar patch, and dragged out a prisoner."

E.C. McClure wrote that the "Tories ran leaving Phillips and his adjutant standing in the yard. Phillips was not hated by the Whigs as much as some of the other Tories. He sometimes favored them."

In Parson's *History of Fairfield District* he wrote that Phillips "had an unaccountable influence over Cornwallis and in the beneficent exercise of that influence, he obtained pardon for all the Whigs condemned to death at the drumhead court while his Lordship occupied Winnsboro". [284]

Gaither's Old Field, South Carolina **Skirmish**
June 1780

John Rosser told Draper that John Land was killed in June 1780. "His muster ground was south of Rosoville. He was mustering his company at the time. There was a general stampede of the militia. Land was pursued and killed at the northwest corner of Richard Gaither's field in the woods."[285]

Fishing Creek Church, South Carolina **Murder**
Presbyterian Rebellion
11 June 1780 [286]

Captain Christian Huck rode towards Simpson's Meeting House with his troop of dragoons from the British Legion, and some mounted Loyalist militia under the command of Lieutenant Colonel James Ferguson. Huck stopped at Walker's Mill and had his men grind wheat taken from local plantations. Colonel Ferguson rode to Rocky Creek and attempted to get his brother Samuel to join his militia, but he declined.

When the militia under Bratton, Winn and McClure learn that Huck's troop was coming for them they moved their camp to Hill's Iron Works on Allison Creek. Reverend Simpson and eighty of his congregation enlisted in McClure and Bratton's militia company, leaving behind Mrs. Simpson, some "negroes" and a boy, William Strong.

On June 10th Lord Rawdon arrived in the Waxhaws and tried to put down the rising Patriot attacks. He told all the inhabitants to return to their farm and take British protection. General Williamson ordered the Ninety-Six District Militia disbanded. When Colonel Andrew Pickens and Colonel John Thomas, Sr. took the British parole, Colonel Thomas's son, John Thomas, Jr. moved his militia and vowed to continue fighting.

Huck and his cavalry rode to the Fishing Creek Church on Sunday, expecting to find the militia, but they had already left. Near the Fishing Creek Settlement Huck's men shot and killed

William Strong, as he walked along the road carrying a bible.[287] Hucks' men raided the home of Janet Strong, the wife of Justice Gaston, and wounded another man, then they continued on to the church. What they didn't know was that "some of the negroes overhearing them declare their intention to go to Mr. Simpson's house and 'burn the rascal out', hastened to carry information to his wife."

Mrs. Simpson heard the shot that killed Strong, and saw the dragoons coming. She gathered up a set of silver teaspoons and went out the back door with her four children, hiding herself in the woods. Huck's men ransacked the house, taking out four feather beds and ripping them up in the yard. They stole all they wanted and then set fire to the house and the small outbuilding beside the house, which was the library and study of the Reverend Simpson. The British force rode away, leaving a dead boy in the dirt road and all the buildings on fire.

Mrs. Simpson rushed into the burning study and carried out two aprons full of books, burning herself badly. She gathered up enough feathers in the yard to fill one bed. Since all she had was in ruins, she went to the house of her neighbors and stayed there for four weeks. Later she moved into a small outhouse in the backyard, but she was still harassed by the Loyalists.

On one occasion she had found some cloth and was cutting out some clothes, when a band of Tories came along and stole her cloth. She complained to the leader of the Tories, who ordered his men to give it back. The gang then found some of Mr. Simpson's clothes and strutted around in front of her, asking her if they weren't better looking than her husband. They told her that one day they would make her a present of his scalp. The Tories then stole her remaining cattle. She begged for them to leave her one milk cow, but they laughed and rode away. The Tories rode on for two miles, when they stopped and put the cattle in a pen. That night two large steers broke out and all the cattle scattered. The next morning Simpson's cattle returned home. Captain Huck and his men returned to Rocky Mount. [288]

Rocky Creek, South Carolina   **Skirmish**
12 June 1780

Reverend William Martin heard Rawdon's proclamation to take British protection, but he was outraged by the massacre at the Waxhaws. He preached a sermon to the Convenanter Church on Rocky Creek telling his congregation that they needed to ignore the proclamation and take up arms against the British.

Turnbull learned of the sermon and sent a troop of dragoons to disperse the congregation that was organizing under Captain Ben Land.[289] The dragoons attacked the congregation seven miles north of Rocky Mount, killing Captain Land.[290]

Two miles away the dragoons attacked another group at a Blacksmith shop, killing one of the militiamen. They then rode on to the Reverend Martin's home and arrested him, taking him to the Rocky Mount jail.[291]

Hill's Iron Works, South Carolina [292]   **Skirmish**
Presbyterian Rebellion
18 June 1780 [293]

The New Acquisition Militia had moved their camp to Hill's Iron Works after they discovered that Huck and his dragoons were after them. When Lord Rawdon learned that they had gathered there he sent an officer to persuade them to put down their arms and take up British protection. The officer "begun by asserting that Congress had given up the two Southern states, & would not contend further for them that as Genl. Washington's army was reduced to a small number of men, & that he, with that small army had fled to the mountains."

William Hill stopped the officer, and told the men gathered there "that Congress had come to a resolution not to give up any of the States, and that Genl. Washington was in a more prosperous way than he had been from some time, that he had actually appointed an officer with a considerable army and was then on their march to the relief of the Southern States."

The militia refused the British offer and the officer left quickly, "for fear of the resentment of the audience." Hill then told them that they should elect two colonels for the New Acquisition Regiment. They elected Andrew Neal as their colonel and William Hill as their lieutenant colonel. Hill wrote that they "then formed camp and erected the American Standard."[294] After a few days men from Georgia and South Carolina came in and the regiment became a force to be reckoned with.

Neal learned that a Loyalist named Mathew Floyd was taking a group of Loyalists to Rocky Mount to form a militia. Neal took most of the men and rode out to intercept Floyd's Loyalists, leaving twelve to fifteen men under Hill to guard the ironworks.

Turnbull wrote to Cornwallis and told him that Bratton, Winn and Patton abandoned their plantations and "gone amongst the Catawba Indians" in North Carolina, instead of taking British protection. He also wrote that the "Irish settlements" have abundant provisions for his men, but they had become violent. He proposed to send troops into the settlement and destroy "Billy" Hill's Iron Works, owned by Colonel William Hill. The Iron Works supplied ammunition for the Continental army.[295]

Refugees came into Rocky Mount and told Turnbull that they were being driven out by the attacks against them by the New Acquisition militia. When Mathew Floyd arrived with his Loyalists, Turnbull made him a colonel, and created the Upper District Loyalist Militia.

On June 16th Huck was ordered to destroy the Iron Works. He took with him sixty men under Captain Abraham Floyd, the son of Colonel Floyd. They went to Moses Ferguson, who was a representative in the legislature, which lived two miles east on Little Ellison Creek. Huck told Ferguson that he must take him to Hill's Iron Works "or they would make mince meat of him."

There were about fifty militiamen at the iron works, consisting of a store, furnace and mills. Hill did not command the militia, since he was with Sumter at the time. Two men from Colonel Bratton's militia arrived at the iron works on June 18th and warned the men there that two or three hundred British dragoons were marching towards them, but they didn't know which road they were on.

Huck's men crossed the ford on Ellison's Creek undetected, and weren't on a road at all. They rode up to the surprised militia and fired. The militia thought that this small force of cavalry had to be the vanguard to the hundreds of British they had been told about. When they heard the shots they all fled, but not before the British killed seven and captured four.

Huck destroyed the forge and burned all the buildings, including Hill's home and the slave's cabins. They confiscated ninety slaves, and took them with him. Mrs. Hill and her family were able to get away and took refuge in the cabin of a neighbor.[296]

When Cornwallis heard of the fight at Hill's Iron Works, he wrote to Clinton in New York and stated that it "put an end to all resistance in South Carolina." Cornwallis also wrote to Clinton and told him that he was going to postpone offensive operations until fall.

Captain Huck rode to Walker's Crossroads and set up camp, ordering all the inhabitants in the area to take British protection and swear allegiance to the King. The men who showed up at the Crossroads were mainly older men, since the younger men had gone off and joined Sumter. When Huck tried to get them to take the protection, he offended the men "in blasphemy by saying that God almighty had become a Rebel, but if there were 20 Gods on that side, they would all be conquered."

Huck could see that his speech was not going to convince anyone to come to the British side, so "he had his officers & men taking all the horses fit for his purpose, so that many of the aged men had to walk many mile home afoot."

McJunkin wrote, "A large portion of this district had been settled by Presbyterians and persons of this persuasion were numerous in adjacent parts of North Carolina, particularly in Mecklenburg County. These were generally known as the staunch advocates of independence. Hence, when the Whigs were expelled from the country lying west of Broad River they found an asylum in the Presbyterian congregations in the Valley of the Catawba."

"Huck commenced his work in good earnest by burning churches, dwelling houses, and murdering the Whigs whenever they fell into his hands. He often used the most profane and impudent expressions while persecuting his work of pillage and carnage. Among other things, he swore that if the rebels were as thick as trees and Jesus Christ Himself were to command them he would defeat them. When his words and doings were reported in Sumter's camp the Presbyterian Irish who rallied around his standard could stand it no longer. They demanded to be led against this vile man, Capt. Huck."

In the end Huck did make an impression on these men. They now considered it a holy war, and "they would be made instrumental in the hand of Heaven to punish the enemy for his wickedness and blasphemy." [297]

Bullock's Fork, Thicketty Creek, South Carolina   Skirmish
June 1780

The British began organizing the Loyalists to end the attacks by the Patriot militia. One of the new regiments was organized at Ninety-Six, under Major Daniel Plummer. Alexander Chesney had been a soldier in the 6th South Carolina Regiment, but after Charleston fell he took the British oath and became a lieutenant in this regiment. Chesney commanded a force of men who skirmished with some Patriots at Bullock's Creek.

He wrote that the "Rebel Party was defeated in attempting to cross the ford; my father was present on this occasion, and hearing the bullets whistle without seeing by whom they were fired, asked me "where are they, where are they?" I placed him near a tree until the affair was over, and resolved he should not be so exposed again."

Joseph McJunkin wrote, "Sumter established his headquarters east of the Catawba River in the territory assigned to the nation of Indians of the same name. Here the whole of July was spent, but not in idleness. His men go out in quest of provisions, arms, and to rally their friends to take a stand under the standard of liberty.

Provisions were obtained with great difficulty, for the want of current funds, so that their fare often consisted of barley meal without meat, salt or any other seasoning, and scarce at that. All the powder which could be obtained was collected. The good ladies in the region round about gave up their pewter vessels to be molded into bullets. Implements of husbandry were converted into swords. While engaged in these preparatory measures they were under the necessity of maintaining the strictest vigilance for the preservation of their lives. The Tories watched their movements, waylaid them and often fired upon them. An instance of this kind occurred to a small party led by Col. Brandon, near Bullock's Creek. A captain by the name of Reed fell behind the party for some purpose or other and was killed by two Tories. His mother, having found out who his murderers were, followed Brandon to North Carolina and implored him to avenge the death of her son. Some of his men volunteered to go with him, and he hunted the Tories and killed them."[298]

Love's Plantation, South Carolina   Skirmish
June 1780

Thomas Young told about a different version of Captain Davie Reid being killed. He wrote "Capt. Reid was at a neighbor's house, in York District, on a visit. The landlady saw two men approaching the house, whom she knew to be tories, and told Capt. Reid he had better escape, for they would kill him. He replied, no! – they had been his neighbors; he had known Love and Saddler all his life, and had nothing to fear from them. He walked out into the yard, offered them his hand, and they killed him."

Reid's mother traveled to North Carolina and found Brandon's camp. As the camp turned out for the morning parade the old woman "came before us, leaning upon the arms of two officers. She drew from her bosom the bloody pocket-book of her son". Colonel Brandon asked for volunteers to go and find the Loyalists who had killed her son, "Twenty-five stepped out at once."

The men rode all night "halted in the day, kept watch in the woods, but slept not." They arrived at the home of the Loyalist named Love the next day. Young wrote "One part of our company was to attack the house, another the barn. The house was attacked and the door broken down by a powerful man by the name of Maddox, who was afterwards killed at King's Mountain. In staving open the door he floored old Love and knocked some of his teeth out. At this moment a cry was raised that they were in the barn, and to the barn we all rushed. One of our men fired through the door and killed one of the murderers, the other was killed in the skirmish. What is most strange about the matter is, that another man was sleeping with them, and in the melee he escaped unhurt. We now felt that we had done all that was required of us and returned to our quarters in North Carolina."[299]

Ramseur's Mill, North Carolina [300]   **Battle**
20 June 1780

American Forces

Commanding Officer	Colonel Francis Locke
State Militia	400
Cavalry	
Major Joseph McDowell	
Burke County Militia Battalion	
Captain Adam Reep	30
Captain Charles McDowell	
Captain Joshua Bowman [301]	
Captain Torrence	
Captain Thomas Kennedy	
Captain Samuel Reid [302]	
Captain William Caldwell	
Captain Daniel McKissick	
Lincoln County Militia	25
Captain James Houston	
North Carolina Partisan Rangers	34

Colonel William Brandon
   2nd Spartan Regiment   Unknown number
     Captain "Killing Stephen" Jackson
     Captain Barry Andrew
     Captain Gavin Gordon
     Captain Samuel Otterson [303]
Captain Galbraith Falls
   North Carolina Partisan Rangers [304]   40
Infantry
Colonel Francis Locke
   1st Rowan Militia Regiment   270
     Captain William Fall
     Captain William "Governor" Knox
     Captain Joseph Dobson
     Captain William Armstrong [305]
     Captain Smith
     Captain Joseph Sharpe
       Fourth Creek Company
     Captain Archibald Sloan [306]
     Captain William "Black Bill" Alexander
     Captain John Hardin
   2nd Rowan Militia Regiment   Unknown number
Colonel William Shepherd
   Surry County Militia   Unknown number
     Captain Richard Goode
     Captain Joseph Philips
     Captain William Armstrong [307]
      Orange County Militia
Major David Wilson
   Mecklenburg County Militia   65
     Captain Patrick Knox
     Captain William Smith
Captain Samuel Martin [308]   Unknown number
Casualties   70 killed, 100 wounded [309]

Loyalist Forces

Commanding Officer	Lieutenant Colonel John Moore	
North Carolina Loyalist Militia		700
Burke County Militia		200
Captain John Morrow		
Captain Nicholas Warlick		
Captain Cumberland		
Captain Carpenter		
Captain Thomas Evans		
Captain Anthony Harmon		
Casualties	100 killed and wounded, 50 captured [310]	

Cornwallis had told the Loyalists in North Carolina to wait until his invasion from the south, in September, before they took any action. He sent Lieutenant Colonel John Moore, of the Royal North Carolina Regiment, to carry them a message. When Moore arrived in Tryon County on June 10th, he met forty Loyalists at his father's house, seven miles from Derick Ramsaur's Mill. He told the Loyalists not to rise in rebellion yet, but to get ready.

During the meeting he learned that General Rutherford had ordered Colonel Francis Locke to raise a militia force that would disperse the Loyalists. He was also informed that Major Joseph McDowell was in the area trying to capture them. Moore knew that the best defense was a good offense, and the Loyalists followed McDowell to the South Mountains, however they did not engage him. [311]

Moore dismissed the Loyalists and told them to assemble at Ramseur's Mill on June 13th. The first few arrived on that day, and continued to come in over the next week. By June 18th Moore had assembled 1,300 men, but only a fourth of them were armed. He led a force to capture Colonel Hugh Brevard, and Major McDowell, but the Patriots evaded them. On the 19th Moore occupied a ridge 300 yards east of Ramseur's Mill, and placed his pickets 600 yards in front of the main force on the Tuckasegee Road. The ridge was a gentle slope, and was mostly open ground with a few trees.

Rutherford was aware of the activities of the Loyalists, and had gathered a force of 1,200 militiamen at Charlotte to oppose them. He did not want to send his forces against them until he knew what Lord Rawdon and his British forces were going to do in Camden. He did order Colonel Locke, and Major David Wilson, to gather their forces and disperse the Loyalists west of Rowan. Wilson marched with sixty-five men and rendezvoused Major Joseph McDowell and his twenty-five men. Both forces then continued towards Locke's army, picking up militia units along the way.

On the 19th Wilson and his force camped at Mountain Creek, sixteen miles from Ramseur's Mill. Locke met up with them with 270 men, and assumed command of this army of "an unorganized crowd of inexperienced, undisciplined, armed civilians." Locke's militia was armed with rifles and fowling pieces. They fired balls made from pewter that had been melted from plates and spoons from their homes.

That night a council of war was held to determine the best method of dealing with Loyalist uprising. The Loyalists outnumbered Locke and his militia by about three to one, and many of the leaders wanted to move towards Whig settlements and defend it against attacks. Others suggested that they ride on to Rutherford, and join his larger force. Finally an insinuation was made that the men were being cowardly and they should attack the next morning before the Loyalists could react. William Graham wrote, "This had the usual effect; not many soldiers or other people can stand an imputation of cowardice, so this plan was adopted." Colonel James Johnston was told to ride to Rutherford and tell him of their plans. That night the Patriot forces began their march.

On the 18th Rutherford did not know that Locke was marching on the Loyalists, and decided to deal with them with his army. He sent a message to Locke to unite with the command of Colonel Joseph Dickson, three miles from Tuckasegee Ford. Rutherford moved his force to Tuckasegee Ford on the 19th, and after a wet morning he had his men discharge their pieces so they could be cleaned and examined. The firing was heard in nearby counties and militiamen showed up, thinking he was being attacked.

Graham rendezvoused with Rutherford on the 20th, bringing his force to 1,200 men. When Johnston told Rutherford of the planned attack at Ramseur's Mill, the army moved out to support Locke.

Before first light on June 20th Adam Reep and thirty men joined Locke's force. Reep informed Locke of the disposition of the Loyalist forces at Ramseur's Mill. Locke arraigned his force into three elements. The mounted force, under McDowell, would approach to the right of the Loyalists on Sherrill's Ford Road. Locke would approach the Loyalist's left, on the Tuckasegee Road. A third element under Captain John Hardin would approach through a ravine, to attack the Loyalists right flank.

The men lined up, with McDowell's mounted men in front, and the footmen of Locke two rows deep, behind the cavalry, to the right. "Without any other organization or orders, they were marched to battle."

The Loyalist pickets detected the approaching horsemen and fired upon them. They ran back towards their camp with McDowell's cavalry pursuing them. When they heard the shooting, many of the unarmed Loyalists fled at once. The rest saw that there were not that many horsemen, and formed a ragged line of battle, firing a volley into their ranks. The mounted militiamen retreated and rode through Locke's infantry. Some of the infantry broke and followed the fleeing cavalry. They did not return. Most of the cavalry rallied at a distance and returned to the fight.

In the initial volley Captain Bowman had been killed, and Captain Falls was mortally wounded. Falls rode 200 yards, and then fell dead from his horse. His 14-year-old son rushed to his father's body, and killed a Loyalist with his father's sword.

Both sides fought each other without any order to their attacks. Joseph Graham wrote that the Patriot line came on "their files were opened six or eight steps, and when the front approached the Tories, the rear was eight poles back. The front fired several times before the rear camp up." [312]

The Loyalists "came into action without order or system. As the rear came up, they occupied those places, and the line gradually extending, the action became general and obstinate on both sides."

No officer was coordinating the Patriot, attack and neither side had bayonets.

The militias of both sides had no uniforms, except for the officers. This made it difficult to tell who was friendly, and who was enemy. The Loyalists wore a sprig of green in their hats, and the Patriots wore a piece of white paper in theirs. These white papers became the point of aim for many Loyalists, because many of Locke's men were shot in the head.

Robert Barkley, one of the Patriot militia, was behind a tree with John Smith. One was shooting to the right and one shooting to the left. Smith was shot through the heart and told Barkley, "Robert, tell Polly I am gone. Fight on, Robert", and he died.

As the fog lifted the fighting intensified. Locke's force surrounded the Loyalists on three sides of a hill that the King's men occupied. Captain Warlick, one of the Loyalist commanders, rallied the men and told them to hold their ground. They were slightly behind the ridge that gave them protection from the intense fire from Locke's militia. The Loyalists that didn't have any weapons were ordered to move to the rear of the ridge, and go behind a creek.

Locke's men were totally exposed against the Loyalists on the high ground, and soon had to move to concealment behind some bushes near a glade. The Loyalists pursued them half way down the hill to obtain better positions, and ran into Captain Hardin's men flanking their position.

Hardin led his men onto the field and "under cover of the fence, kept up a galling fire on the right flank of the Tories; and some of the Whigs, discovering that the ground on the right was more favorable to protect them from the Tories, obliqued in that direction towards the east end of the glade. They continued to oblique until they turned the left flank of the Tories; and the contest being well maintained in the centre, the Tories began to retreat up the ridge. They found part of their position occupied by the Whigs. In that quarter the action became close, and the parties mixed together in two instances, and having no bayonets, they struck at each other with the butts of their guns. In this strange contest, several of the Tories were taken prisoners, and others, divesting themselves of their mark of distinction (which was a twig of green pine top stuck in their hats), intermixed with the Whigs, and all being in their common dress, they excepted unnoticed."

Captain Joseph Sharpe extended his company until they had flanked the right of the line of the Loyalists. Moore's men were now being hit on three sides by a murderous fire. Graham wrote, "they advanced from tree to tree until they obtained a position enfilading the enemy, and with unerring aim picked off their boldest officers. Captain Sharpe's brother placed his gun against a tree to "draw a bead" on a Tory captain; his arm was broken by a shot from the enemy and his gun fell to the ground. A well-directed shot from the Captain felled the Tory captain."

The Loyalist's defense finally collapsed when Adam Reep's sharpshooters killed Captain Nicholas Warlick. They "retreated down the ridge toward the mill, exposed to the fire of the centre and of Captain Harden's company behind the fences. The Whigs pursued until they got entire possession of the ridge, when they perceived to their astonishment that the Tories had collected in force on the other side of the creek, beyond the mill."

Locke had his men pull back, because only eighty-six of his 400 militiamen were able to withstand a counterattack. He quickly sent word to Rutherford, requesting immediate reinforcements. Rutherford sent Major William Davie's cavalry and Colonel Davidson's infantry on at a run, but after covering two miles they were told the Loyalists had retreated from the battlefield.

Moore wasn't about to order any counterattack, because he had been through enough. The Loyalists fled towards Ramseur's Mill, some throwing away their weapons. A few of the fleeing men fell into a pond and in their panic they drowned. Moore had the remaining Loyalists reform at Ramseur's home. Needing to gain time to plan their escape he sent in a flag of truce to make arrangements for the dead and wounded. Locke sent the son of Rutherford, Major James Rutherford, to meet the Loyalists near their lines, and demand that they surrender within ten minutes. Locke did not want the Loyalists to come near his line and learn of his very weakened forces.

During the parley Moore secretly ordered his Loyalists to slip away individually. Four hundred of them were able to escape across the Catawba River. When the flag of truce returned there was only Moore, and fifty Loyalists left, and they immediately fled.

Captain Daniel McKissick, of Major McDowell's force, had been shot through the shoulder early in the battle, and had left the battlefield. He was captured by a group of Loyalists who thought they had won the battle. They marched McKissick back expecting to see a Loyalist victory, but soon discovered that they were now the prisoners.

Major Davie arrived too late to take part in the battle, but his cavalry swept through the area, making prisoners of the Loyalist stragglers.

Shortly after the battle the women and children of the soldiers came to locate their dead. Most of the soldiers were buried in a long trench on the side of the hill, where the Loyalists had made their stand. Fifty-six bodies were found there where they had fallen. Thirteen of the dead were from Sharpe's Fourth Creek Company. Scattered over the rest of the hill were seventy more bodies. Among Locke's dead was William Knox, great-grandfather of President James Knox Polk.

Moore and thirty survivors were the only ones to make it to Cornwallis in Camden. His action was a disaster for the British cause and Cornwallis wanted to court martial him for violating orders. If Moore had waited until the approach of Major Patrick Ferguson, there may have been 2,000 Loyalists to support Cornwallis when he entered North Carolina in September. A year later John Moore was captured in South Carolina, and tried as a spy. He was convicted and hanged on the Congaree River. [313]

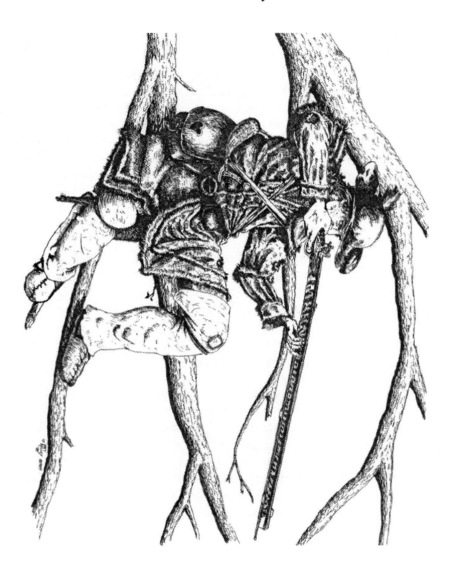

Bullock's Creek Ford, South Carolina
Presbyterian Rebellion
24 June 1780

After the battle of Ramseur's Mill, Colonel Turnbull marched into the New Acquisition with the New York Volunteers and the militia under Captain Matthew Floyd. Turnbull joined Captain Hucks and offered protection to all who will take it, but only a few did. Huck and Ferguson rode west to the Bullock's Creek and Turkey Creek area to put down any rebels. All they managed to do is kill one man at Bullock's Creek ford and "good old Mr. Fleming, a man of 70." [314]

Near Ramseur's Mill, North Carolina   **Murder**
July 1780

Sumter arrived at Ramseur's Mill after the battle and set up camp. Though he missed the battle he obtained much needed supplies. He had been authorized by the State to "impress or take wagons horses, provisions of all kind, from the enemy that was in the action."

A small party of Georgia militia joined him at this location. One of those militiamen was Patrick Carr, commonly known as Paddy Carr. He was one of the most notorious Whigs in the South.

After Carr arrived in camp he and another Georgia militiaman went to the home of a Loyalist. Carr asked the man if he had joined Moore's Loyalists at the battle. The man told Carr that he had been in the battle, but had been captured, and then pardoned by General Rutherford. It was getting dark and Carr asked the man if he knew the way to Sumter's camp. The pardoned Loyalist told him that he had to take the path, and turn where it forked. Carr told the man he would have to show him the way, and the man agreed. When they arrived at the fork the Loyalist pointed the proper direction to go. Carr then shot him dead.

When Carr returned to the camp he told Colonel Richard Winn what he had done. Winn immediately delivered Carr to the local magistrate for committing murder. The next day Carr was back in camp, and no trial ever took place.[315]

Lawson's Fork, South Carolina [316]   **Skirmish**
July 1780

After the battle of Ramseur's Mill, Major Dickson and Captain William Johnston searched for any escaped Loyalists. The Patriots overtook Captain Patrick Moore and his force as they moved toward Cornwallis. Patrick Moore was the brother of Colonel John Moore, who commanded the Loyalists at Ramsour's Mill.

After a brief skirmish, in which Moore and Johnston personally fought each other, Moore was captured. Johnston received several wounds on his head, and his thumb of his right hand. As Johnston escorted his prisoner to the nearby friendly forces he encountered a mounted British patrol. Johnston attempted to fire his musket, but the blood from his wounded thumb had wet the priming of his musket. The musket would not fire and Moore was able to get away. Johnston quickly dodged into a nearby thicket and was able to elude his pursuers.[317]

Williamson's Plantation, South Carolina [318]   **Skirmish**
Presbyterian Rebellion
12 July 1780

American Forces
Commanding Officer   Colonel William Bratton
    South Carolina Militia [319]
        Ninety-Six District Militia   250
           Colonel Edward Lacey [320]   100
           Chester Militia
              Captain John Moffitt

Captain John McClure
Chester Rocky Creek Irish
Captain John Nixon [321]
Colonel Andrew Neal
New Acquisition Militia   80
Lieutenant Colonel William Hill [322]
Captain John Mills
Lieutenant James Jamieson [323]
Colonel Richard Winn[324]   Unknown number [325]
Fairfield Regiment
Captain James Mitchell
Captain John Summers [326]
Captain George Reed

Casualties   1 killed, 1 wounded, 1 captured [327]

Loyalist Forces
Commanding Officer   Captain Christian Huck
Provincials [328]
Captain Christian Huck
British Legion   19
Lieutenant John McGregor
New York Volunteers
Captain Bernard Kane's Company   21
South Carolina Loyalist Militia
Colonel James Ferguson
Camden District Militia
Lieutenant John Adamson
Colonel Henry Rugeley's Regiment 60
Captain Abraham Floyd [329]
Rocky Mount Regiment   20
Lieutenant John Lisle [330]

Casualties   35 killed, 50 wounded, 29 captured [331]

Sumter's force moved back into South Carolina and sent a detachment to test the defenses at Rocky Mount. Turnbull had been reinforced with Kinlock's troop of dragoons from the British

Legion, but once he learned that Sumter was heading towards Rocky Mount he returned to the post.

Sumter learned that Lord Rawdon sent the 23rd Regiment of Foot to the Waxhaws to reinforce the area, and marched on towards the Waxhaws. When he arrived he discovered that the British had left the area. Rawdon had sent both Kinlock and the 23rd Regiment to Hanging Rock to reinforce the post there. Turnbull was also reinforced with a company of Loyalist militia under Lieutenant John Adamson.

Turnbull learned that many of the rebel militia had returned to the New Acquisition area. John McClure was at his home harvesting his wheat, and William Bratton was trying to recruit more men for the militia. Turnbull ordered Captain Christian Huck to capture the rebels. Attached to his troop was a detachment from the New York Volunteers and the Loyalist militia under James Ferguson.

Huck camped at the plantation of Nicholas Bishop and was able to capture Joseph Kerr, a rebel spy. Kerr escaped and told Sumter's partisans that Huck was on his way to New Acquisition. Sumter's men decided to ambush the British force.

On the morning of July 11th Huck stopped at Walker's Mill to have his men grind some grain. He then rode on to the home of John McClure in Chester County and found James McClure, the brother of John. Huck also found McClure's brother in law, Edward Martin, in the house.[332] They had been melting pewter dishes into bullets. Huck arrested them and threatened to hang them. When McClure's mother protested, Huck struck her with the flat of his sword. Huck set fire to the home and then rode on to the home of Colonel William Bratton.

Huck stopped off at the homes of William Adair, John Price and Reuben Lacey, Edward Lacey's father, to get provisions. He arrived at Bratton's home in the late afternoon, but Bratton was not there at the time because he was out raising a force to defeat Huck. Three old men were taken prisoner at Bratton's home, and Mrs. Bratton was forced to make a meal for the invaders. While she was preparing it Huck demanded to know the location of Sumter's camp.

She refused to answer him. One of Huck's officers threatened to cut off her head with a reaping hook, but Captain Adamson of the Camden militia stopped him. Two of the old men were described as "Irishmen, one of them named Moore, was a little intoxicated."

Huck moved a quarter mile north to camp for the night, at the plantation of James Williamson because Williamson had a large field of oats. Huck took his condemned prisoners with him. The prisoners were locked in a corncrib and were told they would be hanged in the morning. Martha Bratton had gone to visit the Williamson's, and was held there by Huck.

The successful raid had gone to the Provincial's heads, because Huck did not place out any proper security for the night. A single sentry was placed on the road in front of the house. The Loyalist militia was not as careless, and placed pickets around their camp, which was away from Huck's men.

The Patriot militia in the area was alerted to the presence of Huck's men. One version of how they were alerted states that James McClure's sister, Mary, saddled a horse and rode thirty miles, and then found her father in Sumter's camp. Another version of this story is that Martha Bratton sent Watt, a family slave, to find Colonel Bratton. Richard Winn doesn't mention either version.

John Craig wrote that they had rode from "Chester into York District. We numbered one hundred and thirty three, when we arrived at Catawba River, the far bank was lined with women and children who had been ordered from their homes by the British and Tories on account of their relations generally having joined themselves to the Whig party. "

"These women who had been forced to leave their homes informed us that Col. Floyd, Capt. Hook, and Capt. Adams, with other officers, commanding about four hundred British and Tories, were lying at White's Mill in Chester County. The situation of these women and children driven from their firesides, excited in every bosom a sympathy for the distressed, and an indignation against the hard-hearted foe who could perpetrate such an inhuman deed. We received our orders to set these distressed people over the river, which we did. Then we received our orders to turn out our horses to graze and meanwhile the officers called a council and soon determined to risk all consequences and attack the inhuman ruffians."

No matter which way alerted them, the Patriot militia was on its way to put an end to Huck, once and for all. Bratton and Colonel Edward Lacey left the camp with about 500 men, but by the time they reached Williamson's Plantation the force had been reduced to 250. Some of the militiamen were not real motivated to fight the same cavalry that had slaughtered Colonel Buford.

Everyone in the area did not support the Patriot cause, and the men had to move to avoid those suspected as being King's friends. At the home of Reuben Lacey they captured Major John Owens of Ferguson's regiment. Owens told them that Huck was camped at the home of Williamson.

Lacey's father, Reuben Lacey, was described as "a little hump shouldered, cynical and unhappy man. He would curse his son by the hour, even after the war, for being a Whig colonel." Edward Lacey had to have his Loyalist father tied into his bed to prevent him from warning Huck.

About an hour before sunrise Bratton's force rode within one mile of Huck's camp and held a council of war. When Bratton learned that his wife and children were at Williamson's Plantation, he "wanted to parley instead of attacking." When this was rejected in the council "he then said he would fire off his gun to draw them from the house. McClure promptly replied that the next gun will be mine and your brains blowed out."

Lacey, Hill and Bratton chose to listen to Winn, since he had the most experience. Winn had been an officer in the 3rd South Carolina Rangers at the Breach Inlet in 1776 and at Fort McIntosh on the Satilla in 1777.

Winn ordered the Patriot militia to dismount on the road and line up. He wrote, "Captain Read, a bold, daring officer, was ordered to pick out twenty-five men and file off to the left of Col. Bratton's plantation and, as soon as the action began in front, he was to attack the enemy's rear and take all stragling parties." The countersign that night was "Washington", answered by "Good Luck".

When the party under Winn came to a fork of the road, they found two Loyalists searching for their horses. They told the Patriots that Huck's men had pitched their tents between the rail fences that lined the road leading to the house. They also said that Colonel James Ferguson had camped with his Loyalist militia 300 yards in front of Huck's men, in an open field.[333]

Winn sent Captain John McClure and Captain John Moffitt around the plantation to attack Huck from a different angle. They were to move as soon as they heard any firing. McClure dismounted his men at a peach orchard and tied off the horses, then moved through the orchard towards the plantation. They thought that moving through the orchard would prevent against a charge by the British cavalry.

The Loyalist sentries placed out by Ferguson spotted McClure's men. They fired and then fled back to camp. McClure and Reed attacked from both sides of the rail fence, with Reed's men firing from less than seventy-five yards. At the same time Winn's force fired upon Ferguson's camp. Even with the early shots by the sentries, the Patriots caught the Loyalists asleep in their camp.[334]

McJunkin wrote, "There were a few women and one old man assembled in Colonel Bratton's house for religious worship. A chapter was read and the old man bowed down and prayed for the destruction of that vile man Captain Huck. Scarcely was the prayer uttered when the roar of arms was heard!"

John Craig wrote, "The alarm gun was given by Col. Neel, who shot the sentinel dead. We then rushed on to the attack, every man his own commander. We heard the words, "boys take over the fence" and our men rushed after the Tories and British as they fled before us."

Ferguson and some of his men were the first to die as they rushed out of their tents. Craig wrote that Ferguson "stood at the end of the lane and was shot down and his clothing was blackened with the gun powder." The rest of Ferguson's men ran to their horses to escape. Huck and his men managed to get out, and mount their horses. The Legion cavalry charged towards the Patriot militia in the peach orchard.

Huck yelled, "Disperse you damned rebels, or we will put every man of you to the sword!" Hill wrote "at the moment the action commenced, he was then flourishing his sword over the head of these unfortunate women & threatening them with death if they would not get their husbands & sons to come in." He was then shot in the neck by two rifle balls, and killed.

McJunkin wrote, "Huck fell under the well directed fire of John Carrolls." John Craig's account agrees with this, when he wrote, "We then pursued the dragoons. John Carroll led the way, I was next to him, and Charles Miles next. We halted to fire and both Miles and Carroll fired at the same time, and brought down the Captain of the British Dragoons. Both claimed the honour, but it was decided that Carroll killed him; he therefore claimed his armour and, David like, took it, and wore it."[335]

Three times the British cavalry charged, but were forced back. The fighting raged around the Williamson plantation. One of the two old men who had been put in the corncrib "lay down on the floor when the bullets hit the crib, but Moore would stand up & shout Hurrah for Liberty".

During the fighting Mrs. Bratton was fearful for the life of her son William, and made him sit in the chimney against his will. She held his hand as the bullets tore through the walls. One bullet passed through the boarding and fell to the floor. William broke loose from his mother's grasp to get the bullet. She quickly seized him and brought him back to the chimney. He kept the bullet as a souvenir.[336]

Winn stated "We was in full possession of the field in five minutes... I am well convinced, the enemy during the action never fired a single gun." McClure lost one man killed due to friendly fire, when the two sides fired from each side of the fence.[337]

McClure's company had been too far away to effectively fire upon Huck's men. Hill wrote that "the party sent to make the attack on the east end of the lane met with some embarrassments, by fences, brush, briars &c that they did not get to the end of the lane until the firing commenced at the west end. The probability is that if that party at the East end had made good their march in time very few of them wd have escaped."

Out of the whole Loyalist force, only twelve Legion dragoons and twelve militiamen escaped.[338] The Patriots captured "about one hundred horses, saddles, bridles, pistols, swords and many other things."[339] The prisoners who were to be hanged by Huck were set free. Captain Adamson, the officer who had spared the life of Mrs. Bratton, was not only spared but was taken into the Bratton home and nursed back to health.[340]

After the battle Captain Floyd's Rock Mount Regiment turned coat, and joined Sumter's Brigade. The leader of this was Lieutenant John Lisle, a former lieutenant in the 3rd South Carolina Regiment, who had joined the Loyalist militia after Charlestown fell. The Rocky Mount Regiment brought with them all their arms and supplies that had recently been issued to them. McJunkin wrote "Huck's Defeat increased Sumter to 600 men."

This was the first battle in South Carolina where a militia force defeated trained troops of the British occupation forces.[341]

Cedar Springs, South Carolina [342]   **Skirmish**
12 July 1780 [343]

Patrick Ferguson had sent Captain Abraham DePeyster to the Spartanburg District to disperse any rebel resistance. When DePeyster arrived at the Fair Forest area he called out the local militia. The Loyalist commanders suggested that he should occupy two redoubts that were still standing from the Cherokee War. Captain James Dunlap and sixty mounted militia occupied the one at Prince's Fort. Captain Patrick Moore with eighty North Carolina militiamen went to the other at Fort Anderson.

The Patriot Spartan Regiment was camped sixty miles south of Ninety-Six. Colonel John Thomas, Jr. had taken command of the 1st Spartan Regiment when his father took parole. Thomas's mother, Jane, was visiting either her sons, or her husband, who had been imprisoned at Ninety-Six.[344] While there she overheard some of the Tory wives talking of Ferguson's plans. She learned that the

Loyalists were going to surprise the camp of her two other sons at Cedar Spring the night of the next day. She rode sixty miles on the night of July 12th to tell her son, John Thomas, Jr., that there would be an attack on his position soon.[345]

Thomas left his campfires burning and moved his men to the rear of the camp. When the Provincials arrived they found the fires still burning. There were 150 Loyalists to oppose the 60 Spartans. The Tories immediately charged into the camp. Thomas fired a concentrated volley into their ranks, killing several, and scattering the rest. The Provincials fled to Gowen's Fort.[346]

Stallion's Plantation, South Carolina [347]   **Skirmish**
12 July 1780 [348]

After William Cunningham had routed Thomas Brandon on June 8th, Brandon moved his militia into New Acquisition. He learned of a party of Loyalists in his area and rode with fifty men to attack their post at Stallion's Plantation, located on Fishing Creek.

McJunkin wrote that after Brandon's men had killed the Loyalists who ambushed Captain Reed, "Their friends in turn sought vengeance; pursued Brandon in considerable force, and he retired before them until he came within the Bethel congregation, where he recruited his force and turned to meet his pursuers. They had followed him to the head of Fishing Creek and turned down that stream. Brandon paused. A short time before he overtook their party Col. Love fell in with him. This Love had encountered the Tories single handed but a short time before, killed two of their number and made his escape by dodging in a briery old field. Brandon soon learned that the Tories had stopped at the house of a man named Sterling to get dinner. This Sterling had married the sister of Col. Love -- he was a Tory and his wife a Whig."

Brandon divided his force into two parties, and sent Captain Andrew Love with sixteen men to attack the front of the house. Brandon moved to the rear of the house with the rest of his militia, to stop any retreat.

Thomas Young wrote in his memoirs that "Mrs. Stallions was a sister of Capt Love, and on the approach of her brother she ran out, and begged him not to fire upon the house. He told her it was too late now, and that their only chance for safety was to surrender. She ran back to the house and sprang upon the door step, which was pretty high. At this moment, the house was attacked In the rear by Col. Brandon's party, and Mrs. Stallions was killed by a ball shot through the opposite door."[349]

Captain Love's men and Brandon's forces attacked the house from two sides. "At the same moment with Brandon's attack, our party raised a shout and rushed forward. We fired several rounds, which were briskly returned. It was not long, however, before the Tories ran up a flag, first upon the end of a gun, but as that did not look exactly peaceful, a ball was put through the fellow's arm, and in a few moments it was raised on a ram-rod, and we ceased firing."

Young wrote that after the shooting had stopped he saw a man "running through an open field near us. I raised my gun to shoot him, when some of our party exclaimed "Don't fire he is one of our own men." I drew down my gun, and in a moment he halted, wheeled round, and fired at us. Old Squire Kennedy (who was an excellent marksman) raised his rifle and brought him down."

Colonel Brandon only had one man wounded. Young wrote that it was Thomas Kennedy, who was shot by his side. "I was attempting to fire in at the door of the house, when I saw two of the tories in the act of shooting at myself and Kennedy. I sprang aside and escaped, calling at the same time to my companion, but he was shot (while moving) through the wrist and thigh." The Loyalists lost two killed, four wounded and twenty-eight captured.[350] The prisoners were sent to Charlotte.[351]

Gowen's Old Fort, South Carolina [352]   Skirmish
13 July 1780 [353]

Captain John Jones and his thirty-five Georgia militiamen were making their way across the mountains to join Colonel Charles McDowell at Earle's Ford, on the Pacolet River. As they traveled Jones and his men pretended to be a party of Loyalists. Their disguise was so good that they were given guides to move them through the area undetected by any Patriot patrols.

Captain DePeyster was the commander at Prince's Fort, and he had detached Captain James Dunlap to find McDowell and Jones, and capture them if possible. Dunlap and Colonel Mills arrived at Earle's Fort at night, and made camp.

Near the headwaters of the Saluda River, Jones's guide, a frontiersman named Benjamin Lawrence, told them that there was a band of Loyalists nearby who were going to pursue the Rebels who had attacked them. They were the American Volunteers who had fled to Gowen's Old Fort after they had been ambushed at Cedar Creek. Jones told his guide to take them to the Provincials. His plan was to trick them into thinking they would join up and pursue the Rebels.

Lawrence had Jones wait in the woods as he scouted the fort. He told Jones that the fort was garrisoned by the Provincials, but no British Regulars. After nightfall Jones and his men approached the fort and claimed to be a group of Loyalists who had come to assist the men in the fort. Jones and his men were welcomed inside and given food and drink. Following dinner Jones gave a signal, and his men immediately seized the fort. One Loyalist was killed and three others wounded. Thirty-two immediately surrendered and called for quarter. Four of the Loyalists fled towards the Pacolet River. These men had enough of the war in the Carolina backcountry. [354]

Jones ordered the prisoner's weapons to be destroyed, except those that would be useful to his men. He then paroled the prisoners and took as many horses as they could move with. [355]

Earle's Ford, South Carolina [356]   **Skirmish**
15 July 1780 [357]

American Forces
Commanding Officer   Colonel Charles McDowell
  State Militia
    Captain John Jones
      Georgia Militia
        Burke County Militia   15
    Colonel Charles McDowell
      South Carolina Militia   248
        Major John Singleton [358]
        Captain Edward Hampton
          Cavalry   52
Casualties   8 killed, 30 wounded, 1 captured

Loyalist Forces
Commanding Officer   Captain James Dunlap
  Provincials
    American Volunteers   14
  North Carolina Loyalist Militia
    Colonel Ambrose Mills   60
Casualties   2 killed, 1 wounded

After Jones defeated the Loyalists at Pacolet River he withdrew east, and joined McDowell's camp on the North Pacolet River. When they arrived at McDowell's camp they were too tired to set up the camp. They dropped down beside the river, posted a single sentry, and went to sleep.

Loyalist Colonel Zacharias Gibbs had learned that there was a Patriot force in the area, and he sent Alexander Chesney to infiltrate the camp. Chesney wrote that he wanted to "learn their numbers, their commanders names, what carriages they had, how many horse and foot, and whenever they made any movement towards Col. Ferguson, to return and let him know, and that there would be a handsome reward."

Chesney "set out immediately and at Pacolet got a man to go with me, who was acquainted with the North Carolina people; we went down to McDole's camp at night without being noticed,[359] counted all their tents and wagons, found out who were their leaders, and that 500 horsemen were gone down to attack Nicholas's Fort. With this news I returned, and on my way found a loyalist in whom I could confide and sent him off with the particulars by one route to Col. Ferguson whilst I went by another." Captain James Dunlap rode to attack McDowell's camp, but neither Dunlap nor DePeyster knew that Jones had joined forces with McDowell.

Early in the morning of July 15th Dunlap discovered the camp and began moving across the North Pacolet River to attack. A lone sentry saw them and ran back to warn the camp. Dunlap rushed into the camp with sabers drawn, and surprised Jones' men still sleeping in their blankets. Jones's men received the bulk of the attack, and he lost two killed and six wounded. Jones received eight cuts on the head with a saber. Lieutenant Freeman rallied the men and moved them back to join Major Singleton behind a rail fence.

Colonels McDowell and Hampton formed the rest of the militia on Singleton's right, and ordered a charge into the Loyalists. Dunlap learned from a prisoner that the Patriots had over 300 men, and he quickly retreated. In the counterattack McDowell lost six men killed, and eighteen wounded.

One of the dead was Hampton's son, Noah. When the Loyalists had him sleeping in the camp, they asked him his name. He said "Hampton." The Loyalists were enraged by the name of the family who had done so much damage to their cause, and ran a bayonet through him. When the Patriots learned of this atrocity they demanded revenge. McDowell picked out fifty-two men from the two commands, and sent them with Captain Edward Hampton to pursue the Loyalists.[360]

Prince's Fort, South Carolina [361]   **Skirmish**
15 July 1780

After attacking McDowell's Camp on the Pacolet River, Dunlap and his men quickly retreated towards their base at Prince's Fort. Before the sun rose Hampton and his cavalry set off in pursuit. Edward Hampton was the brother of Wade, Richard and Henry Hampton in Sumter's army, and he wanted to exact revenge for the death of his son Noah.

Five miles from the fort Hampton caught Dunlap and his dragoons on the Blackstock Road, and attacked.[362] Dunlap's men had been riding quietly and were unaware of their pursuers, when a volley of rifle fire tore into their ranks, killing five men. The Loyalists broke and fled to Prince's Fort, with Hampton's men hot on their heels. They made it to the fort, but only after they lost thirteen men killed, and one captured.

Three hundred yards from the fort Hampton held his men back, unsure of what was inside the fort. What he didn't know was that the only troops inside the fort were the men that they had been pursuing. Hampton returned to his camp with thirty-five horses, and the arms and equipment of the Provincials. He had only lost a single man who had been captured. His son, Noah, had been avenged.

Dunlap questioned their single prisoner and learned that McDowell's strength was around four hundred men. Dunlap sent word to Captain DePeyster of the attack, and then abandoned Prince's Fort. When DePeyster learned of the attack he immediately marched out with 100 American Volunteers and Loyalist militia to support Dunlap. The two parties met at McIlwain's Creek.[363]

Colson's, North Carolina [364]   **Skirmish**
21 July 1780

American Forces
Commanding Officer   Colonel William Lee Davidson
   North Carolina Militia
      Colonel Francis Locke
      2nd Rowan Militia Regiment
      Lieutenant Colonel William Shepherd
         Surry County Militia   100
            Captain Joseph Philips
            Captain Richard Goode
            Captain Eccles
            Captain Absalom Bostick
         Captain Henry Connelly
            Granville County Militia [365]   60
Casualties   2 wounded

Loyalist Forces
Commanding Officer   Unknown [366]
   North Carolina Loyalist Militia   250
Casualties   3 killed, 4 or 5 wounded, 10 captured

After the battle of Ramseur's Mill, Rutherford's 1,200 militia started heading home. By June 22nd Rutherford only had 200 men under his command. He had learned that Colonel Samuel Bryan had persuaded his neighbors and acquaintances to take up arms for the King. This was easily done, since after the fall of Charlestown and the defeat of Buford at the Waxhaws, it seemed that the Patriot cause was lost.

Rutherford sent Davie and his cavalry to keep an eye on the Camden road, leading from Charlotte. The rest of Rutherford's force marched out to find Bryan's Loyalists. As he moved towards the Loyalists his army increased to 600 men.

When Bryan learned of the defeat at Ramsour's Mill, and the approach of Rutherford, he crossed the Yadkin River and marched through territory that was friendly to the King. Bryan's force also increased as he marched, to 800 men. He marched from the Upper Yadkin area, hoping to meet up with Major Archibald McArthur of the 71st Highlander Regiment. McArthur had been ordered to Cheraw Hill on the Pee Dee River. Rutherford continued to force-march around Bryan's Loyalists, trying to cut them off from reaching McArthur. Rutherford dispatched Colonel William Lee Davidson and 160 men to intercept Bryan.[367]

Bryan marched down the east side of the Yadkin River, without stopping to rest, until he rendezvoused with McArthur. Rutherford did not want to attack McArthur's Highlanders, so he broke off the pursuit. Davidson's force continued marching down the west side of the Pee Dee River, and learned of a party of Loyalists camped on a farm near Colson's Mill. Colson's Mill was located at the river junction of the Rocky and Pee Dee Rivers. It consisted of a mill, an ordinary, stagecoach relays, and a ferry crossing.

Davidson decided to attack the Loyalists, but prior to attacking he had his men put white pieces of paper in their hats so they would not shoot their own men. He divided his army so that they would attack from the front and the flank. The Loyalists detected the presence of the Patriots and opened fire. Davidson continued to form his men under fire, without having his men shoot, and then charged forward.

Davidson was wearing his blue Continental uniform, and became a conspicuous target. Loyalist sharpshooters fired upon the only officer visible, and wounded him in the stomach. The loss of their commander did not deter the Patriots and they charged forward at trail arms, attacking from two directions at the same time. After a very short fight, the Loyalists had three killed, and five wounded. The rest fled to their homes.[368]

Flat Rock, South Carolina [369]   **Skirmish**
21 July 1780

William Richardson Davie had been born in England in 1756, and had come to South Carolina when he was eight years old. His uncle, Reverend William Richardson, was a minister in the Waxhaws and had adopted him. Once Davie graduated from Princeton he set up a law practice in Salisbury, North Carolina. In 1777 he was commissioned as a major in General Allen Jones' militia. He served for three months in the local militia, then afterwards helped raise a troop of dragoons under Count Pulaski. He was seriously wounded at the Battle of Stono Ferry in 1779 and returned home to recover. In 1780 he expended his entire estate to raise a cavalry troop in the Waxhaws. It was said, "he was strikingly handsome, graceful and of wonderful physical strength...His voice was so commanding that... it could be heard at an almost incredible distance."

Davie was given the mission to harass British communications between the posts at Hanging Rock and Camden. His dragoons were reinforced by "some South Carolinians under Major Crawford, 35 Catawba warriors under their chief General Newriver, and a part of the Mecklenburg militia commanded by Lt Col^o Heaggins." [370]

The British had thought that they would be able to forage from the local inhabitants, but the continued attacks denied them that source of provisions. The posts at Hanging Rock and Rocky Mount had to rely on supplies from Camden. Davie learned of a convoy coming from Camden and he rode with some of his dragoons to intercept the supplies. He left his camp on the evening of July 20th and rode around the left flank of Hanging Rock, and laid an ambush on the Camden road, five miles south of Hanging Rock at Flat Rock.

The convoy was "captured with little trouble, the spirits provisions and waggons being destroyed, the escorts and waggoners were mounted on the captured horses, and about dark the party commenced its retreat." [371]

Beaver Creek Ford, South Carolina   **Skirmish**
22 July 1780

After Davie had captured the British supply convoy he rode back to his camp at Waxhaw Creek. One of his own men straggled back, and Davie was worried that he would be captured and inform any British patrols that they were in the area. Davie told his guides to take a route back that was the least traveled by anyone. The moon was full and the Patriots were able to pass by the left flank of Hanging Rock again, to reach a plantation on Beaver Creek. At the plantation Davie sent a Captain Petit with an advance force to determine if it was safe. Petit did not see anything suspicious, and Davie ordered the rest of his men to follow. When the rear of his column entered the lane, Davie's advance force "hailed the enemy concealed under a fence and some standing corn; on challenging a second time he was answered by a discharge of Musquetry, which commenced on their right and passed like a running fire towards the rear of the Detachment."

A major in charge of the advance force ordered men to get through the lane, but they charged back against the Loyalists and were hit with a second volley. Once they caught up with the men who made it through the ambush, the whole body filed off to the right and quickly took up a position on a hill overlooking the plantation.

Colonel William Polk had the men guarding the prisoners, and they had suffered some casualties. Casualties in Davie's force was light, "Capt Petit and two men wounded and Lie^t killed; the fire fell principally among the prisoners, who were confined two upon a horse and mixed with the guard presented a larger object than a single dragoon; the advance guard with the prisoners nearly filled the lane, it was owing to these circumstances that the prisoners were all killed or wounded except three or four."[372]

Davie could see the Loyalist forces walking about the plantation with lights, and they did not seem alarmed. His own men were close to a panic and he ordered a retreat. They left the mortally wounded prisoners on the hill and they rode off. Their own guides had fled on the first shots, "but a Tory who was taken from his bed and compelled to serve as guide enabled him to pass the enemys patroles and regain his camp the next day without any further reverse of fortune." [373]

Mars Bluff, South Carolina [374]
25 July 1780 [375]

American Forces
Commanding Officer   Major Tristram Thomas
   South Carolina Militia
      Britton's Neck Regiment   25

British Forces
Commanding Officer   Captain-Lieutenant John Nairne
   British Regulars
      71st Regiment of Foot (Fraser's Highlanders) 106 ill troops
   South Carolina Loyalist Militia
      Lieutenant Colonel William Henry Mills
         Camden District Militia
           Cheraw Regiment   100
Casualties   107 captured, 99 Loyalists deserted

After the defeat of Huck's Loyalists, Lord Rawdon ordered some troops to fall back towards Camden to await the arrival of Cornwallis. Major McArthur was at a post at Cheraw, and was ordered by Rawdon to evacuate the post.

The troops at McArthur's post were the 71st Highlander Regiment. The regiment had some of its troops captured aboard ship in 1776 when it sailed into Boston Harbor, thinking it was still in British hands. The regiment was exchanged in 1778, and saw action in Savannah, Stono Ferry and Charlestown. Unfortunately the climate of South Carolina was defeating the regiment at a rapid pace. Sickness had greatly reduced its effectiveness of defending the fort against any organized force.

McArthur decided to move his ill soldiers to Charlestown by the Pee Dee River. Lieutenant Nairne of the 71st Highlanders was in charge of the flotilla. McArthur called out Lieutenant Colonel William Henry Mills and his Camden District Loyalist militia, to escort the sick soldiers on flatboats to Georgetown. Mills was a physician who had been a delegate to the Provincial Congress in 1775, but had switched sides to the British when they started winning.

Hearing of the British expedition down the river, the Patriot militia under James Gillespie gathered at Beding's Fields, three miles from Cheraw.[376] As the Patriot militia marched towards the Pee Dee River their numbers increased. Major Tristram Thomas, of Sumter's partisans, was assigned to the command of the militia.

The spot Thomas picked to ambush the flotilla was Hunt's Bluff, a bend in the Pee Dee River, which was excellent for cannon. The problem was that they had no cannon, and all they had was small arms that would not stop a boat. Thomas decided to deceive the boats and had his militia construct "Quaker cannons" out of tree trunks, placing them behind a formidable looking parapet.

When the British boats approached the "battery", the Patriots rushed out of hiding, and went through the loading and firing sequence for artillery. Demands were shouted to the boats, telling them they needed to surrender, or be blown out of the water.

Mills' Loyalist militia was thoroughly convinced of the threat of the artillery, and mutinied. They took over the boats, made the Highlanders prisoners, and then surrendered to Thomas.[377]

Colonel Mills did not return to the Patriots, but made his escape to Georgetown. Thomas's deception worked a second time, when they captured another British supply boat coming from Georgetown with supplies.[378]

Thicketty Fort, South Carolina [379]
30 July 1780 [380]

Fort Anderson was built during the Cherokee War in the 1760s, but was known as Thicketty Fort due to Thicketty Mountain that was nearby. The fort was described as a fort that "had an upper line of loopholes, and was surrounded by a very strong abatis; with only a small wicket to enter by." Captain William Johnston had captured the fort's commander, Captain Patrick Moore, a few weeks before, but he had been able to escape.[381]

With Moore and his militia was a sergeant major from the American Volunteers, who had been attached to the fort to train the recruits.[382]

Sumter had learned of Major Ferguson's force moving beyond the Broad River, and he directed Colonel Elijah Clarke and his Georgians to move towards that area.[383] Clarke met up with Colonel McDowell at Cherokee Ford. After the battle at Earle's Ford McDowell had moved his camp there.[384]

More troops arrived increasing their strength, including the forces of Isaac Shelby.[385] McDowell decided to use the reinforcements to eliminate the threat from Moore's Loyalists. He detached Colonels Shelby, Clarke, Andrew Hampton and Major Charles Robertson with 600 men to attack Thicketty Fort.

Shelby's men began their ride at sunset on July 25th, and surrounded the fort at sunrise the next day. Shelby sent Captain William Cocke to the fort to demand their surrender. Moore replied that they would defend the fort to the last extremity. Shelby formed his men within view of the fort, and demanded surrender again. Moore saw the numbers against him, and didn't want to repeat the defeat the Loyalists had suffered at Ramseur's Mill. He surrendered without firing a shot.

Shelby captured 250 muskets, and a considerable amount of ammunition. The muskets had been loaded with buck and ball, and were at the ready at the portholes.[386] This would have been able to stop double the number that Shelby had.

The British authorities censured Captain Moore for the loss of the fort. Shelby moved back to Cherokee Ford with the prisoners, but after they arrived Colonel McDowell sent them back out again to keep an eye of Ferguson's army.[387]

Rocky Mount, South Carolina [388]   Skirmish
30 July 1780 [389]

American Forces
Commanding Officer   Colonel Thomas Sumter
    State Militia   500
        South Carolina Militia [390]
        Colonel William Hill & Colonel Andrew Neal
            New Acquisition Militia
                Lieutenant Colonel Thomas Neal, Jr.
            Lieutenant Colonel James Hawthorne
                Captain James Jamieson
                Lieutenant John Lisle
                    South Carolina Refugees [391]
        Colonel Edward Lacey
            Chester District Militia
                Captain John Thompson
                Captain Samuel Adams
            Lieutenant Colonel James Stein [392]
                Union District Militia
                    Captain Samuel Otterson
        North Carolina Militia [393]
        Colonel Robert Irwin
            Mecklenburg County Militia
                Captain George Reed
Casualties   4 killed, 6 wounded, 2 captured [394]

Loyalist Forces
Commanding Officer   Lieutenant Colonel George Turnbull
    Provincials
    Lieutenant Colonel George Turnbull
        New York Volunteers   150
            Major Henry Sheridan
                Lieutenant Colonel Turnbull's Company
            Captain William Johnston
            Captain Bernard Kane

Patrick O'Kelley

South Carolina Loyalist Militia [395]
Captain Matthew Floyd
Camden District Militia
Rocky Mount Regiment 150
Casualties 12 killed or wounded

Thomas Sumter had been the commander of the 6th South Carolina Regiment until September 1778, when he resigned his commission and returned to his home in the High Hills of the Santee. On May 28th, 1780 he received word that Tarleton was headed his way, in pursuit of Buford's force. Sumter knew what he must do. He put on his regimental uniform, kissed his wife and son goodbye, and then rode off with his slave, Soldier Tom.

He went to North Carolina, following the exiled Governor Rutledge. When he arrived in Salisbury he met with authorities, and received their approval to carry the war back into South Carolina. To do this he was given nineteen $1,000 certificates. Sumter and a few refugees headed down the Catawba River, where 200 Catawba Indians joined his force. [396]

On June 15th the Carolinians held a backwoods convention and elected Thomas Sumter as their leader. He agreed to the appointment, and moved further down the Catawba River to create his Brigade. [397] He quickly built up his army in the heavily wooded area near Hill's Iron Works at Clem's Branch. He camped there for a month and created a fort by ordering "the timber to be felled in different directions round the Camp some what in the form of an Abatis and the body of the trees split and leaned over a strong pole supported by forks or some high stump, the other end on the ground at an angle of 30 degrees elevation and facing the avenues left through the brush or abatis for passage, so that they would answer the double purpose for the men to lay under and for defence. If the enemy's cavalry had come unless they were supported by a large body of Infantry or artillery, they could not have forced the Camp."

The victory over Huck helped increase Sumter's ranks, but he knew this would not last. [398] Draper wrote that Sumter lost men the longer he stayed at Clem's Branch. "While he kept moving and fighting the enemy his men kept with him, but when only attending routine duty and evening formations, they left for home." Sumter decided he needed to use his militia quickly in a strike against the post at Rocky Mount.

After the defeat of Huck, Colonel Winn had employed one of the Loyalists, Major Owens, as a spy for Sumter. Owens told Winn that Rocky Mount only had 300 men, but the fort was "properly prepared for a defence, with abatis." Rocky Mount was a British strongpoint that sat on the crest of a high hill, overlooking the Catawba River. The post consisted of three log buildings, in which firing loopholes had been cut. A ditch and an abatis surrounded the position. Inside the post were 150 New York Volunteers and 150 Camden District Militia, under the command of Lieutenant Colonel George Turnbull.

On July 28th Sumter broke camp and headed towards Major Davie's camp in the Waxhaws. The Waxhaw Meeting House had become a hospital for the eighty wounded survivors of Buford's massacre. Since it was between the two armies it was unable to get any proper medical support and survived due to the assistance of the partisans. McClure joined Sumter's army that night with some prisoners from Huck's defeat. At the Waxhaws Sumter asked Major Davie if he would stage a diversionary attack on Hanging Rock, while he would be attacking Rocky Mount. Davie agreed.

On the 29th Sumter's army received "double rations and a suitable supply of ammunition" and began their march to Rocky Mount. Davies militia marched down the east side of the Catawba "to place himself between the British posts at Hanging Rock and Rocky Mount."

Sumter's men "took the road leading to Lansford, crossed the river at sunset, marched all night and invested Rocky Mount at sunrise." When Sumter's force arrived at Rocky Mount on Sunday morning, July 30th, they ran into a camp of about 100 Loyalist militia. These were men who had arrived at the post late, and had set up camp outside the walls of the fort.

Colonel Winn was leading Sumter's advance force, and fired upon the Loyalists. The Loyalists ran off into the early morning light, many of them leaving "their horses and cloathing." The shots alarmed the garrison at Rocky Mount, and they returned fire on the partisans.

Sumter's men immediately charged the fort. Hill wrote in his memoirs, "This was made under the impression that the Enemy was in a large framed house; the walls of which were only thin clap boards, and we supposed that our balls [would] have the desired effect by shooting through the wall. but ... the enemy had wrought day & night and had placed small logs about a foot from the inside of the wall and rammed the cavity with clay, ...we [could] injure them in no way, but by shooting in their port holes."

Sumter's men attempted three charges. Each time McClure's riflemen covered the partisans as they cut away the abatis surrounding the buildings. Lieutenant Colonel Thomas Neal was able to push through the abatis, and drive the defenders into their cabins, but he was killed, along with two other militiamen and a Catawba Indian.[399]

When Captain Samuel Otterson charged forward "a bullet removed a lock of his hair, another cut his chin and another his cheek." The same bullet that wounded Otterson in the chin, cut off a lock of Lieutenant Joseph Hughes's hair, and hit another man in the cheek. The men were able to get within 30 feet, but each attack was thrown back.

Sumter moved his men to some rocks for protection, and dispatched a note to Turnbull demanding a surrender of the fort. Turnbull requested that the fighting cease for one hour so he could consider Sumter's request. Before the time was up Turnbull refused to surrender, stating "duty and inclination induce me to defend this place to the last extremity." Sumter had no artillery, so he had to devise a different method to defeat the fort's garrison. He observed that if two men could get to a ledge of large rocks, they could throw firebrands onto a small house beside the fort. If it caught fire the fort would burn also.

There was 100 yards of cleared ground between the Sumter's men and the rocks. To do the run would be suicidal. Hill wrote, "the undertaking appeared so hazardous that no two men of the army could be found to undertake it." Colonel William Hill came forward and said, "that if any man would go with him he would make the attempt."

Sergeant Jemmy Johnson volunteered to make the run with him. They strapped "riched lightwood split & bound with cords to cover the most vital parts of our bodies, as well as a large bundle of the same wood to carry in our arms." Both men made it to the rocks with their wooden "armor".

Colonel Hill pulled security, while Johnson tried to start a fire. Turnbull knew what they were doing and forced the men away with a bayonet charge. Hill and Johnson were fired upon by "those who had sallied out, but likewise from a large number of port holes in that end of the house." Sumter's riflemen fired upon the exposed troops, and drove the British back to the fort.[400]

One of Sumter's men, Alexander Haynes, had been hiding behind some black rocks using it for cover. He fired his rifle twice, and after he loaded for a third shot, he looked around the corner of the rocks. His white face stood out in the black rocks, 140 yards from the fort. One of the Loyalist riflemen saw Haynes, and fired at him, hitting him under the eye. "The shot ranged under the brain but missed the vertebrae of the neck; it was thought he was killed, but seeing life was in him when they were about to retire, his acquaintances carried him off." Alexander Haynes lost his eye, but he did not lose his life. He recovered from the wound.

On the second attempt it was decided that Sumter's men would "direct their fire to that space between the small & great house which was about 15 feet." The two volunteers again ran to the ledge, and this time was able to set the small house on fire. The burning smaller house "caused the wall of the great house to smoke." Hill and Johnson ran back to Sumter's men. The run "was more hazardous than the former ones, as the Enemy during the interval, had opened a great many more port holes in that end of the building."

Hill wrote in his memoirs, "Providence, so protected us both, that neither of us lost a drop of blood, altho' locks of hair was cut from our heads and our garments riddled with balls." Unfortunately before the wood on the fort could catch fire, a heavy rainstorm extinguished the flames and soaked the buildings.

After eight hours Sumter called off the attack in frustration. He had lost three men killed, six wounded and two captured. As the rain drove down upon them, Sumter's men marched away in defeat. That night Sumter had his men camp at Fishing Creek.

Sumter wrote, "my loss in killed and wounded did not exceed 20." Turnbull reported that he had only one officer killed, one wounded and ten men killed or wounded.

The day after the attack Colonel Winn rode with 100 men along the road leading to Camden to determine if there were any reinforcements coming to help the British post. Winn's mounted force fell in "with a body of Tories", and dispersed them. Sumter wrote "I interrupted two parties going to reinforce that post." The Patriots captured several of the Loyalists, and they rescued the two men who were captured in the attack the day before. Both of the men had been sentenced to be hanged for desertion, in Camden, when the British discovered that the two partisans had previously served with Colonel Turnbull. Winn returned to Sumter's camp with "several prisoners, a great number of excellent horses, saddalles, guns, etc." [401]

Hanging Rock, South Carolina [402]   **Skirmish**
30 July 1780 [403]

American Forces
Commanding Officer   Major William Richardson Davie
  North Carolina Militia
    North Carolina Partisan Rangers
      Captain David Flenniken
        Mounted riflemen   40
        Dragoons   40

Loyalist Forces
Commanding Officer   Colonel Samuel Bryan
   North Carolina Loyalist Militia
     North Carolina Volunteers [404]   120
       Lieutenant Colonel John Hampton
       Captain Nicholas White

Major Davie had been asked by Sumter to create a diversionary attack on the British outpost at Hanging Rock, while Sumter attacked Rocky Mount. Davie knew that he could not attack the fort garrison of 500 men with his eighty troopers, but he did discover that three companies of Loyalist mounted infantry were camped at a farmhouse within plain view of the fort.

The farmhouse "was placed in the point of a right angle made by a lane of staked and ridered fence; the one end of which opened to the enemy's encampment, the other terminated in the woods."

Davie formed a daring plan to surround the enemy, posing as a band of Loyalists. Davie's riflemen, under Captain Flenniken, looked like the Loyalist militia and would not arouse suspicion as they rode casually to the house. They rode past the sentinels without being challenged, calmly dismounted and then opened fire.

The Loyalists fled to the other end of a lane, where Davie's dragoons had circled around through the wood. The dragoons fired into the panicked Loyalists and then rode through them. The Loyalists "all rushed against the angle of the fence where they were surrounded by the dragoons who had entered the field and literally cut to pieces." Since this was done in view of the garrison, no prisoners could be taken.[405]

Davie's men remounted and took with them sixty captured horses and 100 muskets and rifles, just issued to the Loyalist recruits.[406] Davie only lost one man. The British losses are not recorded.[407]

Davie's force rode to Land's Ford, where he met Colonel Robert Irwin. The two partisan leaders rode on towards Sumter's camp, and stayed there for six days recovering from their attacks. During this week "strong mounted parties traversed the country towards the posts of Rocky Mount and Hanging Rock. McClure was constantly out. While at Landsford the Chester men held an election. McClure was elected colonel, John Nixon was lieutenant colonel". [408]

Tyger River, South Carolina
July 1780 [409]

"Plundering Sam" Brown had been conducting illegal activities before the war began, but when the war arrived in the Carolinas it gave him legitimacy to rob Patriot homes for the British cause.

Sam had started his illegal career with his sister, Charity, and they lived in a cave with Sam's mistress on Island Ford in North Carolina. [410] When the British moved into the South Carolina backcountry Sam Brown took advantage of the defenseless Whig homes in the area.

Brown and another Loyalist, known only as Captain Butler, rode into Fair Forest to find the home of Josiah Culbertson. Culbertson had been at the battle of Wofford's Iron Works. Brown asked Culbertson's wife, Anne, where her husband was, but she refused to answer him. Brown "became very provoked by this spirited woman, and retorted to much abusive and indecent language." He told her the he would come back in a few days, burn her house down and kill her husband. "Plundering Sam" began his return trip home to North Carolina that night.

Josiah Culbertson learned of the abuse of his wife, and gathered up his friend Charles Holloway, William Neal, William McIlhaney and a man called Steedman. They tracked "Plundering Sam" to the home of Dr. Andrew Thompson on the Tyger River. Butler and Brown's horses were tied up in the stable by the roadside. Culbertson and his friends crept up to within rifle shot of the house, and waited. Brown walked outside, having just waked up. He yawned, and stretched with his hands locked over his head. Culbertson fired from 200 yards away and hit "Plundering Sam" right between the shoulder blades. Sam was dead before he hit the dooryard fence. [411]

Butler sprinted out of the house, and fled into the woods. Holloway fired, but missed Butler. When Charity Butler learned of her brother's death, she fled to the mountains of North Carolina.[412] Not long after Brown's death Culbertson learned that another Loyalist had threatened to kill him in an act of revenge. The two met one day and both raised their rifles, firing almost simultaneously. Culbertson's rifle found his mark and killed the Loyalist.[413]

Atlantic Ocean, Near South Carolina
1-6 August 1780

American Forces
South Carolina State Navy
Captain Charles Morgan
Snow *Fair American*   16 guns
Pennsylvania Privateers
Captain Roger Keane
Brig *Holker*   16 guns
Captain James Montgomery
General Green   Unknown guns

Even though Charlestown fell, the South Carolina Navy continued to operate off the coast of the Carolinas. On August 1st the American privateers, the *General Green, Holker* and the South Carolina Navy snow *Fair American*, captured the *Queen Charlotte* off the coast of South Carolina.

The *Queen Charlotte* was laden with turtles and fruit and on her way from Providence to New York. The *Queen Charlotte* was carried into Philadelphia on August 2nd. Five days later the *Fair American* and the *Holker* captured two schooners laden with tobacco. On board the schooners were refugees out of the Chesapeake. [414]

Dooly's Fort, Georgia [415]   Murder
August 1780

Shortly after the surrender of Charlestown Colonel Dooly surrendered his regiment in Georgia to Major Manson. Dooly's home was known as Lee's Old Place, or as Dooly's Fort. The fort was located on the Savannah River. It consisted of a plantation, a fort and a ferry.

In August a party of Loyalists, under Captain William Corker, killed Dooly in front of his family.[416] Dooly's murder was against the rules of war since Dooly was considered a prisoner of war on parole.[417] Dooly's brother, Captain George Dooly, executed several Loyalists in retaliation, and assumed command of his brother's regiment.[418]

Rocky Creek, South Carolina   Skirmish
3 August 1780

Richard Winn wrote that on August 2nd the Rocky Mount garrison was reinforced with "eight hundred men and two field pieces." These troops were the Prince of Wales American Regiment, under the command of Major John Carden, which had marched from Camden to reinforce Hanging Rock.

Sumter was unable to move his campsite until the 3rd, due to the high water at Rocky Creek caused by all the rain. At 11 o'clock in the afternoon Sumter crossed the creek with his force, and halted. The partisans "turned out their horses and scattered about in search of roasting ears and green peaches." This was all the men had to eat at the time.

While they were searching for food an alarm was sounded that Carden's force was less than a mile away, and they had two pieces of artillery. Carden had stopped at Rocky Mount prior to continuing his march to Hanging Rock. Sumter was caught in the open and decided wisely not to fight the Loyalists.

He ordered Colonel Winn to take 100 men and delay Carden until they could all withdraw. Winn sent two men ahead, while he gathered the first 100 men who reached their horses. The two men that Winn sent ahead was Captain Coleman from Georgia, and William Stroud. These two men ventured too close to the British and were captured. The Loyalists had them "stript naked and immediately hung up by the side of the road."[419]

The two sides exchanged long-range fire, but did not get close enough to become engaged in a major skirmish. Colonel Andrew Neal ventured too close to the fight, and was shot out of his saddle. The bullet went in one hip and out the other side. He died on the side of the road, near the Loyalist forces. Another partisan with Winn was wounded.

Major Carden did not anticipate finding hundreds of mounted partisans, and withdrew down the road back to Rocky Mount. Winn pursued them at a distance, but broke off as they neared Rocky Mount.

The day after the skirmish Colonel Hawthorne was sent under a flag of truce to bury Colonel Neal. Hawthorne reported that he thought the Loyalists had lost twelve to fourteen men killed and wounded. [420]

Hanging Rock, South Carolina [421]   **Battle**
6 August 1780

American Forces [422]
Commanding Officer   Colonel Thomas Sumter
   State Militia
     Colonel Thomas Sumter
      South Carolina Militia   300
       Colonel William Bratton
        Ninety-Six District Militia [423]
         Captain James Jamieson [424]
          Lieutenant William Hillhouse [425]
       Colonel William Hill
        South Carolina Refugees
       Colonel Edward Lacey
        Chester District Militia

Lieutenant Colonel James Liles [426]
Captain John Thompson
Captain Samuel Adams
Captain Henry Bishop
Colonel John McClure
    Chester Rocky Creek Irish
      Lieutenant Colonel John Nixon
      Major Robert Crawford [427]
      Lieutenant Hugh McClure [428]
Colonel Samuel Watson
    New Acquisition Militia
      Lieutenant Colonel James Hawthorne
Colonel Richard Winn
    Fairfield Regiment [429]
      Captain John McCool
Captain Coleman [430]
    Georgia Militia
Lieutenant Colonel James Stein
    Union District Militia [431]
      Captain Joseph McJunkin
      Captain Samuel Otterson
Colonel Robert Irwin [432]
    North Carolina Partisan Rangers [433]   200
      Captain George Reed
      Captain Robert Craighead
      Captain James Knox
Major William Richardson Davie
    Charlotte militia (The Bloody Corps) [434]   80
      Captain David Flenniken
      Mounted riflemen
General New River [435]
    Catawba Indians [436]   35
      General Billy Ayers [437]
      Major Jacob Ayers
Casualties   20 killed, 40 wounded, 10 missing [438]

Loyalist Forces

Commanding Officer	Major John Carden
Provincials [439]	500
Major Daniel Manson	
Royal North Carolina Regiment	Unknown number
Captain Kenneth McCulloch [440]	
British Legion [441]	
Legion Infantry	160
Captain John Rousselet	
3-pound artillery	2
Major John Carden	
Prince of Wales American Regiment [442]	181
Loyalist Militia [443]	800
Colonel Samuel Bryan	
North Carolina Volunteers	Unknown number
Lieutenant Colonel John Hampton	
Captain Nicholas White	
Colonel Henry Rugeley	
Camden District Militia	34
Major John Cook, Sr.	
Captain James McCullough	
Captain John Cook, Jr.	
Captain Adam Thompson	

Reinforcements from Rocky Mount

British Legion [444]	
Legion Cavalry	40
Captain Patrick Stewart	
Captain Charles McDonald [445]	
Casualties	25 killed, 175 wounded, 73 captured [446]

After the failed attack by Sumter on Rocky Mount, Davie united with Sumter's forces. The two commanders incorrectly determined that the attack on Rocky Mount had caused the British to reinforce that post with troops from the Hanging Rock garrison. They decided to attack the supposedly weakened Hanging Rock garrison together.

Normally the garrison at Hanging Rock consisted of the Royal North Carolina Regiment, and the North Carolina and South Carolina Loyalist Militia, but the Prince of Wales Regiment and the British Legion were marching towards the post. William Dobein James wrote "Sumter's advance passed themselves off as British and took up all the stragglers on the road."

After traveling all night Sumter and Davie stopped near Hanging Rock, before the sun came up. The men were allowed to "rest on their arms until daylight." Captain McJunkin and "Michael High of Fair Forest lay down by the fire and slept a little. When they awoke High said 'This day I shall die'; he however cheerfully went forward at the signal of attack and fell at the first fire."

Sumter sent out two spies to see if there were any new developments. The spies told Sumter that the British did not have more than 300 men in the camp, and the reinforcements that had been sent to Rocky Mount had not returned. Sumter had around 500 men, but 200 of those men did not have any guns.

After the spies had left, the British reinforcements arrived at Hanging Rock in the dark of night. The Loyalists set up camp at the post, but they neglected sending out any patrols.

McJunkin wrote "The British were encamped south of Hanging Rock Creek, on a hill, something in the shape of a crescent, the Regulars lay about 200 yards from the Tory camp, on Camden Road."

Colonel Winn was to be the main assault against the British, supported by Davie's cavalry. The rest of Sumter's force was divided up into four groups under Colonels Bratton, Lacey, Hill and Hawthorne. The men without arms were to dismount, and take care of the horses. If the British were driven from the field, those men without guns were to follow, and gather up any weapons.

At sunrise Winn captured two Loyalists who told him that the Hanging Rock garrison had been reinforced between twelve and one o'clock in the morning.

Now there were three camps. Davie wrote, "the Regulars were posted on the right, a part of the British Legion and Hamilton's regiment were at some houses in the center, and Bryan's regiment and other Loyalists were some distance on the left and separated from the center by a skirt of wood. The British situation could not be approached without an entire exposure of the assailants."

William Dobein James described the British as being "secured by a strong position, a stockade fort and a field piece; on Sumter's front the wood crossed the Hanging Rock Creek, running between lofty hills; on the right lay the British in open ground; on his left encamped the Tories on a hill side, covered with trees, and between them and the fort ran a small stream of water thro' a valley covered with brush wood."

Sumter held a quick council of war to determine the next course of action. Half of the officers wanted to fight, and the other half wanted to retreat, however no man wanted to be perceived as a coward, so the attack began immediately. Since there was to be an attack Davie argued that the men should dismount prior to the camps, but Sumter wanted to ride into the battle, and each division would attack the camp assigned to it. Davie said that to leave the horses and approach on foot would be better because he "didn't want the confusion always consequent on dismounting under a fire, and the certainty of losing the effect of a sudden and vigorous attack." The rest of the officers present overruled Davie's objections.

There are different versions as to how Sumter attacked. Davie wrote that he led the column on the right, consisting of his Corps, "some volunteers under Major Bryan, and some detached companies of South Carolina refugees. Colonel Hill commanded the left composed of South Carolina refugees; Colonel Irwin commanded the center, entirely of the Mecklenburgh militia."

William Dobein James wrote, "The South Carolinians formed the right and center; Colonel Steene commanded the right and Lacey and Lyles the center; the North Carolinians under Colonel Irvin formed the left. Captain McClure with 50 riflemen and Captain Davie with 60 cavalry were thrown into the reserve."

McJunkin agreed that three divisions made the attack, but "Colonel Steen commanded the right side. Captain McJunkin was ordered to penetrate between the camps. Colonel Lyles, Watson and Ervin commanded the center and left divisions. They were ordered to enfilade and cut off the Regulars. General Sumter, in person, led the center and left." Interestingly, McJunkin doesn't even mention Davie.

The partisans launched their attack between six and seven in the morning. The three divisions were supposed to attack the Loyalist position from the left, right, and center, but the confused command hit the North Carolina Volunteers, on the right flank of the camp. Davie wrote that this was the fault of "the guides, through ignorance or timidity."

Colonel William Hill wrote that the "action commenced under many very unfavorable circumstances...as they had to march across a water course & climb a steep cliff, being all this time under the enemy's fire."

Bryan's corps were undisciplined and fired over the heads of Irwin's forces. Seeing there was no effect by their volleys, the Loyalists broke. They were pursued closely by the Davie's forces, leaving the Loyalist's right flank exposed. Davie wrote that they were "routed with great slaughter. They fled to the center camp."[447]

The British Legion infantry and the Royal North Carolina Regiment tried to make a stand behind a fence, and behind their bush huts.[448] Sumter's partisans soon overran them, shouting the "Indian Hallo".[449]

Sumter's men started the battle with only two to five rounds each, but as they overran the Loyalists they collected more ammunition and weapons from the fallen enemy. The partisans "fired on their enemy as they went, with bullets in their mouths and powder in their pockets, and to load as they run up but by no means to take a tree even where trees was."

Robert Kelsey was a private in Lacey's Regiment and had been at the fight at Rocky Mount. The last time he loaded his weapon at Rocky Mount, he had used green leaves for wadding, and did not fire the weapon. When he went into battle at Hanging Rock his rifle would not shoot because "the green leaves had remained so long and had dampened his powder. He had to unbreach his gun and take out the load before he could take part in the battle." Kelsey said that green leaves were used continuously for wadding while he was a partisan.

The Loyalists soon joined their fleeing comrades, leaving behind their artillery pieces. Sumter wrote that after an hour they had "possession of Bryant's camp."

During the initial attack Lieutenant Colonel James Stein was able to penetrate between the British camp and the Tory camp. Davie wrote, "At this moment Colonel Brown's Regiment nearly changed the fate of the day. They, by a bold and skillful maneuver, passed into a wood between the Tory and center camp, drew up unperceived and poured a heavy fire on the militia forming from the disorder of the pursuit on the flank of the camp."

This was the Prince of Wales Regiment and they poured a deadly fire into Sumter's men, recapturing the fieldpieces.[450] Hill wrote "the British camp, being about one quarter of a mile from this Tory camp, advanced firing in platoons." The firepower was intense. Colonel Samuel Watson was "knocked from his horse, with some broken ribs, by a British ball striking his silver mounted sword. The ball burying itself almost half way in the mettle."[451]

David Wallace told Lyman Draper that McClure led his men through the valley of Hanging Rock Creek and ascended the bluff opposite the enemy's encampment. "The bluff was both steep and rugged. McClure was the first to reach the top and he turned and said, "Come on my brave fellows!" At that moment he was wounded in the thigh by a sentinel. As he was stopping the flow of blood with the wadding for his weapon, a second bullet hit him in the chest."[452]

When McClure's friends came to his aid be urged them to leave him, and pursue the enemy. Lieutenant Hugh McClure took charge of the company after John McClure had been wounded. Two of McClure's cousins, sons of Judge Gaston, fell dead across each other. A third cousin was mortally wounded, and a fourth, Alexander, had a cheek shot away. Captain Samuel Otterson was wounded in the left arm. The rifle bullet "severed the bone between the elbow and the shoulder." Twenty-four men from McClure's company were killed and wounded.

Daniel Stinson wrote "They rushed forward right into Bryant's camp, fired two rounds and then clubbing their muskets, rid the field. The Tories fled towards the British camp about a half mile distant."

Joseph White wrote that a Catawba Indian with Sumter's force ran off in the midst of the battle, pointing to the battlefield he said "Too many bullets there!" Robert Mursh was an Indian with the Catawbas who was a "large and somewhat corpulent warrior...he had adopted the dress and ... the habits of the whites."[453]

Another Catawba, George White, "shot a British officer and saw him and his sword fall... Dick Wright also brought down an officer. He got between him and his men so as to cut off his retreat and he offered his gold watch to spare his life, but Wright scarcely listened to his pleas, but ran his bayonet into his body and nearly disemboweled him and got his watch and some gold from his pockets."

James Saye wrote that "one of the Easten boys thought he was wounded. He could hear blood as it spurt from his body and on the leaves as he ran for a drink from a branch. Once he drank he discovered he wasn't bleeding, but a ball had pierced his powder horn, which spilt powder in a jet every step, on the leaves."

Winn wrote "Here I was eye witness to the British taking trees to defend themselves." Winn remarked to Davie, "Isn't this glorious!" and then was hit by a ball and went down. Captain John McCool and Joseph Hughes were both wounded and carried him from the field.[454]

Militiaman John Ratchford was "shot through the right nipple and out the back while in the act of shooting a Tory, but recovered later." Captain Henry Bishop was mortally wounded. He would be taken to Charlotte, and would die a few months later.

Hill wrote that the Provincials "took to trees & rock; whilst the British were advancing firing in platoons, and they fell so fast by their unseen enemy that their officers were obliged to push them forward by their sabers." Davie wrote that his riflemen "took to the trees and bush heaps and returned fire with deadly effects. In a few minutes there was not a British officer standing."

Hill was hit by a ball "under the shoulder blade and blood spurted out. The surgeon said "let me take you off the field." Hill said, "If I die, I'll die on Flim Nap." He put spurs to his horse, Flim Nap, and dashed from one end of his regiment to the other, encouraging the men, exclaiming in his enormous voice "Fight on, my brave boys, I'm mortally wounded!" Hill did not die that day, and he carried the ball with him to his grave in 1816.

The Prince of Wales Regiment was virtually destroyed. During the battle Davie called out to them "Soldiers, if you value your lives, ground your arms and officers surrender at once", but they continued "to fight with the usual sullenness of the British soldier." Eventually they surrendered and "Threw down their arms."

Hanger wrote that the heavy loss was due to the regiment mistaking the Patriot militia for Loyalists, "they being both dressed alike." When they approached within forty yards of the Patriots, they were fired upon. The weapons of the Loyalists were collected up and given to the partisans who had none.

William Dobein James wrote that "Steen passing up the stream between the fort and the encampment had nearly turned the left of the Tories before he was discovered, but two of his men, contrary to orders, gave the alarm, and both sides were soon warmly engaged along the valley."

McJunkin wrote that this was "where Captain McCullough commenced what was then called street firing upon Steen's command.[455] The right and left, led by Sumter, succeeded in turning their flank, and the whole Prince of Wales American Regiment was killed or taken, except nine.[456] McCullough fell wounded near the Tory camp and surrendered. The British force was driven from the field. McCullough was unable to move and begged for water, which McJunkin gave him in a canteen procured from the Tory camp."[457]

James wrote "Captain McCulloch at the head of 50 British regulars was advancing to the aid of the Tories, Sumter remained in the wood near to the open ground, and Steene in returning from where he had been engaged, formed in his left flank... Steene commenced a galling fire upon the right flank of the enemy, which being soon after followed up by Sumter, McCulloch was mortally wounded and all his men cut off or taken.[458] They brought a second supply of ammunition to the Americans. Major Carden advanced from the fort to rescue McCulloch." Sumter called up his reserve, of McClure's force and "formed them as flankers on his right. They delivered a fire which enfiladed Carden."

The onrushing tide of partisans made the situation look desperate for the Loyalists. When Captain McCulloch of the British Legion was mortally wounded, he had turned over the command of the Legion to Captain Rousselet. In the intense fighting Major Carden lost his nerve, and turned over the command of the whole force to Rousselet, who withdrew to the house. Davie's cavalry pursued them.

Rousselet had his men form a hollow square in cleared ground, supported by the two fieldpieces. When the artillery opened up, the fighting slowed. Sumter's men refused to charge across open ground in the face of both artillery and musket fire. Davie's men concentrated their efforts on the stragglers around the flanks. A heavy, but ineffective fire was loosed upon the Loyalists, but it soon died off. Some of the Legion and the North Carolina Volunteers, that weren't in the British square, tried to reform to attack the partisans, but Davie and his dragoons moved behind the cover of the trees and charged them. The Loyalists thought the square had been defeated and they fled.

The battle had been heard in Rocky Mount, fifteen miles away. Colonel Turnbull sent some British Legion cavalry to reinforce Carden. The British Legion cavalry arrived on the battlefield, led by Captains Stewart and McDonald. They sounded the bugle, and ordered their men to extend their files in order to look larger than they were. They began to advance up the Camden road, driving the militia back. Davie returned from chasing off the Loyalists on the far side of the square, and had his men charge this new threat. The British cavalry were no match for Davie's dragoons. After a brief exchange of fire that killed one of the British Legion, they turned and fled the battlefield.

Lieutenant Alexander Moore had taken cover from the deadly rain of bullets and grapeshot. He looked up and saw Sumter sitting "perfectly erect on his horse, oblivious of his danger." Sumter looked down at him and said "If Tarleton charges I will meet him with my horse."

The Loyalist's 3-pounder on the right of the square continued firing into the trees where Captain Knox's men were located. Knox ordered his men to load their guns and wait until the artillery piece fired. After the cannon discharged Knox's men ran to within forty yards of the gun, and began firing on the crew. The Loyalists quickly retreated, and Knox captured the gun. Unfortunately none of Knox's men knew how to load the gun. The Loyalists rallied and charged with their bayonets, chasing Knox's men back into the cover of the trees.

Sumter wrote, "The action continued without intermission for three hours, men fainting with heat and drought." The Patriots were also almost out of ammunition. Sumter rode along the line and asked how much ammunition they had. They only had three rounds per man. William Dobein James wrote "Sumter was heard everywhere along the line animating his men while Irving called out "Give it to them boys! Give it to them hotter and hotter!"[459]

Sumter's men stayed under the cover of the trees, not wanting to venture out near the British square and their artillery fire. Colonel Robert Irwin of the North Carolina militia had his clothes pierced by four musket balls, but he was unhurt. Lieutenant John Brownfield had gone into action with his captain and 32 men. His captain was killed and only twelve men returned unhurt. Jamieson said, "Many American faces were so blackened by gun powder as to give them the appearance of Africans."

While the Loyalists watched, their camp was plundered. The partisans had not eaten in more than twelve hours, and to make matters worse; hundreds of them found the Loyalist's liquor stores in the camp and got drunk. These were mainly Sumter's men, who were too drunk to fight after drinking captured Jamaica rum.

Sumter took the paroles of the Loyalist officers that had been captured, and prepared litters for the wounded. While they were doing this Loyalist musicians played. At around one o'clock the partisans filed by the Loyalists and withdrew.

When the partisans began to leave, a cheer went up from the Loyalists "three cheers for King George!" The Patriot troops answered with "three cheers for Washington, the hero of American Liberty", and continued to stagger on.

Davie wrote, "the militia at length got into the line of march in three columns, Davies corps covering the rear, but as they were loaded with plunder, encumbered with their wounded friends, and many of them intoxicated, it is easy to conceive that this retreat could not be performed according to the rules of the most approved tacticks, However, under all these disadvantages they filed off unmolested along the front of the Enemy about 1 O'clock."[460]

Two days later both sides flew a flag of truce to collect the dead and wounded still left on the battlefield. John Adair had been in the 3rd South Carolina Rangers when Charlestown fell. He was able to avoid capture and he joined Sumter's partisans as a private. He was in fourteen battles in the war and he wrote "This I believe was the hardest fought battle during the war in the south."

Draper wrote, "Cornwallis was heard to say that no battle fell heavier on the British, considering the numbers engaged, the battle of Bunker Hill excepted." The Prince of Wales Regiment was no longer considered an effective fighting force, having been virtually wiped out. The British Legion had sixty-two of their men killed and wounded.[461] Many of the Loyalist militia simply fled from the field.

The British prisoners and wounded were taken to Charlotte to keep them out of striking distance of the British Regulars. Colonel McClure was carried to Charlotte, where he died two weeks later. Davie wrote that his corps "suffered much while tying their horses under a heavy fire from the Tories." He would not serve under Sumter again.

Captain Robert Craighead had been wounded in the shoulder, and left on the field. S.H. Walkup told Draper that Craighead "would have perished, but for the friendly aid of an Indian who carried him off, and took care of him."[462]

Sumter wrote, "The true cause of my not totally defeating them was the want of led. Having been obliged to make use of arms and ammunition taken from the enemy. I had about twenty kild, forty wounded, ten missing.[463] I took 73 prisoners, 40 odd of which were British, among whom were 3 commissioned officers. I brought off about 100 horses and 250 stands of arms."[464]

Sumter told McJunkin "We have a great victory, but it will scarcely even be heard of, as we are but a handful of raw militia, but if we had been commanded by a Continental officer, it would have sounded loud in our honor." Sumter was wrong about that.

Prior to the battle of Hanging Rock the prospect of peace with the Americans seemed very near. In the *Gentleman's Magazine* of 1780 it wrote of the division of the country upon a cease-fire. The New England States to the Connecticut River would go to the United States. Connecticut to the Delaware River, to include New York and New Jersey, some of Massachusetts and Connecticut, would go to England. From the Delaware River to the northern border of South Carolina would go to the United States, while South Carolina to Eastern Florida would go to England. West Florida would be given to Spain.

Even Governor Rutledge thought that Britain would grant independence to all, except North and South Carolina, and Georgia, and it would be accepted by the doomed Patriot cause. Hanging Rock changed all that. "After Hanging Rock nothing was heard of" a cease-fire again. [465]

Wofford's Iron Works, South Carolina [466]   **Skirmish**
8 August 1780

American Forces
Commanding Officer   Colonel Elijah Clarke
  State Militia   600 [467]
   Colonel Elijah Clarke
    Georgia Militia

Major Burwell Smith
Captain John Clark
Captain John Potts
Colonel Isaac Shelby
Over the Mountainmen
Major Charles Robertson
Captain Valentine Sevier
Colonel William Graham
North Carolina Partisan Rangers
South Fork Boys

Casualties   4 killed, 21 wounded [468]

Loyalist Forces
Commanding Officer   Captain James Dunlap
  Provincials
    Captain James Dunlap
      American Volunteers [469]   14
      Lieutenant Anthony Allaire
  South Carolina Loyalist Militia
    Ninety-Six District Brigade of Loyalist Militia
      Captain Alexander Chesney
      Major Daniel Plummer's Regiment [470]   130 [471]

Casualties   8 -34 killed or wounded, 2 -50 captured [472]

At the end of July Major Patrick Ferguson had mustered 1,800 men into the Loyalist militia. Ferguson's mission was to seek out any Rebel forces and destroy them. He created six regiments in the Ninety-Six District. These were the Long Cane Regiment under Colonel Richard King, the Stevens Creek Regiment under Colonel John Cotton, the Dutch Fork Regiment under Colonel Daniel Clary, the Spartan (or Upper) Regiment under Colonel Zacharias Gibbs, and Moses Kirkland's Regiment.

Cornwallis was having problems arming the new recruits, because when Charlestown surrendered a careless soldier had thrown a loaded musket into a stockpile of arms and ammunition. When the musket fired the powder magazine blew up, destroying

2,000 to 3,000 muskets. On top of that, in January the *Russian Merchant* sank off the coast of South Carolina, taking 4,000 muskets with it.

Lieutenant Colonel Thomas Brown decided that the best way to bring peace to the region was to hang any Whigs that had broken their parole. This was not uncommon, because if a soldier went back on his word he was allowed to be executed. In the Revolutionary War going back on your oath was not looked upon lightly. On June 5th Brown hanged five prisoners. Elijah Clarke and his Georgians decided that Brown's actions were a change in their terms of surrender, and took up arms again. Clarke began recruiting in South Carolina near Ninety-Six.

The Patriots had a force of 1,000 men led by Clarke, Isaac Shelby and William Graham. Four hundred of the Patriots were detached to establish a base of operations, and the remaining six hundred mounted men followed on the outside edges of Ferguson's column, waiting to strike. Clarke fell back to the Spartanburg area, about two miles west of Cedar Springs, to draw Ferguson towards him.

On the morning of August 7th scouts brought word to him that the British were within a half-mile of his camp. One of the Loyalists fired a gun by accident while they were closing in on Clarke's force. Clarke had his men quickly break camp and move to the Wofford Iron Works. The Loyalists arrived at the abandoned camp at 4 a.m., a half an hour after the Patriots had left.[473]

One of Shelby's commanders, Josiah Culbertson, had been out observing enemy movements.[474] He returned to Clarke's abandoned camp expecting to find Clarke still there. Upon his arrival he found Dunlap's Loyalists there. Culbertson didn't panic. Instead he calmly rode through the camp, observing the preparations of the Loyalists to attack Clarke's force. The Loyalists didn't pay much attention to Culbertson, thinking that he was one of their own. As soon as Culbertson was out of the camp he raced his horse to Clarke's position, and warned him of the impending attack.[475]

Ferguson received intelligence that Clarke's supply wagons were only three miles in front of Cedar Springs, and he sent Captain

Dunlap with fourteen mounted American Volunteers and 130 militia, to take the wagons. Along the way Dunlap saw three of Clarke's men and chased after them. He was able to capture two of the horsemen, and pursued the last man into the center of Clarke's camp at the Iron Works.

The Patriots were expecting them, and had set up an ambush. Shelby and Clarke's riflemen fired a volley, emptying many of the saddles. The Loyalists charged the riflemen and a vicious hand-to-hand combat ensued. Clarke received two saber wounds, one on the back of his neck and one on his head. His neck stock buckle stopped the neck wound from being fatal. For a few minutes Clarke was captured by two of Dunlap's men, but he knocked them down and was able to escape. Dunlap was slightly wounded in the fight.

The attack lasted about a half an hour, until Dunlap's mounted riflemen were driven back in a series of running fights. Dunlap's force was pursued for a mile before the action was broken off. Clarke's men returned to their lines at the Old Iron Works, with fifty prisoners.

Dunlap retreated until he rendezvoused with Ferguson and his main army. The combined British units moved to the Iron Works to attack the Patriots, but Clarke and Shelby began a hasty and organized withdrawal. The backwoodsmen continued to form on tactically superior ground, slowing Ferguson's advance so much that the prisoners from the Iron Works went beyond Ferguson's reach. In a last defiant gesture Clarke and Shelby formed their men on a ridge, and ridiculed the Loyalist Forces. The Loyalists held the field, but they had many more casualties than the backwoodsmen.[476]

Little Lynches Creek, South Carolina **Skirmish**
Camden Campaign
8 - 11 August 1780

Following the fall of Charlestown Cornwallis pushed into the backcountry of South Carolina and established a chain of posts from Augusta to Georgetown. Cornwallis's plan was to systematically occupy the enemy's territory, subduing the local population. At the post in Augusta he had placed Colonel Thomas Brown and his King's Rangers; at Ninety-Six was Lieutenant Colonel Nisbet Balfour and three regiments of Provincials; at Camden was Lord Rawdon, the Volunteers of Ireland and two regiments of Regulars; and Colonel George Turnbull was at Rocky Mount with Delancey's Brigade. Tarleton and his Legion were detached to hunt down bands of Rebels in the Low Country, near Georgetown.

Major General De Kalb took control of what remained of the Continental Southern Department's troops.[477] On April 16th De Kalb marched from Morristown, New Jersey, with 1,400 men. These were six Maryland and Delaware Continental regiments, and the 1st Continental Artillery. With the army were their wives, children, laundresses and other camp followers. De Kalb had hoped to be reinforced by state authorities along the way, but little help was given to him. His army had only gone as far as Granville County in North Carolina, when news came of the surrender in Charlestown. De Kalb's army had no horses or wagons, and the men had to carry everything on their backs. Sick and hungry, his army marched on to Buffalo Ford on the Deep River. They made their camp there, 125 miles northeast of Camden.

The state of North Carolina did not welcome De Kalb's army. Former Governor Richard Caswell was the brigadier general of the militia, and he refused to join, cooperate or communicate regularly with De Kalb. The Maryland and Delaware Continentals were abandoned and left to starve by the people they were sent to aid. Some hope arrived when it was learned that the army would soon be placed under the command of Major General Horatio Gates.

Gates had the good fortune in 1777 to be in command at Saratoga when Burgoyne's army had been captured. Gates took the credit for a victory won by Daniel Morgan and Benedict Arnold. Congress looked upon Gates as a successor to Washington, who had lost Philadelphia to Howe. Gates alienated Washington by becoming part of the Conway Cabal, an unsuccessful attempt to replace Washington. In April 1778 Congress appointed Gates to the command of the Northern Department, but he was still under Washington. Washington offered him the command against the

Iroquois Indians, but Gates declined. In November 1779 Gates wrote to Congress about invading Canada, and also of taking command of the Southern Department.

Congress appointed Gates to the Southern Department on June 13, 1780, hoping that the militia would rally to him, as the New England militia had in 1777. General Charles Lee warned him upon his parting, "Beware lest you exchange your Northern laurels for Southern willows."

When Gates arrived in Hillsborough, North Carolina on July 13th, he wrote a letter relieving De Kalb of his command. Gates was angered by the condition he found the army in, and sent letters to North Carolina, Delaware, Maryland and the Congress. Gates was amazed that there were no supply depots for the army. On July 25th Gates linked up with his army of 1,500 hungry men. He ignored the condition of his army and "ordered that the troops to hold themselves in readiness to march at a moments warning." He assured the men that rum and rations were on their way. Within 72 hours of his arrival Gates had his army marching south to attack the British. This confused his officers and even appeared to some to be treasonous.

Thomas Pinckney wrote "When Gen[l] Gates was informed of this state of affairs he said at once — We may then as well move forward & starve, as starve lying here: and immediately gave the order to march. I believe it was his intention when in his power to form a depot at Charlotte to which place he sent off a part of his baggage & the women of the army, from Lynch's Creek."

When the army was east of Mask's Ferry, De Kalb and Colonel Otho Williams proposed an alternate route that would go through Salisbury, Charlotte and the Waxhaws. This was an anti-British, rich, farming countryside. Gates put off the officers by promising to bring up the matter at a meeting of the general officers when the army stopped for lunch. That meeting was never held. Gates decided instead to go directly on to Camden, through the Sand Hills, a poor, barren country that ran through Cross Creek, one of the most pro-British areas in the Carolinas.[478] Along the route to Mask's Ferry the soldiers found none of the promised rum or rations, and the North Carolina Militia had stripped the area of food. Brigadier General Stevens called this area "the desert." Fortunately a small amount of Indian corn was found at Mask's Ferry, which they ground into one meal for the army.

None of the officers openly questioned Gates' orders. He finally explained his actions to Otho Williams. Gates knew that Caswell and his militia would not join his army, so he decided to move his army to Caswell's force. He knew that if the militia were defeated in a battle before he could unite their forces, he would not be able to muster them again. This would be another defeat that the United States may not be able to recover from. Gates had thought Caswell was still at Mask's Ferry, but Caswell had moved his militia to attack to British post at Lynches Ferry. Gates moved his army in that direction, hoping to save the Patriot militia from themselves.

Lieutenant Colonel Charles Armand joined Gates from Wilmington, with his Legion of Horse and Foot. Armand was a French volunteer, who had a cavalry force that included the few survivors of Pulaski's Legion, and a large number of recruited Hessian prisoners of war. Charles Lee did not care for Armand's Legion, calling them a body of cavalry consisting of foreigners and deserters. General Washington stated Armand was a very gallant and excellent officer.

In Gates' military career he had not had much experience using cavalry. In the battles around Saratoga he had defeated the British army without cavalry. What he didn't know was that in the South every man rode whenever possible. Every Continental dragoon regiment would serve in the Carolinas, and most Patriot militia was mounted. The only way to outmaneuver the enemy was to put the cavalry to full use. Gates did not use the cavalry the way they should have. In one instance he had the cavalry horses pull the wagons through the marshes along the route.

A lack of order and discipline plagued the officers. Wagon masters had to be told repeatedly not to let anyone ride on the wagons, especially the women. Baggage was tossed aside as the waggoners ignored these orders. There was ongoing plundering of supplies. To control the men the regimental commanders were required to conduct roll calls four times each day. The soldiers were told that if they were absent from the formation they would "suffer death."

At the end of July Colonel Charles Porterfield joined Gates' army with his light infantry troops.[479] Virginians and North Carolinians who had escaped Charlestown and the Waxhaws came in next.

Crossing into South Carolina Gates' army found the fields of green corn growing on the banks of the Pee Dee River, and the men ate their fill. These were the "5,000 hills of green corn" of farmer Benjamin Thurman. The men also found Thurman's eight hundred unripe peach and apple orchards. The officers resorted to using their hair powder to thicken soup. The result was diarrhea to add to all the other miseries of the march. The men were soon fatigued and weak and even talked of mutiny as they marched on, covering seventeen to eighteen miles a day.

On August 4th Francis Marion rode into camp. Williams wrote "Colonel Marion, a gentleman of South Carolina, had been with the army a few days, attended by a very few followers, distinguished by small black leather caps and the wretchedness of their attire; their number did not exceed twenty men and boys, some white, some black, and all mounted, but most of them miserably equipped; their appearance was in fact so burlesque that it was with much difficulty the diversion of the regular soldiery was restrained by the officers; and the general himself was glad of an opportunity of detaching Colonel Marion, at his own instance, towards the interior of South Carolina, with orders to watch the motions of the enemy and furnish intelligence."

Gates had decided that Marion's comical army was of no use to him in the swamps of South Carolina, and sent them out to gather intelligence and deliver a proclamation to the citizens that he would protect them from "acts of barbarity and devastation."

At Deep Creek foragers brought in enough old corn for the men, grinding it with their little hand mills, to have about a half a pound of cornmeal apiece. They used the flour to make johnny cakes, to go with their ration of half a pound of stringy beef and mush for breakfast. The officers allowed the men this "luxury" to stop a threatened mutiny. Williams was amazed at the change in the men once they received rations. He wrote, "the mill was set to work, and as soon as a mess of meal was ground it was delivered out to the men; and so, in rotation, they were all served in the course of a few hours — more poor cattle were sacrificed — the camp kettles were all engaged — the men were busy but silent until they had each taken his repast; and then all was again content, cheerfulness and mirth. It was as astonishing as it was pleasing to observe the transition."

Lord Rawdon had learned of the battle at Hanging Rock, and thought that Sumter had captured the post. He knew that Gates's Army was approaching Camden, but he felt that Sumter's mounted force was a larger threat to the British post. Rawdon called upon all the male inhabitants in and around Camden to take up arms against the Rebel army. Some of the inhabitants did serve in the Loyalist militia, but 160 of the town's residents refused. These men were thrown into a small common jail. Twenty men of the highest standing were manacled to the walls. Rawdon's army marched to the west branch of Lynches Creek towards Granny's Quarter. Rawdon learned the next morning that Sumter had been defeated at Hanging Rock by the British Legion infantry, and the post was still in British hands. He moved immediately to occupy the bridge across the western branch of Lynches Creek.

On August 7th Gates rendezvoused with 2,100 North Carolinians under Brigadier General Richard Caswell. Both commanders were cordial to each other. Williams wrote "The reception was gracious, and the general and his suite were regaled with wine and other novelties, exquisitely grateful and pleasingly exhilarating; but, a man must have been intoxicated, not to perceive the confusion which prevailed in the camp — tables, chairs, bedsteads, benches, and many other articles of heavy and cumbrous household stuff, were scattered before the tent doors in great disorder."

The army marched toward Lynches Creek the next day. Williams wrote that the army was "encumbered with a great multitude of women and children, with immense amount of baggage." Major Dean was ordered to escort these women and children back to Charlotte. Most of them remained behind to witness the battle of Camden because there were no wagons to take them back. Caswell had been preparing to attack the British outpost at Lynch's Creek, and now the combined forces continued marching towards that objective. What they didn't know was that the British had evacuated their post and moved back to Little Lynches Creek, where they were met with reinforcements from Camden.

Lord Rawdon had posted the Volunteers of Ireland, the 33rd Regiment, 23rd Regiment of Welch Fusiliers, and the 71st Regiment Highlanders at the creek. Rawdon wanted delay the approach of Gates while he waited for British cavalry from Charleston, and light infantry from Ninety-Six. He was outnumbered by four to one, and if he attacked, Gates would have easily defeated him. He did not want to retreat to defend Camden, since Gates would be able to capture the British stores there.

Gates made a move as if to flank the British defenses located there. A skirmish followed when Armand's Legion drove in some of the British sentries, but the creek banks were too steep, muddy and slippery and the swamp was too wide. A cornet of Armand's Legion was captured in this skirmish. Gates did not want to make a frontal attack on the British, remarking that to do so would be "taking the bull by the horns." The Patriots did engage the British sentries with long-range rifle fire, but did not hit any of them. After a two day wait, Gates moved up the creek and crossed over.

Since he had been flanked, and not wanting to risk a major fight, Lord Rawdon withdrew back to Camden, and set up camp in Log Town. Rawdon later wrote that his main objective at the time of Lynches Creek was to slow down Gates's army, so that Cornwallis would have time to collect reinforcements, with the option of attacking if circumstances were sufficiently favorable.

Neither army could see each other across the river, due to the thick woods. Neither side wanted to attack, for fear of being detected and ambushed. Rawdon had the upper hand when he discovered a pass through the swamp that came out two miles from the Patriot camp. He did not want to attack since he was outnumbered, but he wanted to delay Gates until Cornwallis arrived. In the end Rugeley was successful. Gates could not move across the river, so he had to move his army to Rugeley's Mill by way of Hanging Rock. This took him thirty-five miles from Camden, where before he had only been fifteen miles away at Lynches River.

Thomas Pinckney wrote that Gates's "principal reliance for intelligence was in the officers of the country acting in the neighborhood particularly in Gen[l] Sumpter for the west side of the Wateree, Col Hampton for upper Pedee & Gen[l] Marion in lower Pedee & Santee."

Gates arrived there on August 15th and waited for the arrival of Sumter and his partisans. Tarleton wrote that Gates might have crushed British opposition if he had flanked Lord Rawdon, and marched into the lightly defended Camden. Tarleton wrote in his memoirs that Gates could have marched around Rawdon up a creek bed and "he could have passed Lord Rawdon's flank, and reached Charleston; which would have been an easy conquest, and a fatal blow to the British."

Rawdon answered the criticism in an 1810 letter when he wrote, "Tarleton, with a childish pretension to Generalship, censures me for not having thus collected my troops at Camden, & arraigns Gates for incapacity in not comprehending that the getting round me & destroying my magazines must be fatal... Gates did know, namely, that there was no turning my right flank without going fifty miles down Lynche's Creek, there was no turning my left by a shorter process than heading the Creek & getting into the other road above Hanging Rock. Lynches Creek runs thro' swamps of perhaps a mile in breadth on each side; impenetrable, except where a causeway has been made at the passing-places on the great road." [480]

Cary's Fort, South Carolina [481]   **Skirmish**
Camden Campaign
9 August 1780

After the battle of Hanging Rock Sumter wrote to Gates, and told him that "Both British and Tories are panic struck, and seem well convinced that fifteen hundred men can go through any part of the State with ease, this will not be the case ten or fifteen days hence."

Sumter also learned that a "rich convoy of stores, consisting of 42 wagons, with a proper escort, coming from Ninety-Six to the army at Camden and that they would soon reach the ferry one mile below." Sumter urged Gates to strike into South Carolina with a small force, and take possession of the high hills and Nelson's ferry. The ferry commanded both the water and land routes to Charlestown. Sumter figured that 1,200 to 1,500 men would be enough for this purpose.

Gates did send Sumter three hundred Maryland Continentals and some artillery to cut off any British reinforcements from Camden to Charlestown. While Sumter waited for the Maryland troops he marched on Hanging Rock again, to determine the strength of the post. He found the post abandoned by Turnbull, who had moved his men into Camden. Sumter followed with his army, and began occupying crossing sites for Gates' army on the Wateree River, above and below Camden.

A leading Loyalist officer, Lieutenant Colonel James Cary, had built a fort that guarded the main ferry crossing a mile from Camden. It was located on the west bank of the Wateree River, on McCaa's Hill. The fort was built on his plantation that was called Cary's Place.[482] Cary had originally supported the Patriot cause, and had provided slaves, along with Joseph Kershaw, to help construct defenses against the British siege of 1780.

When Cornwallis marched towards Camden some of the residents met him at the town limits, and offered their services. Cary offered his, and was given a commission in the Royal Militia. Thirty-seven Loyalists of Cary's Regiment garrisoned the small redoubt that guarded the ferry that crossed to the eastern entrance to Camden.

Sumter sent Colonel Thomas Taylor and Edward Lacey to Cary's Fort to determine if it could be taken. Taylor surprised the fort, and found it's whole garrison asleep. The partisans quickly rushed in the fort and captured all of the occupants, along with thirty-six wagons with supplies, including a load of rum.

One of Taylor's men, "a chunky, plucky little man" named Johnny Dinkins chased "Carey around a tree at the fort, with his gun cocked, to get a shot at the Tory leader. John Taylor ordered him desist."[483]

Taylor learned that a supply train was coming to the fort from Ninety-Six, and since all of his men looked like the Loyalist militia he set a trap. By the time the Loyalists in the convoy knew differently, they were prisoners. Taylor had captured thirty-two wagons of supplies from Augusta, and seventy more men from the 71st Highlanders, mostly ill from disease. [484]

Sumter's entire force moved in and occupied Cary's Fort. He was supposed to supply Gates' army with provisions, but he didn't know where Gates was going. Williams wrote "the obscure route the army had marched, actually kept their friends ignorant of their movements."

Not all of Cary's men had been captured. Sumter wrote "the boats are all upon the opposite side of the river; the ground upon this side very bad. The enemy keeps up a constant fire, but I have received no damage yet."

Lieutenant Hicks Chappell was sent off with two other men to determine if there were any British reinforcements that were marching from Ninety-Six to Camden. They found fifty British marching down the road. They had placed their arms in six wagons. Chappell "hid his men until the British army came up, they rushed them and took the whole party without firing a shot." Sumter wrote, "Many of the prisoners are sick."

On the 11th Sumter wrote that he had taken possession of all the crossing points over the Wateree River, and that all the British guards had been ordered into Camden. He reported that the British Regulars in Camden did not exceed 1,200 men, and the militia was less than one thousand. These were "generally sickly and dispirited", and that a reinforcement of five hundred was expected from Charlestown to arrive in two days. Sumter's information was accurate. Sumter captured Elias Langham, a sergeant with the British artillery, and he reported that on August 11th the force at Camden was 2,365 men. Of these 1,770 were British Regulars. [485]

Brown's Creek, South Carolina   **Skirmish**
12 August 1780

This is a skirmish that is mentioned in Alexander Chesney's Journal. After the fight at Wofford's Iron Works Chesney moved with the Loyalist militia "down towards the Fish Dam Ford on Broad River." He wrote that at Brown's Creek "there was a fight near the mouth of Brown's Creek with Neale's Militia where we, made many prisoners." This was the New Acquisition Militia of Andrew Neal, Sr. It was not the same Andrew Neal who had been killed twelve days earlier at Rocky Mount. That was Andrew Neal, Jr., his son.[486]

Parker's Old Field, South Carolina [487]   **Skirmish**
Battle of Camden
16 August 1780

American Forces
Commanding Officer   Lieutenant Colonel Charles Porterfield
   Continentals
      Lieutenant Chevalier Georges, chevalier de Fontevieux
         Armand's Legion of Horse and Foot
           Dragoons   60
   State Troops
      Lieutenant Colonel Charles Porterfield
         Light Infantry   168
           Captain Thomas H. Drew
              Virginia Light Infantry [488]   200
           Major John Armstrong
              North Carolina Light Infantry   68

British Forces
Commanding Officer   Lieutenant Colonel Banastre Tarleton
  British Regulars
    Captain Charles Campbell
      Light Infantry
        Captain Charles Campbell
        71st Regiment of Foot (Fraser's Highlanders)
          Light Company   70
        Lieutenant John Skinner
        16th Regiment of Foot
          Light Company   78
      Captain Forbes Champagné
      23rd Regiment of Foot (Royal Welch Fusiliers) Unknown
      Lieutenant Colonel James Webster
        33rd Regiment of Foot   Unknown number
  Provincials
    Lieutenant Jeremiah Donovan
      British Legion
        Mounted Infantry   20
        Cavalry   20

When Cornwallis learned of the attacks on Hanging Rock and Rocky Mount he began his march from Charlestown to Camden. He continued to get exaggerated reports of the size of Gates' army as it marched through North Carolina. Cornwallis knew he had to keep Camden, or else he may lose Charlestown. He expected to be joined by a party of the 63rd Regiment, who had seized horses on the march up from Charlestown. These men would ride on to Camden and help guard the town during the impending battle. Cornwallis arrived at Camden on the night of August 13th. He ordered the British garrisons to withdraw from Hanging Rock, Rugeley's Mill and Rocky Mount. Four other companies were brought in from Ninety-Six. He was not a timid field commander and did not plan to wait for Gates to get any stronger. He resolved to force a battle with Gates.

After eighteen days of walking, and eating very little, the army of Gates camped ten miles north of Camden, near Clermont, the plantation of Loyalist Colonel Henry Rugeley. Seven hundred Virginia militiamen, under General Edward Stevens, arrived on August 14th. What Gates didn't find at Rugeley's Mill was Sumter, or any provisions. All the army found at the mill was molasses. Sumter had not known where Gates and his army were going, so he did not know where to send the supplies.

On the afternoon of August 15th Cornwallis sent Tarleton out to gain intelligence on Gates' army. Tarleton intercepted a Patriot patrol and brought back three prisoners. They told Cornwallis that their unit was to join Gates as he marched on Camden that night. Cornwallis asked Rawdon for his opinion on what should happen next. Rawdon told him that Camden was unsuitable to meet an enemy and that as soon as Gates was within an easy march, the army should move out and attack him. Rawdon told him that he could strike him at Kingsley's Plantation, and told him that his spies had found a trail away from the main road, where there was a possibility that they could approach Gates' flank undetected.

Cornwallis decided to leave the town of Camden under the command of Major McArthur, with a small number of provincials, militia and the weakest convalescents of his army. Stedman wrote, "Nearly eight hundred British troops were sick at Camden. The number of those who were really effective, amounted to something more than two thousand, including officers, of whom about fifteen hundred were regulars, or belonged to established provincial corps, and the rest, militia and refugees from North Carolina." The provincials were Major Carden and his Prince of Wales American Regiment. After the battle at Hanging Rock they could only muster fifty-one men present for duty, and no officers.

Cornwallis's move was daring, because Gates had a numerically superior force that was marching towards Camden. Gates had protected his flanks by sending Harrington to the west, on the upper Pee Dee River; Marion to the east, to the lower Pee Dee, and Sumter was on the west side of the Wateree. If Cornwallis was not able to act quickly, and decisively, he could be surrounded and defeated, just like Gates had defeated Burgoyne at Saratoga.

Sumter had sent a message asking for reinforcements to attack the British detachment at Hanging Rock. Gates did not expect an attack that soon, and detached 300 North Carolina militia, 100 Maryland Continentals and two guns under the command of Colonel Woolford. This was 10% of his force, and 25% of his artillery. Gates further depleted his force by ordering Captain Hawkins Martin to go with his cavalry troop of volunteers to St. Bartholomew's Parish, to enlist as many men as he could. Gates did not think the British would attack, since Lord Rawdon had retreated from him with a smaller force. From Sumter he learned that the British only had from 1,200 to 2,000 men, but this was before Cornwallis had brought reinforcements.

That night Gates ordered his men to move their camp closer to the British in Camden. Some accounts mistakenly state that Gates was marching to attack Camden. Thomas Pinckney, Gates's Aide de Camp, wrote that he had asked whether or not they were to attack the British at Camden. "He answered, No! assigning as his reason the number of Militia who formed the bulk of his army."

Gates' intention was to occupy the position five and a half miles north of Camden, at the ford on Saunder's Creek. He would prepare defensive works there. The "great road" leading to Camden was only fordable at this strategic location. Gates chose ground that would require the enemy to attack him in a defensive position. An indicator that had had not planned to attack Camden was because he had not left his baggage behind, but had it move with his army. His army now consisted of about 4,100 men, but he thought he had 7,000. When Colonel Williams showed Gates the true numbers, he said that it was on no great significance and that "there are enough for our purpose."

Thomas Pinckney wrote, "That purpose he did not explain to him, but it certainly could not have been to attack a fortified post, we garrisoned. They were however sufficient to have repulsed any force the Enemy had in the vicinity, if so posted as to have rendered the Militia force efficient."

For the evening meal that night the Patriots were issued rations that were hastily eaten. Williams wrote "One gill of molasses per man and a full ration of corn meal and meat were issued to the army previous to their march...But at this time a hasty meal of quick-baked bread and fresh meat, with a dessert of molasses mixed with mush or dumplings, operated so cathartically as to disorder very many of the men, who were breaking ranks all night, and were certainly much debilitated before the action commenced in the morning."

At 8 o'clock that night the Continental army began to march towards Camden. Gates had expected some encounter with British forces and had given the order that "The troops will observe the profoundest silence upon the march, and any soldier who offers to fire without the command of his officer must instantly be put to death."

Cornwallis knew that the best defense was a good offense, and he formed his men. John Robert Shaw, of the 33rd Regiment, wrote that Cornwallis said, "Now my brave soldiers, now an opportunity is offered for displaying your valor, and sustaining the glory of British arms; -- all you who are willing to face your enemies; -- all you who are ambitious of military fame stand forward; for there are eight or ten to one coming against [us]; let the men who cannot bear the smell of gunpowder stand back and all you who are determined to conquer or die turn out. Accordingly we all turned out except a few who were left to guard the sick and military stores. We marched out of Camden about 10 o'clock at night, August 15, 1780; in being the intention of our general to surprise the enemy in his quarters at Ruggles."

Stedman wrote "The front division, commanded by lieutenant-colonel Webster, consisted of four companies of light-infantry, and the twenty-third and thirty-third regiments, preceded by twenty cavalry, and as many mounted infantry of the legion, as an advanced guard. The center division consisted of the volunteers of Ireland, the legion infantry, Hamilton's North Carolina regiment, and colonel Bryan's refugees, under the command of lord Rawdon. And the two battalions of the seventy first regiment followed as a reserve; the dragoons of the legion forming the rear-guard."

Marching twice as fast as the Patriots, he was able to march the eight miles to Saunder's Creek in four hours. The British had become disorganized at the crossing of the creek, but they were quickly put back in order and continued the march. The vanguard of the British force was forty men of the British Legion, under the command of Lieutenant Jeremiah Donovan, but only half of them were mounted.

Leading the advance of the Continentals was Chevalier de Fontevieux, of Armand's Legion, with sixty dragoons. On the Patriot's right flank, in the woods, was Porterfield's Virginia Light Infantry of 100 men, marching in "Indian file." On the left were sixty-eight men of Major John Armstrong's North Carolina Light Infantry, doing the same. Guilford Dudley wrote that the Light Infantry "moved by files through the open piney woods plain, 25 yards out of the great Waxhaw road; the right flank headed by Col. Porterfield (commandant of the whole corps in person,) whilst Capt. Drew with his Virginia regulars, (about 55, and mostly raw levies,) composed the leading company of that flank. The left flank of infantry, under the care of Major Armstrong, moved in like order, having the Halifax volunteers, headed by Capt. Lockhart, for his leading company. Col. Armand, with his dragoons in column, occupied the road which was here a dead level and very spacious."

Colonel Johann Senf and Porterfield had done a reconnaissance earlier, and "returned & reported that they had found a position 5 or 6 miles in advance, with a thick swamp on the right, a deep Creek in front & thick low ground also on the left; but this flank not being so well secured as the right, Col: Senf proposed to strengthen it with a Redoubt or two & an Abbatis." [489]

Gates had given orders to Armand, "In the case of an attack by the enemy's cavalry in front, the light infantry upon each flank will instantly move up and give and continue the most galling fire upon the enemy's horse. This will enable Colonel Armand not only to support the shock of the enemy's charge, but finally to rout him.

The Colonel will therefore consider the order to stand the attack of the enemy's cavalry, be their numbers what it may, as positive."

The men marched through the humid Carolina night, with only the sound of loose equipment occasionally clanking. The dust kicked up from thousands of feet would have made breathing difficult, and the sand from the road would have collected in the sweat soaked uniforms. It was to the surprise of both sides when they met at 2:30 in the morning, on a slight rise near Saunder's Creek called Parker's Old Field.[490] The British Legion hailed Armand's Legion then spotted Porterfield's light infantry on the flank by the light of a full moon. Dudley wrote "The moon was at full and shone beautifully; not a breath of air was stirring, nor a cloud to be seen big as a man's hand. Consequently, we could see to fight in the open piney wood plains, destitute of brush wood almost, as well in the night as in the day."

A single pistol shot from Armand's lead horseman rang out in the night. The trooper rode quickly back to the security of the light infantry, 300 yards to their rear. Armand rode over to Porterfield and told him in a whisper, "there is the enemy, Sir — must I charge him." Porterfield replied, "by all means, Sir." Armand rode back to his troops in the road, but it was too late,

Tarleton's Legion charged first. He "came on at the top of his speed, every officer and soldier with the yell of an Indian savage — at every leap their horses took, crying out, "charge, charge, charge," so that their own voices and the echoes resounded in every direction through the pine forest."

Armand's men held their ground, and emptied their pistols at the charging horsemen. They then drew their sabers and rode at the enemy. Armand ordered his right flank to come up on line, instead of retreating. He knew that Porterfield's light infantry was on their flanks and would protect them.

Dudley wrote, "Porterfield ordered, "Halt, face to the road and fire." This order was executed with the velocity of a flash of lightning, spreading from right to left, and again the piney forest resounded with the thunder of our musketry; whilst the astonished British dragoons, looking only straight before them along the road, counting no doubt with certainty upon extirpating Armand's handful of cavalry, and not dreaming that they were flanked on the right and on the left by our infantry, within point-blank shot, drew up, wheeled their horses, and retreating with the utmost precipitation, were out of our reach before we could possibly ram down another cartridge."

The light infantry on both sides of the road caught Tarleton's Legion in a crossfire, and forced them to withdraw. The Virginia militia with Porterfield had never been in a fight and fled back to the main body on the road. Armand's Legion retreated with them, causing confusion for a few minutes. Disorder reigned throughout the 1st Maryland Regiment, but Porterfield's light infantry stopped any possible advantage the British forces may have been able to use.

Lieutenant Donovan had been wounded but he would recover. Gates and his staff rode up to the head of the column, and "remained there until the firing grew slack and the troops were beginning to be formed."

The British 23rd and 33rd infantry moved up the road in column, and deployed across the road to counter the attack by the flanking Patriot light infantry. Armstrong's men fell back to the main army, leaving Porterfield's force and Lockhart's Halifax militia to face the British army alone. Porterfield would have normally fallen back sooner, but the British advance force had captured one of the Continental artillery pieces.

After twenty minutes of disorganized fighting around the broken artillery piece in a wagon, both sides fell back to regroup.[491] Porterfield ordered a retreat back to the main body. He had lost his horseman's hat, and most of his troops in the withdrawal.

Dudley wrote "At this fire, Porterfield with horse's head reined directly to the enemy, received a horrid wound in his left leg, a little before the knee, which shattered it to pieces, when falling forward upon the pommel of his saddle, he directed Captain Drew, who was close by his side, to order a retreat, which was done in a very deliberate tone of voice by the Captain, and instantly our little band retreated obliquely from the road, which was wholly secluded from us by the enemy."

William Seymour wrote in his journal that it was "a very hot fire, in which the infantry and advance picquet suffered very much." Dudley was there when Porterfield was wounded, and he later wrote that "Locking my left arm in the Colonel's right to support him in the saddle on that side, and having completely turned his horse, we received another hot fire from the enemy directed solely upon us at the distance of thirty yards or less. Upon this the Colonel's horse, very docile and standing fire with the same steady composure as his master, having no doubt been grazed by a ball which he sensibly felt, reared, plunged forward and dropt his rider on the spot, who had a severe fall in his maimed condition, and had liked to have dragged me off my horse with our arms locked, and the horse going off with his accoutrements at the top of his speed, followed the track of the retreating soldiers. At the very instant Porterfield's horse reared and plunged forward, Captain Drew fell prostrate on his face, and that to naturally, that I entertained no doubt but he was killed. The Captain, however, receiving no injury, and being an active, nimble little man, was presently on his feet, and wheeling around the stern of my horse, was in a moment out of sight. Thus left entirely alone with the Colonel, who was flat upon the ground with his head towards the enemy and his shattered leg doubled under him, entreating me not to leave him, I sprang from my horse and seizing him with an Indian hug around the waist, by a sudden effort jerked him up upon his well leg. Then again the Colonel, in the most pathetic manner, apparently dreading instant death, brave as he was, or captivity, entreated me, as he had done before, not to forsake him; the blood, in the meantime gushing out of his wound in a torrent as big as a large straw or goose-quill, which presently overflowed the top of his large, loose boot and dyed the ground all around him. Pale as a piece of bleached linen, and ready to faint with the loss of blood and the anguish of his wound, he made another appeal to my feelings."

Dudley did not leave him, even though they were now alone on the battlefield. Dudley tried to throw Porterfield on his horse, without attracting any attention from the British on the road. Unfortunately Porterfield was 6 feet 2 inches tall and weighed 210 pounds. Dudley could not get him on the horse. He wrote "In this dilemma I ceased to make any further efforts to throw him upon my horse and resolved calmly to wait the result whatever it might be, nor did Porterfield attempt to give me any direction in this emergency, or express an opinion how I ought to act for his relief or my own preservation, but appeared to be entirely resigned to whatever fate might await him in his exhausted and fainting condition."

Dudley was able to see "two men at the distance of about 150 yards in my rear, running back with great speed, half bent and with trailed arms, towards where they supposed the main body, under Gates, was by this time halted. Although I could not at the moment divine where these men came from, I yet, nevertheless, with joy as well as surprise recognized them for American troops by their garb, their manner and by their clumsy wooden canteens slung over their shoulders upon their blankets and knapsacks." At first the troops would not halt but Dudley yelled, "by G-d, come and help me away with Colonel Porterfield." The two men laid down their muskets and fixed bayonets by my direction, than they seized Porterfield by both his arms" and placed him on Dudley's saddle. The three men were able to carry Porterfield off while British "balls whizzed along six feet above our heads, while others struck the ground before they reached us, and rebounding passed off without doing much injury that I could perceive."

The three men moved Porterfield to some persimmon trees and bandaged Porterfield's leg with a piece of cloth, cut from one of the soldier's blanket. Dudley splinted the leg by cutting "a bundle of twigs 10 or 12 inches in length and hastily trim them to apply all around the Colonel's leg before the bandage was wrapped over them." After the bandage was put on it became drenched in blood, but the trio moved on for another mile and a half to an open field, where Dudley laid the colonel down to await the dawn. Back on the road Gates discovered that he had stumbled into Cornwallis and his 2,000 British Regulars. Thomas Pinckney wrote, "Armand approached the General and urged him to retire, because the firing was pretty smart where he was — Gates refused, saying it was his business to be where his orders might be necessary."

Gates retreated and took up a defensive position across the Charlotte road, deciding to wait until morning to attack. Lord Rawdon dismounted and felt the coats of the dead Patriots in the road. He suspected that they may have been Continentals, due to the way they were fighting and their clothing proved his assumption. He informed Cornwallis of his discovery, and advised him that they were on good ground to fight a larger force, since the swamps to either side protected their flanks. Cornwallis decided to wait to daylight before attacking.[492]

Camden, South Carolina [493]   **Battle**
16 August 1780

American Forces
Commanding Officer   Major General Horatio Gates
Major General Johann-Alexandre von Robaii, Baron De Kalb [494]
    Continentals
        Major General William Smallwood
            1st Maryland Brigade   400
                Lieutenant Colonel Peter Adams
                    1st Maryland Regiment
                    Major Levin Winder
                    Captain George Anderson
                    Captain William Bruce
                Major Archibald Anderson
                    3rd Maryland Regiment
                    Captain Jacob Brice
                    Captain John Smith
                    Captain Lilburn Williams
                Colonel William Richardson
                    5th Maryland Regiment
                    Captain Perry Benson
                    Captain Richard Bird
                    Captain James Bruff

Captain Adam Hoops [495]
Colonel John Gunby
7th Maryland Regiment
Captain Jonathan Morris
Brigadier General Mordecai Gist
2nd Maryland Brigade   500
Lieutenant Colonel John Eager Howard
2nd Maryland Regiment
Captain-Lieutenant John Hardman
Captain Edward Duvall
Captain John Gassaway
Colonel Josiah Carvel Hall
4th Maryland Regiment
Captain Edward Oldham
Lieutenant Colonel Benjamin Ford
6th Maryland Regiment
Captain-Lieutenant Nathan Williams
Captain James Somervell
Lieutenant Colonel Joseph Vaughan
The Delaware Regiment   280
Major John Patton
1st Company
Captain Robert Kirkwood
2nd Company
Captain John Rhodes
3rd Company
Captain John Learmonth
6th Company
Captain Peter Jacquett
8th Company
Captain George Purvis
Additional Company
Lieutenant Colonel Charles Tuffin Armand
Armand's Legion of Horse and Foot [496]
Count Nicholas Dietrich, Baron von Ottendorff
Cavalry   60

Lieutenant Richard Heard
1st Troop Dragoons
Captain Henry Bedkin
2nd Troop Dragoons
Captain Jerome Le Brun de Bellecour
3rd Troop Dragoons
Infantry
Captain Jost Driesbach
Corps of German Volunteers   40
Captain Jacob Baner
Chasseur Company   20
Captain Edmund Read   62
Major Nelson's Regiment of Virginia State Cavalry
Captain Edmund Read
1st Troop
Captain Martin Armand Vogluson
2nd Troop
Captain Charles Fierer [497]
3rd Troop
Major Thomas Pinckney
South Carolina Volunteer Mounted Infantry   70
Colonel Charles Harrison
Continental Artillery   100
Captain William Meredith
1st Continental Artillery Regiment of Virginia
Captain-Lieutenant John Blair
Captain William L. Pierce
Brass 2-pounders   2
Captain Richard Dorsey
1st Maryland Continental Artillery Company [498]
Captain-Lieutenant Ambrose Bohannon
Brass 3-pounders   2
Captain Anthony Singleton
2nd and 3rd Maryland Continental Artillery [499]
Captain-Lieutenant Lewis Booker
Captain-Lieutenant Richard Waters

Brass 6-pounders   4
Lieutenant Colonel Elias Edmunds
Virginia State Artillery Regiment
Captain John Watlington
Major John Armstrong
Light Infantry   Unknown number
Captain Thomas H. Drew
Lieutenant Colonel Porterfield's State Detachment
Captain Thomas Upshaw
Captain John Holliday [500]
Captain Thomas Downing [501]
Captain Thomas Minor [502]
Captain Edmund Curd [503]
Major John Armstrong
North Carolina Troops
Caswell's Brigade
Light Infantry Company
Captain Samuel Lockhart [504]
Halifax District Militia
State Militia [505]
Brigadier General Richard Caswell
North Carolina Division   1,800
Brigadier General John Butler
1st Brigade of North Carolina Militia
Colonel John Collier
Randolph County Militia
Major Joseph Sharpe
Captain Chambers
Wake County Militia
Captain David McFarland
Caswell County Militia
Captain Joseph Johnson
Orange County Militia
Captain John Graves
Caswell County Militia

Colonel Porterfield
Captain Trice
Orange County Militia
Colonel Etherington
Northampton County Militia [506]
Major Robert Peebles
Captain Samuel Lockhart
Brigadier General Griffith Rutherford
2nd Brigade of North Carolina Militia [507]
Colonel Martin Armstrong [508]
Surry County Militia
Captain William Meredith
Captain Absalom Bostick
Colonel George Alexander
Lincoln County Militia
Major Joseph Dixon
Captain William Armstrong
Lincoln County Militia
Captain Samuel Givins
Mecklenburg County Militia
Captain Samuel Reid
Rowan County Militia   33
Colonel Francis Locke
2nd Rowan Militia Regiment
Captain Richmond Pearson
Colonel John Lynch
Lieutenant Colonel David Love
Brigadier General Isaac Gregory
3rd Brigade of North Carolina Militia
Lieutenant Colonel Henry "Hal" Dixon
Caswell County Militia
Lieutenant Colonel Stephen Moore
Captain Daniel Odom
Captain Edward Yarborough
North Carolina Continentals [509]   25

Captain Ray
Orange County Militia
Colonel William Polk [510]
Captain Joshua Hadley
Rowan County Militia
Colonel Benjamin Exum[511]
Captain David Roach
Craven County Militia
Captain John Macon
Warren County Militia
Colonel William Brickell
Franklin County Militia
Captain Harrison Mason
Captain Julius Alfred
Captain John Patterson
Brigadier General Edward Stevens
Virginia Militia Brigade   700
Colonel George Stubblefield
Louisa County Militia [512]
Lieutenant Colonel Joseph Spencer
Major William Moseley
Captain John Byers
Captain Thomas Roberts
Pittsylvania County
Captain William Stanton
Culpepper County
Captain Elias Edmunds [513]
Fauquier County Militia
Lieutenant Colonel Holt Richardson [514]
Amelia County Militia
Major John Bias
Captain William Craddock
Captain James Johnson
Caroline County Militia
Captain John Price
Hanover County Militia

Bedford Militia
    Captain Nathaniel Tate
    Captain Thomas Leftwich
Lieutenant Colonel Ralph Faulkner
    Chesterfield County Militia
        Captain Archibald Walthal
        Captain Booker
    Captain Walker
        Lunenburg County Militia
    Captain George Pegram
        Dinwiddie County Militia [515]
Colonel James Lucas
    Mecklenburgh County Militia [516]
        Captain Azariah Martin
        Amherst County Militia [517]   46
Colonel Lawson
    Captain Paul Wattington
        Halifax County Militia
Colonel Downman [518]
    Charlotte County Militia
        Major Henry Conway [519]
        Captain Thomas Williams
    Pittsylvania County Militia
        Captain Isaac Clement
        Captain William Dix
        Captain Peter Perkins
    Henry County Militia[520]
        Captain Cunningham
        Captain George Waller[521]
    Colonel William Mayo
        Powhatan County Militia
Captain Benjamin Carter
    South Carolina Militia   Unknown number [522]
    Lieutenant John Cathey, Jr. [523]
Total American Forces engaged   4,100 [524]
Casualties   683 -733 killed, wounded and captured [525]

British Forces
Commanding Officer   Lieutenant General Lord Cornwallis
   Lieutenant Colonel James Webster
      British Regulars   1,000
         Lieutenant Colonel Nesbit Balfour [526]
            23rd Regiment of Foot (Royal Welch Fusiliers) 292
               Major Frederick Mackenzie
               Captain William Keppel
               Captain Sir William Howe
               Captain Forbes Champagné
               Captain Thomas Saumarez
               Captain James Drury
               Charles Ward Apthorp
         Major William Dancey
            33rd Regiment of Foot [527]   238
               Captain Frederick Cornwallis
               Captain Allen Malcolme
               Captain James Campbell
               Captain John Manley
               Captain John Kerr
               Captain Hildebrand Oakes
                  Grenadier Company
         Lieutenant Colonel Alexander McDonald
            71st Regiment of Foot (Fraser's Highlanders) [528]
               Captain Hugh Campbell
                  1st Battalion   144
               Unknown Captain
                  2nd Battalion   110
         Captain Charles Campbell
             Light Infantry [529]   148
               Captain Charles Campbell
                  71st Regiment of Foot (Fraser's Highlanders)
                  Light Infantry Company [530]   70
                  Lieutenant Archibald Campbell

Lieutenant John Skinner
16th Regiment of Foot
Light Company   78
Unknown commander
New York Volunteers
3rd Battalion
Light Company   Unknown number
Royal Regiment of Artillery   19
Lieutenant John MacLeod
3rd Battalion
Number 1 Company
Brass 6-pounders   2
Brass 3-pounders   2
Lieutenant William Marquois
4th Battalion
Number 6 Company
Brass 6-pounder   2
Additionals [531]   126
Brass 2-pounders   2
Swivel guns   3
Artillery manned by the British Legion
Iron 3-pounder   1
Lieutenant Andrew Husband
Corps of Guides and Pioneers   28
Colonel Francis Lord Rawdon
Provincials   800
Lieutenant Colonel Banastre Tarleton
British Legion
Captain Patrick Stewart
Legion Infantry   126
Major George Hanger [532]
Legion Cavalry   182
Colonel Francis Lord Rawdon
Volunteers of Ireland [533]   303
Captain Lieutenant David Dalton
Captain John Campbell

Captain John Doyle	
Captain Charles Hastings	
Captain James King	
Captain John McMahon	
Lieutenant Colonel John Hamilton	
Royal North Carolina Regiment	267
Loyalist Militia	
Colonel Samuel Bryan	
North Carolina Volunteers [534]	202
Lieutenant Colonel John Hampton	
Captain Nicholas White	
Total British Forces engaged	2,239
Casualties	66 killed, 256 wounded [535]

After the initial engagement at Saunder's Creek, Gates placed his army astride the Charlotte road, on Parker's Old Field. Throughout the night shots were constantly being exchanged by both sides, but to no effect, except to cause both armies to lose any sleep that was possible. Williams wrote "Frequent skirmishes happened during the night between the advanced parties — which served to discover the relative situations of the two armies and as a prelude to what was to take place in the morning."

Guilford Dudley had a mounted British patrol come within twenty-five yards of his hiding place, but he was not detected. He heard what he thought was the morning gun in the town of Camden; just as some surgeons arrived to take care of the wounded colonel.[536] They placed him in a fabricated stretcher, and members of his light infantry carried him back to the main force. Dudley rode on to the main force and told Porterfield he would see him later. Unfortunately Porterfield would die from his wounds a few days after the battle.[537]

The British soldiers lay upon the ground for the next two hours, until the morning twilight. Very few of them slept. Both sides had captured men during the night, and some deserters had come into the British army. Cornwallis learned that Gates had his entire army and that the force he faced outnumbered his. Williams learned from a British prisoner that the force laying 500 yards in front of his soldiers was the whole British army, commanded by Lord Cornwallis himself. Both sides were surprised to learn what appeared before them on the morning of the 16th.

Gates had formed his line with Gist's 2nd Brigade of Maryland Continentals on the right of the road. On the left of the road was the North Carolina and Virginia Militia, with Armand's Legion in support. Since the flanks were covered by marshes, Smallwood's 1st Maryland Brigade was moved from the line, and placed in reserve two hundred yards in the rear of the line. Seven artillery pieces were placed in the center of the road, between Caswell and Stevens's militia. De Kalb commanded the right wing, while Gates and his staff took post 600 yards to the rear. The Patriot line stretched over a mile of "sandy area of widely spaced pines." On the flanks of Gates' army was Gum Swamp, impassable to an army with wheeled equipment. In the tradition of 18th century battles, Gates had placed his Continentals in the position of honor, on the right flank.[538]

Cornwallis described the ground as "being narrowed by swamps on the right and left" and was "extremely favorable to my numbers." From left to right on the road was the Royal North Carolina Regiment, the infantry of Tarleton's Legion and the Volunteers of Ireland. Bryan's North Carolina Volunteers were slightly behind their left flank.

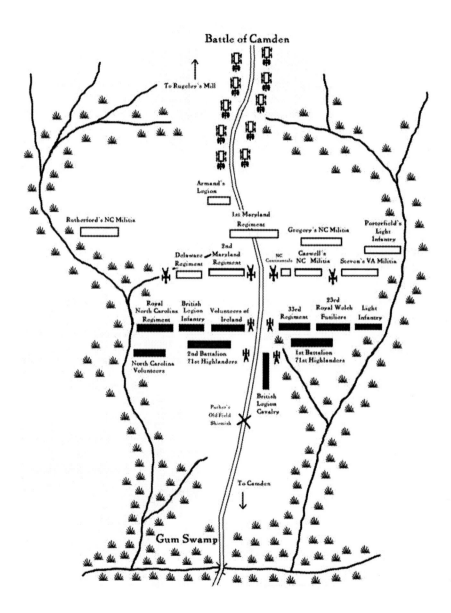

Battle of Camden

Bryan's Loyalists wore "red Rags in their Hats, for Distinction" so that they wouldn't be confused with the Patriot militiamen. The right wing, from the swamp to the road, was composed of the Light Infantry, the 23rd Regiment and the 33rd Regiment. Two 6-pounders and three 3-pounders were placed in front of the British center, under the command of Lieutenant MacLeod.

Tarleton's dragoons were in column in the rear, waiting to exploit any retreat by the enemy. The 71st Highlanders were in reserve, two hundred yards behind the two 6-pounder field guns. Cornwallis had also placed his Regulars on the right flank, in the position of honor. What faced the British Regulars was the fatigued, hungry and inexperienced Patriot militia.

Williams informed Gates of the information he learned from the British prisoners. Gates was astonished that the entire British army was only a musket shot away, and called for a council of war. When all the general officers formed Gates asked, "Gentlemen, what is best to be done?" General Stevens asked, "Is it not too late now to do anything but fight?" No other officer offered any advice. They were stunned by the realization that the entire British army was to their front.

Even though Cornwallis was outnumbered two to one, defeat never entered his mind. At dawn he ordered his men forward, in a line of columns. The British typically are depicted as standing in two to three ranks, shoulder to shoulder, with the front rank kneeling, but this was not the case with the war in the South. The British had learned from the deadly American style of warfare and adapted to the changing tactics. The three ranks had become two, with the front rank no longer kneeling. The men did not always stand shoulder-to-shoulder, and sometimes they fought at "open order". This distance varied, but it was generally between two to five feet between men. The British had learned that if they could close quickly with the Patriots, they would flee from their bayonets. For this battle Cornwallis had his light infantry deploy in only a single rank, with five feet between the men.

As the darkness gave way to the coming dawn Captain Anthony Singleton was standing beside his artillery and spied the British 200 yards to his front. He informed Colonel Williams, and he was given the order to fire. As Singleton's artillery opened up the battle Williams quickly rushed back to report to General Gates. The British artillery returned fire upon Singleton's guns.

Thomas Pinckney was told by a British officer that "the first discharge of our Field pieces put sixty men *hors de combat*" He was later "carried over the field of battle in the night where as far as I could see they were thickly strewn and I heard the groans of many." John Shaw of the 33rd Foot verified this when he wrote, "the Americans gave the first fire, which killed and wounded nearly one half of our number."

It took Gates awhile to deploy the militia into a line of battle, and the army did not get any rest at all the night before. Pinckney wrote that "soon after the troops were formed, the General (Gates) moved along their front, saying a few words of encouragement to the men; & that it was but a short time after he had proceeded along the front of Smallwood's Brigade composing the reserve, when our Artillery opened up on the enemy."

Seeing that Gates had not ordered the troops to move, Williams suggested that Stevens should move his troops forward and hit the British while they were deploying from columns into a line. Gates thought the suggestion was worthwhile, and ordered it done. Gates told Major Pinckney to "go to Baron de Kalb, & desire him to make an attack on the Enemy's left to support that made by Genl. Stevens on the Right." This was the last order that Williams remembers Gates giving.

The sunrise that morning was at 5:24 and the morning was hot and humid. The artillery smoke hung in the air, not dissipating at all. Tarleton wrote "The morning being hazy hung over and involved both armies in such a cloud that it was difficult to see." The British swiftly deployed from column into open order line, and charged towards Stevens' Virginians. The British light infantry quickly drove in the pickets.

Williams rode to Stevens and requested that he be given forty or fifty volunteers to run ahead of the brigade, take to the trees, and keep up a brisk a fire as possible. Unfortunately it was too late.

The British right flank, under the command of Webster, advanced on the Virginians in such a way as to cause panic.

The Virginia militia had barely deployed when they were met by shouting British infantrymen, coming at them with bayonets. Williams and his fifty volunteers had moved ahead of the Virginia militia as advance skirmishers, but the British Regulars passed through his men as if they weren't there. Stevens ordered his men to fix bayonets, and stand firm, shouting out "Come on, my brave fellows, you have bayonets as well as they." Stevens's men did have bayonets, but they had only received them the day before. When they saw the veterans of the British army charging forward, the Virginia militia fled, followed by Butler and Gregory's North Carolinians. Most of them "threw down their loaded weapons without ever firing a shot."

The Craig brothers, James, Robert and Samuel, were firing from behind some trees. When they were told to retreat another man, Henry Ray, told Samuel "Lets run!" Samuel said, "No, I will shoot again." Ray left him, as he was loading his rifle. After he had ran a short distance, Ray looked back to see if Samuel was coming. He saw Tarleton's dragoons cutting him down. James Craig was killed near his brother, and Robert wounded.

Pinckney wrote that as soon as the firing commenced General Gates hastened to the front line of battle, "where he met Armand retreating, who urged the General to retire, as a smart firing was carried on where he was." Gates "rode about 20 yards to the rear" of the fleeing militia and tried to rally them, "which he found impossible to do there."

As the left wing collapsed, and was swept away, De Kalb's Maryland and Delaware troops held firm against Rawdon's attack. One regiment of North Carolina militia was led by General Gregory and stood with the Continental line. Gregory's regiment had fled in the panic, but he stayed and assumed command of Colonel Henry Dixon's regiment. Their commander had been wounded in the neck and withdrew in "his large cocked hat ... [with] a broad laugh." The 600 men stood against 2,000 British troops.

Williams wrote, "Dixon's regiment...next in the line to the second Maryland brigade, fired two or three rounds of cartridge." However, "the regular troops, who had the keen edge of sensibility rubbed off by strict discipline and hard service, saw the confusion with but little emotion."

The fleeing militia ran through the second line of the Maryland troops 200 yards to the rear. The smoke from the battle made everything even more confusing. Tarleton wrote that the smoke made it "difficult to see the destruction on either side."

When De Kalb's horse was shot out from under him he continued to fight on foot. His head was slashed by a saber stroke, but after getting it bandaged by a captain of the Delaware Regiment, he stepped in front of his men, drew his sword, and simply said, "Follow me." He led a last desperate counterattack, which momentarily drove the enemy back.

General Gregory was wounded twice by bayonet, and his North Carolinians only received wounds from the bayonet, showing their ability to stand toe to toe with the British Regulars.

The British chose not to pursue the fleeing militia, and instead stopped when they were opposite the flank of the Continental's right company. They then wheeled into the Patriots. The 2nd Maryland Brigade, led by De Kalb, stood in their path. They had not run from the British, and instead moved forward into the fight. Many of the Maryland troops thought they were winning, and even took fifty prisoners as they inflicted heavy losses on the Volunteers of Ireland.

Senf wrote "Gen[l] Gates rode up to Gen[l] Gist, gave orders to advance slowly with the Brigade, to reserve their fire till proper distance, fire & charge Bayonets which has been according to orders Executed. They came close, Gen[l] Gist's Brigade took a Field Piece from the Enemy and kept it some time." Major McGill verified this in his letter when he wrote, "Gist's Brigade charged Bayonets and at first made the Enemy give way, but they were reinforced."

Williams assumed command of the 1st Maryland Brigade when General Smallwood moved back to try and rally the fleeing militia. The 1st Maryland struggled to advance up to the exposed flank of the 2nd Maryland Brigade, but the British were between the two brigades.

The Maryland units were separated by 200 yards, and in the smoke and heavy humidity Williams only had the sound of fighting to determine where De Kalb's Brigade was located. Williams rode from the 1st Brigade to the 2nd Brigade, hoping to restore communication. He told his own 6th Maryland Regiment to not flee the field. Lieutenant Colonel Ford said "They have done all that can be expected of them; we are outnumbered and outflanked; see the enemy charge with bayonets!"

Cornwallis had his regiments concentrate on both the Maryland Brigades. Three times the Continentals drove the British back, but an intense fire was slowly reducing their ranks. Finally Cornwallis ordered Major Hanger and his cavalry to charge the Patriot's left, while Tarleton led his cavalry forward. When the cavalry charged, the British infantry came forward with bayonets.

De Kalb had been wounded eleven times in the intense fighting, and fell. When his men saw him go down, and saw the charging Regulars and cavalry, they finally broke and ran. De Kalb did not know that the army had fled, and while lying on the ground, wounded, could not believe that Gates had been defeated. De Kalb's Aide-de-Camp, Chevalier de Buysson, rushed towards his commander's body. He received several bayonet wounds as he tried to shield De Kalb's body. De Kalb would die three days later.

General Rutherford of the North Carolina militia was captured. Peter Francisco, a Virginia soldier, speared a British cavalryman with a bayonet, and hoisted him from his horse. He climbed on the horse and escaped through the enemy line, pretending to be a Tory sympathizer. Francisco gave the mount to his colonel, saving the exhausted officer's life.

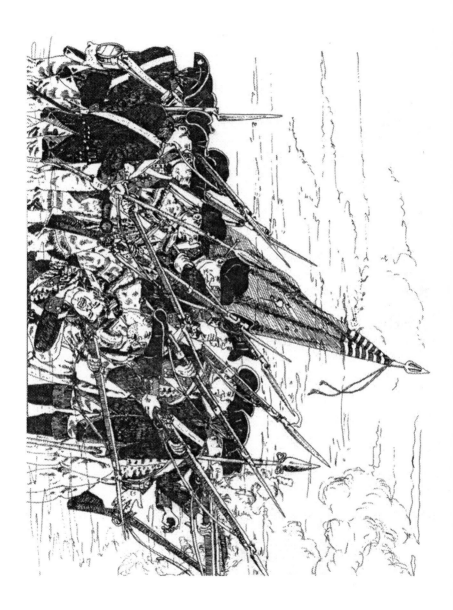

The Patriot's waggoners sensed defeat, cut loose the horses, and left the loaded wagons behind for the British to capture. Some of the waggoners sped off without cutting loose the horses, and the baggage and equipment was strewn along the road. Thomas Pinckney wrote "the causeway at Rugeleys was rendered impassable for carriages, by the waggons by which it was covered."[539]

Some of the camp followers had stayed with the army, and were in these wagons. Many were thrown from the wagons as they smashed into stumps, and were killed. Guilford Dudley wrote "some of them" had "new-born infants in their arms, a sight lamentable to view." The waggoners threw off their baggage to lighten their load, so they could move faster. Dudley wrote "a man might almost walk upon it without touching the ground."

Armand's force in reserve had not come into play. Williams later accused them of plundering the Patriot wagon train, but Tarleton stated that he had to send a body of men to dislodge Colonel Armand, who had been employed in rallying the militia. As they left the field the North Carolina and Virginia Militia had stopped to loot the baggage. Tarleton and his dragoons came up and ruthlessly cut down whatever resistance was offered. After capturing the baggage he continued the pursuit. At Rugeley's Bridge some officers had rallied a small force, but Tarleton discovered them and routed the Patriots. Tarleton continued his pursuit until he reached Hanging Rock, twenty-two miles away.

Gates initially had rode back a half a mile behind the lines to rally the men, but it proved fruitless. When Tarleton's cavalry came riding upon them, everyone fled. Gates rode to the former campsite at Clermont, hoping to rally sufficient men to cover the retreat of the Continentals, but the militia could not be organized again. The historian John Austin Stevens wrote, "The misfortune which befell Gates is not alone in history. It was not unlike that which befell the great Frederick, who was swept off the field of Mollwitz by a part of his own routed army to a great distance, and returned to find the battle had been won by those who remained."

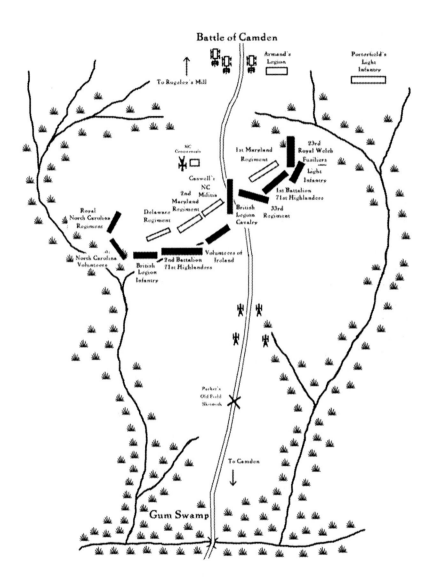

Battle of Camden

The Virginia militia fled towards Hillsborough, and the North Carolina militia fled into the "wilderness which lies between the Wateree and the Pee Dee Rivers." Gates sent word to Sumter of the loss at Camden, and told him "retire in the best manner you can." He then abandoned his army. William Richardson Davie met Gates as his men advanced towards Camden. Dan Alexander wrote that he was wearing "a pale blue coat with epauletts and velvet breeches, riding a bay horse."

Without stopping Gates told Davie that he should retire to Charlotte, or the British dragoons would be upon him. Davie replied, "His men were accustomed to Tarleton, and did not fear him." Gates was riding hard and probably did not hear him. Davie sent an officer in pursuit of Gates with a message that asked if the General wanted Davie to bury the dead. Gates answer was "I say retreat! Let the dead bury the dead!" Davie asked General Isaac Huger how far should he obey Gates' order. Huger replied, "Just as far as you please, for you will never see him again."

The only escape for the Continentals left on the field was to wade through the swamps, on either side of the battlefield. This was the only place that the cavalry could not follow. Many officers and men made their way out individually, or in small groups. These small company or regiment-sized units continued to fight while withdrawing. Major Archibald Anderson of the 3rd Maryland kept 100 of his men together and made it safely to Charlotte. The senior ranking member of the Delaware Regiment to make it out was Captain Robert Kirkwood.

In fleeing from their pursuers the Continental army lost all the supplies it had, including "eight brass field pieces, Twenty-two ammunition wagons, a large supply of fixed ammunition, 2,000 stand of arms, many musket cartridges, and a number of colors" fell into the hands of the British.[540]

The British supply train had been captured, but it was recaptured when Tarleton caught the guards asleep. The Patriot dead included 162 Continentals, twelve South Carolina militiamen, three Virginia militiamen, and sixty-three North Carolina militiamen. Gates's army had lost about 65% of their army. "The road was heaped with the dead and wounded. Arms, artillery, horses and baggage were strewn in every direction."[541]

Cornwallis continued to advance with his army until he reached Rugeley's Mill. The fight was not one-sided. Cornwallis lost 324 of all ranks, which was 14% of his whole force. The 33rd Regiment lost 36% of its men and half of its officers; Rawdon's Irish Volunteers lost more than 20%. Francis Marion wrote, "Their great loss is equal to a defeat."

As soon as the news of the victory of Camden arrived in New York Clinton ordered Major General Leslie to make a diversion in the lower part of Virginia, and try to rendezvous with the Cornwallis's army. This was the last action in the Carolinas of the Pulaski's Legion. Armand and his Legion were sent into North Carolina, where, on December 15th, General Nathaniel Greene ordered them to Virginia, under the command of Baron Von Steuben. For a second time, another entire Southern Continental army had been captured. All that was left for the defense of the Carolinas were the partisans.[542]

Fishing Creek, South Carolina [543] **Skirmish**
Camden Campaign
18 August 1780

American Forces
Commanding Officer   Brigadier General Thomas Sumter
    Continentals
        Lieutenant Colonel Commandant Thomas Woolford
            5th Maryland Regiment   100
                Captain Jonathan Gibson
                Captain John Lynch
                Captain George Hamilton
        Captain William Brown
            1st Maryland Continental Artillery Company
                Brass 3-pounders   2

State Troops and Militia
   Sumter's Brigade of Partisans [544]   300
      Lieutenant Colonel Henry Hampton
         Henry Hampton's Regiment of Light Dragoons
            Captain Jacob Barnett
            Captain John Mills
               Lieutenant Archibald "Mad Archy" Gill [545]
      Colonel William Hill
         Colonel William Hill's Regiment
            Captain James Giles
            Captain William McKinzey
      Colonel Edward Lacey
         Chester District Militia
            Captain John Steele
            Captain James Pagan [546]
            Captain John Moffitt
            Captain John Thompson
            Captain Samuel Adams
      Colonel Thomas Taylor [547]
         Lieutenant Hicks Chappell
   North Carolina Militia
      Lieutenant Colonel Elijah Isaacs
         Wilkes County Militia   300
            Captain John Cleveland
            Captain Jonathan Smith [548]
Casualties   50 killed, 100 wounded, 310 captured [549]

British Forces
Commanding Officer   Lieutenant Colonel Banastre Tarleton
   British Regulars
      Captain Charles Campbell
         71st Regiment of Foot (Fraser's Highlanders)
            1st Battalion
               Light Infantry Company   40

Provincials
    Lieutenant Colonel Banastre Tarleton
        British Legion
            Dragoons   100
            Captain David Kinlock
            Infantry   20
Casualties   9 killed, 6 wounded [550]

After Sumter's men captured Cary's Fort he had his army occupy the fort. When the British started crossing below the fort, Sumter retreated up the Wateree. He made a slow retreat because he had fifty captured supply wagons, 300 head of cattle, and 250 prisoners slowing his men down. After the defeat of Gates at Camden Sumter's force was now the largest organized Patriot unit in South Carolina, and this made him a prime target for Cornwallis. Davie saw that Sumter was in danger, and sent ten dragoons to alert him and tell him to meet below Charlotte. Charlotte had become the rallying point for the survivors of the battle of Camden.

Cornwallis pushed his main body to Rugeley's Mill and waited for Tarleton's return from pursuing Gates and his army. The British commander learned of the capture of the convoy from Ninety-Six by Sumter's men. Cornwallis eagerly wanted to make a move on Sumter, who had taken the desperately needed wagon trains. Colonels Turnbull and Ferguson were on Little River and were told to cut off Sumter's retreat. Early in the morning of August 17th Tarleton led his Legion along the Wateree to overtake Sumter's partisans.

After an exhausting march, without a break, Sumter's column reached his old campsite at Rocky Mount on the 17th. Sumter had known about Ferguson and Turnbull, and had eluded their forces, but he did not know about Tarleton.

Tarleton covered thirty miles with his typical speed and arrived at the Catawba at the same time as Sumter. He observed Sumter's campfires from the east bank, and waited to see if the partisans would cross the river at Rocky Mount. Sumter learned that Tarleton was opposite him on the west bank, and continued his march without crossing the river. As soon as Tarleton saw that Sumter was staying on the west side, he crossed the river by using boats. Sumter thought he was safe and marched only eight miles to Fishing Creek, where he halted at noon and made camp.

Tarleton's Infantry were not able to keep up, so he did the same thing he had done when pursuing Buford. He chose 100 dragoons of the Legion, and sixty men of the Light Infantry, and doubled up on the horses. He also left behind his 3-pound cannon. Tarleton did not care that his 160 troopers would face 800 partisans.

At Fishing Creek Sumter relaxed in camp. His men had camped on the main road, near the creek. He seemed to have a good position between Fishing Creek and the Catawba River, with ravines to the north and south. Sumter lay partially undressed, under the shade of a wagon, sleeping after the long march.[551]

McJunkin wrote "It happened that two Tory women passed the place soon after Sumter halted and went on in the direction whence Sumter had come. They had passed the rear guard about half a mile when they met Tarleton's force. They gave Tarleton precise information as to Sumter's position and the arrangement of things connected with his army. They also informed him of a way by which he could leave the main road and fall into a road leading to Sumter's position at right angles to the main road."[552]

The Continentals had stacked their arms, and the men bathed in the river, slept, or strolled to a neighboring plantation. Many of the men lay under the wagons parked along the road, to get some relief from the oppressive heat. Some of the men began shooting some cattle so that they could get the meat.[553] A Tory named Reeves had a large peach orchard there, and the men lay around eating the fruit. Sumter was not totally careless. He had placed out sentries near the ravines.[554]

Colonel Winn wrote that "the men were very hungry, had marched for three days, very hot weather and very weary." There were "many prisoners" with them from Cary's fort.

When Tarleton's advance guard under Captain Charles Campbell came into view, Sumter's sentries shot and killed one of the Legion dragoons. The dragoons charged, and the sentries were hacked to death by the Legion sabers.

Colonel Thomas Taylor had just pulled off one boot, preparing to lie down and rest, when Tarleton appeared. Sumter awoke and asked about the shooting, but he was told it was the sentries shooting the cattle. Lacey heard the shots and ordered his men to take post behind the captured baggage wagons and put up a resistance.

Samuel Martin, one of Sumter's men, wrote that Sumter had ten companies of militia, and "the men were engaged in drinking, having taken two hogsheads of rum from some Tories who were conveying it to the British ... Many of the men were so drunk that they couldn't succeed in stopping Tarleton."[555]

Tarleton reacted immediately by ordering his cavalry and infantry into one line and, with a shout, charged into the partisan camp. Tarleton's green-jacketed horsemen cut the few defenders to pieces. [556]

Elizabeth Peay had been riding with Sumter's army so that she could be near her husband. Her "house was burned, everything destroyed, and she followed the army to escape starvation." She had been shadowing Sumter's army, and had fallen in with them a couple of days before. She had an infant that rode with her on one horse, and "her servant, a Negro man, riding another horse and carrying the other child."

She had been sitting on a log, breast-feeding her baby, when she heard Tarleton's boys sound the trumpet to charge.[557] "Tarleton's horsemen dashed and jumped over the logs on each side of her, without injuring her."

Samuel Morrow stated, "I seized my gun and shot a Capt. Campbell of the British light horse. I looked around me and saw Sumter's men running in every direction. I snatched up another gun and saw Col. Bratton rallying on a little eminence near me. I joined the little band that stood with him, fired again and the man at whom I took aim dropped. By this time the British were passed us in pursuit of those retiring and we saw no chance and our escape."

Elizabeth Peay "saw Tarleton's men cutting down the whigs and she grew faint and sic, until she heard the bullets whistling past her and breaking limbs. She lay down beside the log, pulling her children down beside her."

Captain James Pagan called to his men to rally behind the fence. He was able to make a stand with part of his company, but when the Legion charged down upon them, the company fled. Pagan was unable to escape the sabers of the dragoons and was cut down at the fence. [558]

Sumter saw Colonel Woolford, and some of his Maryland officers, trying to get to their stacked weapons, but they were cut down by the sabers of the Legion. Woolford was "badly wounded four times." The artillery was able to fire one shot, but then was overrun. To add to the chaos of Tarleton's raid "there were many horses running helter skelter".

Many of the men who were bathing in the water were killed as they tried to swim away. Winn wrote, "Many of the men who were swimming were called upon to surrender, with the promise of good treatment and upon emerging from the stream were mercilessly cut down by the enemy."

Sumter was picked up by Captain John Steele, and carried to a horse. Winn wrote "Sumter had given his horse to a messenger who had ridden to General Gates. Joe Gabby of York County hastened with his horse to Sumter, who mounted it."

Sumter was hatless, bootless, and unable to rally his men, he yelled, "let every man take care of himself" and galloped into the woods. He didn't travel far because he ran under a low hanging branch, and knocked him to the ground unconscious. A few minutes later he came to, remounted his horse and rode away to join Davie in his camp two days later. [559]

There were briar patches around the camp, which "enabled some Americans to dodge among them and escape." Matthew Johnston was one of Sumter's militia, and his group grabbed their weapons off the ground before they fled. They met some of Tarleton's dragoons on the road and Matthew Johnston was "shot down." His brother, James "turned and taking deliberate aim at one of the dragoons, fired, & saw him fall from his horse. At the same instant he was himself severely wounded by a ball. He happened to have a pocket book in his vest, against which the ball struck, driving it under his ribs. When the dragoons saw one of their fellows fall, they wheeled about. The loose horse ran up to where James lay, unable to move, his friend, Samuel Morrow, being a powerful man, caught the horse and flinging Johnston upon him, mounted himself behind & bore him safely to Charlotte."

Colonel Taylor, still only wearing one boot, "received a sword cut, some four inches across his head. Since he had no weapon he fell, playing possum. He was stripped of his boots and everything except his shirt, pants or drawers." He was discovered when "He was struck by Captain Mc_____."

Draper wrote that Alexander Ferris said "while some were butchering beeves, he and two others were ordered to take a parcel of horses and put them in a field of corn between the camp and the river and returning saw two British troopers who demanded his surrender and making no reply he fired and shot one of them and he fell off and the other dashed up and slashed Ferris, severely cutting him under the ear and he fell and was taken prisoner and carried with many others to Camden."

Tarleton captured all the Continentals, forty-four wagons, the artillery, and 1,000 stands of arms. The British prisoners of Fort Cary had been rescued.[560] Captain Campbell of the 71st Highlanders was killed during the fighting. Ironically Campbell was the officer that burned down Sumter's home, and started him on his partisan career.

Elizabeth Peay roamed the battlefield after the fight, until she found her dead husband, George Peay.[561] "The tories took her horse, but she found an old gray shot through the neck. She mounted it with her children, one in her lap and one behind and the negro man walking." She rode towards her husband's relatives in Virginia.[562]

Her brother, John Starke, had tried to swim to safety, but he was shot at across the river and was severely wounded. "He was captured by treachery of a Tory, but afterwards escaped."

Sumter stopped off at Susannah Smart's house. She was only a little girl then, but she told Lyman Draper that Sumter had stopped there for some any food that her mother could offer. While he ate some stew, a girl tied his hair up. Susannah described his hair as "very long, rather of fair or light color."

The next day the survivors of the massacre returned to the battlefield. Tarleton had left the dead unburied, knowing that the neighbors and relatives would bury the corpses. James Collins was a 17-year-old militiaman with Captain Moffitt's cavalry. He wrote "The dead and wounded lay scattered in every direction over the field; numbers lay stretched cold and lifeless; some were yet struggling in the agonies of death, while here and there, lay others, faint with the loss of blood, almost famished for water, and begging for assistance." The wounded were placed in a horse cart and taken home.[563]

Colonel Taylor had covered his face with blood and mud "so as to be unrecognizable as an officer. He feared being hanged. He joined the other prisoners and huddled with them, none of who recognized him. The British had captured Henry Hampton, stripped him of nearly all of his clothing and had pinioned his hands behind him, leaving his rope fastened around his neck and fastened to a cavalry horse beside him. The prisoners were placed between two lines of Tarleton's cavalry and marched towards Camden."

During the march to the Camden jail Taylor was able to get a knife from a soldier who was also a tanner. He and Hampton cut their ropes and then pushed between the British horses and made a run for the woods. "Hampton worried his white shirt would make him a conspicuous mark for British marksmen." Taylor didn't worry since the mud and blood he had smeared on himself acted as camouflage. The British did not shoot at either man.

William Taylor told Draper "after Fishing Creek many of the men escaped during a rainy night." Captain Joel McLemore had not been captured and followed behind the British, gathering the militia as they escaped. When two brothers escaped in the darkness he blew a whistle to gather them in the rainy night. Unfortunately the whistle drew the attention of some of Tarleton's men, and they were pursued. When it seemed they had lost the British, they both stopped and "were enjoying a pot of mush." As they were eating the dragoons appeared.

"One of them, a very fine looking and well dressed officer dashed up ... to my grandfather and Captain McLemore (a fence being between the parties) and demanded a surrender. McLemore cautioned the officer not to advance or he would kill him." He didn't want to do it, but the officer continued to move forward and was killed by McLemore. Taylor said "McLemore always after the event...regretted having to kill so brave and fine looking fellow." [564]

Musgrove's Mill, South Carolina   Battle
18 August 1780 [565]

American Forces
State Militia	200 - 300
Colonel Isaac Shelby	
North Carolina Militia	
Over the Mountainmen	
Sullivan County Militia	
Major Charles Robertson	
Captain Valentine Sevier	
Josiah Culbertson	
Mounted militia	40
Major Jonathan Tipton	
Washington County Militia	100
Captain Godfrey Isbell	
Captain John McNabb	
Captain James Stinson	
Captain John McCampbell	

Captain William Trimble
Major Joseph McDowell
Burke County Militia Battalion
Colonel Elijah Clarke
Georgia Militia
Wilkes County Militia   Unknown number
Captain Shadrick Inman   25
Colonel James Williams
South Carolina Militia   Unknown number
Lieutenant Colonel James Stein
Union District Militia
Major Samuel Hammond [566]
Laurens District Militia
Captain Andrew Barry
2nd Spartan Regiment
Captain William Smith

Casualties   4 killed, 9 wounded [567]

Loyalist Forces
Commanding Officer   Lieutenant Colonel Alexander Innes
Provincials
Major Thomas Fraser
South Carolina Royalists   100
Captain Peter Campbell
New Jersey Volunteers
3rd Battalion
Light Company   50
Captain James Kerr
DeLancey's Brigade
1st Battalion   50
Loyalist Militia
Captain David Fanning
Fanning's Loyalist Militia of North Carolina   14

Colonel Daniel Clary
   Ninety-Six District Brigade of Loyalist Militia
      Dutch Fork Regiment   100 - 300
          Captain William Hawsey
          Captain Vachel Clary
          Captain Humphrey Williamson
            Captain William Ballentine
          Captain George Stroup
          Captain James Wright
          Captain William Thompson

Total Loyalist forces engaged   Approximately 600
Casualties   63 killed, 90 wounded, 70 captured [568]

After McDowell had captured the Loyalists at Thicketty Fort, he sent Shelby and Clarke to disperse an assembly of Loyalists camped at Musgrove's Mill, on the Enoree River. The enlistments of the men with Shelby were almost up, and he wanted to get one more engagement in before they returned home. Unlike Gates and his army, Shelby's men had been eating well. William Smith was with the Patriots and told Draper that "Roasting ears were plenty…a week or two before the fight at Musgrove's Mills."

Shelby left Smith's Ford at around sunset. Along the way Colonel James Williams and some of Sumter's men joined them.[569] The militia army "travelled through the woods until nearly dark then took the road, & traveled fast all night, a great part of the way in a canter, never stopped even to let their horses drink, & arrived within ½ mile of the enemy camp just at the break of day." They had rode forty miles in one night, and passed within four miles of Major Patrick Ferguson's camp.

Shelby discovered that Ferguson had been joined by a detachment of Provincials under Colonel Innes, who wore red coats. They also discovered that they were caught between a camp of Loyalist militia and Ferguson's Provincials.

Hill wrote "The Americans after a hard travel all night of 40 miles, or upwards were too much broke down to retreat." Shelby decided to lure the Provincials into an ambush and annihilate them.

Shelby, Williams and five to six men went out on a reconnaissance and ran into a five man Loyalist patrol that was returning to their camp.

The two sides fired at each other. The Patriots killed one Loyalist and wounded two others. The two Loyalist survivors rode back to their camp and warned them that the backwoodsmen were near. Shelby's scouts had two slightly wounded, and they returned to the main force.

Shelby immediately fell back and set up a defensive line on a low ridge across the road. He had his men fell trees and make breastworks. They realized they were now outnumbered two to one and the best chance of survival was to erect fortifications, hold off the British throughout the day, and then try to get away under cover of night.

The backwoodsmen formed a semi-circular defense along a ridge that was 300 yards long. In thirty minutes the breastworks were chest-high. Shelby commanded the right of the defense, with his North Carolinians. Colonel James Williams had his South Carolinians in the center, and Colonel Elijah Clarke and his Georgians were on the left. Two small mounted detachments of twenty horsemen were placed on the flanks. These men were under the command of Josiah Culbertson and were hidden from the view of the Loyalists. Clarke also had a reserve force of forty men to the rear of the line. Like similar backwoods battles there was no overall commander, and Clarke, Shelby and Williams worked together.

Lieutenant Colonel Alexander Innes was in command of the Loyalists, and quickly convened a council of war at the home of Edward Musgrove. Innes wanted to immediately attack, but Major Fraser and two other officers wanted to wait until after breakfast because 100 mounted men would return from a patrol. Innes over-ruled them, and immediately set out "to bag" the backwoodsmen. Innes left 100 men to guard the camp, and moved forward in three columns.

Captain Shadrick Inman asked to go forward to skirmish with the enemy, and Shelby sent him with twenty-five expert riflemen to ride close to the approaching Loyalists, and open fire on their three wings. "The sound of their drum and bugle horns soon announced their movements." Inman fired upon the approaching Loyalists, and then fell back, drawing the Loyalists towards the defensive line. He engaged a second time, and drew back, then engaged a third time. The Loyalists dismounted their horses at 150 yards, fired a volley and then advanced with their bayonets shouting "Huzza for King George!"

Shelby had the Patriots withhold their fire until the Loyalists were seventy yards away. [570] McJunkin wrote that the command was "Reserve your fire until you can see the whites of their eyes!" Another wrote that they were to hold their fire "till they could distinguish the buttons on their clothes."

The backwoodsmen opened up with a devastating volley on the Loyalists who were "in full exposure to the American riflemen." The rifles at that range tore through the Loyalist line and they fell back and rallied, then advanced again. It took an hour, but the Provincials came from the left flank, and drove Shelby's men from their breastworks by bayonet.

Clarke sent in the reserve force of forty men, and the Provincials began withdrawing. There rose above the battle wild shouts that chilled the Loyalists blood, sounds they would always remember. Captain Abraham DePeyster called the backwoodsmen the "yelling boys." Shelby's men came on giving the shrill Indian war cry, which in another war would be known as the "Rebel yell." Culbertson's horsemen burst out of their hiding place, and charged with Clarke's riflemen. Clarke was wounded in the exchange.

William Smith, a rifleman with the Over the Mountainmen, shot Alexander Innes through the back of the neck. Smith yelled above the noise of battle, "I've killed their commander." Innes had been shot in both the neck, and in the thigh, which broke the bone. He was quickly taken to the rear. Major Fraser, of the Royalists, was shot out of his saddle by another frontier rifleman, Robert Beene. Captain Hawsey, a noted leader of the Loyalist militia, was shot down. All of the officers in the New Jersey Volunteers were wounded in this counterattack.

Colonel William Hill wrote that "This action was one of the hardest ever fought in the United States with small arms. The smoke was so thick as to hide a man at a distance of 20 yards."

The fighting was so confusing that Loyalist militia commander, Colonel Clary, had his horse grabbed by two of Clarke's men. Looking down on the men he yelled, "Damn you, don't you know your own officers!" and was released. Clary then rode to safety. The Loyalist militia saw the Provincials being forced back, and turned and fled. Hill wrote, "The Tories upon the fall of Capt Hawsey broke in great confusion."

The Provincials noticed that they carried on the fight alone, and retreated, running towards the river with the militia. Hill noted "The slaughter from thence to the Enoree River about half a mile was very great. Dead men lay thick on the ground over which our men pursued the enemy." The fighting only lasted fifteen minutes, and it was a complete rout. Hill wrote that the battle had been "bloody & obstinate for upwards of an hour & a half." Inman was killed as he pursued the Loyalists. Draper wrote "He received seven shots from the Tories, one, a musket ball, piercing his forehead."

Golding Tinsley was in the fight and he told L. Miles "they Killed many British & Tories as they fled across the Stream & shot them while in the act of crossing. After they had got over one fellow squatted down, turned his buttock & slapped in derision at the Americans. Tinsley's commander said to him "Cant you turn that fellow over?" Tinsley replied, "I can try." Tinsley had a good rifle, sat down, took good aim, shot & turned him over. They took him up & carried him off."

Shelby wrote that the British and Patriot strength during this battle was both at about 700, William Hill wrote that there was between 700-800 men, but James Williams wrote that the British had 500 and the Patriots only 200. Casualties for the battle vary depending on the different sources. Lyman Draper wrote that the Loyalists had 63 dead, 90 wounded and 70 captured, almost 50% of the men engaged. The Patriots lost four dead and eight or nine wounded.

Shelby was determined to continue with his force to the British post at Ninety-Six, twenty-five miles away, but an express rider from General McDowell told him of the defeat of Gates. Shelby knew that Patrick Ferguson would be coming soon. He mounted the prisoners double with his militia, made them carry their weapons with the flints removed, and withdrew to the northwest. The backwoodsmen rode for 100 miles in the next 48 hours, without stopping for a rest. Hill wrote, "The excessive fatigue to which they were subjected two nights & two days effectually broke down every officer so that their faces & eyes swelled & became so bloated in appearance as scarcely to be able to see." Major John Alexander said, "He was without food for nearly four days. When his engagements permitted and the opportunity offered he pulled some corn and ate it raw and found it delicious."

Riding for that distance was a good choice, since the early morning patrol of 100 Loyalists returned and quickly rode to the battlefield, only to find that Shelby was gone. The Loyalist's patrol became an ambulatory detail to remove the wounded to the newly created hospital at Musgrove's home.

Most of the casualties were from the Loyalist and Provincial forces. One of the reasons for the differences in the losses of both sides may have been because the Loyalists were firing downhill towards the Patriots.

Lyman Draper commented "forest hunters…often shoot too high when their object is below them." Richard Thompson "stated that there were marks of battle for two miles along the road on the east side of the river and that he made this observation in regard to the shooting of the different parties: The marks of the balls shot by the Whigs on the trees were generally from three to five feet above the ground, while their antagonists had generally shot entirely above the heads of the Whigs."

Women showed up for miles around to turn over the bodies and examine the faces, to see if it was their loved ones. Sixteen Loyalists were buried in a mass grave near the mouth of Cedar Shoal Creek; others were buried in the yard of Patriot Captain Philemon Waters.[571]

Enoree River, South Carolina   **Skirmish**
20 August 1780

This is another skirmish that is only mentioned in Alexander Chesney's Journal. Chesney was a captain in the Loyalist militia attached to Colonel Ferguson's force. He wrote that after the defeat of Gates' army at Camden the "news made us happy as people in our position could possibly be." They then learned of the defeat by Innes at Musgrove's Mill, and Ferguson's army marched quickly to intercept the Patriot militia before they got away.

Chesney was placed in command of the rear guard as the army crossed the Enoree River. An unidentified force of Patriot militia fired upon the Loyalists. Chesney was able to hold them off throughout the night. The next day Ferguson arrived with the main body, "and the Americans retreated, on August 21st, after suffering some loss." Ferguson's army camped there on the Enoree for a few days, then marched up to Fair Forest.[572]

Nelson's Ferry, Great Savannah, South Carolina [573] **Skirmish**
25 August 1780 [574]

American Forces
Commanding Officer   Colonel Francis Marion
     Continentals
        1st South Carolina Regiment [575]   16
           2nd Battalion
             Major Hugh Horry
               Captain Lemuel Benton
     South Carolina Militia
        Major John James
           Williamsburg Township Militia   134
             Captain William Robert McCottry
               Cedar Swamp and Black Mingo Company
             Captain Henry Mouzon
               King's Tree Company

Captain John James of the Lake
Lynch's Lake Company
Captain John McCauley
Black River Company

Casualties   2 wounded

British Forces
Commanding Officer   Captain Jonathan Roberts
  British Regulars
    63rd Regiment of Foot   22
  Provincials
    Unknown Subaltern
      Prince of Wales American Regiment   14
Casualties   24 killed or captured

Gates had not thought much of Marion or his men and had sent them out on an intelligence-gathering mission in the Pee Dee region. On July 1st Captain Ardesoif of the Royal Navy sailed into Georgetown harbor, and captured the town and all the vessels in the harbor. So far there had been no resistance from possible Patriot forces in the area, but on August 1st Cornwallis ordered Tarleton to cross the Santee River and determine the size of any possible rebel forces in that area. Tarleton found nothing, but did hear of a force of 500 men led by Major John James at Indiantown. When James learned of Tarleton's raid into Williamsburg County, he asked Gates to send an experienced commander for the resistance. Gates did not think Marion could do much, so he gave him orders to go to the Williamsburg Township, and destroy all the boats to prevent Cornwallis from escaping his approaching army. This began Marion on his legendary career as a partisan.

Irish emigrants had settled Williamsburg in 1730, and in the mid-18th century a large amount of Scottish settlers moved there. James had been sent to Williamsburg to organize the people into a fighting force. He went to the different clan leaders of this Scotch-Irish community, and told them, "Something must be done." He then went to the British commander in Georgetown, and asked him what was expected of the people in Williamsburg. James told Captain Ardesoif that he represented the people. Ardesoif drew his sword and stated, "I shall require unqualified submission from them; and as for you, I shall have you hanged." James parried the sword with a chair, and escaped on his horse *Thunderer*.

James told his story to the clan at King's Tree, and the word was passed to Pudding Swamp, then to Cedar Swamp, then to Thorntree Swamp and finally to Lynch's Lake. Two days later four companies formed in Williamsburg, and called on James to command them. This battalion would be the nucleus of Marion's partisans.

Colonel Marion was the commander of the imprisoned 2nd South Carolina Regiment. As an officer of the Continental Line on special assignment, and without rank in the militia, he had no legal authority over the Williamsburg Township Militia. This did not faze him and he immediately took command on August 10th. The men in the district knew Marion. James and Mouzon had both served with him, as did many of their men.

It was said that Marion "did not talk much. He did things. Williamsburg called Francis Marion to command and he came." He was described as "lean and swarthy. His body was well set, but his knees and ankles were badly formed, and he still limped upon one leg. His eyes were black and piercing. He was dressed in a close round-bodied crimson jacket of a coarse texture, and wore a leather cap, part of the uniform of the 2nd Regiment, with a silver crescent in front, inscribed with the words, 'Liberty or Death!!'" Marion had his partisans wear white cockades to distinguish them from the Tories and he armed his men with swords fashioned from saw blades by blacksmiths in the area.

Marion learned that Gates had been defeated at Camden, but fearing his men would disperse, he kept this information to himself. He learned that Captain Jonathan Roberts and the 63rd Regiment had one hundred and fifty Continental prisoners taken at Camden, and were holding them at Sumter's abandoned plantation at Great Savannah. Cornwallis had been sending his Continental prisoners from Camden down the Santee Road to Charlestown, one hundred and fifty at a time. Marion decided to free these men.

He sent Major Hugh Horry with sixteen men to seize the pass over Horse Creek. Horry's patrol stumbled over a sentry who fired a shot. At the alarm Horry rushed the house, with Marion's men closing from the rear. They found the British muskets stacked outside the front door. In the brief fight they killed or captured twenty-two British Regulars and two Loyalist guides. One of the prisoners, Captain Perry Benson of the 5th Maryland Regiment, was wounded. [576]

Marion's men released 147 of the Continentals captured at Camden. Seventy-five were from the Maryland Line, and seventy-two were from the Delaware Continentals. Eighty-five of the freed prisoners refused to obey Marion's commands or follow him. They did not want to go with the miserable looking group, and insisted that they be allowed to go on to Charlestown to a British prison ship. After all attempts to get them to change their minds failed, Marion took his British prisoners and the few Continentals who would leave with him to Port's Ferry in the swamps, near Snow's Island. By the time Marion reached his destination all but three of the Continentals had deserted him.

Marion captured two field pieces at some time during this period, and after returning to Port's Ferry he created a redoubt on the east bank of the Pee Dee. He placed a few men in there to guard the position. He did not want the artillery pieces, but knew that placing them there would impress the Loyalists in the area, and perhaps lure the British into a trap.[577]

Kings Tree, South Carolina   Skirmish
27 August 1780

Major James Wemyss was a British officer, who would soon have a reputation for cruelty, which was only surpassed by Tarleton. Most of Tarleton's image was incorrect and used as propaganda, but Wemyss's cruelty was well founded. Marion's partisans came to the attention of the British after his successful prisoner rescue, in what was supposed to have been a subdued area. Wemyss was sent into the Williamsburg Township to organize the Loyalist militia, and put down the partisans.

Wemyss brought with him 200 regulars of the 63rd Regiment, and 100 men of Harrison's South Carolina Rangers, the Royal North Carolina Regiment and Colonel Samuel Bryan's North Carolina Volunteers. Wemyss had been ordered by Cornwallis to punish the concealment of arms and ammunition with a total destruction of the plantations. This attempt at seizing the arms of the farmers would drive more men into Marion's ranks.

Marion sent James and a small party of men to determine the strength of Wemyss's force. James hid his men in a thicket and counted the British as they marched past. When the rear guard started past their position, the partisans rushed out and killed or captured thirty of the British. They then quickly made their escape. James suffered almost as much as the British in the ambush, losing five killed, fifteen wounded and ten captured.

After the attack, four hundred Regulars and Loyalists, out of Kings Tree and Georgetown, reinforced Wemyss. Marion decided that the force was too strong for his small partisan force, and withdrew to North Carolina with sixty of his men and the two fieldpieces he had captured. The artillery slowed him down, so after crossing the Little Pee Dee River he wheeled them into a swamp and continued on.[578]

After marching day and night Marion ended up at Amy's Mill, on Drowning Creek, where he stayed for several days.[579] Marion dispatched James with a small party of volunteers back to South Carolina to gain intelligence, and raise the militia.[580]

Ocracoke Inlet, North Carolina
September 1780

In September 1780 Captain Deshon captured two Brigs with his North Carolina privateer, *General Nash*. The brig *General Nash* was a privateer of twenty guns owned by John Wright Stanley of New Bern. Deshon brought the captured ships into the port at Cape

Fear. One brig was from St. Christopher with a cargo of rum and sugar and the other from Scotland. Both ships amounted to £50,800.[581]

Blue Savannah, South Carolina [582]   **Skirmish**
4 September 1780

American Forces
Commanding Officer   Colonel Francis Marion
   Continentals
      1st South Carolina Regiment   16
        2nd Battalion
          Major Hugh Horry
   South Carolina Militia
      Major John James
        Williamsburg Township Militia   53
      Captain William Robert McCottry
        Cedar Swamp and Black Mingo Company
      Captain Henry Mouzon
        King's Tree Company
      Captain John James of the Lake
        Lynch's Lake Company
      Captain John McCauley
        Black River Company
Casualties   4 wounded

Loyalist Forces
Commanding Officer   Major Micajah Ganey
   Loyalist Militia
      Captain Jesse Barfield   205
      Major Micajah Ganey
        Colonel Robert Gray's Regiment
          Georgetown Militia [583]
            Little Peedee Company   45
Casualties   30 killed and wounded

Marion's Partisan Operations

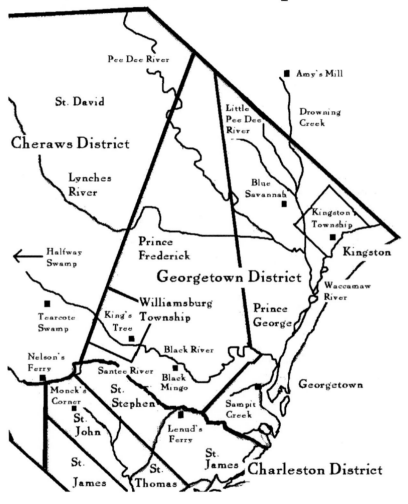

Pee Dee River

Amy's Mill

St. David

Little Pee Dee River

Drowning Creek

Cheraws District

Lynches River

Blue Savannah

Kingston Township

Prince Frederick

Kingston

Halfway Swamp

Georgetown District

Waccamaw River

Williamsburg Township

Prince George

Tearcote Swamp

King's Tree

Black River

Nelson's Ferry

Santee River

Black Mingo

Georgetown

Monck's Corner

St. Stephen

Sampit Creek

St. John

Lenud's Ferry

St. James

St. Thomas

St. James

Charleston District

After Marion's attack at Great Savannah, he quickly rode to North Carolina with his band of partisans. After several days they returned to South Carolina and set up camp at Port's Ferry. Major Micajah Ganey found out that Marion was camped there and gathered his Loyalist militia to attack. Ganey had served in the 2nd South Carolina under Francis Marion, but when he felt slighted by an officer, he swore allegiance to the King. Loyalist Colonel Robert Gray told of Ganey's militia when he wrote, "Marion could only call out Williamsburg Township, due to Loyalist partisans in the Cheraw District. Cheraw Patriots had to be released to guard their homes." Ganey led the way down the Little Pee Dee River with an advance guard of forty-five horsemen. Marion knew that Ganey was coming, and knew that his force was outnumbered, so he decided to attack first.

Since his men only wore homespun clothing and had no uniform, Marion had them wear white cockades in their caps. Marion's men were armed with shotguns, hunting rifles, British muskets, cavalry carbines, pistols and sabers hammered by local blacksmiths from wood saws. Their favorite close range load was goose shot. At thirty yards it would tear a man apart.

At a Loyalist settlement on the Little Pee Dee Marion ran into a troop of Ganey's horsemen who were blocking the road. Major James charged the Loyalists. Ganey took off down the road and his men scattered. James pursued him, until he had outrun his own men. He ran into a thicket that held several Loyalists, and shouted, "Come on boys! Here they are!" in an attempt to fool the then enemy. The Loyalists fled, thinking they were outnumbered.

Marion learned from the prisoners that Ganey's infantry was three miles away. He rode towards them and in ten minutes met the Loyalists in full march towards him. Captain Jesse Barfield formed his men into line and stood his ground. Marion knew to attack a larger force would be foolhardy, so he signaled a retreat and moved back to set up an ambush. He concealed his men at Blue Savannah, an open sandy area surrounded by scrub pines. Barfield led his excited regiment right into the ambush.

Marion charged with fifty men, weapons firing and swords slashing. Barfield delivered one volley that knocked three men from their horses, and then his men broke and ran. Marion's men pursued the Loyalists to the edge of the swamp, but did not want to penetrate it. They knew that a cornered enemy was extremely dangerous. They prowled the rim of the swamp, screaming, cursing, and firing at the hiding Loyalists. Marion eventually called them off and turned back to Port's Ferry. That same day sixty volunteers came in to join Marion's partisans, effectively doubling his force. His fame had grown, and he was becoming known as the most successful partisan in the Carolinas.[584]

Graham's Fort, North Carolina   Skirmish
September 1780

Colonel William Graham had been a delegate to the Fifth Provincial Congress, and had taken part in the deliberations that produced North Carolina's first state constitution. He fought at Moore's Creek Bridge and Ramseur's Mill, and was now a wanted man by the Loyalists. Graham had constructed a large log cabin on Buffalo Creek, which became known as Graham's Fort. Because of the increased activity by Loyalists in the area many people would gather at the strongest house in the region, and in Lincoln County that was Graham's Fort.

In September a band of Tory raiders approached the fort and demanded entrance. Inside the fort were Graham, two other men, and many young, old and infirmed settlers. When Colonel Graham refused to let the Loyalists enter the fort, they attacked. The Tories fired at the house, and after each volley they demanded Graham to surrender, yelling, "Damn you, won't you surrender now?"

Since they were doing no damage Graham refused. One of the Loyalists, John Burke, left the ranks and raced up to the cabin. Burke placed his musket through a crack, and aimed at 19-year-old William Twitty. When Burke fired, Twitty's 17-year old sister, Susan, pulled him to safety. The musket ball missed and hit the opposite wall. Susan looked through the crack, and saw that Burke was on his knees reloading. Susan shouted, "Brother William, now's your chance – shoot the rascal!" Twitty fired, and sent a ball into Burke's head. Susan ran out of the fort and grabbed Burke's gun and ammunition. The Loyalists were stunned to see one of their own fall, and held their fire. Once Susan was inside she started firing at the Loyalists as fast as she could load.

After losing one Burke and having four others wounded, the Loyalists withdrew. Graham sent his pregnant wife, and all the others in the fort to a safer location. He then moved his men to a better site. [585] After Graham had left, the Loyalists returned, plundered the fort, and carried off six of his slaves.[586]

Pee Dee Swamp, South Carolina
September 1780

Marion continued to send out reconnaissance patrols to determine the movements of the British in his area of operations. Captain Gavin Witherspoon and four of Marion's men were in one of these patrols, and while he had been hiding in the Pee Dee Swamp, he discovered a Loyalist camp.[587] His men did not want to venture into the camp, but he would not be deterred and went alone. He crept up to the camp and found the Loyalists asleep with their muskets leaning up against a pine tree. Witherspoon secured the muskets, and then woke the Loyalists by loudly demanding their surrender. The seven Loyalists surrendered when they saw Witherspoon's timid followers drawing near to finally assist him.[588]

Anson County, North Carolina   Skirmish
9 September 1780

As the British moved into the low country looking for Marion, many of the partisans moved up into North Carolina to wait for a better time to strike. While they were there they conducted actions against the North Carolina Loyalists, with very little threat of retaliation by British forces. On September 9th Colonel Abel Kolb led eighty to one hundred South Carolina militiamen against

Loyalists in two locations in Anson County, North Carolina. The Loyalists lost three men killed and five wounded.[589]

Mask's Ferry, North Carolina   Skirmish
10 September 1780

On September 10th Captain Herrick and his light horse militia attacked a party of Loyalists, near Mask's Ferry on the Pee Dee River. Herrick killed some of them and took eleven of them prisoner.[590]

Cane Creek, North Carolina [591]   Skirmish
12 September 1780

Captain James Dunlap was the commander of the advance party of Major Patrick Ferguson's army and as they moved towards the mountains there was constant skirmishing with the partisans. Alexander Chesney wrote "We continued some time at the Iron Works, and whilst there, a party of loyalist with whom I was, defeated Colonel Beauman, destroyed some of his party, and scattered the rest. I was present also, at a small affair at Fair Forest, the particulars of which, as well as numerous other skirmished, having escaped my memory, scarcely a day passed without some fighting…we marched with horse and some foot past Gilbert's Town towards Colonel Grimes' who was raising a body of rebels to oppose us, when we succeed in dispersing, taking many prisoners, and then joined the foot at Gilbert's town."[592]

Chesney continued, "Colonel Ferguson soon got intelligence that Colonel McDowell was encamped at Cain and Silver Creeks, on which we marched towards the enemy, crossed the winding creek 23 times, found the rebel army strongly posted towards the head of it near the mountains"

Colonel Charles McDowell had been riding along the Broad River, and was retreating towards the Watauga settlements, in what would later become east Tennessee. McDowell learned that Ferguson was approaching, and decided to lay in an ambush where the Loyalists would cross at Cane Creek Ford. McDowell's men were positioned on a hill that "was a small round elevation about a quarter of a mile from the base of the South Mountain then covered with timber and surrounded by a soft swamp."

When the Loyalists crossed the ford, McDowell sprung his ambush. Dunlap was severely wounded in the thigh.[593] The American Volunteers counterattacked and took seventeen prisoners, along with twelve horses of the partisans.

Major Joseph McDowell, the Colonel's brother, hollered out to the men to never yield, and to stand with him and die. The Loyalists fell back from the spirited defense, and retreated from the ford. McDowell realized that his forces were outnumbered and retreated across the mountains to Watauga. Ferguson's advance party withdrew to Gilbertown.[594]

Anthony Allaire wrote "We totally routed them, killed one private, wounded a Capt. White, took seventeen prisoners, twelve horses, all their ammunition, which was only twenty pounds of powder, after which we marched to their encampment, and found it abandoned by those Congress heroes. Our loss was two wounded and one killed. Among the wounded was Capt. Dunlap, who received two slight wounds."

As a result of this victory Ferguson came to the erroneous, and fatal conclusion that the resistance to the Crown in western North Carolina was at an end.[595]

McKay's Trading Post, Augusta, Georgia [596] Siege
14 – 18 September 1780

American Forces
Commanding Officer   Colonel Elijah Clarke
   Georgia Militia
      Colonel Elijah Clarke
         Wilkes and Burke County Militia   300
            Captain Patrick "Paddy" Carr
            Captain William Bugg [597]

South Carolina Militia
Major James McCall
Sumter's Brigade of Partisans   300
Major Samuel Taylor
Captain Anthony Ashby
Captain Ranal McCoy
Captain William Martin
Artillery captured from Fort Grierson
4-pounder   1
6-pounder   1
Casualties   60 killed and wounded, 100 captured [598]

Loyalist Forces
Commanding Officer   Lieutenant Colonel Thomas Brown
Provincials
Lieutenant Colonel Thomas Brown
King's Rangers   150
Captain Andrew Johnston
Captain Joseph Smith
Captain Alexander Campbell Wylly
Captain Samuel Roworth
Artillery
3-pounder   2 brass pieces
Major Robert Drummond
New Jersey Volunteers   27
Indians
Captain William McIntosh
Little Prince of the Tuckabatchees
Creeks   250
Captain Alexander McGillivray
Cherokees   50
Casualties   16 Loyalists killed, 6 wounded, 1 missing,
19 captured, 20 Indians killed or wounded [599]

Relief Force from Fort Ninety-Six
Commanding Officer   Lieutenant Colonel John Harris Cruger
   Provincials
      Lieutenant Colonel John Harris Cruger
        DeLancey's Brigade
          1st Battalion   105
      Unknown Captain
        New Jersey Volunteers
          3rd Battalion   40
      Colonel Alexander Innes
        South Carolina Royalists   198

Colonel Thomas Brown had been having a general conference of the Creeks and Cherokees at McKay's Trading Post in Augusta. The Creek Indians were camped near Indian Springs, outside Augusta. Captain Johnston's company was posted at Robert MacKay's house, guarding all the Indian supplies worth £4000.[600] Brown and some of the New Jersey Volunteers were at Grierson's fortified house, also known as Fort Grierson.[601]

Elijah Clarke and James McCall joined forces to march on Augusta and disrupt Brown's conference. Clarke's scouts had ridden to the outskirts of Augusta, and captured a British officer. The officer was forced to reveal the disposition of Brown's forces in Augusta. Clarke divided his command into three elements to strike each of the positions. Clarke would attack Fort Grierson, Major Samuel Taylor would attack the Creek Indian camp and McCall would attack McKay's House, a mile and a half west of the town.

On the morning of the 14th the first element, under Major Taylor, attacked the Creek camp near Hawk's Creek to the west of town. Brown led his Rangers to the sound of firing, and joined forces with the retreating Indians. Clarke had taken the Savannah road and had come in behind Brown, capturing Fort Grierson and its garrison without a fight. Clarke then advanced with McCall on the MacKay house and captured the men and Indian supplies there. Captain Johnston, of Brown's Rangers, was killed in the fight at house.

Brown's Rangers and the Indians formed a line of battle with bayonets fixed, on a slight elevation called Garden Hill. The Indians deployed to the left of Brown's men, and had their rifles at the ready. Two artillery pieces flanked the left and right of the line. The cannons fired upon Clarke's men, while Brown's troops charged, recapturing MacKay's house and the outbuildings. Some of Clarke's men circled through a thicket, and captured one of the artillery pieces. Clarke's riflemen continued to fire sporadically at the British until the afternoon, when they broke away to plunder the fort.

Brown did his best to fortify the MacKay house. The Indians manned the earthworks dug around the house. Bails of cloth and blankets found in the store at Garden Hill were made into a breastwork. Loopholes were cut in the building to increase their field of fire. Brown also sent a message to Lieutenant Colonel Cruger at Ninety-Six to come to his aid.

Clarke brought two cannons down from Fort Grierson, and dug his own earthworks around MacKay's house. He opened a heavy fire with his rifles. Brown was hit with a rifle ball that penetrated both thighs. Captain Martin was the only experienced artillerist with Clarke's militia, and he kept up an accurate barrage until a rifle ball killed him. That evening Clarke asked for Brown's surrender. Brown defiantly replied that if Clarke's men did not lay down their arms, there would be serious retaliation. Sporadic shooting continued throughout the night, and neither side slept. That night fifty Cherokees crossed the river and joined Brown's forces inside the White House.

Brown had no food or water in the house. The men at raw pumpkins for nourishment, and Brown had his men collect the urine in earthen vessels, which was served out to the men when it was cold. He continued to direct the defense, but he was in considerable pain due to his wounds.

On September 16th Lieutenant Colonel Cruger placed Colonel Moses Kirkland and 100 militiamen in charge of Fort Ninety-Six, then he set out for Augusta. Cruger's force approached MacKay's house on the evening of the 18th. Clarke's men kept up a continuous fire, but after Cruger had gained the Georgia side of the riverbank Brown ordered the Rangers and Indians to assault the backwoodsmen. Casualties and desertions had already weakened Clarke's force, and his men fled before the Rangers. The Rangers recaptured their artillery, while the Indians pursued Clarke's militia. They resorted to "savage warfare" when they caught up with any unlucky frontiersmen.

Thirteen of the prisoners who had broken their parole were hanged. Because of the continued threat of Clarke and other backwoodsmen Cornwallis sent Ferguson back into the mountains to subdue them. Brown marched into Wilkes County and took twenty-one prominent citizens hostage. He kept them at Augusta to insure the county would remain neutral. The twenty-one citizens were kept in close confinement in the fort, until June of 1781.

In retaliation for Clarke's attack on Augusta, a combined force of Loyalists and Indians burned over one hundred Whig plantations in Wilkes County, in September and October. They also destroyed Zachariah Phillips' Fort, at the mouth of Lick Creek on the Little River. [602]

McGill's Plantation, Williamsburg Township, South Carolina
Wemyss's Raid
15 – 20 September 1780

Major Wemyss laid waste to a path fifteen miles wide, along the seventy-mile route from Kings Tree to Cheraw. He was under order by Cornwallis to disarm "in the most rigid manner" all those who joined in the uprising. Wemyss's force consisted of 200 Regulars of the 63rd Regiment and 100 Provincials of the Royal North Carolina Regiment and the South Carolina Rangers. He did not consider the South Carolina Rangers to be very effective. He wrote to Cornwallis "Harrison's Corps are not worth anything. There is but 50 of them, irregulars and plunderers."

Wemyss had his men break up looms and burn the mills. He even had his troops shoot milk cows and bayonet sheep. His destruction of the looms and the sheep was to deprive the people of clothing. He burned, and laid waste to fifty plantations, carried off their slaves for use as slave labor by the British, and hanged several men who opposed his actions. Wemyss burned the Presbyterian Church at Indian Town because he said all churches were "sedition shops." His destruction would be very similar of another invading army, 85 years later. Fortunately for the people of the low country the corn was not housed yet and was able to be saved.

There was some opposition to the invaders. Captain James had fired upon Wemyss's men at McGill's Plantation, but this only enraged them more. Adam Cusack shot at a Loyalist officer, but missed and killed the officer's black servant instead. Cusack's wife and children threw themselves in front of Wemyss's horse, begging for mercy for her husband. If it hadn't been for the interference of his own officers, Wemyss would have rode over the kneeling woman. He hanged Cusack in front of his wife and children. Dr. James Wilson tried to stop the hanging, but had his home burned for his trouble.

Dr. Wilson traveled to North Carolina with many others from the area, and joined Marion. Wemyss became the second most hated man in the Carolinas, and Francis Marion's best recruiting officer. Once Marion heard what Wemyss had done, he rode back into to South Carolina to stop the carnage. [603]

Wahab's Plantation, North Carolina   Skirmish
21 September 1780

American Forces
Commanding Officer   Lieutenant Colonel William Davie
   North Carolina Militia
     North Carolina Partisan Rangers
      Lieutenant Colonel William Davie
        Mecklenburg Regiment [604]   80
         Captain James Wauchope [605]
      Colonel George Davidson
        Anson County Militia [606]   70
Casualties   1 wounded by accident

British Forces
Commanding Officer   Major George Hanger
   British Regulars
      Lieutenant Colonel Alexander McDonald
        71st Regiment of Foot (Fraser's Highlanders)   300
   Provincials
      Major George Hanger
        British Legion
           Legion Cavalry   60
Casualties   20 killed, 47 wounded, 1 captured

After Cornwallis defeated Gates at Camden he rested his army at the Waxhaws. Many of the men were not from the South and came down with malaria. Major George Hanger of the British Legion had his camp near "Wahab's" Plantation and conducted raids from his camp spreading, "havoc and destruction" in the area.

Colonel Davidson wrote that he had sent "small parties of observation in every disaffected quarter. The Tories are quiet, except about 500, who plunder the country under pretense of being part of their King's army and even those apprehend great danger."

Davie, along with Colonel William Davidson, decided to put a stop to these raids. Governor Nash had appointed Davie "Colonel Commandant of all the cavalry of North Carolina" and he had set up his camp at New Providence, twenty-five miles from the British camp. He rode around Cornwallis's main camp to avoid detection, and found that the Loyalists they were looking for had moved to the plantation of Captain James Wauchope, who was riding with Davie. The plantation was about two miles in the rear of the British lines.

Davie reached Wahab's plantation at dawn and found it surrounded not only by Loyalists, but also by the 71st Highlander Regiment. Davie was unwilling to back off, and divided his forces into three elements. They would attack the house from three sides. Captain Wauchope led some of the cavalry from one end of the lane, while Davie led the rest of the cavalry from the other end. Some infantry and dismounted men would come from the west. He told his men to take no prisoners.[607]

The battle began when the company of riflemen worked their way through a cornfield, and began firing on the house. The British Legion ran from the house, right into Davie's waiting riflemen on the flanks. The withering fire drove them back upon the two elements of cavalry that had rode around the cornfield. The Loyalists tore down the farm fence and fled in panic.

One of Davie's men, Jack Barnett, rode up and saw something move at the edge of the fence around the cornfield. He was surprised to find a Loyalist that he recognized. It was a Tory named Dixon, who threw down his gun and ran away. Barnett dismounted to get the gun, right at the moment that Davie's cavalry charged forward. Barnett's horse charged forward without him, following the other horses.

Barnett could see the flashes coming from the cornfield, and hear the bullets whistling around him. He picked up Dixon's gun and took cover behind a tree. Two British dragoons rode forward, and he fired his two weapons at the mounted men, and then ran to rejoin his forces.

He was almost killed by his own men, but he was quickly able to answer the countersign. He had been hit three times in the side by friendly fire.[608] While they held the house Captain Wauchope was able to see his wife and children briefly, before he had to withdraw.

Davie collected ninety-six horses, and "as many saddles", along with 120 muskets lying on the field. He was able to retreat just as the 71st Regiment had formed to attack. Barnett was picked up by William Polk and rode off.[609] Captain Wauchope watched as the British burned his houses and barn.

Cornwallis was so irritated by this incident that he decided to break camp and march on Charlotte to eliminate the threat from the North Carolina partisans.[610]

Charlotte Town, North Carolina [611]   **Skirmish**
North Carolina Campaign of 1780
26 September 1780

American Forces
Commanding Officer   Colonel William Richardson Davie
    North Carolina Militia [612]
        North Carolina Partisan Rangers
            Mecklenburg Regiment   150
                Captain James Wauchope
                Captain Joseph Graham
                    Lincoln County Militia   14
                        Captain John Brandon
                            Rowan County Militia
                    Captain Henry Connelly
                        Granville County Militia   Unknown number
                Major Joseph Dickson
                    Lincoln County Militia   20
                Colonel George Davidson
                    Anson County Militia   70
Casualties   5 killed, 6 wounded, 12 captured

British Forces
Commanding Officer   Lieutenant General Lord Cornwallis
    British Regulars
        Lieutenant Colonel James Webster
            33rd Regiment of Foot
                Captain William Gore
                    Light Infantry   Unknown number
            Captain Campbell
                71st Regiment of Foot (Fraser's Highlanders)
                    1st Battalion
                        Light Infantry   Unknown number
            Royal Regiment of Artillery
                3-pounders   2
                6-pounder   1

Provincials
    Major George Hanger
      British Legion
        Legion Cavalry   100
           Captain David Kinlock
           Captain Charles Campbell
        Legion Infantry   60
           Captain Patrick Stewart
           Captain Charles McDonald
      Captain John Doyle
        Volunteers of Ireland   60
Casualties   33 wounded [613]

In 1780 Charlotte Town was a small town of twenty houses. After the defeat of Gates the town became the rendezvous point for the survivors of Camden. Officers quickly molded what was left of the army into units, and then began the long march to Salisbury.

The wounded of the battle were transported on wagons, litters and on horseback. Refugees traveled with the column, mostly made up of women and children. In the rear came the 300 "half-naked" Catawba Indians.

The Charlotte Town militia under Davie stayed behind. Davie and Captain Joseph Graham were considered the two most competent soldiers in the state. Graham had been a quartermaster sergeant with Colonel Malmedy at Stono Ferry, and had been discharged in August of 1779. He had taken a fever and was exempted from duties for three years. When Buford was defeated the North Carolina militia was called out "en masse", and Graham became an adjutant to the Mecklenburg Regiment.

Cornwallis decided to go into North Carolina because he thought that large numbers of North Carolina Loyalists would join his army. He also wanted to destroy the remaining opposition that had escaped from Camden. He began his North Carolina invasion by marching to Charlotte Town. When he crossed the North Carolina border on September 25th General Davidson issued a call for militia volunteers, and then ordered his 400 Mecklenburg militiamen under Davie to delay Cornwallis at Charlotte Town.

On the night of the 25th Davie's men "hovered around the British army" and captured a number of prisoners. The partisans moved into and occupied Charlotte Town.

On the morning of the 26th Graham's pickets discovered the British advance guard moving towards the town. Davie had placed Captain John Brandon's militia under the Courthouse in the town. Graham's militia had protection from a chest-high stonewall at the courthouse. Major Dickson and his men were posted in front of Graham, in houses to the left and right of the courthouse. The Patriots were hidden from the approaching British.

Tarleton arrived with his Legion, but within five minutes he turned over command to Major Hanger, because he was sick due to having yellow fever. Graham's pickets sniped at the British as they deployed into line 300 yards in front of the courthouse. The British deployed the cavalry in subdivisions, and the infantry in platoons, with 100 yards between the columns.[614]

Hanger charged Davie's men in typical Tarleton-like fashion, but Davie was not Buford. When the Legion had galloped to within sixty yards of the courthouse, the Patriots at the wall rose and fired. The volley broke the Legion's charge and they fled. The British Light Infantry pressed on.

As the Light Infantry engaged the flanks, the Legion Dragoons reformed and charged the center. After another volley from Davie's men they withdrew in confusion. The Legion Infantry and the Light Infantry were able to turn Davie's flank, and he had his companies withdraw and form a single line at the end of the street, 100 yards from the courthouse. The Legion Dragoons again attempted to break Davie's line, but after receiving an intense fire from the militia they retired behind the houses. Cornwallis had ridden to the front and shouted to Hanger's men, "Legion, remember you have everything to lose, but nothing to gain!"

The Legion Infantry pressed the partisans and Davie gave the order to disperse through the woods. The men withdrew to the Salisbury road, and out of the town. Graham's men collected at

Kennedy Creek and waited for the British to appear. The men waited on horseback until a full platoon of British infantry appeared. They fired on the British, then immediately withdrew. The British returned fire, but the musket balls smashed through the trees, doing little damage.

After the war Major George Hanger described this type of fighting. In "*An Address to the Army*" he wrote, "The crackers and militia in those parts of America are all mounted on horseback, which renders it totally impossible to force them to an engagement with infantry only. Whey they chuse to fight, they dismount and fasten their horses to fences and rails; but if not very confident in the superiority of their numbers, they remain on horseback, give their fire, and retreat, which renders it useless to attack them without cavalry: for though you repulse them and drive them from the field, you can never improve the advantage, or do them material detriment."

At Sugar Creek Church Graham and Brandon's men held a hill, and began to fire on the Light Infantry that were 250 yards away. The Light Infantry moved behind trees and fences, and fired for nearly half an hour at long range. Graham's men returned fire in the same manner, but no damage was done to either side. Hanger arrived with the Legion cavalry and charged into Graham's men.

Graham was wounded badly, and sustained three bullet wounds in the thigh, a saber thrust in the side, a gash on the neck, and four cuts to the forehead. He wrote of his head wound that, "some of my brains exuded."

Lieutenant George Locke, the son of General Matthew Locke, was cut to pieces by the sabers of the Legion. He tried to shield himself with his rifle barrel and it was cut in many places. Graham's men fled to the woods.

When the British withdrew to Charlotte Town, they came up on the badly wounded Graham. One of the British aimed a pistol at Graham's head, but Hanger stopped him, saying, "Put up your pistol, save your ammunition, he has enough." Graham was left to die, but instead he crawled to a spring near a church.

At sunset Susan Wilson discovered him. Susan rushed to get her mother and they brought Graham back to their home. They nursed his wounds and hid him from the British. Five months later Graham would be back in the fight, trying to stop Cornwallis again at Cowan's Ford.

Cornwallis stayed in Charlotte until October 14th. When it became time to leave, many of his men were unable to march due to the break out of Yellow Fever. Major Hanger soon became sick with yellow fever and left the Legion, never to return to duty with that regiment.[615]

Yadkin River, North Carolina   **Skirmish**
North Carolina Campaign of 1780
September 1780

Colonel John Peasley and his North Carolina militia marched to Salisbury to join General Davidson's Brigade.[616] Richard Vernon was in Captain George Pray's Company, and wrote that when they reached McCalpine's Creek in Mecklenburg County they spotted a British patrol, and "retreated to the north side of the Yadkin River. On our retreat we were overtaken by the English and had a skirmish with them." Vernon wrote that several men were killed "among whom were William Rankin, and a Mr. Sock of my acquaintance."
[617]

Black Mingo Creek, Shepherd's Ferry, South Carolina[618]
28 – 29 September 1780

American Forces
Commanding Officer   Colonel Francis Marion
     Continentals
         1st South Carolina Regiment
             2nd Battalion   Unknown number
                Major Hugh Horry
     South Carolina Militia
         Williamsburg Township Militia   75

Colonel Hugh Giles
    Captain John Huggins
Major George King
Captain Thomas Waities
Captain John Melton
Captain John James of the Lake   10
Captain Henry Mouzon   5
Captain George Logan   6
Lieutenant John Scott   4

Casualties   2 killed, 8 wounded

Loyalist Forces
Commanding Officer   Colonel John Coming Ball
    South Carolina Loyalist Militia
    Craven and Berkeley County Regiment of Militia   46
Casualties   3 killed, 1 wounded, 13 captured

When Marion had heard about the destructive raid of Major Wemyss, he moved at daybreak from North Carolina to the Williamsburg Township. He gathered his forces, traveling forty-two miles and crossing three rivers by nightfall. Captain George Logan had been sick near the White Marsh, but hearing that Marion was marching for South Carolina, he rose from his bed and rode eighty miles to join him. Marion learned that Colonel John Coming Ball and his Loyalist militia were at Dollard's Tavern, on Black Mingo Creek.[619] Colonel Ball's mission was to serve as an advance outpost for the recently completed British post at Georgetown, twenty miles to the east.

As Marion's horsemen crossed the Willtown Bridge, a mile from the Loyalist camp, the planks began to rumble. The noise carried down the Mingo, and one of Colonel Ball's sentries fired an alarm gun. Marion heard the shot and rode hard towards Dollard's Tavern. The partisans dismounted at three hundred yards and decided to do a frontal assault onto the Tavern. Marion sent the rest of his cavalry to the left.

Ball had roused his men at the sound of the gunshot, and rushed them out into the open field west of the Tavern. This was unexpected by Marion, as he thought Ball would fight from the tavern. As Hugh Horry's infantry charged through the field, Colonel Ball gave the command to fire. Horry's men were thirty yards away when the volley hit them. Three of his officers fell. Captain Logan was killed, and Captain Henry Mouzon and Lieutenant John Scott were knocked to the ground, severely wounded. Horry's men fell back in disorder from the unexpected counterattack. Captain James rallied Horry's men and stopped the retreat.

Marion's partisans crept forward, loading and firing at every moving shadow. When Captain Waties moved up on the right with his men, the Loyalists began to break. Ball's men fired an ineffective volley, and then fled into the Black Mingo Swamp.

The battle only lasted fifteen minutes, but for the few number of men involved it was bloody. Marion lost three of his officers; Captain Mouzon and Lieutenant Scott were so severely wounded that they would no longer be fit for service. Marion's troops captured the enemy's guns, ammunition, baggage, and horses.

Marion took Ball's horse, and renamed him "Ball." Marion did learn from his mistakes, and would try to cross a river at a ford instead of using a bridge. If he had to cross a bridge near the enemy, he would cover the planks with his men's blankets to reduce the noise.[620]

Richmond Town, North Carolina
North Carolina Campaign of 1780
3 October 1780

Most of the North Carolina militia rendezvoused at Quaker Meadows on September 25th to oppose the Ferguson's expedition into the western region of South Carolina.[621] The Over the Mountainmen from Virginia and Tennessee joined them, then marched on to find Major Patrick Ferguson.

Since the local Whig militia was absent, Gideon and Hezekiah Wright raised a large band of Loyalists in Surry County. On October 3rd Colonel Gideon Wright attacked the Surry Courthouse in Richmond Town. They killed the Sheriff of the County, and took several prisoners.[622] They also raided the home of Captain William Shepherd, because he had marched off to fight Ferguson.[623]

The Battle of the Bees, North Carolina [624]   Skirmish
North Carolina Campaign of 1780
3 October 1780

After a week in Charlotte Town, Cornwallis needed to send out foraging parties to replenish his supplies. A large foraging party of 450 Provincials under the command of Captain John Doyle moved out on Beattie's Ford Road with sixty wagons.[625] A local boy notified the McIntyre family that the Loyalists were coming.

The boy rode on and told Captain James Thompson of the local militia. Thompson quickly rounded up Captain James Knox and thirteen local farmers to harass Doyle's troops, and then hid the riflemen in two sections at the McIntyre farm.

Thompson watched as Doyle's sixty men plundered the McIntyre's barns and raided the livestock pens.[626] The British tied their horses to the farm wagons while they went about their work. When the baggage wagons arrived they loaded bags of corn and oats onto the wagons.

During the pillaging the Loyalists accidentally knocked over some beehives, and found themselves under attack by the bees. One of the Loyalist officers stood in the doorway and laughed as the men swatted at the bees and ran from the danger.

As they were occupied Thompson and his men approached the raiders. Thompson yelled out that he would take a captain that he spotted, and every one of his men should pick a target. Thompson and a militiaman named Francis Bradley fired at the same time.[627] Thompson's shot found it's mark, and the man who he had thought was a Loyalist captain fell dead. The British quickly mounted their horses and formed a line, but Thompson and his men were able to reload and fire a second time.

The British set dogs loose on the Patriots, and they pursued one group of Thompson's men. "The dogs came on the trail of these retreating men, and the leading one sprung upon the heels of a man who had just discharged his rifle. A pistol-shot laid him dead; and the other dogs, coming up to him, paused, gave a howl, and returned."

Doyle believed that his men were being attacked by a much larger force and ordered a speedy retreat back to Charlotte. More of the local farmers showed up and began firing at the British from concealment, in a skirmish that resembled the start of the war at Concord, Massachusetts.

In the 19th century Reverend William Henry Foote wrote "The leading horses of the wagons were some of them shot down before they ascended the hill by the branch, and the road was blocked up; and the retreat became a scene of confusion in spite of the discipline of the British soldiers, who drew up in battle array and offered to fight the invisible enemy that only changed their ground and renewed their fire." Doyle's men rode so hard that "many of their horses fell dead in the streets." Eight of the Loyalists were killed in the attack, along with two horses. Twelve others were wounded. [628]

Hollingsworth Mill, Brown's Creek, South Carolina
North Carolina Campaign of 1780
5 – 8 October 1780

A party of eight or ten Whigs were patrolling around King's Mountain to gain intelligence on where Ferguson was, and trying to determine where the other Patriots militia units had gone. Within this patrol were Joseph Hughes, John Savage, William Sharp, William Giles and Charles Crade. They captured a "pet Tory" and learned that there was 250 Loyalists camped at the schoolhouse near Hollingsworth Mill on Brown's Creek.[629] Since the schoolhouse was on top of a hill, and surrounded by thick woods, the small patrol decided to "give them an alarm."

That night the Patriots surrounded the hill, and approached at different angles. The plan was to continue to move close to the house until a sentry challenged them, then lie down and fire into the camp. Each man would shoot, then rush into the camp after they fired. As they approached the camp a huge bonfire lit the trees and the surrounding woods. "All was joy and gladness in the camp. The jovial song and merry laugh told the listening ears of the approaching Whigs that good cheer abounded among the friends of King George around the fires."

One of the sentinels did detect the approaching Whigs and fired upon them. The Patriots charged towards the Tories, screaming like Indians and firing their muskets. The Loyalists must have thought they were outnumbered and fled into the night. When the Patriots had moved to the fire there was not a Loyalist to be found, but they could hear them running through the woods in the distance.

They found "wagons standing hither and thither, horses hitched to them and at the surrounding trees, guns stacked, cooking utensils about the fires, clothing and hats and caps scattered in merry confusion, but not a man could they find."

When the sun came up they were faced with the problem of determining what to do with all the wagons and horses. It was too much for them to carry off. They moved all of the captured equipment away from the hill, and then watched it for several days, hoping to ambush any Tories that attempted to come back for the goods.

Finally a small mounted force of fifteen Loyalists approached the area. The Patriot militiamen fired upon the Loyalists, scattering the men into the woods. One horse and rider were not able to get away, and he surrendered. He told the Patriots that he had been at the battle at King's Mountain and he was trying to flee the area. The Patriots were able to find some fellow militiamen who were returning from the battle, and they helped carry away all of the captured goods.[630]

King's Mountain, South Carolina   **Battle**
North Carolina Campaign of 1780
7 October 1780

American Forces
Commanding Officer   Colonel William Campbell [631]
  State Militia
    Virginia Militia   200
      Colonel Arthur Campbell [632]
        Washington County Militia
          Captain David Beatie
          1st Lieutenant Reece Bowen
            Captain William Bowen's Company
          Captain Andrew Colville
          Lieutenant Colonel Robert Craig
          Captain James Dysart
          Captain William Edmondson
            Captain Robert Edmondson, Sr.
          Lieutenant Thomas McCullough [633]
          1st Lieutenant William Russell, Jr.
            Captain William Neal's Company
        Colonel William Bowyer
          Rockbridge Rifles
        Captain Samuel McCutcheon
          Augusta Militia
    North Carolina Militia   700
      Colonel Benjamin Cleveland
        Wilkes County Militia [634]   110
          Captain Benjamin Herndon   60
          Captain Robert Cleveland [635]
          Captain "Devil John" Cleveland
          Captain Jesse Franklin
          Captain William Lenoir
            North Carolina Partisan Rangers [636] 6
          Captain John Barton
          Captain William Meredith

Captain William Jackson
Captain John Brown
Major Joseph Winston
   Surry County Militia   60
     Major Micajah Lewis
     Captain Joel Lewis
       Captain Samuel Johnson [637]
     Captain Minor Smith
Burke and Rutherford County Militia   90
   Colonel Andrew Hampton
     Rutherford County Militia
       Major James Porter
       Captain Richard Singleton
       Captain James Withrow
       Captain James Miller
   Colonel Joseph "Quaker Meadows Joe" McDowell
     Burke County Militia Battalion
       Major Joseph McDowell [638]
       Captain Thomas Kennedy
       Captain David Vance
       Captain Samuel Wood
       Captain Edmund Fear
       Captain John Sigman
Colonel William Graham
   Lincoln County Militia [639]
     Major Joseph Dickson
     Captain George Wilfong   25
     Captain James White
     Captain James Johnson
     Captain Samuel Espey
Lieutenant Colonel Frederick Hambright [640]
   Tryon County Militia [641]   90
     Major William Chronicle   20
     Captain John Mattocks
     Captain Samuel Martin   20

Over the Mountainmen
  Colonel Isaac Shelby
    Sullivan County Militia   120
      Major Evan Shelby, Jr.
      Captain Moses Shelby
      Captain Gilbert Christian
      Captain James Elliot
      Captain John Sawyers
      Captain George Maxwell
      Captain John Pemberton
      Captain David Webb
  Lieutenant Colonel John Sevier
    Washington County Militia
      Major Jonathan Tipton
      Captain Valentine Sevier
      Captain Christopher Taylor
      Captain Jacob Brown
      Captain Samuel Wear
      Captain Samuel Williams
      Captain James Stinson
      Captain Jesse Bean
      Captain Thomas Price
      Captain George Russell
      Captain Joel Callahan
    Captain William Bean
      Watauga Riflemen
        Captain Joseph Lusk
        Captain Thomas Preston
      Captain James Crabtree
      Holston Militia
South Carolina State Troops and Militia   200
  Colonel Thomas Brandon [642]
  2nd Spartan Regiment
    Captain Andrew Barry
    Captain Robert Hannah

Lieutenant Colonel James Stein [643]
   Union District Militia   60
Colonel Edward Lacey
   Chester District Militia
      Captain James Syles
      Captain John Moffitt
Colonel John Nixon
   Chester Rocky Creek Irish
Lieutenant Colonel James Hawthorne
   Sumter's Brigade of Partisans   100
      William Hill's Regiment of State Troops [644]
         Lieutenant Colonel Benjamin Roebuck
         Major Samuel Tate
         Captain James Giles
         Captain William McKinzey
         Captain John Hollis
      Major Samuel Hammond
      Hammond's State Troops
Colonel James Williams
   Laurens District Militia
      Little River Regiment
         Major George Anderson [645]
         Captain Gabriel Brown
         Captain Joseph Hayes
         Captain James Dillard
         Captain John Thompson
         Captain Daniel Williams [646]
      Captain John Douglas
      Caswell County Militia
Georgia Militia [647]   30
   Major William Candler
      Elijah Clarke's Brigade
         Captain Patrick "Paddy" Carr
         Captain Stephen Johnson
         Captain John Clark [648]

Total American Forces engaged [649]	1,100
Casualties	28 killed, 64 wounded [650]

Loyalist Forces
Commanding Officer   Major Patrick Ferguson
  Provincials
    Major Patrick Ferguson [651]
      American Volunteers   70
        Captain Abraham DePeyster
        Captain Charles McNeill
        Captain John Taylor
        Captain Samuel Ryerson
  Loyalist Militia
    North Carolina Loyalist Militia   450
      Colonel Ambrose Mills
      Major William Mills
      Colonel Vezey Husbands
      Major William Green
        Rutherford County Loyalist Militia
          Captain James Chitwood
          Captain Walter Gilkey
          Captain Aaron Biggerstaff
          Captain Grymes
    South Carolina Loyalist Militia
      Ninety-Six District Brigade of Loyalist Militia   350
      Major Daniel Plummer
        Major Daniel Plummer's Regiment [652]
          Captain Alexander Chesney
          Captain Robert Wilson
          Captain William Gist
          Captain James Campbell
          Captain James Shearer
          Captain Phillip Coleman
        Captain David Larimore
          Colonel Richard King's Regiment [653]   35

Lieutenant William Elliot
    Colonel John Hamilton's Regiment [654]
        Captain Elisha Robinson's Company
Captain William Young
    Zacharias Gibbs' Regiment[655]
Captain William Cunningham
    Major Patrick Cunningham's Regiment [656]
        Captain William Payne
        Captain William Helms
Unknown commander
    Colonel Daniel Clary's Regiment [657]
Unknown commander
    Colonel John Cotton's Regiment [658]
        Captain Henry Rudolph
        Captain Denas Knowland
            Captain Thomas Whitehead
            Captain William Kirkland
            Captain Hezekiah Williams
        Captain Bailey Chaney

Wagonners	10
Total Loyalist forces engaged	1,016
Casualties	157 killed, 163 wounded, 698 captured [659]

Major Patrick Ferguson had been tasked by Cornwallis with subduing the local rebels around Ninety-Six. Prior to the British arrival in the mountainous backcountry, the frontiersmen living in the Appalachian Mountains had not been involved much in the war. They had fought Indians, but not the British and Loyalists.

With Loyalist activity increasing everywhere after the fall of Charlestown, some of the backwoodsmen had become involved and fought several engagements with British forces. Alarmed at this threat to the rear of his main force Cornwallis ordered Ferguson out on an expedition into the backcountry aimed at crushing rebel resistance.

Early in September Ferguson arrived in Gilbert Town and sent a paroled prisoner into the mountains with a message for the backwoodsmen. He threatened to lay waste to their country with fire and sword, and hang their leaders should they stay with the Rebel cause. These were the wrong words to use to the men from the mountains. Instead of frightening them, it unified them with a common goal of wiping out Ferguson.

On September 25th a thousand of the backwoodsmen gathered at Sycamore Shoals on the Watauga River.[660] Amongst these backwoodsmen was the Over the Mountainmen. These were mainly North Carolinians who had moved to the Tennessee country. William Sparks was one of the backwoodsmen and he described them as "all mounted gunmen, and nearly all armed with Rifles, tomahawks, and butcher knives, each man, and myself amongst the rest, furnishing his own horse arms and equipment."

The men pursuing Ferguson were traveling without a commissary as regular armies did; each man had a rolled blanket to sleep in and a wallet or saddlebags filled with corn meal mixed with maple sugar. The horses foraged wherever they were hobbled for the night.

On the 26th the men left Sycamore Shoals to find Ferguson's trail. Reverend Samuel Doaks sent them off with a sermon that told the men to smight the British with "the sword of the Lord and Gideon."

Ferguson had heard of the force coming after him, and decided to avoid a confrontation. He favored picking off the small groups of militia as they marched to join the backwoodsmen. One group of Loyalists was able to ambush some of the Patriot militia at Lovelady Shoals on the Catawba River, but most of the Patriots were able to get through without any distractions. Ferguson asked Cornwallis for reinforcements, but there were none to spare, since Cornwallis was fighting his own war against Davie's partisans attacking the British foraging parties. On October 6th Ferguson had withdrawn to King's Mountain in what he thought was an impregnable position.

The man who was the driving force behind the backwoods army was Isaac Shelby, but no overall commander had been picked. Shelby argued that all of the colonels who were there were North Carolinians, but since Colonel Campbell was from Virginia, and commanded the largest regiment, he should command the force. Campbell was the least experienced of them all, but Shelby also noted that the decisions were to be regulated and directed by the determinations of all the Colonels.

Scouts were sent out by Shelby to find the British force. Near the Broad River two of the scouts, John Martin and Thomas Lankford, rode into an ambush. Lankford escaped, but Martin was shot in the head and knocked out of his saddle. Luckily the bullet's force had been broken by his hat and only skinned him along the temple. The ambushers thought he was dead and left him. Martin awoke and walked back to camp. He recovered from the wound after returning home.

The North Carolinians and Virginians rendezvoused with the South Carolinians at Hannah's Cowpens on October 6th. The Cowpens was a place in the backcountry where cattle were penned and fattened prior to being driven to the coast for sale. A Loyalist named Saunders carried on a business at the Cowpens, and when the frontiersmen arrived he asked that they spare his cattle and corn. The militia ignored him. Several cattle were slaughtered, and in ten minutes fifty acres of corn were harvested. Thomas Young wrote, "As soon as we got something to eat, for we were very hungry and weary, we retired to sleep at random in the woods."

At 9 o'clock that night the men began their march in the direction of Ferguson's force, and continued until the next day. It poured down rain and they kept their rifles dry by wrapping their hunting shirts around the locks. At Solomon Beason's house they learned that Ferguson was eight miles ahead. The backwoodsmen captured two Loyalists and gave them a simple choice, guide them or die. The rain stopped at noon and Sevier's men came across a girl who pointed at a ridge three miles away. She told them, "He is on that mountain".

Thomas Young's group had stopped "At a meeting-house on the eastern side of the river." He was under the command of Colonel Brandon. The men were ordered to halt, "and were on the point of sending out for some beeves, when we met George Watkins, a whig, who had been taken prisoner and was on his way home on parole.

He gave us information of the position of the enemy… Watkins had informed us were within a mile of the enemy."

They had chased Ferguson's force for eleven days. On October 7th nine hundred mounted men went ahead of the main force to make sure he was still on King's Mountain. The mountain is a ridge about 600 yards long, and 60 to 120 feet wide. Ferguson had built no fortifications because he believed that the rocks and trees would protect his men.

Colonel William Hill wrote that Ferguson "was so well pleased with the goodness of his position, as well as the courage & skill of his men who he had been training for some time with great success, that he defied God Almighty & all the rebels that could be collected to drive him from that camp." Unfortunately for him these same rocks and trees would be perfect cover to backwoodsmen used to warfare against the Indians.

Two miles from Ferguson's camp Lieutenant Colonel Frederick Hambright captured John Ponder, a young Loyalist. Ponder was carrying a dispatch from Ferguson for Cornwallis, imploring him for help. Ponder was questioned, and told the backwoodsmen that Ferguson was in full British uniform, but he wore a checkered shirt over it. Hambright laughed and said with his German accent, "Poys, hear dot! Shoot for the man mid the pig shirt!"[661]

A mile further the backwoodsmen ran into Henry Watkins, a prisoner who had just been released by Ferguson. Watkins was able to give the men detailed information on Ferguson's camp.

The backwoodsmen arrived and were told to "dismount and tied horses; tie up blankets and coats to the saddle." Some men were detailed to take care of the horses. The final command was to "Fresh prime your guns; go in resolved to fight till you die or win."

Cleveland talked to his men before going into the battle. "Every man must consider himself an officer and act from his own judgment. Fire as quick as you can and stand as long as you can. When you can do no better get behind trees, or retreat; but I beg of you not to run quite off. If we be repulsed, let us make a point to return to renew the fight. Perhaps we may have better luck in the second attempt than in the first."

Brandon told his men that "at the firing of the first gun, for every man to raise a whoop, rush forward, and fight his way best he could." Some of the men took off their hats and tied handkerchiefs around their heads, so limbs and bushes would not slow them.

The battle started at three o'clock in the afternoon when Ferguson's pickets discovered the backwoodsmen advancing up the slopes. The frontiersmen marched in two files that were two men deep, with the officers in the lead.[662] Once the battle started there was no overall field commander in charge of the backwoodsmen. Their plan was to ascend the mountain and surround the enemy on all quarters. Campbell was on the south side of the mountain and Cleveland was on the north. Chesney wrote, "so rapid was their attack that I was in the act of dismounting to report that all was quiet and the pickets on the alert, when we heard their firing about half a mile off."

At the approach of the frontiersmen the drum was sounded in the Loyalist camp, and Ferguson's whistle was distinctly heard, notifying his men to form for battle. Chesney wrote "I received a wound which however did not prevent my doing duty; and on going towards my horse I found he had been killed by the first discharge."

Ensign Robert Campbell wrote that the Loyalists "formed on top of the mountain behind a chain of rocks that appeared impregnable, and had their wagons drawn up on their flank across the end of the mountain, by which they made a strong breast work." Ferguson's Provincials were armed with muskets and the bayonet. His Loyalist militia was armed with muskets and rifles. Ferguson had plug bayonets made for the Loyalist's weapons.[663]

Shelby observed "their situation and what a destructive fire was kept up from behind those rocks, ordered Robert Campbell...to advance and post themselves opposite to the rocks, and near to the enemy, and then return to assist in bringing up the men in order, who had been charged with the bayonet." The frontiersmen were told not to fire until they heard an "Indian war whoop." When the Loyalists opened up on Shelby's force he had to restrain his men from returning fire until the signal was given. Shelby ordered his men to "Press on to your places, and your fire will not be lost."

Campbell had designated the troops of Major Micajah Lewis, Captain Andrew Colville and his brother Captain Joel Lewis, to rush into the British camp as soon as the firing had started. They were to sweep away the British main guard, then fall back and join the others. When the men rushed the British lines there was a vicious fight that left several of the Loyalists dead and wounded. Both of the Lewis brothers were wounded in the fight.

Campbell and his Virginians did not get into the initial fight, and had been delayed for ten minutes by a swampy marsh to his front. As they began the climb up the mountain, Ferguson's Loyalists fired downhill upon them. Their shots went high, taking the bark off the trees above the Virginian's heads. As the backwoodsmen wheeled into line, Campbell's voice could be heard shouting, "Here they are boys; shout like hell and fight like devils!" What would later be known as the "Rebel Yell" echoed off the mountain. Captain Abraham DePeyster turned to Ferguson and said, "This is ominous. These are the same yelling devils that were at Musgrove's Mill. These are the damned yelling boys!"

Ferguson ordered a bayonet charge down the slope into Campbell's men, who stood their ground for a short time. Lieutenant Anthony Allaire rode up to a mountaineer that was six feet high, and killed him with a single blow. William Robertson wrote that when he had advanced within thirty paces of the Loyalists, "I received a slight wound in my side, and another in my left arm; and, after that, a bullet went through my hair above where it was tied, and my clothes were cut in several places."

After a fierce fight, where some of the Virginians were run through with the bayonet, they backed away from the bayonet wielding Loyalists. Campbell's men ran to the next ridge over and rallied. The backwoodsmen had no bayonets, and simply thinned out the Loyalist ranks by well-aimed rifle fire. Once the bayonet charge was spent the Loyalists returned to the top of the mountain to get away from the galling rifle fire. Shelby said, "The mountain was covered with flame and smoke, and seemed to thunder."

Some historians believe that Ferguson could have escaped at this point. Ramsay wrote that, "Had he pursued his march on charging and driving the first party of the militia which gave way, he might have got off with the most of his men." Gordon also wrote that Ferguson "might have made good his retreat, if not with the whole, at least with part of his men, had he pursued his march immediately upon his charging and driving the first detachment." However Ferguson did not believe in fleeing or surrendering.

Shelby's Over the Mountainmen was forced down into a ravine. They turned and fired one volley, then used their tomahawks and knives and fought their way back to the top. Captain Charles Gordon grabbed one Loyalist officer by his hair, and dragged him down the mountain. When he was shot in the arm by the officer's pistol, he drew his sword and killed his prisoner.

Captain Moses Shelby, the brother of the Colonel, had been wounded twice, once in the thigh. He was carried down the mountain, and given his rifle to defend himself. When one of the backwoodsmen came off the mountain to get a drink from a stream, Moses Shelby told him it was not time to shirk his duty, and he would shoot him if he returned to the stream.

Three times the Loyalists charged with the bayonet, and three times they were driven back. Each time the Loyalists charged down one side of the mountain, the frontiersmen on the other side shouted, "They retreat! They retreat!" pouring rifle fire into their backs. On the final time that the Patriots were pushed down the mountain, the men began to hear shouts that Tarleton and his Legion had arrived. The men began to be demoralized by this news, and were upon the verge of leaving the field. Colonel Sevier rode along the line telling the men that Tarleton was not there, it was only a deception from the enemy. The backwoodsmen returned to engage the Loyalists, fighting hand to hand. The fighting was so close that some of Campbell's men were pushed over the cliffs.

On the third time that the Loyalists were pushed back up the mountain, they were pushed to the narrow end of the ridge where their camp was. The mountain men came at them yelling and screaming like Indians. Shelby shouted to them, "Now boys, quickly reload your rifles and let's advance upon them and give them another hell of fire…Shoot like hell and fight like demons!"

Chesney wrote that some of the Ninety-Six Loyalist Militia fled early, by placing white scraps of paper in their hats and moving through the backwoodsmen.

Graham had asked to leave before the fighting started. His wife was in a "precarious position" having his child. During the battle Major William Chronicle took command of his "South Fork Boys". As Graham headed home he heard the firing on the mountain. He quickly returned and arrived in time to take part in the battle. Chronicle had led his men up the mountain on horseback, and gave the command "Face the hill." He then fell, mortally wounded in the heart.

Major Dickson ordered the men to charge, and Colonel Frederick Hambright assumed command of the force. Hambright had his hat perforated by three balls, and then was wounded in the thigh. The ball passed between the thighbone and his saddle, but he continued to lead his men, mounted on his horse and bleeding over the tops of his boots. Hambright never did recover from his wound and walked with a limp for the rest of his life.

Thomas Young, a soldier in Roebuck's command, wrote of the attack, "Ben Hollingsworth and I took right up the side of the mountain, and fought our way, from tree to tree, up to the summit. I recollect I stood behind one tree and fired til the bark was nearly all knocked off, and my eyes pretty well filled with It. One fellow shaved me pretty close, for his bullet took a piece out of my gun-stock. Before I was aware of it, I found myself apparently between my own regiment and the enemy, as I judged, from seeing the paper which the Whigs wore in their hats, and the pine knots the Tories wore in theirs, these being the badges of distinction."

Sevier's North Carolinians reached the summit of the mountain first. Using the rocks for shelter, they poured a murderous fire into the Loyalist's flank. Captain Robert Sevier, the brother of the colonel, was mortally wounded by buckshot in the kidney as he bent down to pick up his ramrod. Major Samuel Hammond and a small squad broke through the lines of the Provincials, and noticed that they were about to be cut off from escaping. Hammond immediately ordered his men back, having to cut their way through the Loyalists.

The Loyalists were pushed to the southwestern side of the ridge, and were surrounded by the frontiersmen. Robert Campbell wrote "Ferguson, being pressed heavily on all sides, ordered Capt. DePeyster to reinforce some of the extreme post with a full company of British Regulars.[664] He marched, but to his astonishment, when he arrived at the place of destination, he had almost no men, being exposed in that short distance to the constant fire of rifles. He then ordered his cavalry to mount, but to no purpose. As quick as they were mounted they were taken down by some bold marksman."

Two white flags were raised in an attempted surrender, but Ferguson rode over and cut them down with his sword. He swore he "would never surrender to such banditti!"[665] DePeyster urged Ferguson to surrender, but instead he decided to break through the lines of backwoodsmen with a few chosen officers.

Ferguson tried to ride through the file of frontiersmen. He slashed at all that came near him, breaking his sword on a rifle barrel. He was heard to have cried, "Which way I fly is hell!" Shelby constantly admonished his men to "never shoot till you see your enemy and never see him without bringing him down." Eight to twelve marksmen saw Ferguson and fired. One of them was Robert Young, firing his rifle "Sweet Lips." Ferguson was hit numerous times, including once in the forehead, knocking him out of the saddle. His foot hung up in the stirrup and he was dragged over the rocky terrain for a short distance. As his body was being dragged past a group of backwoodsmen, they fired into it. Two riders with Ferguson, Colonel Vezey Husbands and Major Daniel Plummer, were both shot dead in the same volley.

James Collins, the 17 year old militiaman, wrote in his autobiography, "On examining the body of their great chief, it appeared that almost fifty rifles must have been leveled at him, at the same time; seven rifle balls had passed through his body, both of his arms were broken, and his hat and clothing were literally shot to pieces."

Abraham DePeyster saw Ferguson fall, and he took command of the surviving Loyalists. He tried to rally the panicked men in a sunken hollow, but he was forced to surrender. As fresh groups of mountain men reached the summit they fired into the cowering prisoners. Some of the backwoodsmen were unaware of the cease-fire and some didn't care. They sought revenge for Tarleton's Quarter at the Waxhaws. When the Loyalists raised white handkerchiefs they soon became the point of aim for the frontiersmen's rifles.

Captain DePeyster tried to raise a white handkerchief, but a rifle ball hit him. According to *Appleton's Cyclopedia of American Biography* Captain DePeyster had been paid that morning, and his life was saved when a bullet was stopped by a coin in his waistcoat pocket. The white handkerchief was taken out of DePeyster's "hand by one of the officers on horse back and raised so high that it could be seen by our line, and the firing immediately ceased."

Shelby advanced on the Loyalists huddled around their tents and wagons, and said, "Damn you, if you want quarter, throw down your arms!" Campbell waded into the midst of the Loyalists, to get his men to stop the killing. DePeyster rode up to Colonel Campbell and said, "Colonel Campbell, it was damned unfair!" Campbell told him to dismount his horse, and have his men take off their hats and sit down. Campbell had to personally stop some of his men from killing, by knocking their rifles up. He yelled at one private, Andrew Evins, "for God's sake, don't shoot! It is murder to kill them now, for they have raised the flag!"

Chesney wrote, "the Americans surrounded us with double lines, and we ground arms with the loss of one third our numbers." Campbell "was stalking around among the enemy in his shirt sleeves and his collar open, and when some of the Americans pointed him out as their commander, the British, at first, from his unmilitary plight, seemed to doubt it, but a number of officers now surrendered their swords to him, until he had several in his hands, and under his arm."

After about an hour of fierce fighting the mountain was littered with the dead of the Loyalists. One hundred and sixty three were too badly wounded to be moved. Graham left the battlefield, and immediately rode to his wife's side. She gave birth to Graham's only child, Sarah, a few hours later.

Some accounts have claimed that Colonel James Williams was killed during the fighting. Thomas Young wrote in his memoirs, "On the top of the mountain, in the thickest of the fight, I saw Col. Williams fall, and a braver or a better man never died upon the field of battle. I had seen him once before that day; it was in the beginning of the action, as he charged by me full speed around the mountain; toward the summit a ball struck his horse under the jaw when he commenced stamping as if he were in a nest of yellow jackets. Col. W. threw the reins over the animal's neck – sprang to the ground, and dashed onward. The moment I heard the cry that Col. Williams was shot, I ran to his assistance, for I loved him as a father, he had ever been so kind to me, and almost always carried carrying cake in his pocket for me and his little son Joseph. They carried him into a tent, and sprinkled some water in his face. He revived, and his first words were, "For God's sake boys, don't give up the hill!" I remember it as well as if it had occurred yesterday. I left him in the arms of his son Daniel, and returned to the field to avenge his fall. Col. Williams died next day, and was buried not far from the field of his glory."

However Williams was not killed during the fighting on the mountain, but was killed as the Loyalists were surrendering. A small party of Loyalist militia led by Colonel Moore had returned from a foraging party. [666] When Moore saw the backwoodsmen he began firing upon them. Campbell yelled that he would kill all the prisoners unless the firing stopped. Williams was riding to the British campsite when the Loyalists fired and mortally wounded him. Williams turned to one of Campbell's men, William Moore, and said, "I'm a gone man." He thought that the Loyalists had been Tarleton and his Legion bringing reinforcements.

Campbell ordered Williams and Brandon's men to fire upon the prisoners. The soldiers quickly obeyed Campbell and began blasting into the Loyalists. Lieutenant Joseph Hughes, of Brandon's command, wrote, "Colonel Campbell then ordered a fire on the

Tories and we killed near a hundred of them after the surrender of the British and could hardly be restrained from killing the whole of them."

There are accounts that said Ferguson died immediately, and others that state he died later from his wounds. Chesney incorrectly wrote that Ferguson shot Williams with a pistol as he came to assist the wounded officer. However, Williams was shot and killed on the opposite side of the mountain where Ferguson fell, and Chesney was not there to witness it.[667]

Ferguson was wrapped in a rawhide of beef and buried where he died. Local legend states that Ferguson was buried with a female camp cook, Virginia Sal, who was one of his two mistresses and had died in the battle. Also according to the legend the other mistress, Virginia Pol, rode about after the battle as if nothing unusual had happened.[668]

The American Volunteers ceased to exist. Of the seventy men that marched into the mountains with Ferguson only twenty were not killed or wounded. In the morning the wives and children of the Loyalists came in to find their loved ones. The backwoodsmen proceeded to bury the dead, but it was badly done; they were thrown into piles and covered with old logs and the bark of trees. It was said that after the battle the wolves were so numerous that it was dangerous for anyone to be out at night. Hogs from the area gathered and ate the exposed bodies. For a long time afterwards the local farmers did not eat pork.

There are numerous conflicting reports as to the numbers of wounded and killed with the backwoodsmen. An accepted number is 28 killed and 64 wounded. Of the twenty-eight killed, thirteen of these were officers leading from the front. One third of the killed and wounded were from Campbell's regiment.

That day the prisoners were marched away between two rows of mounted backwoodsmen. The prisoners carried the 1,500 captured weapons with the locks removed. Each prisoner was forced to carry two muskets in this fashion. The Patriot wounded who could travel was placed on litters of tent cloth, suspended on poles between horses. Colonel James Williams was taken to a farm near Derry's Ferry, where he died on October 8th.

Captain Robert Sevier had been wounded by buckshot in the kidney, and the Loyalist doctor Uzal Johnson had told them that if he stayed he could possibly recover, but if he left his kidneys would inflame and he would die. Robert Sevier feared staying on the mountain, and possible Loyalist retaliation. He left with the rest of the backwoodsmen and died on the ninth day of the march.

During the march "one very large Tory, weary in North Carolina, dodged into a hollow sycamore tree. When he was discovered Brandon dragged him out and hacked him into mince meat with his sword."

On October 11th Colonel Campbell issued a General Order to have the men stop "slaughtering" the prisoners. By the time the army reached Cane Creek the men were "near starving to death." The men ate fried green pumpkins. The prisoners were thrown raw corn on the cob, and pumpkins.

On October 14th a trial was held at Gilbert Town. Officers had demanded Campbell convene a court martial for prisoners who were parole breakers, robbers, house burners, and assassins. Thirty Loyalists were condemned to death. Nine, including Colonel Ambrose Mills, Captains Chitwood and Wilson, were actually hanged. The rest escaped as the mountain men drifted back to their home, and left them unguarded. Captain Carr, of Georgia, pointed at the nine dangling Loyalists and said, "Would to God every tree in the wilderness bore such fruit as that."[669]

After the departure of the militia Mrs. Martha Biggerstaff cut down the bodies. Mrs. Mills had sat beside the body of her husband, Aaron, with her child in her arms, all night in the rain, without even a blanket to cover her from the weather.

The prisoners were marched seven more days to the Moravian settlements at Salem. Many more of Loyalists escaped, and one of them was executed for attempting it. Several were unable to keep up and were cut down and trampled to death in the mud.

There was little food for either the prisoners, or their guards on the march. Thomas Young wrote, "We all came very near starving to death. The country was very thinly settled, and provisions could not be had for love or money. I thought green pumpkins, sliced and fried, about the sweetest eating I ever had in my life!"

Lieutenant Allaire wrote of the death march, "On the morning of the fifteenth, Col. Campbell had intelligence that Col. Tarleton was approaching him, when he gave orders to his men, that should Col. Tarleton come up with them, they were immediately to fire on Capt. DePeyster and his officers, who were in the front, and then a second volley on the men. During this day's march the men were obliged to give thirty-five Continental dollars for a single ear of Indian corn, and forty for a drink of water, they not being allowed to drink when fording a river; in short, the whole of the Rebels' conduct from the surrender of the party into their hands is incredible to relate. Several of the militia that were worn out with fatigue, and not being able to keep up, were cut down, and trodden to death in the mire. After the party arrived at Moravian Town, in North Carolina, we officers were ordered in different houses. Dr. Johnson (who lived with me) and myself were turned out of our bed at an unseasonable hour of the night, and threatened with immediate death if we did not make room for some of Campbell's officers; Dr. Johnson was, after this, knocked down, and treated in the basest manner, for endeavoring to dress a man whom they had cut on the march. The Rebel officers would often go in amongst the prisoners, draw their swords, cut down and wound those whom their wicked and savage minds prompted. This is a specimen of Rebel lenity-you may report it without the least equivocation, for upon the word and honor of a gentleman, this description is not equal to their barbarity. This kind of treatment made our time pass away very disagreeably"

Allaire and three other men were able to escape and travel 200 miles to Fort Ninety-Six, then on to Charlestown. Cleveland threatened Chesney with death, because he would not "teach his regiment for one month the exercise practised by Colonel Ferguson". Chesney escaped by hiding in a cave near his home for most of the year.

Many battles were claimed to have been the turning point in the Revolution, but for the war in the South King's Mountain was the turning point. This battle marked the beginning of the end of British occupation in the South. Fresh militia flocked in to join the Patriot army when news of this victory reached them. This battle forced Cornwallis to delay his invasion of North Carolina, and sent him marching to Winnsboro to protect his rear.

William Woolford wrote his brother, Colonel Thomas Woolford, prisoner at Haddrell's Point, "Our men are in High Spirits, and I hope, with the blessing of God, we shall be in Charleston by Christmas Day."

All of the victories achieved by the Patriot forces in the Carolinas, from the fall of Charlestown to King's Mountain, had been the work of the militia, but the Continentals were returning.[670]

South Carolina coast   **Naval Skirmish**
7-15 October 1780

American Forces

South Carolina State Navy	
Captain Charles Morgan	
Snow *Fair American*	16 guns
Philadelphia Privateer	
Captain Roger Keane	
Brig *Holker*	16 guns
Casualties	1 killed, 1 wounded on the *Holker*

British Forces

Commanding Officer	Captain Jameson
Royal Navy	
Armed Transport *Richmond*	16 guns
Casualties	*Richmond* captured

On October 7th the South Carolina ship *Fair American* teamed up once again with the Privateer *Holker,* and captured the brig *Rodney* out of Liverpool. The *Rodney* had been bound for Charlestown. The next day the two ships captured another brig from Plymouth, bound for Charlestown.

A week later, on October 14th, the two brigs captured the *Richard* from Glasgow, also bound for Charlestown . The next day they attacked the armed transport, *Richmond.* After a short action the *Richmond* struck her colors. All of the vessels that were captured in the two weeks had valuable cargoes of dry goods, wine, porter, cheese, and pork. The captured ships were taken to Delaware. On the 17th of October the *Fair American* and the *Holker* returned to sea to hunt for more prizes.

The *Holker* would meet her fate in between the waters of St. Lucia and Martinique, when Captain Keane tried to outrun the Royal frigate *Alcmene* in a violent squall. During the run she capsized. The British frigate rescued forty-seven men.[671]

Richmond Town, North Carolina
North Carolina Campaign of 1780
8 October 1780

By October 8th the Loyalist militia in Surry County, under Gideon and Hezekiah Wright, had increased to 300 men. In the absence of the local Whig militia the county was left exposed. The Wright brothers lost no time in taking advantage of the situation, and attacked Richmond again. Captain John Crause was wounded as he stood guard. The rest of the Whig militia in the town fled into the countryside. After the raid Colonel Wright moved his army to Bethabara.[672]

Polk's Mill, North Carolina   **Skirmish**
North Carolina Campaign of 1780
9 October 1780

After Cornwallis occupied Charlotte Town he established a post at Thomas Polk's Grist Mill so that the army could forage. Major Joseph Dickson returned from King's Mountain with a detachment of 120 mounted riflemen and attacked Lieutenant Stephen Guyon, and twenty Royal Welch Fusilier's at Polk's Mill. With Guyon was a detachment of Loyalist militia.

Dickson was able to capture the sentinel of the Fusiliers and eight of the militia, but Guyon defended the blockhouse and drove the Patriots off. Dickson had one man killed and one man wounded. Later that night a small party of fifty riflemen stole fifty horses from Polk's plantation.[673]

Tarleton wrote about the country around Charlotte Town describing that "The town and environs abounded with inveterate enemies; the roads were narrow and crossed in every direction and the woods were close and thick. It was evident, as had been frequently mentioned to the King's officers, that the counties of Mecklenburg and Rowan were more hostile to England than any others in America. No British commander could obtain any information in that position which would facilitate his designs or guide his future conduct. The foraging parties were every day harassed by the inhabitants, who did not remain at home to receive payment for the produce of their farms, but generally fired from covert places to annoy the British detachments." [674]

Evacuation of Charlotte Town, North Carolina   Skirmish
North Carolina Campaign of 1780
13 October 1780

After he learned of the defeat at King's Mountain Cornwallis decided to leave Charlotte Town, and withdraw to Winnsboro. Cornwallis's goal of gaining Loyalists to fight for his army was not met, and now his flank was open.[675]

The British placed their dead in Liberty Hall, at the college in town, and burned it down. They then marched out of Charlotte on October 12th. William McCafferty, a Charlotte merchant, guided the British, but he feared reprisals from the Patriots, so he deserted as soon as it was dark. The British wandered through the night and became extremely disorganized. They were not reunited with the army until noon on the following day.

McCafferty rode all night to Davie's camp on Sugar Creek, and informed him of the British retreat. Davie immediately sent a large detachment back to harass the British. The detachment skirmished with the enemy, with unknown results.

The British left Charlotte in a virtual panic after hearing that Davidson and 5,000 soldiers were pursuing them. In reality General Davidson had hardly more than 300 men. It began to rain and the roads turned into a muddy morass. Five miles from Charlotte the British abandoned thirty wagons so they could move faster. Those wagons and supplies were recovered by Davie. Inside the wagons was a printing press, supplies for the army, and the knapsacks of the Light Infantry and the British Legion.

Because they abandoned their wagons the British lacked provisions, and for five days lived only on corn gathered from the fields they passed by. Since they had no tents they slept on the open ground, with only their blankets. Many of the men, including Cornwallis, were sick with yellow fever. The men took tin canteens and broke them apart, then punched holes in them with their bayonets. They would use these homemade rasps to grate the Indian corn they could find.

The British Regulars did not treat the Loyalist militia very well. Charles Stedman wrote, "The militia were maltreated by abusive language, and even beaten by some of the officers in the Quarter-Master General's department. In consequence of this ill usage, several of them left the army the next morning forever, choosing to run the risk of meeting the resentment of their enemies, rather than submit to the derision and abuse of those to whom they looked up as friends." After fifteen days of being hounded by Davie's partisans, the British finally arrived in Winnsboro.

Local legend has it that as Cornwallis prepared to leave Charlotte on October 12th he had remarked, "This place is a damned hornet's nest." The phrase stuck, and the people of Charlotte adopted the title permanently. [676] Today the official seal of Charlotte bears a hornet's nest.[677]

Gilberttown, North Carolina
October 1780

Captain James Dunlap had been wounded at Cane Creek in September, and was recovering at the house of Mrs. Gilbert in Gilberttown. As Cornwallis retreated from North Carolina, two or three men, led by Captain Gillespie, rode up from Spartanburg to find Dunlap. Gillespie was an officer in the Spartan Regiment. When the men came to the Gilbert home, Mrs. Gilbert let them in thinking that they were Loyalists and had some important communication for Dunlap.

Gillespie and his men told her that they were there to kill Dunlap because he had put some of their friends to death, and had abducted Mary McRea, the fiancée of Captain Gillespie. Dunlap had kept Mary McRea in hopes that she would yield to his wishes. It was said that she died of a broken heart instead. Gillespie mounted the stairs and approached Dunlap as he lay in his bed.

"Where is Mary McRae?" he asked.

"In heaven," was Dunlap's reply.

Gillespie then shot Dunlap through the body, leaving him for dead, and rode away. The story of Mary McRae may be romantic lore of the mountains, but Gillespie did shoot Dunlap as he lay in his bed. Dunlap did not die. He was concealed by friends and carried to Ninety-Six.[678]

Shallow Ford, North Carolina   Skirmish
North Carolina Campaign of 1780
14 October 1780

American Forces
Commanding Officer   Major Joseph Cloyd
   State Militia
      North Carolina Partisan Rangers
         Charlotte Militia
            Captain Andrew Carson   52

Salisbury Militia	
Captain Jacob Nichols	30
Captain James Miller	30
Surry County Militia	80
Captain Henry Smith	
Captain David Humphreys	
Virginia Militia	
Major Joseph Cloyd	
Montgomery County Militia	160
Captain Henry Francis	
Captain Isaac Campbell	
Captain George Parris	
Captain Abraham Trigg	

Casualties   Captain Francis killed, 4 wounded [679]

Loyalist Forces

Commanding Officer	Colonel Gideon Wright
North Carolina Loyalist Militia	
Surry County Loyalist Militia	500
Colonel Gideon Wright	
Colonel Hezekiah Wright	
Captain James Bryan	
Captain Kyle	
Captain Lakey	
Captain Ben Burke	

Casualties   15 killed, 4 wounded [680]

The Loyalists under the Wright brothers continued to grow in Surry County. On October 13th 500 Loyalists arrived in Bethabara, then marched south to join the British army in Charlotte Town the next day. Some reports counted their number as high as 900. They plundered Whig homes along the way.

Andrew Carson lived about fifteen miles west of the Shallow Ford. When he heard the first reports of a Loyalist uprising he mounted his horse and rode to the headquarters of General William Lee Davidson. Davidson commanded the western North Carolina militia near Charlotte Town, and had assumed command of the militia when Rutherford was captured at Camden. Davidson gave Carson fifty-two men and sent them out to meet the Loyalist forces under the Wright brothers.

After a previous skirmish on the north side of the Yadkin River, Richard Vernon's company commander, Captain Pray, became sick and Vernon commanded the company. He wrote that Colonel John Peasley was also dispatched with 750 militia to find and "to disperse a body of about 380 Tories collected on the shallow ford of the Yadkin, in Surry County."

General Jethro Sumner dispatched two companies under Captains Nichols and Miller to do the same. Four companies from Montgomery County, Virginia under Major Cloyd had followed the forces headed to meet Ferguson. When they learned of Ferguson's defeat they were sent to Surry County. These four companies from Virginia joined with the North Carolina militiamen who had not pursued Ferguson.

On the morning of October 14th the Patriot force of 350 men were on the west side of a small stream, near the Shallow Ford crossing of the Yadkin River. They saw the Loyalist force that had threatened the county for the past weeks. The Loyalists had crossed the Yadkin River and were moving westward, on the Mulberry Fields Road. A single cry of "Tory! Tory!" was quickly echoed among the ranks of the Patriots. From across the branch came similar cries of "Rebel! Rebel!" Officers on both sides hastily formed ranks and fired across the river.

Captain Bryan of the Loyalists was the first to fall. Five rifle balls passed through him and his horse. Captain Isaac Campbell of the Virginia militia fled under the intense fire, and left his men to themselves. The Patriots advanced towards the ford as the Loyalists fell back and formed again. Captain Henry Francis of the Virginia militia was shot through the head, and fell dead on the ground a few steps from his son Henry. His other son John took careful aim and fired at the Tory who had killed his father. Though outnumbered, the Patriots quickly gained the advantage and took down several Loyalists. After exchanging several shots, the Loyalists fled back across the Yadkin River, shouting, "we are whipped, we are whipped."

The Patriots clubbed the wounded Loyalists to death after their comrades had fled. A Black Loyalist named Ball Turner continued to fire at the Patriots, until they charged his location and riddled his body with bullets.

At the close of the battle the 300 militiamen under Colonel John Peasley arrived, along with Colonel Joseph Williams of Surry County, who had heard the rifle fire from his home. General William Smallwood arrived in Salem the next day with about 150 horsemen, 30 infantry, and three wagons. He had set out from Guilford Courthouse the day before. Finding that the militia had already defeated the Loyalists, he ordered his militia to pursue those who had fled.

Richard Vernon wrote, "We killed several and took 30 or 40 prisoner. Among the killed was Captain Jas. Bryant. Col. Pasely took charge of the prisoners and we conducted them to Moravian town and left them under guard."

The victory at Shallow Ford dispersed Wright's Loyalist force in Surry County, and they were never able to gather in such numbers again. Hezekiah Wright was later shot and wounded in his own home. His brother Gideon fled to the safety of Charlestown, where he would die on August 9, 1782.[681]

Antioch, South Carolina   **Murder**
14 October 1780

Robert Harrison, one of the brothers of Major John Harrison, was in bed sick with small pox. A Whig scouting party discovered where he was and burst in the house, shooting him dead in his bed.[682]

Tearcoat Swamp, South Carolina [683]   **Skirmish**
25 October 1780

American Forces
Commanding Officer   Colonel Francis Marion
   South Carolina Continentals and Militia
      Williamsburg Township Militia [684]   150
         Major Hugh Horry
           1st South Carolina Regiment
            2nd Battalion
         Captain Thomas Waite
         Captain William Robert McCottry
           McCottry's Riflemen
         Captain Gavin Witherspoon
         Major John James
         Captain John McCauley
         Major Peter Horry
           Captain Bonneau [685]
         Captain Mitchell [686]
         Captain Lemuel Benton
         Captain Abram Lenud

Loyalist Forces
Commanding Officer   Lieutenant Colonel Samuel Tynes
   South Carolina Loyalist Militia
      Camden District Militia
         Santee Militia
           Lieutenant Colonel Samuel Tynes' Regiment   80
             Captain Amos Gaskens
             Captain William Rees
             Captain Benjamin Rees
Casualties   6 killed, 14 wounded, 23 captured

After Gates suffered his disastrous defeat at Camden, Lieutenant Colonel Samuel Tynes had called out his Loyalist militia from Nelson's Ferry. The men were given new English muskets, blankets, saddles, shot and powder. They were proud of their militia, but they were not disciplined. Tynes had been ordered by Lieutenant Colonel Nisbet Balfour to replace the force commanded by Wemyss, since he had been ordered to return to Camden.

Marion had been on the trail of Major Harrison and his South Carolina Rangers when he learned of the location of Tynes' encampment. Marion called out his own militia, and once he collected one hundred and fifty men he crossed the Pee Dee. Marion sent out two boys to scout the position of Colonel Tynes.

The Loyalists were camped in an open field, in the fork of the Black River, with Tearcoat swamp to the rear. Some of them were sleeping in the grass, others were around three large fires, singing and laughing. Loyalist Captain Amos Gaskens was winning at cards, because Marion's men could hear him shout, "Hurrah! At him again, damme! Aye, that's a dandy! My trick, by God." Marion waited until midnight to attack.

Marion divided his troops into three forces, one to the left, one to the right, and his detachment towards the center. At the firing of Marion's pistol his partisans rode in. The Loyalists bolted from their beds, and ran into the swamp, as Marion's men fired at their backs.

In the short firefight the Loyalists lost six men killed and fourteen wounded. Marion's men captured eighty horses, eighty muskets and the baggage, food and ammunition. Among the dead was Captain Gaskens. He was holding in his hand the ace, deuce, and jack of clubs. Marion did not lose a single man. This attack so impressed the Loyalists that many joined Marion's partisans after they came out of the swamp. This earned the swamp the nickname "Turncoat" swamp. [687]

Myhand's Bridge, North Carolina   Skirmish
October 1780 [688]

Captain John C. Williams had been a private in the Duplin militia at the Battle of Moore's Creek Bridge in 1776. He was commissioned as a lieutenant in the 2nd North Carolina Regiment, and served in Washington's Grand Army, until he resigned in 1778. He was born with a harelip, which in turn caused a speech impediment. He slurred the letter "c" into "she" or "shay," and became known as "Shay" Williams. Williams had formed a militia company in Duplin County when the British army invaded the Carolinas.

Williams' men were hard fighters, well-drilled and excellent horsemen. Their discipline was not as excellent, and the men fought among themselves when not patrolling for Loyalists. Williams wrote "one of my troopers was slashed about the face by one of the 'sorefoots,' and had to be sewn together by Judge Moore's wife. They regularly settle petty differences with long knives and fists, and drink to excess whenever they can find a dram."

Senator Fleet Cooper would later write, "to command such men requires one who is not faint of heart." After the war Williams told Richard Clinton that his men could drill "as neatly as any militia could hope for, afoot or mounted, and fight like savages when needed."

When Cornwallis had invaded North Carolina, the Loyalists became motivated and began to assemble and organize. Williams and his men patrolled in Duplin County to put down any Loyalist activities. One of the leaders of the Loyalists in Duplin County was Middleton Mobley. Mobley gathered some of his followers, and laid an ambush at Myhand's Bridge to disrupt any traffic going through the county. Mobley had already captured some wagons when he spotted Williams and his mounted militia.

When the Loyalists fired upon the horsemen, the Patriots became badly disorganized. One of William's men was killed and several were wounded. Had Mobley pushed them he would have saved his wagons, but his followers escaped into the swamps and down the Cross Creek Road, sniping at Williams' men when they were pursued.

Williams demanded that the last man standing, a wagon driver, surrender a load of meal and cloth that he thought had been stolen by a raiding party. The waggoner refused, threatening Williams and two men with a musket and a sword. Williams shot the man through the face with his pistol. He then ripped a piece of the striped fabric from the cargo, wiped his face and coat, and folded the rag over his belt. Williams men followed suit, some pinning a square piece of the cloth to their hats, others wrapping longer sections over their belts or around their waists. The "striped sash" became Williams' version of a cockade. From that time on Whigs moving about in West Duplin were advised to obtain a piece of striped cloth to show their loyalties.[689]

Great Swamp, North Carolina   Skirmish
3 November 1780

Engineer Colonel John Senf, and ninety men of the Camden Militia, attacked some Loyalists in Bladen County. They killed two and wounded several others. The Patriots only had one man wounded in the fight. [690]

Ocracoke Inlet, North Carolina
November 1780

In November the North Carolina privateer *General Nash* struck again, capturing the brigs *Aggie, Prince of Wales* and *Kattie* near the Ocracoke Inlet.[691]

Williamsburg Township, South Carolina
7 – 8 November 1780

Colonel Samuel Tynes had been able to escape when Marion raided his camp at Tearcoat Swamp. Marion wanted to capture him, so he sent Captain William Clay Snipes to the High Hills of Santee to bring back the Loyalist. Snipes was able to capture Tynes and several other Loyalist officers, and Justices of the Peace.

Lieutenant Colonel Turnbull was outraged that Marion had the ability to do this in an area under his command, and asked Tarleton to find the partisans. Marion learned of Tarleton's mission and tried to surprise him, but Tarleton had set up a trap of his own to ensnare

Marion at Woodyard Swamp. Marion was warned of this and immediately rode away.

Enraged that Marion had detected his ambush, Tarleton began burning thirty plantations and houses, from Jack's Creek to the High Hills. He punished the Widow Richardson for warning the partisans by digging up her husband, General Richard Richardson.[692] The Richardson's home was plundered.

After Tarleton forced them to feed him dinner, he ordered his troops to drive all the cattle, hogs, and poultry in the barn, and set it on fire. Tarleton was aware of Marion's skills, and each night he brought his Legion together to form a defensive perimeter.

Marion tried every trick he knew to lure Tarleton into an ambush, but the men were evenly matched, neither falling for the other's traps. The chase soon ended when Tarleton was ordered back to find Sumter's partisans. It seems that from this point on, Tarleton's luck changed for the worse.[693] Due to his actions, Tarleton, like Major Wemyss, became the best recruiting officer for Marion's Partisans.[694]

Jenkin's Cross Roads, South Carolina   Skirmish
8 November 1780

Colonel Edward Lacey had seized a barrel of whiskey from a Tory named Knight, five miles west of Chester Courthouse, on the Fishdam Road. He used the whiskey to influence 150 men to enlist into his regiment in a single day. William Wylie described them as "the warm hearted whiskey loving Irish."

After drinking their fill they grabbed "milk pails, milk piggins, noggins, pitchers, cups and any vessel" and mounted their horses.[695] "They kept swigging at it till they all soon became gloriously befuddled and courageously brave."

They rode four miles to Jenkin's Cross Roads, which was located about seven miles from Fishdam Ford. They spotted a British patrol and Lacey's men yelled "There's the red coats, by G__, lets at them!" The British heard the loud hooping and hollering and fled from the wild sight.

Lacey quickly regained control of the men, and steered them away from the road leading to Fishdam Ford. Lacey knew that it was the place he was supposed to rendezvous with Sumter, and he didn't want the British to follow his drunken mob and find the partisan force. Lacey told his men that the British were just ahead and to continue to ride forward. They rode on for a mile, until Lacey was sure that they were not being followed, and then they turned on a road leading to Fishdam Ford.

As the men rode into the partisan camp they "made frequent ludicrous tumbles from their horses, over the horse's heads, when drinking at their piggins."[696]

Fishdam Ford, Broad River, South Carolina [697]   Skirmish
9 November 1780

American Forces

Commanding Officer Brigadier General Thomas Sumter	
South Carolina State Troops and Militia	300
Colonel Thomas Taylor	50
Captain George Avery	
Captain John Taylor	
Colonel Edward Lacey	
Chester District Militia	
Major James McCall	
South Carolina State Dragoons	
Captain Stephen Carr	
Colonel Richard Winn	130
Fairfield Regiment	
Captain John Winn[698]	
Colonel William Bratton	
Ninety-Six District Militia	
Colonel William Hill	
Colonel William Hill's Regiment of State Troops	
Lieutenant Colonel James Hawthorne	

Georgia Militia   100
    Colonel Benjamin Few
       Upper Richmond County Militia Battalion
    Colonel Elijah Clarke
       Major William Candler
    Major James Jackson
Casualties   4 killed, 10 wounded [699]

British Forces
Commanding Officer   Major James Wemyss
    British Regulars
       Lieutenant Henry Bethune Stark [700]
          63rd Regiment of Foot [701]   63
    Provincials
       Lieutenant Moore Hovenden
          British Legion
             Legion Cavalry   40
Casualties   4 killed, 23 wounded [702]

After the battle of King's Mountain Sumter moved his forces to Stallion's Plantation on Fishing Creek. He was joined there by the Georgia militia of Colonel Few, Elijah Clarke, and James Jackson. Colonel Thomas Taylor and "60 choice riflemen from the region" also joined Sumter.

On the advice of Colonel Winn he moved his forces closer to the British at Moore's Mill. This was definitely a show of arrogance, since he would only be thirty miles from Cornwallis's camp at Winnsboro. Sumter wanted Cornwallis to divide his forces, so he'd be easier to attack.

Cornwallis learned that Sumter was in the area from a British patrol. He would have preferred sending Tarleton after Sumter, but Tarleton was busy chasing Marion in the swamps of the Low country. Cornwallis sent Major James Wemyss instead.

Wemyss had obtained enough horses from around his headquarters area to convert 100 men of his 63rd Regiment into mounted cavalry. Cornwallis gave Wemyss forty of Tarleton's cavalry that had been left at headquarters, but with the instructions that he could not place them in the lead forces, or use them at night. Wemyss agreed, but he did not relay Cornwallis's commands to his second in command, Lieutenant John Stark.

With Wemyss was a man named Sealy, who offered to guide him to Sumter. Wemyss took the offer and gave Sealy a second objective on the raid. He mission was to take five dragoons, penetrate the camp, then find Sumter and kill or capture him.

On the night of November 8th Wemyss left Winnsboro, and arrived at Moore's Mill by midnight. Sumter moved down the Broad River to Fishdam Ford, twenty-five miles northwest of Winnsboro. Wemyss moved out at a brisk pace to intercept the partisans. This went against Cornwallis's orders of not attacking at night.

Sumter spread his five regiments around Fishdam Ford, and then he went to his tent, partially undressed, and fell asleep. William Wylie wrote "Sumter had a lot of prisoners at Fishdam on a high hill south of the camp and guarded by a squad of men." Sumter did not feel concerned that the British would attempt to attack the camp.

There was one officer who did not want to take that chance. McJunkin wrote, "That man was Col. Thomas Taylor of Congaree. He had been out with his command during a part of the previous day toward the Tyger River. In his excursions he had heard of the approach of the party under Wemyss, and from his intelligence of their movements he conjectured their purpose. He went to Sumter and remonstrated in regard to the state of things in his camp. Sumter gave him to understand that he feared no danger, and felt prepared for any probable result. Taylor's apprehensions were not allayed by the security of his commander. He determined to take measures to guard against surprise, and to this Sumter gave his hearty assent. Taylor conjectured that if the enemy came that night his approach would be along the road leading from the mouth of the Tyger and hence must cross the creek at the ford to reach Sumter's position."

"He placed himself at the head of his own men, marched them across the creek, built up large fires of durable material, sent out a patrol party in the direction of the enemy, examined a way for a safe retreat for his party down the creek, and took all other precautions deemed proper in the circumstances. He withdrew his men from the fires some distance in the direction of the main army and directed them what to do in case of alarm."

Draper wrote, "There was a manifest want of watchfulness...there was no attention to order in Sumter's camp. Sumter made light of his apprehensions." Taylor "gave orders to his men to refrain from sleep."

Winn also did not trust their situation, and had told his men to "sleep with their guns in their arms and shot-bags under their heads." Pickets were placed out to warn of any approaching danger.

Draper wrote, "about midnight Taylor heard a great sound in the direction from which he expected. The enemy came to the top of the hill above Taylor, formed and the charged down on Taylor's fires, expecting to butcher a slumbering foe. As soon as they were in the light of the fires Taylor's men fired upon them and a few rounds decided the contest."

Taylor's men were told to not shoot until you could see their buttons, and he ordered his men to "shoot at their belts". The first shots from Taylor emptied twenty British saddles. Wemyss was one of the injured, with a broken arm and a shattered knee.

The command then fell to Lieutenant Stark, who knew nothing of Wemyss's plan, or of the limitations placed on them by Cornwallis. Stark led his men in a charge towards the invisible partisans, giving the "Indian Halloo", but the British were easy targets against the light of the campfires. Some of Stark's men were shot down as they stopped to loot the bedrolls and baggage around the campfire.

Draper wrote, "The utmost consternation ensued in Sumter's camp. The sleeping militia was roused by the clash of arms and ran hither and thither, supposing Taylor's corps to have been annihilated and many of them ran clear off."

Lieutenant Stark yelled out to the shadows, "God Damn your souls; who are you?" One of Winn's officers, Captain Kirkland, yelled back, "God Damn your souls and who are you?" In an instant Stark had his men dismount and attack with bayonets.

Colonel Thomas Taylor fired a volley into the British at close range, but they still came on with the bayonets. One of the partisans was Moses, a Black slave, who was "shot between the body and shoulder and bayoneted in three different places in the body."

The fight was evenly matched until Colonel Lacey fired a volley into the British flank from the woods. After a few minutes of confused fighting, both sides withdrew. Taylor gave the retreating British two more volleys, but in the dark it did very little damage.

Sealy's detachment of assassins found their way to Sumter's tent, but he had gone out the back of the tent and hid under a bank of the river.

The regiments of Colonels Bratton and Hill were not involved in the battle, since it took place away from their positions. The entire action only lasted twenty minutes. Lacey's regiment arrived at the end of the battle to fire one volley. He told Winn that he didn't attack because he "was afraid of killing some of you."

McJunkin wrote, "It is said that when Taylor's men delivered their first fire, a scene of confusion resulted in Sumter's camp utterly beyond description. The soldiers and officers ran hither and thither, whooping and yelling like maniacs. Some got ready for action and joined in it, while others ran clear off and did not join Sumter again for weeks. Hence this action was denominated in the region round about as Sumter's Second Defeat, though the rout of the enemy was complete and the American loss was nothing."

Wemyss had been left behind with thirteen other wounded, under a flag of truce, with a sergeant major to guard over them. In the morning they were the only ones on the battlefield.

Sumter returned to the field two hours later and found them.[703] He paroled the British prisoners, but found a list in Wemyss' pocket of the houses that he had burned along the Pee Dee. It also listed the men he had hanged during his search for Marion. Sumter threw the list in the fire because he knew that if the men had found it they would kill Wemyss.

A British doctor tending to the wounded told Captain John Winn "I have not seen such damage done by so few men in so short a time since I have been in America."

Taylor's brother, Captain John Taylor, had been wounded by random fire when the British fired blindly at their unseen enemy. The ball "penetrating the body near the shoulder blade." John Taylor told the British surgeon "Take it out carefully, I'll give it back to your people to-morrow." However John Taylor did not survive. After his wound was tended to, he contracted small pox and died.[704]

After taking parole Sumter sent Wemyss and his men to Charlestown. Sumter spread the word throughout the countryside that he had a victory, not over Tory militia, but over Regulars. Recruits flocked to his camp and his command grew to 1,000 men. Cornwallis was furious and called Wemyss a "Mad Trooper." He knew the answer to stop Sumter was Tarleton, so he recalled him from chasing Marion and ordered him to eliminate Sumter's partisans.[705]

Bradley's Plantation, North Carolina
14 November 1780

Francis Bradley had been with Thompson in the "Battle of the Bees" at McIntyre's Farm. Afterwards Bradley had become a terror to the Loyalists in Mecklenburg County by harassing enemy scouts and foraging parties. He had killed a number of British sentries at long range with his rifle during Cornwallis's stay in Charlotte. On November 14th the Loyalists had enough. Four of them ambushed and killed Bradley at his plantation.[706]

Enoree River, South Carolina   **Skirmish**
November 1780

This is another account that is only mentioned in Alexander Chesney's Journal. After his escape from the backwoods militia Chesney "raised a company with great difficulty and joined a strong party at Col Williams's house on Little River, where there was a strong party under General Cunningham."

His militia commander, Major Daniel Plummer, had been killed at King's Mountain and Major Jonathan Frost took over command. Frost ordered Chesney and his militia to "join him at an appointed place on the Enoree."

The Patriots had learned about the rendezvous site also, and when Chesney's militia arrived Lieutenant Colonel Benjamin Roebuck and his men captured them. Chesney's Loyalists were "immediately disarmed" and marched away.

When Major Frost arrived at the rendezvous and learned of the capture of Chesney he immediately pursued Roebuck. Frost caught up with Roebuck's militia twelve miles up the river, but Roebuck had his men in defensive position inside a cabin. When Frost attacked the house he was killed, and the rest of his Loyalists fled. After the skirmish Roebuck paroled Chesney and the other Loyalist prisoners.[707]

White's Plantation and Ashton's Plantation, South Carolina[708]
15 November 1780

American Forces

Commanding Officer	Colonel Francis Marion
South Carolina Militia	
Williamsburg Township Militia	
Major Peter Horry	33
Captain Bonneau	
Captain Mitchell	
Captain Lemuel Benton	
Captain Abram Lenud	
Captain John Melton	Unknown number
Casualties	2 killed, 3 wounded

Loyalist Forces
Commanding Officers   Captain James "Otterskin" Lewis
   South Carolina Loyalist Militia
      Georgetown Regiment
         Captain James "Otterskin" Lewis   100
         Captain Miles Barfield   100
Casualties   4 killed, 2 wounded, 16 captured

Colonel Marion wanted to take Georgetown, because he needed supplies of salt, clothing and ammunition for his men. The capture of Georgetown would also be a huge blow to British morale in the region.

Marion moved across the swamp at "White's Bay" at the mouth of the Black and Sampit Rivers.[709] He sent Peter Horry and his horsemen across White's bridge, on a reconnaissance towards the Black River. He sent Captain John Melton to the Sampit road. He concealed the rest of his force in the swamp north of town, at a location near Alston's Plantation that became known as The Camp. From The Camp Marion was able to raid either in the direction of Black River Road, coming into Georgetown from the north, or the road along the Sampit River, entering from the west.

At White's Plantation Horry's force found Captain James Lewis's Loyalists killing cattle. At the approach of Horry they fled, firing as they ran. Upon hearing the sound of the shooting, Horry's men ran out of the village. Horry and a boy named Gwinn found themselves alone. Ten men galloped up and Horry shouted, "Are you friends?"

"Friends!" was the reply, "Friends of King George!" Gwinn fired his musket and Captain Lewis fell from the saddle, struck by buckshot. Lewis fired as he fell, killing Horry's horse. The firing brought Horry's partisans racing back, chasing off the Loyalists.

Captain Melton's patrol was moving down the Sampit Road, when he learned of a Loyalist party camping at The Pens, the plantation of Colonel William Alston. Riding with Melton was Francis Marion's nephew, Lieutenant Gabriel Marion.

As Melton's horsemen were passing through a dense swamp, they stumbled onto Captain Barfield and his Loyalist troop. Both sides fired at the same time. Barfield took a load of buckshot in his face and was killed. His brother Jesse Barfield was wounded. Gabriel Marion's horse was killed. A schoolmaster riding with Melton, named Swaineau, was killed.

The Loyalists seized Gabriel, and began clubbing him with their muskets until he was knocked senseless. When he was recognized as the nephew of Francis Marion, a mulatto named Sweat put a musket against Gabriel's chest and fired a load of buckshot into his heart, killing him instantly. The barrel was so close that it set his linen shirt on fire.

The next day Marion's Partisans captured Sweat. As they were crossing the swamps that night, a militia officer rode up to Sweat, put his pistol to his head and shot him dead. Marion was furious and publicly reprimanded the officer that killed him. Marion did not condone any acts that were against the rules of war, and demanded his men adhere to the strict discipline of the regular army.[710]

Brierly's Ferry, South Carolina [711]   Skirmish
18 November 1780

Tarleton force-marched from the Lower Peedee River, where he had been pursuing Marion, to Brierly's Ferry to find Sumter. Major Archibald McArthur had hurried to secure the ferry with his Highlanders and the eighty survivors of the 63rd Regiment.

Sumter wanted to capture Ninety-Six, but could not do so without artillery. On November 13th Sumter crossed the Enoree River and camped at Nixon's Plantation to build up his forces. Since Sumter had defeated a group of Regulars at Fishdam Ford his ranks swelled. He moved his partisans to Shirar's Ferry, and issued a challenge to the 71st Highlanders to "come out and fight him". This act of bravado also helped him increase his ranks.

Sumter did not run like Gates, but went out to find the British. He sent 150 mounted men, under Colonel Taylor, to spy on the

Highlanders at Brierly's Ferry. With Taylor were Major William Candler and his men.

Tarleton reached Winnsboro eager to fight Sumter, but did not want the Patriots to know that he was in the area. He had his men take off their green jackets so that any spies would think that the Legion was only a regular British patrol.

At nine o'clock in the morning on November 18th Tarleton's tired troops were on the edge of the Broad River, washing up and cleaning their horses. Taylor's men spotted them and ran to the top of the opposite bank. They fired a volley, knocking down a horse and soldier of the 63rd Regiment. McArthur quickly responded by firing two 3-pound cannons to disperse Taylor's riflemen. The Highlanders crossed the river and secured the west bank.

During this hit and run attack Tarleton had kept his men hidden in the woods, near the ferry, so that Taylor's partisans would not know his Legion was there. Taylor went downriver to Summer Mills, and then went into the countryside for thirteen miles to set up camp away from Tarleton's forces. The next morning Major Candler was detached with his fifty men, and they returned to Summer Mills to destroy it by cutting the running gear. They then marched day and night to catch up to Sumter.

Tarleton received word that Sumter was moving towards Williams' house, fifteen miles from Ninety-Six, with up to 1,000 men. He had his men wait until dark, and then marched until ten o'clock then next morning, where they set up a camp on the Enoree River. A soldier of the 63rd Regiment deserted during the march and alerted Sumter to the approaching Legion.

Sumter did not want to be caught in the open while retreating from Tarleton, because this would place him in the same position as Buford at the Waxhaws. Sumter instead decided to move to William Blackstock's Farm, on the Tyger River, and set up a defensive position.[712] Tarleton followed after him.[713]

Blackstock's Plantation, South Carolina [714]   **Battle**
20 November 1780

American Forces
Commanding Officer   Brigadier General Thomas Sumter
   State Troops and Militia
      South Carolina State Troops and Militia   900
         Sumter's Brigade of Partisans
            Lieutenant Colonel Henry Hampton
               Hampton's Regiment of Light Dragoons
            Colonel Thomas Brandon
               2nd Spartan Regiment
                  Major William Smith
                  Captain George Avery
            Colonel William Hill
               Colonel William Hill's Regiment of State Troops
                  Lieutenant Colonel James Hawthorne
            Colonel William Bratton
            Colonel Edward Lacey
               Chester District Militia   100
                  Captain Samuel Adams
                     Chester Rocky Creek Irish
                     Captain John Nixon
         Major James McCall
            South Carolina State Dragoons
        Colonel Thomas Taylor   150
        Colonel Richard Winn
            Fairfield Regiment
        Major Samuel Hammond
            Hammond's State Troops
        Colonel Joseph Hayes
            Captain-Lieutenant William Harris
      Georgia Militia   100
         Colonel John Twiggs
            Burke County Militia

Colonel Elijah Clarke
   Wilkes County Regiment
      Captain Patrick "Paddy" Carr
      Major William Candler
   Major James Jackson
   Colonel Benjamin Few
      Upper Richmond County Militia Battalion
   Major Joseph McJunkin
      Refugees from South Carolina and Georgia

Total American Forces engaged [715]   420
Casualties   3 killed, 4 wounded, 50 captured [716]
British Forces
Commanding Officer   Lieutenant Colonel Banastre Tarleton
   British Regulars
      Lieutenant John Money
         63rd Regiment of Foot   80
      Major Archibald McArthur
         71st Regiment of Foot (Fraser's Highlanders) [717]
            1st Battalion   100
   Provincials
      Lieutenant Colonel Banastre Tarleton
         British Legion   170
         Cavalry Troops
            Captain David Kinlock
            Captain Richard Hovenden [718]
            Lieutenant Nathaniel Vernon
               Captain Jacob James's Troop [719]
            Captain Thomas Sanford
            Captain David Ogilvy
            Lieutenant John Skinner [720]
Casualties   52 killed and wounded [721]

On the morning of November 20th Tarleton discovered that
Sumter and his army were only two hours ahead of him at
Blackstock's Farm. He used the same tactic that he had used
against Buford, because it had worked for him so far. He left his

infantry and artillery and moved quickly with his Legion cavalry and the mounted infantry of the 63rd Regiment.

Captain Samuel Otterson had been sent out on patrol, with "one Virginian and another". They detected Tarleton's approach and hid beside the road, counting the British as they went past. The men quickly rode around the approaching British and came out on the main road, two miles from Blackstocks. The British saw them and pursued.

The other two men with Otterson were "poorly mounted, were overtaken and cut down, killed, hallooing for quarters without avail." Otterson had a better horse and was able to escape. As he got near Sumter's camp he fired his musket in the air, to give Sumter notice. Some of Sumter's men rode out to help Otterson. The advanced British troopers saw the force against them, and retreated.[722]

Major Joseph McJunkin wrote that Sumter halted his men at the plantation house of Captain William Blackstock "for the purpose of permitting his men to cook and eat. Their fires, however were but just lighter and the simple preparation to cook, of rolling dough around sticks, and placing them before the fires" was interrupted.

"Sumter told the troops to abandon their cooking and take post in and at the house." Hill wrote "The Americans having been pursued for 2 days and nights took this ground under firm determination to defend it & not to retreat further."

Sumter placed his men around the plantation house, with the Tyger River to their rear. Colonel Henry Hampton and his riflemen were placed inside a large log barn. Sumter left Captain Paddy Carr at the Enoree to give early warning of Tarleton's approach. Carr had been able to take "three loyal militia, unarmed, and two boys who had been to mill, prisoners, and was conducting them to Camp."

The outbuildings around Blackstock's house were not chinked between the logs, and provided openings for the riflemen to fire through. Twiggs and his Georgians were placed on the left side of the road, which led from the rear of the house to the Tyger River. Hill described the location, "On the west side of this lane was a thick wood and at the mouth of this lane was placed a strong picket." They had a strong fence to fight behind. Hill described the fence as "not made with common rails but with small trees notched one on to the other."

To the right of the house, below a wooded ridge, Sumter placed Lacey and Hill. Winn held a reserve force behind the house on top of a hill. Sumter still had the humiliation of Fish Dam Ford on his mind and did not want to be surprised again. Captain Blackstock was away with Colonel Roebuck's militia, but his wife Mary was there at the plantation. Mary approached Sumter and told him that she did not want any fighting around her house, however it was no longer in her hands.

Joseph Hart, observing the battlefield many years later, wrote, "The place Sumter selected was admirably chosen & in a military point of view could be scarcely be equaled in the vicinity. Covered by the woods, and supported right and left by the hill and trees, he was able to place his untrained men in a position that would give them confidence. The gentle ascent immediately in his front would prevent an advantageous charge from the enemy – a move Sumter, with his undisciplined forces, no doubt much dread."

Tarleton's force spotted Captain Carr at the Enoree River and immediately charged. Carr left the five prisoners at the Enoree, and galloped off. The Legion dragoons did not let the prisoners identify themselves, and they were hacked down. One of the prisoners was the Loyalist called Sealy, who had the mission of capturing Sumter at Fishdam Ford. Sealy cried out "I am a prisoner!" but the dragoons cut him down.[723]

Major William Candler returned from the foraging expedition, and entered Sumter's lines when Tarleton's Legion came into view. Sumter's pickets fired on the British cavalry just as Colonel Taylor's other raiding party appeared, with captured British wagons loaded with flour.

These wagons were from Tarleton's baggage train and Taylor had urged "the teams under whip and spur to avoid being captured." The wagons full of flour had burst their heads and "the road behind them was whitened with the scattered flour." Taylor's force slipped into Sumter's lines with moments to spare. Taylor's men rode over a corduroyed causeway, and it made a "great noise."

When Tarleton's dragoons ran into the Georgians "they kept the cavalry from entering the Lane." Joseph Hart wrote, "Tarleton could very easily discover Sumter's position form the road, nearly half a mile before reaching it." Not wanting to attack a thousand well-posted militia, Tarleton waited for his infantry and artillery to catch up.

Charles Myddleton wrote, "They appeared within 400 yards of our camp, dismounted, and formed in a field." They took off their knapsacks and grounded them on the bank of the Tyger River. He then had his men "let down the fence opposite to them."

Sumter noticed that Tarleton had divided his force and he also knew that Tarleton was probably waiting for artillery support. He decided to start the battle by sending volunteers against the 63rd Regiment.

McJunkin said, "Sumter called for volunteers to act as the advance and bring on the action. Colonel Farr of Union and Major McJunkin were the first to volunteer.[724] They were followed by others, until the General said there were enough." These men were ordered to go forward, until they met Tarleton's advance, which they were to engage and if not strong enough to resist, they were directed to fall back gradually, facing about and firing on occasion."

Myddleton wrote, "The parties detached kept up a loose fire, and the enemy retired to a wood, under cover of which they made their disposition of cavalry and infantry for an attack, and immediately advanced to the charge."

Eighty men of the 63rd Regiment charged with the bayonet. The militia were unnerved and fell back through the farmhouses. Sumter sent 100 horsemen under Colonel Lacey around the 63rd Regiment's right, to block any reinforcements. The Legion cavalry under Lieutenant Skinner was watching the 63rd Regiment's charge, and did not see Lacey's mounted riflemen until they were seventy-five yards away.

Hill wrote, that they "very judiciously advanced within fire of them undiscovered, as they were then on horse back near the end of the lane [they] then gave fire so well directed that upwards of 20 of them fell from their horses as well as a number of their horses killed, the woods being so thick that the regular horse dare not penetrate it. And a number of the men dismounted occasionally crept up so as to kill many of them in their ranks." Dead horses and riders covered the road. Lieutenant Skinner quickly recovered and drove Lacey's cavalry back to their lines.

The back and forth action continued for two hours. William Taylor wrote, that the British "over shot and the twigs and acorns would rattle down." Henry Hampton's riflemen fired on the 63rd Regiment, taking special aim at the officers. Lieutenant Cope and Gibson were shot dead immediately.

Hampton's riflemen mortally wounded Lieutenant Money, but he had pushed the partisans back into the woods behind Blackstock's house. Tarleton sprang to Money's side, and in defiance of Hampton's sharpshooters, lifted him into the saddle and rode off.[725] One third of the 63rd fell to the rifles "dropping some of them…at a distance of 200 yards."

During the battle Winn had his men in reserve, and had not been utilized. Major Jackson ran to Winn and told him the front was giving way to the British. Jackson yelled out, "I will tell you the Salvation of this country depends on this single fight." Soon the fighting died down on every quarter as the men on both sides became fatigued. Hill wrote "The action commenced at one oclock and neither horse nor foot advance to our camp between the lane & the river until the going down of the sun."

Winn had his men all lie down on top of the hill so that the British would not know they were there. He told them that when he gave the order they should all "jump up, set up the Indian hallo and run down the hill on the enemy and to fire as they run, at the same time have bullets in their mouths and powder in their pockets." He also had the men spread out five yards between each man, so as to make them seem larger than they were.

A few minutes later Tarleton's cavalry advanced towards the Patriot lines. Hill wrote, "Their horse then advanced in the lane to attack our body of reserve that stood between the lane & the river where the charge was made by their horse." When they were at the bottom of Blackstock's Hill, Winn gave the command to charge.

"The Americans having the advantage of the before mentioned fence together with the thick wood just by the fence that before they got through the lane their front, both men and horse, fell so fast that the way was nearly stopt up." Tarleton's horse was shot from under him. He saw what appeared to be a large reinforcement arrive, and "A retreat was then ordered ... so many falling either by wounds or stumbling over the dead horses or men. They were pursued by the Americans with loud shouts of victory."

The 63rd Regiment continued the attack across the open field towards the houses on the hill. Sumter told them to hold their fire until the British were 60 yards away. "There they received such a heavy fire from those in the houses as well as from a number of the reserve that had got round to that quarter they made their retreat in as great confusion as the horse."

Samuel Morrow told Lyman Draper that he "fired three times with double loads, twice with effect." William White told Draper that Twiggs made an "obstinate resistance" and drove the British back. Thomas Charlton observed one rifleman kill a dragoon, then fall on the ground and reloaded his rifle. He sprang up and shot a second dragoon who was trying to charge him from the rear.

The British rallied their exhausted men and retreated in order, but they left the field with half of their men lost to the action. Daniel Stinson wrote, "The British made three charges and after the final one, sounded the bugle for retreat, which was known in Sumter's camp."

Sumter was badly wounded during the battle, but there are conflicting statements on when he was shot. Some accounts state that he was wounded in the middle of the battle, but many of the men who were there wrote that it happened after the battle was over.

Thomas Starke wrote, "Sumter and others took the trail and dashed towards the ford and discovered the British forming and Sumter and party became suddenly exposed, when Sumter received a shot and, one Brown, only second in the rear of Sumter, was killed."

Draper wrote, "Otterson, Winn and Sumter rode out after the battle and near sunset to see if the British were retreating or were designing to renew the fight. Sumter saw them in line, evidently awaiting the arrival of reinforcements. Sumter got a good view, and was in the act of turning when he received the wound in the shoulder and an artery was cut by the bullet and bled nearly to death."

J. S. Sims wrote that Major Otterson told him that "Tarleton withdrew his force & at the same time Sumter mounted his men & each party made for the ford on Tyger river – Sumter led his men in single files by a small path in the woods. All of a sudden the British formed on the big road & fired at them, when Sumter was wounded in the shoulder & a man by the name of Brown, the next man to Sumter was killed."

Sumter was wounded with six buckshot. Five of the buckshot went in his chest and the sixth chipped his spine and lodged in his left shoulder. Captain Robert McElvey, Sumter's aide-de-camp, was with Sumter when he heard "a trickling sound in the dry leaves." He told Sumter, "General, you are wounded!" Sumter replied, "I am wounded – say nothing about it" Sumter did not want to panic his men. Winn told Hampton not to tell anyone that Sumter had been wounded, and had him carried from the field. Sumter told Colonel Twiggs to take command.[726]

Tarleton withdrew his force, and had his men spend the night on a hill two miles from Blackstock's. Twiggs was left holding the field for two hours after the battle. This was considered a victory in the 18th century. [727]

Sumter was placed in a large piece of rawhide suspended between two horses, and carried to the mountains of North Carolina with a guard of five men. Twiggs sent Jackson after the British, and he was able to capture thirty of their horses. The British also left most of their backpacks grounded on the bank of the Tyger River. That night Twiggs left the campfires burning and forded the Tyger River.[728] Once on the other side he disbanded the militia.

Tarleton pursued the partisans for two more days, and went as far as the Pacolet River. While there he picked up the survivors of

King's Mountain. At the end of the month Tarleton returned to Brierly's Ford. When Colonel Winn returned to New Acquisition he learned that his brother, Captain John Winn, had been taken prisoner by the British.

John and Minor Winn had decided to capture Lord Rawdon. They knew that Rawdon rode out from Winnsboro from time to time, and went to the fruit orchard of John Woodman. The Winns knew that they could capture him at the orchard, so they rode to an ambush site and had their slave hold their horses. The slave betrayed them and warned Rawdon of the trap. The two Winns were captured, and were ordered to be executed. Their execution was delayed because John Winn's wife had died and he was allowed to go to the funeral. Afterwards they were moved to the Camden jail. Captain William Nettles was able to capture four British officers near Camden.[729] He sent a message to Cornwallis that he wished to exchange the officers for the Winns. At first Cornwallis would not do it, but Nettles told him that if the Winns were executed, he would kill the four British officers.

Colonel Winn sent his own message, that said if his brother were hanged he would execute 100 of the British officers and men that had been taken prisoner in the month of November. Cornwallis knew that this was not an idle threat, and let the Winns, and Captain Thomas Starke, go on parole. [730]

Rutledge's Ford, South Carolina [731]   Skirmish
November 1780

After the battle of Blackstock's, Sumter's forces proceeded northward. When they passed Lawson's Fork Creek the Georgians under Colonel Clarke, Twiggs and Few separated and headed westward. South Carolina militia under Samuel Hammond, James McCall and Moses Liddell joined the Georgians. The combined forces moved to a Loyalist fort known as Hoil's Old Place on the Saluda River.

When the Loyalists heard of the approaching army they abandoned the fort, and crossed the Saluda River at Rutledge's

Ford. The two parties exchanged rifle fire at long range, killing several men on both sides of the river.[732]

Elijah Clarke and his army continued on to the pro-Whig settlement of Long Canes. The objective of Clarke's militia army was the fort at Ninety-Six, under the command of Colonel Cruger.[733]

Chester District, South Carolina   Skirmish
November 1780

Robert Cooper had been born in County Armagh, Ireland, on Christmas Day. His father moved to America when he was young. He initially lived in New Jersey, learning the trade of a blacksmith. When he was 22 years old he married 16 year old Jane Hamilton, and moved to Fishing Creek, South Carolina.

Cooper had been a lieutenant under Colonel Winn on the Florida Expedition. After Charlestown fell he became a captain under Colonel Lacey.

About the time that "Tarleton was plundering the country" he learned of a "squad of Tories who had collected for the purpose of organizing to commit depredations in the neighborhood".

Cooper gathered his militia and rode towards the Loyalists, who had fortified themselves in a new log cabin. Cooper and his men approached the house at night, riding down a lane, hoping to be undetected. The Tories heard them approach and fired a volley at them. Cooper was wounded in the side with a flesh wound, and William Hale was severely wounded in the foot.

The Tories refused to surrender and Cooper tried unsuccessfully to burn them out. Since the first volley there had been not shots from the house, and Cooper determined that they were out of ammunition. He had his men construct a battering ram out "by swinging a log with ropes & battered down the door".

All of the Loyalists were captured. William Hale "was rendered lame all of his life afterwards." The next day Cooper found a young girl who had been killed while walking down the lane. She had been going to a neighbor's house and had been hit in the first volley by the Tories.[734]

Sandy River, South Carolina   Skirmish
December 1780 [735]

McJunkin wrote "in early December Brandon, McJunkin, and such as they could collect, took post at Love's Ford on Broad River to prevent intercourse between Cornwallis and the Loyalists west of the Broad River."

"While there a Scout, under the command of Captain McCool, was ordered to cross the Broad River and attack the Tories on Sandy River.[736] McCool was defeated and Daniel McJunkin was taken captive and sent to Winnsboro."

Captain Robert Wilson wrote that the Loyalists were under the command of Captain Manning Gose. He also wrote "I lost a valuable horse shot under me in the battle. In this engagement we defeated the Tories."

Brandon wrote Greene that he "proceeded after them and fell in with a small party – we killed three and wounded three, most notorious villains." The rest of the Loyalists were able to get away with their prisoners.

"Colonel Brandon sent a flag to Cornwallis and proposed to exchange Colonel Fanning for Daniel McJunkin.[737] Cornwallis declined and sent Daniel to jail in Camden.[738] He remained there till April 1781, when he and some others made their escape, but nearly perished for the want of food before they reached their friends."[739]

Rugeley's Mill, South Carolina [740]
4 December 1780 [741]

After Camden Gates reorganized his Continental forces into a light corps of three companies. These companies were made up of the survivors of Camden, the Waxhaws, and of seventy dragoons under William Washington. Otho Williams wrote, "Each man in the brigade was supplied with one new shirt, a short coat, a pair of woolen overalls, a pair of shoes, and a hat or a cap."[742]   The commander of this new light corps was Daniel Morgan.

Morgan had become angered when he was passed over for promotion after his riflemen helped win the victory at Saratoga. He resigned in 1779 and returned to his home in Virginia. In June 1780 Congress ordered Morgan back into service to be "employed in the Southern army as Major General Gates shall direct."   Morgan ignored the order, and stayed home. However after the defeat at Camden he realized the country needed his services, and he joined Gates in Hillsborough. When Morgan was placed in command of the new light corps Congress finally promoted him to Brigadier General.

Gates learned that Loyalist parties were moving out of their posts at Winnsboro and Camden, and intercepting Patriot supply trains at Lynches Creek. General Morgan received permission to escort the wagons that were to procure pork and corn.   Morgan's force consisted of three hundred infantry and eighty cavalry under William Washington. When the Loyalists heard of this covering force they returned to their posts.

Colonel Henry Rugeley was a Loyalist officer who had a plantation ten miles north of Camden. He named the plantation Clermont, but it became known as Rugeley's Mill, or Rugeley's Fort. The fort consisted of Rugeley's barn, built of strong logs, with loopholes cut in the walls. A platform had been erected inside for a second tier of muskets. Around the whole fort was a strong abatis.

Rugeley was a gentleman more than a soldier, and believed in the ancient traditions of hospitality. When Governor Rutledge fled Charlestown after its surrender, he stopped for the night in Rugeley's plantation. When Rugeley learned that Tarleton was on Rutledge's trail, he warned the governor and allowed him to escape.

Morgan released Washington and his dragoons to raid Rugeley's Fort. Major Joseph McJunkin and Thomas Young were guides for the dragoons. When Washington approached the fort on December 4th Rugeley was inside the fort with Major John Cook and 112 Loyalist militia. Washington found that the fort was impregnable to his 100 cavalry, and he needed artillery to capture the Loyalists. He decided to make "Quaker Guns". These were fake cannons made from tree trunks. From a distance these pine logs took on the shape of a cannon.

Williams wrote that Washington "humourously ordered his men to plant the trunk of an old pine tree, in the manner of a field-piece, pointing towards the garrison — at the same time, dismounting some of his men to appear as infantry, and displaying his cavalry to the best advantage, he sent a corporal of dragoons to summon the commanding officer to an *immediate* surrender."

Aware that a cannon would annihilate his flimsy fort, and encouraged by his junior officers, Rugeley surrendered the fort and garrison without firing a shot. Washington captured all 114 men, ninety muskets, fourteen horses and four wagons. Only one wagon was taken with Washington, the rest were destroyed. Williams wrote "The corporal was made a sergeant of dragoons — the old fort was set on fire; and Washington retired with his prisoners without exchanging a shot."

The next morning a patrol sent out from Camden by Lord Rawdon found only the smoking ashes of the fort. Cornwallis wrote to Tarleton, "Rugely will not be made a brigadier." Morgan's wagons returned without any pork or corn. On their return Morgan and Washington learned that they had a new commanding officer, General Nathanael Greene.

Congress finally decided to let General Washington make the next selection, since they chose three consecutive losers for the command of the Southern Department. Washington immediately appointed his Quartermaster General, Major General Nathaniel Greene. Washington also ordered General Von Steuben south with Greene to help train new soldiers.[743]

Black River, South Carolina
7 December 1780

Peter Horry was Francis Marion's cavalry commander. He was brave and ambitious, but a very poor rider. Several times in combat he fell off his horse. Horry had a speech impediment, he stuttered.

It increased when he was excited. During one ambush he attempted to initiate the shooting, but all he could say was, "fi-fi-fi!" Angered by the men who knew what to do, he shouted, "SHOOT, damn you, Shoot! You know what I would say! Shoot, and be damned to you!"

Marion sent Horry out to reconnoiter Colonel Tynes' militia at Fort Upton. Tynes had been released by the North Carolina jailers and had returned to the area. Horry complained often that the North Carolinians released the men as quick as he caught them. Many of the North Carolina jailers that Marion used were Loyalists. After a night of riding, Horry's troops stopped at a tavern kept by a well-known Loyalist. Horry questioned the frightened Loyalists about Tynes. The tavern-keeper's wife was not afraid of the partisans and showed them a barrel of apple brandy in a storehouse. She let the men fill their canteens and drink as much as they want. Horry did not know his men had been drinking the brandy, but began to suspect, as they continually drank from their canteens and were in high spirits. Some grinned in his face "like monkeys, others looked stupid as asses, while the greater part chattered like magpies."

Horry was the only sober man in the whole troop, so he decided to retreat while he still had a troop. The men whooped and hallooed down the road, by the Black River. Even though his mission was a failure Horry's patrol was effective. His drunken troopers had terrified the Loyalists along the Black River, and twenty militiamen deserted from Tynes' command.[744] When Tynes noticed how small his force was he deserted himself, and resigned his command.[745]

Lynch's Creek, South Carolina   Murder
December 1780

Colonel Marion sent out a patrol, led by Lieutenant William Gordon, to reconnoiter Lynch's Creek. While Gordon's men stopped at a house to rest, Captain Butler and a Loyalist patrol surrounded the house. When Gordon's men wouldn't come out Butler set the house on fire. Gordon knew he was outnumbered and surrendered. When Gordon and his men grounded their arms, they were all shot down and murdered.

The British South Carolina Gazette condemned Marion's men and wrote that the "State of South Carolina no longer exists. Marion and the men who follow him are blue parties and traitors against rebellion itself, and are to be sacrificed by any regular enemy.[746] Their violence and rapine mark their steps. The King will not always be merciful."[747]

French Broad River, Tennessee [748]   **Skirmish**
Cherokee Campaign of 1780
8 December 1780 [749]

American Forces
Commanding Officer   Lieutenant Colonel John Sevier
   State Militia
      Major Jonathan Tipton
         Washington County Militia   100
           Major Joseph Wilson
           Captain Benjamin Gist
           Captain Joseph Martin
           Captain Godfrey Isbell
           Captain William Trimble
           Captain John McNabb
           Captain James Stinson
      Lieutenant Colonel John Sevier
         Greene County Militia   200
           Captain William Pruett
           Captain Hawkins
           Captain Landon Carter
           Captain Samuel Handly
           Captain George Russell
           Captain James Hubbard
           Captain Thomas Gist
Casualties   Colonel Sevier and Major Tipton wounded

Loyalist Forces
Chicamauga Indians   70
Casualties   16 killed

After King's Mountain Cornwallis had finally decided to release the Indians upon the Carolina frontier. This would force the victors of King's Mountain back into the backcountry to protect their settlements. This plan worked, but the Indians did not expect any resistance, since the men were off fighting Loyalists. In December Colonel Sevier marched towards Chota Town with men from the backcountry militias.

The Chicamaugas had set an ambush in a field of tall grass at Boyd's Creek. Sevier's Scouts detected the Indians and sprung the ambush early. The backwoodsmen immediately attacked from their horses and commenced firing. The Indians fled from the intense fire of the riflemen into a canebrake, where they took refuge. In the baggage of the Indians the frontiersmen found Clinton's proclamation for the Indians to rise up. Sevier ordered his men back to Buckingham's Island on the Broad River, to wait for reinforcements from Virginia.[750]

McKown's Mill, South Carolina   Murder
11 December 1780

John Nuckolls was a partisan who lived near Thicketty Creek. Early in December he had returned home to visit his home at Whig Hill. He took his young son John to McKown's Mill on Broad River to get more meal for his family. McKown was a Tory, but Nuckoll's decided he could trust him.

McKown told Nuckolls that he would not be able to grind any meal for him until the next day, and then gave him a room at the mill for the night. What Nuckolls did not know was that McKown could not be trusted and he had just been trapped. McKown sent for some other Loyalists and they went to Nuckolls' room. They woke him up, saying, "We've come for you."

Nuckolls realized the deadly mistake he had made, and asked if he could wake up his son so he could give some messages for his people at home. The Loyalists told him that if they woke the boy, they would kill him too. They walked Nuckolls a short distance from the mill and he asked if they would give him five minutes to pray. They told him to go ahead and pray, but one of the Loyalists named Davis said "If he continues praying that way much longer we will not be able to kill him," and shot him through the head.

They threw the body into a hole where a tree had blown over, and covered the hole with brush. A few months later an old woman found his bones. His family gathered them up and buried him at Whig Hill, his home.

A few months later the Loyalist Davis and several of the other men that murdered Nuckolls were captured by a Whig patrol, and executed in the same way they killed John Nuckolls. The Whigs went to the house of Mrs. Nuckolls and asked if they could have a pick and a shovel because "they were going to settle her some new neighbors." She said that she "hoped they would be good neighbors." The men laughed and said that they "they would guarantee them to be quiet ones." [751]

Long Cane, South Carolina   **Battle**
12 December 1780 [752]

American Forces
Commanding Officer   Colonel Elijah Clarke
   State Troops and Militia   100
     Major James McCall
      South Carolina State Dragoons
       Major John Lindsay
       Captain Samuel Carr
     Georgia Militia
      Colonel Elijah Clarke
       Wilkes County Regiment

Colonel Benjamin Few
Upper Richmond County Militia Battalion
Casualties   14 killed, 7 wounded, 9 captured [753]

British Forces
Commanding Officer   Lieutenant Colonel Isaac Allen
   Provincials   150
     Lieutenant Colonel Isaac Allen
     New Jersey Volunteers
       3rd Battalion
         Lieutenant Edward Steele
           Lieutenant Colonel Isaac Allen's Company
         Lieutenant John Jenkins
           Captain Robert Drummond's Company
         Captain John Barbarie
         Captain Peter Campbell
         Captain Daniel Cozens
         Captain Charles Harrison
         Captain Thomas Hunloke
         Captain Thatcher Bartholomew
         Lieutenant John Hatton
           Captain Joseph Lee's Company
     Unknown commander
       DeLancey's Brigade
        1st Battalion
        Artillery   1 fieldpiece
    South Carolina Loyalist Militia
      Brigadier General Robert Cunningham
        Ninety-Six District Brigade of Loyalist Militia   110
         Captain James Dunlap [754]
           Dunlap's Corps of Provincial Cavalry   50
Casualties   2 killed, 9 wounded

Some of the militia who fought with Sumter at the Blackstocks joined Colonels Clarke and Few of Georgia, and marched to the Long Cane settlement. They intended to encourage the people there to join the Patriot cause, and eventually raise enough men to attack the fort at Ninety-Six.

Lieutenant Colonel John Harris Cruger was the commander of the fort at Ninety-Six, and when he learned of the plans of the Patriot militia, he dispatched Lieutenant Colonel Isaac Allen to put down the militia. Colonel Allen moved to White Hall where the partisans had been camped, but only found an old campsite. He continued to search, but he did not find any partisans at all. Ironically Allen had camped only three miles from the partisan's camp. When he sent out foragers they bumped into a patrol sent out by Clarke. After a brief skirmish the partisans drove the foragers back, only to discover the Loyalist camp. Clarke and McCall engaged the Loyalist camp and sent back a message to Colonel Few to bring up his main force.

The partisans thought that only the Loyalist militia was present, and did not know of the Provincials under Allen. Allen had his men form on the other side of a hill, so as not to be seen. Clarke had his men tie their horses up within 100 yards of the Loyalist force, and then moved to engage the militia. When they were within forty yards of the Provincials, Clarke discovered the trap. He knew he was outnumbered and sent another message to Colonel Few, urging him to hurry. Clarke was seriously wounded in the shoulder and taken from the field. McCall and Lindsay were also wounded, and Lindsay lay where he fell. A Loyalist Captain named Lang ran forward and cut off Lindsay's right hand.[755]

When the Provincials charged with their bayonets the Patriots had enough, and retreated. Allen threw Dunlap's mounted militia into the battle, and the Patriots fled. As the men made it back to their camp and told Colonel Few what was charging after them, he retreated, leaving six wagons and thirty head of cattle to be captured by the British. [756]

Halfway Swamp, Singleton's Mill, South Carolina [757]
13 December 1780

American Forces
Commanding Officer   Colonel Francis Marion
   South Carolina Militia
      Williamsburg Township Militia   700
         Captain James Postelle
           Colonel Joseph Kershaw's Regiment
         Lieutenant Colonel Hugh Horry
           Colonel Richard Richardson's Regiment
             Captain Thomas Waite
             Captain William Robert McCottry
               McCottry's Riflemen
             Captain Gavin Witherspoon
             Captain Samuel Price
             Captain John McCauley
         Captain Lemuel Benton
           Colonel Abel Kolb's Regiment
             Captain Tristram Thomas
             Captain Daniel Williams
             Captain John Butler
             Captain Guthridge Lyons
             Captain Alexander McIntosh
             Captain Moses Pearson
             Captain Daniel Sparks
             Captain William Standard
         Major Peter Horry
           Colonel Archibald McDonald's Regiment
             Major John James
             Captain William Clay Snipes
             Captain John Baxter
             Captain John Postelle
             Captain Daniel Conyers
             Captain James McCauley

Captain William Allston of Clifton

Casualties   4 killed, 6 wounded

British Forces
Commanding Officer   Major Robert McLeroth
  British Regulars
    Major Robert McLeroth
      64th Regiment of Foot   200
    Captain George Kelly
      7th (Royal Fusilier) Regiment of Foot   100
Casualties   3 wounded [758]

On the 20th of November Major Robert McLeroth crossed the Santee River at Nelson's Ferry, and marched into the Williamsburg Township. He camped on the village green in Kings Tree. This was a direct challenge to Marion, because any British unit going into the Williamsburg Township was tempting fate.

The villagers sent a message to Marion in Black Mingo, but instead of mounting an attack, he hastily assembled his partisans and slipped away. On November 22nd McLeroth feared an attack by a larger unit, and abandoned Kings Tree.

Three weeks later Marion learned the Major McLeroth was marching two hundred recruits of the 7th Fusiliers, from Charlestown to Camden. Marion immediately rode off searching for the British soldiers. He stopped at the house of a lady who had always been friends to the Whigs, and asked her if she had known of any movements of McLeroth. The woman told Marion that she could not help him because McLeroth had been so honorable and gentle, that she didn't wish to see him harmed. Her opinion did not sway Marion from his intended target, but it may have lessened the aggression he normally went into battle with.

Marion overtook the recruits on the road, and drove in the British pickets from the rear. McCottry's Riflemen skirmished with the rear guard, while Marion attacked the flank and front of the 64th Regiment. He drove them into a field enclosed by a rail fence. As the veterans of the 64th dragged in the frightened recruits behind them, Marion drew up his troops in the swamp and waited.

After Marion's snipers hit several pickets McLeroth sent out a British officer under a flag of truce. McLeroth argued that shooting pickets was contrary to all the laws of civilized warfare. He dared the partisans to come out of the woods and fight in the open field. Marion replied that the burning of houses by Tarleton and Wemyss was worse than shooting pickets, and as long as the British burned houses, then he would shoot pickets.

He took McLeroth's challenge of fighting in the open by having twenty of his men fight twenty British Regulars. McLeroth accepted the challenge. Marion chose Major John Vanderhorst to command the fighters, and then he chose the bravest and most accurate marksmen. Vanderhorst marched forward to within a hundred yards of the British, but the British shouldered their muskets and retreated. Vanderhorst and his men gave three huzzahs, but they had been tricked.

McLeroth had been stalling for time. While the preparations for the challenge had been going on, McLeroth had sent couriers racing for help. They met Captain Coffin and one hundred and forty mounted infantrymen. Coffin did not come to rescue them from Marion, but instead turned back and camped his men in Swift Creek.

During the night McLeroth's men built huge bonfires, they shouted and sang, then quieted down at midnight. This was a deception because in the dark of night they abandoned their baggage and slipped quietly away on the road to Singleton's Mills. Marion discovered the trick at daylight and dispatched Hugh Horry and a hundred horsemen to intercept the British.

Horry couldn't overtake McLeroth, so he told Major John James to ride to Singleton's Mills and seize the houses there. James beat the British to Singleton's Mills, just as McLeroth's men came into sight. James had his men fire one volley, and then to the amazement of the British soldiers, they fled in a hurry. The Singleton family had smallpox![759]

Before James fled from the diseased house one of his men rested his rifle against a tree, took careful aim, and shot the captain of the British advance party. McLeroth had beaten the great partisan leader, and he had not done it by burning houses or killing wounded partisans, but instead outfoxed Marion.[760]

The day after the action at Singleton's Plantation Marion's men boldly blocked all traffic on the Santee Road and the Santee River. Due to Marion's actions Lieutenant Colonel Balfour ordered the wagon trains to take to the longer, harder route from Monck's Corner to Friday's Ferry on the Congaree. All supply boats were to remain below Murry's Ferry. Unfortunately one captain of a supply boat coming from Camden docked at Nelson's Ferry. Before the crew realized their danger, Marion's men had swarmed aboard and seized the vessel. After removing the stores, sails, hardware, and everything else of value, they burned it.

Major McLeroth approached Nelson's Ferry with his 64th Regiment, but did not attack. Marion's men contented themselves with an occasional random shot at the British. Marion remained on the road until he received orders from Nathaniel Greene to conduct intelligence gathering for his army.[761]

Indian Creek, South Carolina [762]   Skirmish
14 December 1780

Colonel Joseph Hayes, Captain Thomas Blassingame and their fifty militiamen attacked a force of twenty-five Loyalists, under the command of Major Moses Buffington. Buffington and his Dutch Fork Militia had been posted at Colonel Dugan's place on Indian Creek, four miles south of Enoree River.

Buffington and three of his men were wounded; seven or eight others were captured. Buffington is said by some accounts to have died of his wounds, but he did not die for two more years. The British commander in the area stated that the fault of his defeat was probably due to Buffington, "who as usual had no centry out."[763]

Hopkins Place, Broad River, South Carolina   Skirmish
December 1780

Major Samuel Otterson had been sent from Union District, with eight or ten men, to spy on the Tories in the western Chester District. The Patriot patrol crossed the Broad River at Fishdam Ford, and then rode to the home of Captain David Hopkins. The house was deserted, but Otterson noticed a fire on the west side of a ridge, a quarter of a mile away.

Otterson crawled up to the ridge by himself and "discovered Tories, double his strength. They must be Tories or they would have been at Hopkins". He "snaked" his way back to his men so he would not be seen, and ordered his me to approach the Loyalist camp the same way. His men were to fire when he gave a signal.

While they were moving into position, the commander of the Tories, Captain Moore "who was advanced in his years", rose out of his bed and went to the fire to build it up. "He was on his knees blowing up a blaze" when Otterson gave the signal to fire. Several of the Tories were killed in their beds. Captain Moore had been hit from behind and fell into the fire. "A few escaped like wild turkeys".

One of the Loyalists grabbed up his musket and clubbed one of Otterson's men. He would have smashed in his skull, but another Patriot "who had just knifed his antagonist, came to the relief of the overpowered man and dispatched the Tory with his knife."[764]

Chota Town, Chilhowee and Telassee, Tennessee   Skirmish
Cherokee Campaign of 1780
22-26 December 1780

After Lieutenant Colonel Sevier's backwoods militia defeated the Cherokee at Boyd Creek, they withdrew to Buckingham Island, and waited for the arrival of Colonel Campbell. Campbell and his Virginians arrived eight days later and took control of the entire force.

On December 22nd the frontiersmen crossed the French River and found Major Jonathan Tipton and his Watauga Riflemen. They needed provisions. Campbell gave them supplies and then continued the march to the Tennessee River. The frontiersmen received word that the Cherokee knew of their approach and had blocked all the normal fording places.

On the 24th Campbell divided his force for the attack on Chota Town. He could see the Indians on the hills around the town, but he could not decoy them to come down to attack. He burned Chota Town and continued to search the town for several days to find any stores. One Indian was killed at this town and seventeen horses loaded with clothing, skins and household furniture were captured. Major Joseph Martin discovered the escape path of the Indians, and determined that it led towards the towns of Tellico and Hiwassee.

Captain James Crabtree of the Virginia militia was detached with sixty men to burn the town of Chilhowee. Crabtree succeeded in burning part of the town, but a superior force of Cherokees attacked him. Crabtree retreated back to Campbell's force with no losses.

On the 26th Major Tipton and 150 mounted men were detached from Campbell's force to cross the river and dislodge the Indians at the town of Telassee. Major Gilbert Christian was also detached with 150 dismounted men to burn the remaining part of the town at Chilhowee that had not been burned by Crabtree. The town at Chilhowee was burned and three Indians were killed. Christian's force was able to take nine prisoners. Major Tipton's mounted men did not fare so well, since they were unable to cross the river. [765]

Georgetown, South Carolina   **Skirmish**
25 December 1780

Cornwallis reorganized his forces in South Carolina by ordering Lieutenant Colonel Nisbet Balfour to command Charlestown, and placing Lieutenant Colonel John Cruger in command of Ninety-Six. Captain John Saunder's and his troop of Queen's Rangers sailed to Charlestown in order to join Cornwallis in the interior of the Carolinas. Once the Queen's Rangers arrived in Charlestown they were ordered to Georgetown by Colonel Balfour. Captain Saunders wished to return to New York, so he sent Lieutenant John Wilson with the troop to Georgetown, while he rode on to Winnsboro to meet with Cornwallis.

After their arrival the Queen's Rangers were sent out on a patrol around Georgetown led by Lieutenant Colonel George Campbell. The patrol encountered fifty mounted Patriot militia. Lieutenant Wilson immediately charged with his thirteen troopers.

The Patriots dispersed, but Wilson was wounded in the melee. He was able to capture one of the Patriot officers, but the rest of the militia escaped into the woods. The Rangers were not able to capture them due the militia horses being faster than the horses of the Rangers.[766]

Ninety-Six, South Carolina   **Murder**
25 December 1780

Lieutenant Colonel Isaac Allen and his 3rd Battalion of the New Jersey Volunteers shared the fort at Ninety-Six, with Lieutenant Colonel Cruger and his 1st Battalion of DeLancey's Brigade. While the Loyalists were garrisoned in the stockade, the South Carolina partisans conducted some minor raids on the fort.

On Christmas day Ensign John Massey Camp was captured outside the walls of the fort. The partisans murdered Camp and left his body outside the walls.[767]

Georgetown, South Carolina   **Skirmish**
27 December 1780

American Forces
Commanding Officer   Lieutenant Colonel Peter Horry
    South Carolina Militia
      Williamsburg Township Militia
        Colonel Archibald McDonald's Regiment   33
          Captain John Baxter
          Captain John Postelle

Loyalist Forces
Commanding Officer   Cornet Thomas Meritt
   Provincials
     Cornet Thomas Meritt
      Queen's Rangers
       Captain John Saunder's Troop of Cavalry   18
Casualties   16 captured

To determine the strength of the British forces in Georgetown Marion sent Peter Horry and, Captain Baxter, with thirty men from Indiantown, on a reconnaissance.

In Georgetown Marion's men set up an ambush and waited for an enemy to appear. Cornet Meritt was commanding a troop of green-coated Queen's Rangers in Georgetown. Meritt had been sent into the countryside around Georgetown to provide cover for some slaves, which were sent to the neighboring plantations to bring back cattle that had wandered away from the garrison.

About midmorning Meritt, another officer and a squad of the Queen's Rangers were escorting two young ladies past Horry's ambush. Horry decided not to ambush these men, since the women were with them, and let them pass. Horry and his men then went to a house to seek a late breakfast because they had not eaten in thirty-six hours. They rode to White's Plantation and discovered that inside the house was Mrs. White, her daughter, and the two ladies that had been escorted by the Rangers.

Mrs. White asked Horry what he wanted, and he replied that he wanted food and drink for his men. The family begged Horry to go away because they were all poor and had no provisions. Horry was confused, because he knew these people were Marion supporters, so he followed Mrs. White to the kitchen and asked what the matter was. She told Horry that the two women in the room were Tories, and that if Horry wanted anything, he had to pretend to take it by force. This was a situation that Marion's men were used to, because if the people appeared too friendly the British may burn their house down and place the inhabitants in jail.

Horry had gone back into the room with the Tory women, when the sentries outside fired a warning shot and came running back to the house. They told Horry that the Queen's Rangers were charging down the road. The partisans quickly mounted their horses and charged the Rangers. The Rangers saw they were outnumbered, and fled back towards Georgetown.

Cornet Meritt stayed in the rear, fighting off each of Horry's men as they caught up with him. Captain Baxter fired pistols at Meritt, but missed. Captain Postelle and another partisan came at Meritt with swords, but they were driven back. Meritt had two horses killed under him, and was so stunned by the fall of the last one that he was left for dead. Marion's men took his boots, helmet and weapons. When he recovered his senses he escaped into the swamp and hid.[768]

Two of the prisoners captured by Horry were both men who had been in the 3rd South Carolina Regiment. They said that they had enlisted from the prison ship in Charlestown so that they would have a better chance to escape.[769]

Chota Town, Sietego, Little Tuskeego and Kaiatee, Tennessee
Cherokee Campaign of 1780
27-28 December 1780

Nancy Ward was a Cherokee who came into Colonel Campbell's camp at Chota Town. She was sent there to make an overture for peace on behalf of some of the Chiefs. Campbell refused to consider peace, because he still "wished first to visit the vindictive part of the nation, mostly settled at Hiwassee and Christowee, and to distress the whole as much as possible by destroying their habitations and provisions."

On the 28th Campbell set fire to Chota, Sietego and Little Tuskeego, and moved his force to Kaiatee, a town on Tellico River. That night as Major Joseph Martin was returning from a patrol he discovered a band of Indians. Martin's men killed two of the Cherokees and drove several others into the river.

That same evening, in another skirmish, Indians gathering corn fired upon Captain Elliot of the Virginia Militia. One of Elliot's men wounded an Indian. When Elliot rode up to the wounded man, he rose up and shot Elliot in the head. The Indian grabbed Elliot's gun, but was shot dead by the rest of the men in the patrol. Three other Indians were killed in this skirmish. Captain Elliot was buried beneath one of the cabins, and then the cabin was burned to prevent the mutilation of his corpse.[770]

Hammond's Store, South Carolina [771]　　　　　Skirmish
30 December 1780

American Forces
Commanding Officer　　　Lieutenant Colonel William Washington
　　Continentals
　　　　Lieutenant Colonel William Washington
　　　　　　3rd Regiment of Continental Light Dragoons　　　75
　　　　　　　　Major Richard Call
　　　　　　　　Captain William Parsons
　　　　　　　　Captain William Barrett
　　　　　Captain John Watts
　　　　　　1st Regiment of Continental Light Dragoons　　　10
　　　South Carolina State Troops
　　　　Unknown commander[772]
　　　　　South Carolina State Dragoons
　　　　　　Major James McCall's Troop　　　　　　200
Loyalist Forces
Commanding Officer　　　　　　Colonel Thomas Waters [773]
　　Loyalist Militia
　　　Savannah Militia　　　　　　　　250
Casualties　　　　　150 killed and wounded, 40 captured

When Greene assumed command of the army he found an ill-equipped and demoralized army. He established discipline by ordering men to be executed that were caught plundering, or deserting. Greene was a man of his word, and had the entire army watch as a deserter was executed by firing squad. He decided to move the men from their huts in the depleted area of Charlotte, and have them march to Cheraw in South Carolina. He ordered Daniel Morgan to march deep into South Carolina and harass the enemy while this move was being conducted.

Sergeant Major William Seymour, of the Delaware Line, wrote "Here the manly fortitude of the Maryland Line was very great, being obliged to march and do duty barefoot, being all the winter the chief part of them wanting coats and shoes, which they bore with the greatest patience imaginable."

Morgan camped on Pacolet River and received intelligence that Colonel Thomas Waters had banded together the Loyalist militia at Fair Forest. These Loyalists were destroying the settlements of Whig families between Ninety-Six and Winnsboro. Morgan sent Colonel Washington's dragoons and 200 men of McCall's mounted militia to attack the Loyalist raiders. Waters learned of Washington's advance and fell back twenty miles to Hammond's Store.

Washington caught up with Colonel Waters after a forty mile ride behind British lines. Thomas Young was a militiaman riding with Washington that day, and he wrote in his memoirs, "When we came in sight, we perceived that the Tories had formed in line on the brow of the hill opposite to us. We had a long hill to descend and another to rise. Col. Washington and his dragoons gave a shout, drew swords, and charged down the hill like madmen. The Tories fled In every direction without firing a gun. We took a great many prisoners and killed a few."

Washington's men were infuriated at the outrageous treatment inflicted on the settlements, and they did their best to kill everyone in sight. One hundred and fifty of the raiders were hacked to death or mutilated. Young wrote of an incident during the massacre, "In Washington's corps there was a boy of fourteen or fifteen, a mere lad, who in crossing Tiger River was ducked by a blunder of his horse. The men laughed and jeered at him very much, at which he got very mad, and swore that boy or no boy, he would kill a man that day or die. He accomplished the former. I remember very well being highly amused at the little fellow charging round a crib after a Tory, cutting and slashing away with his puny arm, till he brought him down."

A few of the Loyalists escaped to a small fort on Williams' Plantation. Washington understood that he was deep behind enemy lines, and he rode towards Morgan's camp.[774]

Williams' Fort, South Carolina [775]   Skirmish
31 December 1780

American Forces
Commanding Officer   Colonel Joseph Hayes
    Continentals [776]
      Cornet James Simons
        1st Regiment of Continental Light Dragoons   10
    South Carolina Militia
      Colonel Joseph Hayes
        Little River Regiment   40
Loyalist Forces
Commanding Officer   Brigadier General Robert Cunningham
    South Carolina Loyalist Militia
      Ninety-Six District Brigade of Loyalist Militia
        Major Patrick Cunningham's Regiment [777]   150
          Captain William Payne
          Captain William Parker
          Captain William Griffin
          Captain John Mayfield

Captain Christopher Neily
Captain John Brown
Captain David Jones
Captain William Cradock
Captain William Helms
Captain James Campbell
Captain Arthur William
Captain William Hendricks
Captain John Dalrymple
Captain Joseph Person
Captain William Cunningham [778]
Dunlap's Corps of Provincial Cavalry
Cunningham's Troop

The day after the action at Hammond's Store Washington detached a small body of troops under Colonel Joseph Hayes to capture Williams' Fort. After James Williams had been killed at King's Mountain, Loyalist Colonel Moses Kirkland occupied his plantation, and removed Williams' wife and kids from the main house. Mary Williams and her six children moved into some outbuildings on other land that Williams had owned. After Robert Cunningham defeated the Patriot militia at Long Cane he also joined Kirkland at the plantation.

When Hayes arrived at the gate of the fort, he demanded the surrender of the fort. The commander of the fort, Brigadier General Robert Cunningham, asked for time to consult with his officers. While Cunningham was doing this some of his Loyalists slipped out the rear of the fort and into the woods. A few of them were spotted and killed, but most escaped.

The Patriot dragoons gathered up all the supplies they could, then destroyed the fort and the mills. Washington wisely decided to return to the Pacolet River and rejoined Morgan.[779]

Christowee, Tennessee
Cherokee Campaign of 1780
31 December 1780

On December 29th Colonel Campbell left Kaiatee and marched forty miles to Hiwassee Old Town. Campbell left Major Christian at Kaiatee with a force of 150 men. Campbell and Sevier found Hiwassee abandoned, but captured a young warrior that told them that some Indians were twelve miles away at Christowee, waiting to ambush them. They were with the British Agent McDonald and some Loyalist militia.

Campbell knew the Indians were watching him, so he ordered the camp to be laid out and cooking fires to be kindled. This gave the impression that they were going to stay all night. After dark Campbell took 300 men and crossed the River. Not all the men went, because the Watauga men refused to go.

The frontiersmen discovered that the Indians had fled in a hurry, leaving behind almost all their corn and other provisions. They also left behind many of their utensils for agriculture, all their heavy household furniture, and part of their stocks of horses, cattle and hogs. Campbell destroyed 1,000 Indian cabins, and 50,000 bushels of corn. After the town was burned the men returned to Kaiatee.

On the return march Major Martin captured four prisoners. Campbell learned from them that the Chicamauga chiefs wished to seek peace. He sent the chiefs a message that if they wanted peace then they should send six of their headmen to the Great Island, and meet with Major Martin.

The rest of the army decided to head back home. In the entire campaign against the Chicamaugas the frontiersmen killed twenty-nine Indians and took seventeen prisoners, mostly women and children. The frontiersmen only lost one man killed and two wounded. Campbell stated that "No place in the Over Hill country remained unvisited, except the small town of Telassee, a scattering settlement in the neighbourhood of Chickamogga, and the town of Calogee, situated on the sources of the Mobile."

The Chicamaugas moved farther down the Tennessee River to the foot of Lookout Mountain, and built the "Five Lower Towns". These towns were Lookout Town, Crow Town, Long Island, Runningwater, and Nickajack.[780]

Discontented Creeks, Shawnees and Loyalists joined the Chicamaugas. Dragging Canoe and his men continued their raids on white settlements.[781]

Bibliography

Primary Sources

Allaire, Anthony. *Diary of Lieut. Anthony Allaire, of Ferguson's Corps, Memorandum of Occurrences during the Campaign of 1780*, New York, 1968

American Antiquarian Society, *Letter from William Washington to Nathaniel Greene, July 28, 1781, McCord's Ferry*, Worcester, Massachusetts

Aspinall, A. Editor, *The Correspondence of George, Prince of Wales, 1770-1812, Volume 4*, Oxford University Press

Brooke, Francis J. *A Family Narrative, Being the Reminiscences of a Revolutionary Officer, Afterwards Judge of the Court of Appeals, Written for the information of his children*, McFarlane & Fergusson, 1849

Brooklyn Historical Society, *Mss Book 42*, folio 27, New York

Brown, Tarleton. *Memoirs of Tarleton Brown, A Captain in the Revolutionary Army, Written by himself*, New York, 1862

Bulger, William T. editor, *Journal of the Siege of Charleston, 1780*, The South Carolina Historical Magazine, Volume 66, Number 3, July 1965

Campbell, Archibald. *Journal of An Expedition against the Rebels of Georgia in North America Under the Orders of Archibald Campbell Esquire Lieut. Colonel of His Majesty's 71st Regiment 1778*, The Ashantilly Press, 1981

Campbell, Charles, editor. *The Orderly Book of That Portion of the American Army Stationed at or Near Williamsburg Under the Command of General Andrew Lewis,* Richmond, 1860

Chesney, Alexander. *Journal of Alexander Chesney, a South Carolina Loyalist in the Revolution and After,* Ohio State University Bulletin, Volume XXVI, Number 4, October 30, 1921

Chesnutt, David R., editor, *The Papers of Henry Laurens,* Model Editions Partnership, 1999

Clinton, Henry. *The American Rebellion, Sir Henry Clinton's Narrative of his Campaigns, 1775-1782, with an Appendix of Original Documents,* Yale University Press, 1954

Collins, James. *A Revolutionary Soldier,* revised and prepared by John M. Roberts, Esq. Felician Democrat, Print, 1859

Conrad, Dennis, editor. *The Papers of General Nathanael Greene,* Model Editions Partnership, 1996

Cornwallis, Earl. *An Answer to that Part of the Narrative of Lieutenant General Sir Henry Clinton, K.B.*

Cross, Jack L. editor, *Letters of Thomas Pinckney, 1775-1780,* The South Carolina Historical Magazine, Volume LVIII, Number 1, January 1957

Dickson, William. *Historical Sketch of Old Duplin County, by Col. William Dickson,* The Raleigh Star, 1810

Dickson, William. *Duplin County History to 1810,* The North Carolina Historical Review, 1928

Dudley, Guilford. *A Sketch of the Military Services Performed by Guilford Dudley, Then of the Town of Halifax, North Carolina, During the Revolutionary War, Parts I-V,* Literary Messenger, 1845

Draper, Lyman. *Thomas Sumter Papers, Draper Manuscript Collection*, State Historical Society of Wisconsin

Elliot, Bernard. *Diary of Captain Barnard Elliot, 1st South Carolina Regiment*, Laurens Collection, South Carolina Historical Society, Charleston, South Carolina

Fanning, David. *The Narrative of Colonel David Fanning (A Tory in the Revolutionary War with Great Britain;) Giving an Account of his Adventures in North Carolina, From 1775 to 1783, As Written by Himself, with an Introduction and Explanatory Notes.* The Reprint Company, 1973

Farr, Thomas. *Revolutionary Letters*, South Carolina Historical and Genealogical Magazine, Volume XXXVIII, Number 1, January 1937

Forster, Thompson. *Diary of Thompson Forster, Staff Surgeon to His Majesty's Detached Hospital in North America, October 19th 1775 to October 23rd 1777*

Georgia Historical Society. *Mark King Papers*, Collection Number 462

Goss, Thomas, editor. *Primary Source Reference Book For the 1781 Guilford Courthouse Campaign.* Department of History, United States Military Academy, West Point, 1998

Gray, Robert. *Colonel Robert Gray's Observations on the War in Carolina*, South Carolina Historical and Genealogical Magazine, Volume XI, Number 3, July 1910

Great Britain, Public Record Office
Admiralty, Class 51, Volume 968

    Audit Office, Class 13, Volume 4, folios 305-307; Volume 34, folio 356, 357; Volume 119, 130

    Chancery, Class 106, Volume 90, Part 2, Bundle 13

    Colonial Office, Class 5, Volume 97-99, 104, 182

    Cornwallis Papers, Class 30, Volume 11

    Headquarters Papers of the British Army in America, Class 30, Volume 55

    Treasury Office, Class 1, Volume 650, folio 154; Class 50, Volume 2, folio 372

    War Office, Class 12, Volumes 247, 3960 and Muster Rolls; Series 12 5637/2 Company Pay Rolls, return of 25 December 1775-24 June 1776; Class 34, Volume 159, folio 9; Class 65, Volume 29, the annotated Army List for 1779; for 1780; for 1781; 30 June 1780. *A List of all the Officers of the Army: viz. The General and Field Officers; The Officers of the Several Troops, Regiments, Independent Companies, and Garrisons: with an Alphabetical Index to the Whole*

Grimkè, John Faucheraud. *Journal of the Campaign to the Southward, May 9th to July 14th, 1778*, The South Carolina Historical and Genealogical Magazine, Volume XII, Number 4, October 1911; Number 4, October 1912;

Volume XIV, Number 1, January 1913; Number 2, April 1913; Number 3, July 1913; Number 4, October 1913; Volume XVI, Number 2, April 1915; Number 4, October 1915; Volume XVII, Number 2, April 1916; Number 3, July 1916; Number 4, October 1916; Volume XVIII, Number 2, April 1917; Number 3, July 1917; Number 4, October 1917; Volume XIX, Number 2, April 1918; Number 4, October 1918

Hanger, George. *An Address to the Army in Reply to Strictures, by Roderick M'Kenzie (Late Lieutenant in the 71st Regiment) on Tarleton's history of the Campaigns of 1780 and 1781.by the Hon. George Hanger, Major to the Cavalry of the British Legion, commanded by Lieut. Col. Tarleton, and Captain in the Hessian Jäger Corps,* London, 1789

Hanger, George. *The Life, Opinions and Adventures of Col. George Hanger, Written by Himself, Interesting Particulars relative to Col. George Hanger when in America; being a Continuation of his Life and Adventures, Vol. 2,* London, 1801

Harden, William, editor. *Order Book of Samuel Elbert, Colonel and Brigadier General in the Continental Army, Oct 1776 to November 1778,* Georgia Historical Society Collections, 1902

Harriet Irving Library, *Saunders Family Papers, Correspondence, 1780-1803,* University of New Brunswick, Canada

Hill, William. *Colonel William Hill's Memoirs,* Library of Congress, Washington, D.C.

Horry, Peter. *Order Book of Peter Horry*, The South Carolina Historical and Genealogical Magazine, Volume XXXV, Number 2, April 1934

Huntingdon Library, San Marino, California
Francis Marion's 2nd South Carolina Regiment Orderly Book, 1775-1782

American Loyalists Papers, HM 15228

House, Ezrael. *Ezrael House's Statement to the clerk of court in 1811*, House-Autry Mills Company

Johnson, William. *Sketches of the Life and Correspondence of Nathanael Greene, Major General of the Armies of the United States, In the War of the Revolution, Volume I,* Charleston, 1822

Johnson, Uzal. *Memo of Occurrence During the Campaign of 1780*, South Carolina Historical Society, Military Manuscripts.

Jones, George Fenwick, editor. *The 1780 Siege of Charleston as Experienced by a Hessian Office, Part One, (Journal of the Hochfuerstlichen Grenadier Battalion Platte from 16 February 1776 to 24 May 1784 by the Regimental Quartermaster: Carl Bauer,* South Carolina Historical Magazine, Volume 88, Number 1, January 1987; Number 2, April 1987

Kentucky Archives, *Kentucky Pension Accounts*, Frankfort, KY

Lamb, Roger. *Journal of Occurrences During the Late American War, from Its Commencement to the Year 1783.* Wilkinson and Courtney, Dublin, 1809

Lee, Henry Jr. *The Campaign of 1781 in the Carolinas*, Quadrangle Books, Inc., 1962

Lee, Robert. E, editor, *The Revolutionary War Memoirs of General Henry Lee*, Da Capo Press, 1998

MacKenzie, Frederick. *The Diary of Frederick Mackenzie, Giving a Daily Narrative of his Military Service as an Officer of the Regiment of Royal Welch Fusiliers During the Years 1775-1781 in Massachusetts, Rhode Island and New York, Volume II*, Harvard University Press, 1930

Mackenzie, Roderick. *Strictures on Lieut. Colonel Tarleton's History of the Southern Campaigns of 1780 & 1781*, London, 1787

Mathis, Samuel. *The Battle of Hobkirk's Hill*, South Carolina Archives, Columbia

Magallon de la Morlière, Louis-Antoine. *A French Account of the Siege of Charleston, 1780*, translated by Richard K. Murdoch, The South Carolina Historical Magazine, Volume 67, Number 3, July 1966

Moultrie, William. *Memoirs of the American Revolution So Far as it Related to the States of North and South Carolina and Georgia, Compiled from the most Authentic Materials, the Author's Personal Knowledge of the Various Events, and Including an Epistolary Correspondence on Public Affairs, with Civil and Military Officers, at that Period, by William Moultrie, Late Governor of the State of South Carolina, and Major General in the Army of the United States During the American War, Vol. I. & Vol. II*, New York, 1802

Nase, Henry. *Diary of Henry Nase, King's American Regiment,*
Nase Family Papers, The New Brunswick Museum,
Department of Canadian History, Archives Division

National Archives and Records Administration, Washington, D.C.
Compiled Service Records of Soldiers, Revolutionary War,
Army, M881-785

Letter from Wayne to Greene, 24 May 1782, Papers of the
Continental Congress, M 247, Reel 175, item 155, V. 2,
Pages 461–464

Papers of the Continental Congress, M247, r175, i155, v2,
Page 83

William Beasley Pension File, #W9352, Willoughby
Blackard Pension File, # S29638, Sanford Berry Pension
File, #S1638, Thomas Crawley Pension File, Abraham
Elledge Pension File, #S10625, Robert L. English Pension
File, #R3354, James Hopkins Pension File, #W3553,
William Kelly Pension File #W25993, Benjamin
Richardson Pension File #W4061, Mathew Sparks
Pension File, #S31385, Samuel Walker Pension File
#S3448, Dan Alexander Pension File #S2905

Revolutionary War Pension Applications and Bounty-Land
Warrant Application Files, RG 15, Microcopy 804

National Archives of Canada
RG 8, "C" Series, Volume 1902, *Muster Roll of Captain*
Atwood's Troop, King's American Regiment, 24 December
1781

RG 8, "C" Series, Volume 1883, 1887, 1899, *Muster Roll of*

Captain Frederick Starcloff's Troop of Light Dragoons, from their Commencement, Vizt. 1st April to the 24th June 1781 Inclusive Being 85 days

Ward Chipman Papers, MG 23, D 1, Series 1, Volume 25

New York Historical Society
Gates Papers, Reel 12

Official Letters of Major General James Pattison, Collections, 1875

North Carolina Department of Cultural Resources, Division of Archives and History, Raleigh, North Carolina
Brigade of Guards Orderly Book (A British Orderly Book)

List of Capt. James Houston's Company of North Carolina Rangers, Microfilm Roll 79; Misc.

Troop Returns, Military Collection

O'Donnell, James, editor. *A Loyalist View of the Drayton-Tennent-Hart Mission to the Upcountry*, The South Carolina Historical Magazine, Volume 67, Number 1, January 1966

Pennsylvania State Archives, *Revolutionary War Military Abstract Card File Indexes*, Philadelphia, PA

Saye, James Hodge, editor. *Memoirs of Major Joseph McJunkin, Revolutionary Patriot*, Richmond, VA Watchman and Observer, 1847

Senf, Johann Christian. *Extract from a Journal Concerning the*

Action of the 16th of August 1780 between Major General Gates and Gen. Lord Cornwallis, Manuscript Division, Library of Congress, Washington, D.C.

Seymour, William. *A Journal of the Southern Expedition, 1780-1783*, The Historical Society of Delaware, Wilmington, 1896

Simcoe, J.G. *A Journal of the Operations of the Queen's Rangers*, The New York Times and Arno Press, 1968

South Carolina Archives, *Benjamin Lincoln Papers*, Columbia, South Carolina

South Carolina Historical and Genealogical Magazine, *Letters to General Greene and Others*, The, Volume XVI, Number 3, July 1915; Number 4, October 1915

South Carolina Historical Society, Charleston, South Carolina
Benjamin Marion's 1st South Carolina Regiment Orderly Book, 1776-1780

Divers Accounts of the Battle of Sullivan's Island In his Majesty's Province of South Carolina the 28th June 1776

Emma Richardson Papers. Regiment Book of Captain James Bentham 1776-1780

Moultrie/Lincoln Order Book, 1779

Troop Returns, Military History Section

Southern Historical Collection, University of North Carolina, Chapel Hill
The Halifax Resolves, April 12th 1776

Mecklenburg Declaration (copy)

Stedman, Charles. *The History of the Origin, Progress, and Termination of the American War, Volume II*, London 1794

Stevens, Daniel. *Autobiography of Daniel Stevens, 1746-1835*, The South Carolina Historical Magazine, Volume LVIII, Number 1, January 1957

Tarleton, Banastre. *A History of the Campaigns of 1780 and 1781 in the Southern Provinces of North America*, Ayer Company Publishers, 1999

Tilden, John Bell. *Extracts from the Journal of Lieutenant John Bell Tilden, Second Pennsylvania Line, 1781-1782*, The Pennsylvania Magazine of History and Biography, Volume XIX (1895)

Tucker, Joseph Brown, editor. *The Journal and Order Book of Captain Robert Kirkwood of the Delaware Regiment of the Continental Line, Part I, "A Journal of the Southern Campaign" 1780-1782*, Kennikat Press, 1970

Virginia Records, *Officers nominated by Committee Sept. 27, 1778,* Deed Book 4, Pittsylvania County, VA

William L. Clements Library, University of Michigan
Sackville Germain Papers, Volume 15,

Sir Henry Clinton Papers, Volume 83, item 38; Volume 87, item 9; Volume 91, item 7; Volume 95; Volume 99; Volume 101; Volume 103; Volume 232

George Wray Papers, Volume 6, 7

Williams, Samuel C. editor, *General Richard Winn's Notes –
1780*, The South Carolina Historical and Genealogical
Magazine, Volume XLIII, Number 4, October 1942;
Volume XLIV, Number 1, January 1943

Wilson, John. *Journal of the Siege of Charleston*, edited by
Joseph Ioor Waring, The South Carolina Historical
Magazine, Volume 66, Number 3, July 1965

Young, Thomas. *Memoir of Major Thomas Young*, Orion
Magazine, October and November 1843

Primary Newspapers

Caledonian Mercury, August 2, 1776

Charlestown Royal Gazette, July 10, 1781

Connecticut Gazette, August 17, 1781

The Leeds Intelligencer, June 26, 1781

London Chronicle, May 26,1778

The New York Commercial Advertiser, Volume XXXI, No. 48,
August 15, 1823

The New York Gazette and the Weekly Mercury, August 6, 1781

The Pennsylvania Gazette

The Pennsylvania Packet

The Royal American Gazette, April 27, 1780

The Royal Georgia Gazette

Patrick O'Kelley

Ruddiman's Weekly Mercury, 28 February 1781

Contemporary Sources

Amblard, Marie. *Marins et Soldats Fran◊ais en Amérique pendant La Guerre de l'Indépendence des États-Unis (1778-1783)*, Librairie Académique Didier, 1903

Babits, Lawrence E. *A Devil of a Whipping, The Battle of Cowpens*, University of North Carolina Press, 1998

Babits, Lawrence E. and Howard, Joshua B. *Fortitude and Forbearance, The North Carolina Continental Line in the Revolutionary War, 1775-1783*, not yet published, 2003

Babits, Lawrence E. *Research Notes and Maryland Miscellany, The "Fifth" Maryland at Guilford Courthouse: An Exercise in Historical Accuracy,* Maryland Historical Magazine, Volume 84, Winter 1989

Bailey, Reverend J. D. *History of Grindal Shoals and Some Early Adjacent Families*, 1900, pp. 75-83

Baker, Thomas E. *Another Such Victory, The Story of the American defeat at Guilford Courthouse that helped win the War for Independence*, Eastern Acorn Press, 1992

Balch, Thomas. *The French in America during the War of Independence of the United States, 1777-1783, Volume II,* Porter and Coates, 1895

Barefoot, Daniel W. *Touring North Carolina's Revolutionary War Sites,* John F. Blair, Publisher, 1998

Bass, Robert D. *Green Dragoon*, Columbia SC, 1973

Bass, Robert D. *Swamp Fox, The life and campaigns of General Francis Marion*, Sandlapper Publishing Company, 1974

Batt, Richard John. *The Maryland Continentals, 1780-1781*, Tulane University Dissertation, 1974

Bearss, Edwin C. *Battle of Cowpens*, The Overmountain Press, 1996

Bennett, C. P., *The Delaware Regiment in the Revolution, Narrative of the Services of the Delaware Regiment with Captain McKennan During the Revolutionary War*, Pennsylvania Magazine of History & Biography, Volume 9 (1885)

Bennett, Charles E. and Lennon, Donald R. *A Quest for Glory, Major General Robert Howe and the American Revolution*, The University of North Carolina Press, 1991

Bennett, John. *Marion – Gadsden Correspondence*, The South Carolina Historical and Genealogical Magazine, Volume XLI, Number 1, January 1940

Blythe, Brockman. *Hornet's Nest. The Story of Charlotte and Mecklenburg County,* Public Library of Charlotte and Mecklenburg County, 1961

Boatner, Mark M. *Encyclopedia of the American Revolution*, David McKay Company Inc, 1966

Bodinier, Gilbert. *Les Officiers De l'Armee Royale Combattants de la Guerre d'Indépeendance des Etats-Unis De Yorktown a l'An II,* Service Historique de L'Armée de Terre at Château de Vincennes, 1983.

Borick, Carl P. *A Gallant Defense, The Siege of Charleston, 1780,* University of South Carolina Press, 2003

Brumbaugh, Gaius Marcus. *Revolutionary War Records, Volume 1, Virginia,* Baltimore: 1936.

Buchanan, John. *The Road to Guilford Courthouse,* John Wiley and Sons, Inc. 1997

Burgoyne, Bruce E. *Diaries of Two Anspach Jaegers,* Heritage Books, Inc. 1997

Burgoyne, Bruce E. *Enemy Views,* Heritage Books, Inc. 1995

Butler, Lewis. *The Annals of the King's Royal Rifle Corps, Volume I, "The Royal Americans",* John Murray, London, 1913

Cann, Marvin. *Ninety-Six, Old Ninety-Six in the South Carolina Backcountry 1700-1781,* Sleep Creek Publishing, 1996

Cannon, Richard, *History of the Twenty-Third Regiment, or Royal Welsh Fusiliers, 1689-1850,* Parker, Furnival & Parker, London 1847

Cannon, Robert. *Historical Record of the Seventeenth Regiment of Light Dragoons; Lancers: Containing an Account of the Formation of the Regiment in 1759, and of its Subsequent Services to 1841,* John W. Parker, London, 1843

Carrington, Henry B. *Battles of the American Revolution, 1775-1781, Historical and Military Criticism, with Topographic Illustration*, A.S. Barnes & Company, 1876

Caruthers, Eli W. *The Old North State in 1776, Volumes I and II with Index*, Guilford County Genealogical Society, 1985

Cary and McCance. *Regimental Records of the Royal Welch Fusiliers (Late the 23rd Foot), Volume 1 & 2*, Forster Groom and Company, LTD, 1921

Cashin, Edward J. *The King's Ranger, Thomas Brown and the American Revolution on the Southern Frontier*, University of Georgia Press, 1989

Clark, Murtie June. *Loyalists in the Southern Campaign of the Revolutionary War, Volume I, II, III* Genealogical Publishing Company, Inc. 1981

Clark, Walter. *Roster of North Carolina Soldiers in the American Revolution*, Winston, 1976

Clark, Walter. *The State Records of North Carolina, Vol. XIII – 1778 – '79*, Winston, 1895; *Volumes XIV – 1779 – '80; Volumes XV – 1780; Volumes XVI – 1781; Vol. XVII, 1781-1785*, Winston, 1896; *Vol. XIX – 1782 – '84. With Supplement – 1771 -'82, Volume XXII, Miscellaneous*, Nash Brothers, 1907

Clark, William B., editor, *Naval Documents of the Revolution (NDAR), Volume 1; Volume 2*, Washington DC: Government Printing Office, 1968

Coakley, Robert W. and Conn, Stetson. *The War of the American Revolution*, Center of Military History, United States Army, 1975

Coggins, Jack, *Ships and Seaman of the American Revolution*, Stackpole Books, 1969

Commager, Henry Steele and Morris, Richard B. *The Spirit of Seventy-Six*, Bonanza Books, 1983.

Conner, R.D.W. *Revolutionary Leaders of North Carolina*, North Carolina Normal & Industrial College Historical Publications, 1916

Cowan, Bob. *The Siege of Savannah, 1779*, Military Collector and Historian, Volume XXVII, Number 2, Summer, 1975

Crow, Jeffrey J. *A Chronicle of North Carolina during the American Revolution, 1763 – 1789*, North Carolina Division of Archives and History, 1975

Crow, Jeffrey J. *The Black Experience in Revolutionary North Carolina*, Division of Archives and History, North Carolina Department of Cultural Resources, 1992

Dann, John C. *The Revolution Remembered, Eyewitness Account of the War for Independence*, University of Chicago Press, 1980

Davies, K.G. *Documents of the American Revolution 1770-1783 (Colonial Office Series) Volume IX Transcripts 1775, January to June; Volume XI Transcripts 1775, July to December,* Irish University Press, 1972

Davies, K.G. *Documents of the American Revolution 1770-1783 (Colonial Office Series) Volume XII Transcripts 1776,* Irish University Press, 1973

Davies, K.G. *Documents of the American Revolution 1770-1783*

(Colonial Office Series) Volume XV Transcripts 1778, Irish University Press, 1976

Davies, K.G. *Documents of the American Revolution 1770-1783 (Colonial Office Series) Volume XVII Transcripts 1779,* Irish University Press, 1977

Davies, K.G. *Documents of the American Revolution 1770-1783 (Colonial Office Series) Volume XVIII Transcripts 1780,* Irish University Press, 1978

Davies, K.G. *Documents of the American Revolution 1770-1783 (Colonial Office Series) Volume XX Transcripts 1781,* Irish University Press, 1979

Davis, Marianna W. *South Carolina's Blacks and Native Americans, 1776-1976,* The Bicentennial Project Editorial Board, 1976

Davis, Robert S. *The Battle of Kettle Creek,* State of Georgia Department of Natural Resources, Office of Planning and Research, Historical Preservation Section, 1974

Davis, Robert S. *Georgia Citizens And Soldiers of the American Revolution,* Southern Historical Press, 1979

Davis, Robert S. *Georgians in the Revolution: At Kettle Creek (Wilkes Co.) and Burke County,* Southern Historical Press, Inc. 1986

Davis, Robert Scott. *The Loyalist Trials at Ninety-Six in 1779,* South Carolina Historical Magazine, Volume 80, Number 2, April 1979

Davis, Robert Scott. *Thomas Pinckney and the Last Campaign of*

Horatio Gates, South Carolina Historical Magazine, Volume 86, Number 2, April 1985

DeMond, Robert. *Loyalists in North Carolina During the Revolution*, Duke University Press, 1940

Draper, Lyman. *Kings Mountain and its Heroes: History of the Battle of King's Mountain, October 7th, 1780, And the Events Which Led To It*, The Overmountain Press, 1996

Dull, Jonathan R. *The French Navy and American Independence, A Study of Arms and Diplomacy, 1774-1787*, Princeton University Press

Duncan, Francis. *History of the Royal Regiment of Artillery*, London: John Murray; 1879

Ellet, Elizabeth F. *Domestic History of the American Revolution*, New York, Charles Scribner, 1859

Ellet, Elizabeth F. *The Women of the American Revolution*, New York, Baker and Scribner, 1849

Ervin, Sara Sullivan. *South Carolinians in the Revolution*, Genealogical Publishing Company, Inc. 1971

Fleming, Thomas J. *Cowpens, "Downright Fighting"*, National Park Service, 1988

Foote, William Henry. *Sketches of Virginia, Historical and Biographical, 2nd Series, 2nd Edition, revised*, J.B Lippencott, 1856

Ford, Worthington Chauncey. *British Officers Serving in the American Revolution 1774 – 1783*, Brooklyn, NY, 1897

Fortescue, Sir John W. *A History of the British Army, Vol. III,* London, 1902

Furches, D. M. *A Leaf of History - A Reminiscence of the Revolutionary Battle of Shallow Ford,* The Landmark, Statesville, NC, February 17, 1887

Garden, Alexander. *Anecdotes of the Revolutionary War in America with Sketches of Character of Persons the Most Distinguished, in the Southern States, for Civil and Military Services,* A.E. Miller, Charleston, 1822

Gibbes, Robert Wilson. *Documentary History of the American Revolution, Volume 1, 1764-1776; Volume 2, 1776-1782; Volume 3, 1781-1782,* The Reprint Company, 1972

The Guilford Genealogist, Volume 14, Number 1, Number 35, Fall 1986

Graham, William. *The Battle of Ramsaur's Mill, June 20, 1780, Major on Staff of Adjutant General of North Carolina,* North Carolina Archives, 1910

Graves, William T. *James Williams: An American Patriot in the Carolina Backcountry,* Writers Club Press, 2002

Griffiths, John William. *To Receive Them Properly, Charlestown Prepares For War, 1775-1776,* University of South Carolina, Department of History, 1992

Gruber, Ira D. *John Peebles' American War, The Diary of a Scottish Grenadier, 1776-1782,* Stackpole Books, 1998

Hairr, John. *Colonel David Fanning, The Adventures of a Carolina Loyalist,* Averasboro Press, 2000

Patrick O'Kelley

Hatch, Charles E. Jr. *The Battle of Moore's Creek Bridge*, National Park Service, 1969

Haun, Weynette Parks. *North Carolina Revolutionary Army Accounts: Secretary of State, Treasurer's & Comptroller's Papers, Journal "A", (Public Accounts) 1775-1776* part I, Weynette Parks Haun, 1989

Hayes, Jim. *James and Related Sea Islands*, Walker, Evans and Cogswell Co., 1978

Hayes, John T. *Stephen Jarvis, The King's Loyal Horseman, His Narrative, 1775-1783*, The Saddlebag Press, 1996

Hayes, John T. *A Gentleman of Fortune, The Diary of Baylor Hill, First Continental Light Dragoons, 1777-1781, Volume 2 and 3*, The Saddlebag Press, 1995

Hayes, John T. *The Saddlebag Almanac, September, 1996, Volume IV; January 1997, Volume V; January 1998, Volume VI; January 1999, Volume VII; January 2000, Volume VIII; January 2001, Volume IX; 2002, Volume X; 2003, Volume XI*

Heitman, Francis B. *Historical Register of Officers of the Continental Army during the War of the Revolution, April 1775, to December 1783*, Genealogical Publishing Company, 1967

Hibbert, Christopher. *Redcoats and Rebels, The American Revolution Through British Eyes*, Avon Books, 1990

Hough, Franklin B. *The Siege of Savannah by the Combined American and French Forces under the command of Gen. Lincoln and the Count D'Estaing in the Autumn of 1779*, J. Munsell, Albany, 1866

Howard, Joshua. *Things Here were a Melancholy Experience, The Battle of Briar Creek, Georgia, 3 March 1779, An Analysis* (April 2002)

James, William Dobein. *A Sketch of the Life of Brig. Gen. Francis Marion, and A History of his Brigade, From its Rise in June 1780, until Disbanded in December, 1782; With Descriptions of Characters and Scenes not heretofore published*, Gould and Riley, Charleston, S. C., 1821

Johnston, Henry P. and Iris Rose Guertin. *Collections of the Connecticut Historical Society Revolution Rolls and Lists, 1775-1783, Vol. VIII.* Hartford: Connecticut Historical Society, 1901, 1999

Jones, Charles Colcock. *The History of Georgia. Volume 2: Revolutionary Epoch.* Houghton-Mifflin, 1883

Jones, Charles Colcock. *The Siege of Savannah in 1779 as described in two contemporaneous journals of French Officers in the Fleet of Count D'Estaing*, Joel Munsell, 1874

Jones, Lewis Pinckney. *The South Carolina Civil War of 1775*, Sandlapper Store, Inc. 1975

Kell, Jean Bruyere. *North Carolina's Coastal Carteret County During the American Revolution, 1765-1785, A Bicentennial Project of the Carteret County Bicentennial Commission,* Era Press, 1975

Kirkland, Thomas J. and Kennedy, Robert M. *Historic Camden,* State Company, 1905

Lambert, Robert Stansbury. *South Carolina Loyalists in the*

American Revolution, University of South Carolina Press, 1987

Landers, H. L., *The Battle of Camden, South Carolina, August 16, 1780*, United States Government Printing Office, Washington, 1929

Lawrence, Alexander A. *Storm Over Savannah, the Story of Count d'Estaing and the Siege of the Town in 1779*, University of Georgia Press, 1951

Lawrence, James Walton. *Hogback Country*, The News Leader, 1982

Lee, Albert. *History of the Thirty-Third Foot*, Jarrold & Sons Ltd, The Empire Press, Norwich. 1922

Lee, E. Lawrence. *Indian Wars in North Carolina, 1663 – 1763*, North Carolina Division of Archives and History, 1968

Lewis, James A. *The Final Campaign of the American Revolution, Rise and Fall of the Spanish Bahamas*, University of South Carolina Press, 1991

Lipscomb, Terry W. *South Carolina Revolutionary Battles: Part I,* Names in South Carolina, Volume XX, Winter 1973, *Part II,* Names in South Carolina, Volume XXI, Winter 1974; *Part Three,* Winter 1975; *Part Four,* Winter 1976; *Part Five,* Winter 1977; *Part Six,* Winter 1978; *Part Seven,* Winter 1979; *Part Eight (With Map),* Winter 1980; *Part Nine,* Winter 1981; *Part Ten,* Winter 1983, South Carolina Historical Society

Lossing, Benson J. *The Pictorial Field-Book of the Revolution;*

or, Illustrations, by Pen and Pencil, of the History, Biography, Scenery, Relics, and Traditions of the War for Independence, Volume II, 1850

Lowell, Edward J. *The Hessians and the other German Auxiliaries of Great Britain in the Revolutionary War*, Harper and Brothers Publishers, 1884

Lumpkin, Henry. *From Savannah to Yorktown*, University of South Carolina Press, 1981

Maas, John. *"That Unhappy Affair" Horatio Gates and the Battle of Camden, August 16, 1781*, The Kershaw County Historical Society, 2000

Massey, Gregory D. *A Hero's Life: John Laurens and the American Revolution*, University of South Carolina Press, 1992

McAllister, J.T. *Virginia Militia in the Revolutionary War, Mcallister's Data,* McAllister Publishing Co., 1913

McGeachy, John, *"Revolutionary Reminiscences from the "Cape Fear Sketches"*, NCSU History Paper, 2001

Meyer, Duane. *The Highland Scots of North Carolina*, Carolina Charter Tercentenary Commission, 1963

Miller, A.E. *Sketches of the Life and Correspondence of Nathaniel Greene, Volume I,* Charleston, South Carolina

Milling, Chapman J. *Red Carolinians*, The University of South Carolina Press, 1969

Mooney, James L., editor, *Dictionary of American Naval Fighting*

Ships, Volume VII, Naval Historical Center, Department of the Navy, Washington D.C. 1979

Moore, Frank. *Diary of the American Revolution from Newspapers and Original Documents, Volume I,* Charles Scribner, 1858

Mouzon, Harold A. *The Ship "Prosper," 1775-1776,* South Carolina Historical Magazine, Volume LIX, Number 1, January 1958

Morgan, Thurman T. *The Fate of the Ship Prosper,* South Carolina Historical Magazine, Volume 93, Numbers 3&4, July/October 1992

Morgan, William J., editor, *Naval Documents of the Revolution (NDAR), Volume 3, Volume 4, Volume 5,* 1970; *Volume 6,* 1972; *Volume 7,* 1976; *Volume 8,* 1980; *Volume 9,* 1982, Washington DC: Government Printing Office

Moss, Bobby Gilmer. *Roster of the Patriots in the Battle of Moore's Creek Bridge,* Scotch-Hibernia Press, 1992

Moss, Bobby Gilmer. *Roster of the South Carolina Patriots in the American Revolution,* Genealogical Publishing Co., Inc. 1983

Neuffer, Claude Henry. *Names in South Carolina, Volume I-XII, 1954-1965,* State Printing Company, 1967

Neeser, Robert Wilden. *Statistical and Chronological History of the United States Navy, 1775-1907, Volume II,* Burt Franklin, 1971

Newlin, Algie I. *The Battle of Lindley's Mill,* The Alamance Historical Association, 1975

Newlin, Algie I. *The Battle of New Garden*, North Carolina
    Friends Historical Society, 1977

Newsome, Anthony. *A British Orderly Book, 1780-81* North
    Carolina Historical Review, vol. 9

Nichols, John L. *Alexander Cameron, British Agent Among the
    Cherokee*, 1764-1781, South Carolina Historical
    Magazine, Volume 97, Number 2, April 1996

The North Carolina Daughters of the American Revolution, Roster
    *of Soldiers from North Carolina in the American
    Revolution*, Durham, NC, 1932

O'Donnell, James H. *Southern Indians in the American
    Revolution*, University of Tennessee Press, 1971

O'Donnell, James H. *The Cherokees of North Carolina in the
    American Revolution*, North Carolina State University
    Graphics, 1976

Olson, Gary D. *Loyalists and the American Revolution: Thomas
    Brown and the South Carolina Backcountry, 1775-1776*,
    The South Carolina Historical Magazine, Volume 68,
    Number 4, October 1967

Olson, Gary D. *Dr. David Ramsay and Lt. Colonel Thomas
    Brown: Patriot Historian and Loyalist Critic*, The South
    Carolina Historical Magazine, Volume 77, Number 4,
    October 1776

Pancake, John S. *This Destructive War, The British Campaign in
    the Carolinas, 1780-1782*, University of Alabama Press,
    1985

Peckham, Howard H. *The Toll of Independence, Engagements & Battle Casualties of the American Revolution*, The University of Chicago Press, 1974

Powell, William S. *The Regulators in North Carolina, A Documentary History, 1759-1776*, North Carolina State Department of Archives and History, 1971

Powell, William S. *The War of the Regulation and the Battle of Alamance*, North Carolina State Department of Archives and History

Ramsay, David. *Ramsay's History of South Carolina from Its First Settlement in 1670 to the year 1808, Volume 1*, W.J. Duffie, Newberry, S.C, 1858

Rankin, Hugh F. *The Moore's Creek Bridge Campaign, 1776*, University of North Carolina Press, 1953

Rankin, Hugh F. *The North Carolina Continentals*, University of North Carolina Press, 1971

Rhode Island Historical Magazine, April, 1886

Ripley, Warren. *Battleground, South Carolina in the Revolution*, Evening Post Publishing Co., 1983

Robinson, Blackwell P. *The Revolutionary War Sketches of William R. Davie*, North Carolina Department of Cultural Resources, 1976

Robinson, St. John. *Southern Loyalists in the Caribbean and Central America*, South Carolina Historical Magazine, Volume 93, Numbers 3&4, July/October 1992

Rogers, Thomas G. *Victory Snatched Away*, Military History

Magazine, Volume 13, Number 7, March 1997

Rosengarten, J. G. *The German Allied Troops in the North American War of Independence, 1776-1783, by Max Von Eelking,* Joel Munseill's Son's Publishers, 1893

Sabine, Lorenzo. *Biographical Sketches of Loyalists of the American Revolution, Volume 1, Volume 2,* Baltimore, 1994

Saffell, W.T.R., *Records of the Revolutionary War: containing The Military and Financial Correspondence of Distinguished Officers; Names of the Officers and Privates of Regiments, Companies, and Corps, with the Dates of their Commissions and Enlistments; General Orders of Washington, Lee and Greene at Germantown and Valley Forge; With a List of Distinguished Prisoners of War; The Time of Their Capture, Exchange, Etc. To Which is Added the Half-Pay Acts of the Continental Congress; The Revolutionary Pension Laws; And a List of the Officers of the Continental Army who Acquired the Right to Half-Pay, Commutation, and Lands,* Baltimore: Charles C. Saffell, 1894

Salley, Alexander S. *Horry's Notes to Weems's Life of Marion,* The South Carolina Historical Magazine, Volume LX, Number 3, July 1959

Salley, Alexander S. *Records of the Regiments of the South Carolina Line in The Revolutionary War,* Genealogical Publishing Co. Inc., 1977

Salley, Alexander S. *South Carolina Provincial Troops named in Papers of the First Council of Safety of The Revolutionary Party in South Carolina, June-November, 1775,* Genealogical Publishing Co. Inc., 1977

Sanchez-Saavedera E.M. *A Guide to Virginia Military Organizations in the American Revolution, 1774-1787,* Richmond, VA 1978

Schenck, David. *North Carolina 1780-'81, Being a History of the Invasion of the Carolinas by the British Army under Lord Cornwallis in 1780-'81,* Edwards & Broughton, Publishers, 1889

Scott, Ruth. *Loyalist Anthony Allaire,* Officers Quarterly, Summer, 1997, York-Sunbury Historical Society of Fredericton, New Brunswick

Simms, William Gilmore. *The Life of Francis Marion,* New York, 1844

Smith, Charles R. *Marines in the Revolution,* History and Museums Division, Headquarters, U.S. Marine Corps, 1975

Smith, D. E. Huger. *Commodore Alexander Gillon and the Frigate South Carolina,* South Carolina Historical and Genealogical Magazine, Volume IX, Number 4, October 1908

Southern Studies Program *Figures of the Revolution in South Carolina, An Anthology, Florence,* University of South Carolina; *Figures of the Revolution in South Carolina, An Anthology, Spartanburg, Anderson, Beaufort, Aiken, Florence, Georgetown.,* University of South Carolina, 1976

Sparks, William H., *The Memories of Fifty Years,* J.W. Burke & Co. 1870

Stevens, John Austin, *The Southern Campaign, 1780, Gates At Camden,* (Magazine of American History, Volume V, No. 4, October 1880)

Stewart, Robert Armistead. *History of Virginia's Navy in the Revolution,* Richmond, Virginia, 1933.

Still, William N. *North Carolina's Revolutionary War Navy,* Theo. Davis Sons, Inc. 1976

Stokeley, Jim. *Fort Moultrie, Constant Defender,* National Park Service, 1985

Stone, William L. *Letters of Brunswick and Hessian Officers During the American Revolution,* Da Capo Press, 1970

Stryker, William. *The New Jersey Volunteers in the Revolutionary War,* Trenton, 1887

Thomas, Sam. *The Dye is Cast: The Scots-Irish and Revolution in the Carolina Back Country,* The Palmetto Conservation Foundation, 1994

Toth, Charles W. *The American Revolution and the West Indies,* National University Publications, Kennikat Press, 1975

Troxler, George. *Pyle's Massacre, February 23, 1781,* Alamance County Historical Association, 1973

Trussell, John B. B. Jr. *The Pennsylvania Line, Regimental Organizations and Operations, 1776-1783,* Pennsylvania Historical and Museum Commission, 1977

Tustin, Joseph P. *Diary of the American War, A Hessian Journal, Captain Johann Ewald, Field Jägers Corps,* Yale University Press, 1979

Uhlendorf, Bernard A. *The Siege of Charleston, With an Account of the Province of South Carolina: Diaries and Letters of Hessian Officers From the von Jungken Papers in the William L. Clements Library*, University of Michigan, 1938

Wallace, Lee A. *The Orderly Book of Captain Benjamin Taliaferro, 2d Virginia Detachment, Charleston, South Carolina, 1780*, Virginia State Library, 1980

Ward, Christopher L. *The Delaware Continentals*, Historical Society of Delaware, 1941

Warren, Mary B. *Revolutionary Memoirs and Muster Rolls*, Heritage Papers, 1994

Watson, Harry L. *An Independent People, The Way We Lived in North Carolina, 1770 – 1820*, University of North Carolina Press, 1983

Weinmester, Oscar K. *The Hessian Grenadier Battalions in North America, 1776-1783*, Military Collector & Historian, Winter 1975

White, Katherine Keogh. *The King's Mountain Men, The story of the Battle with Sketches of the American Soldiers who took part,* Genealogical Publishing Company, 1966

Williams, Samuel Cole. *Tennessee During the Revolutionary War*, Nashville, 1944

Williamson, Joel. *New People: Miscegenation and Mulattoes in the United States*, The Free Press, 1980

Index

84th Regiment of Foot (Royal
  Highland Emigrants)
  Light Infantry, 50
Abbot
  British Ensign, 53
Abercromby
  Robert, 49, 122, 131
Adair
  John, 232
  William, 192
Adams
  Peter, 256
  Samuel, 211, 222, 278, 365
Adamson
  John, 191, 192
  William, 193, 197
Agers
  Militia colonel, 46
Agnew
  Stair, 58
Aksom
  Benjamin. *See* Exum
Aldington
  John, 53
Alexander
  Dan, 276
  George, 260
  John, 292
  Reverend, 165
  William "Black Bill", 181
Alexander's Old Field
  Skirmish of, 167
Alfred
  Julius, 261
Allaire
  Anthony, 64, 110, 144, 145,
    146, 234, 304, 332, 340
Allen
  Isaac, 382, 383, 390
Allston

William, of Clifton, 385
Alston
  William, 362
Amelia County Militia, 45, 261
American Engineer Corps, 42
American Volunteers, 56, 63,
    123, 140, 141, 143, 145, 146,
    152, 200, 201, 203, 210, 234,
    236, 304, 326, 338
Amherst County Militia, 262
Anderson
  Archibald, 256, 276
  George, 256, 325
  John, 60
  Robert, 135
Andrè
  John, 64
Andrew
  Barry, 181
Anson County, 303
  Skirmish at, 302
Anson County Militia, 40, 309,
    312
Antioch
  Murder at, 349
Apthorp
  Ward, 263
Arbuthnot
  Mariot, 25, 26, 59, 66, 69, 79,
    81, 83, 86, 89, 90, 95, 96,
    101, 110, 112, 136, 137,
    138, 144, 145, 152
Ardesoif
  Royal Navy captain, 294
Arent
  Nash County Captain, 44
Armand
  Charles, 239, 251, 255, 257,
    270, 274, 277

Cane Creek
  Skirmish at, 303
Cannon's Company of
  Volunteers, 46
Cape Hatteras
  Naval skirmish at, 162
Carden
  John, 220, 221, 223, 230, 248
Carnes
  Jacob, 160
Caroline County Militia, 261
Carpenter
  Loyalist Captain, 182
Carr
  Patrick "Paddy", 189, 304,
    325, 339, 366, 367, 368
  Samuel, 381
  Stephen, 355
Carrington
  Mayo, 48
Carroll
  John, 196
Carson
  Andrew, 346, 347
Carter
  Benjamin, 262
  John Champe, 158
  Landon, 379
Cary
  James, 244, 245, 283
Cary's Fort
  Skirmish at, 243
Cary's Fort, 279
Caswell
  Richard, 156, 237, 239, 241,
    242, 259
Caswell County Militia, 259,
  260, 325
Caswell's Brigade, 139, 156,
  239, 259, 266

Catawba
  Indians, 127, 176, 206, 212,
    214, 222, 313
Cathey
  John, 262
Catlett
  Thomas, 154
Cedar Springs
  Skirmish at, 197
Chambers
  Militia captain, 259
Champagné
  Forbes, 247, 263
Chaney
  Bailey, 327
Chapman
  Thomas, 55
Chappell
  Hicks, 245, 278
Charles Town Forresters, 45
Charles Town Volunteers, 46
Charleston Bombardiers, 41
Charlestown
  Siege of, 35
Charlestown Battalion of
  Artillery, 28, 41, 83, 89, 105
Charlestown Militia, 28, 45, 47,
  106, 151
Charlotte, 160, 199, 228, 232,
  276, 279, 316, 319, 343, 344,
  345, 347
  Evacuation of, 344
  Skirmish at, 312
Charlotte County Militia, 262
Charlotte Militia, 222, 346
Charlton
  Thomas, 371
Cheraw, 394
Cherokee, 305, 306, 307, 388,
  389, 392

Gowen's Old Fort
  Skirmish at, 200
Graff
  Wilhelm, 32, 55
Graham
  Charles, 57, 125
  Colin, 55
  James, 50
  Joseph, 184, 186, 312, 313,
    314, 315
  Sarah, 337
  William, 45, 183, 234, 235,
    301, 323, 334, 337
Graham's Fort
  Skirmish at, 301
Grant
  Alexander, 78
  James, 55
Granville County Militia, 204,
  312
Granville County Regiment of
  Foot, 43
Graves
  John, 259
Gray
  Peter, 36, 40
  Robert, 55, 300
Great Savannah
  Skirmish at. See Nelson's
    Ferry
Great Swamp
  Skirmish at, 353
Green
  William, 326
Greene
  Nathanael, 151, 277, 375,
    377, 387, 393
Greene County Militia, 379
Gregory
  Isaac, 260, 270, 271

Griffin
  William, 396
Grimball
  Thomas, 41
Grimes
  Joseph, 44
  Militia colonel, 303
Grimkè
  John Faucheraud, 40, 88, 108
Grymes
  Loyalist captain, 326
Gum Swamp
  Skirmish at. See Parker's Old
    Field
Gunby
  John, 257
Guyon
  Stephen, 343
Gwinn
  Partisan boy, 362
Hacker
  Hoysteed, 21, 46
Haddrell's Point
  Skirmish at, 144
Hadley
  Joshua, 261
Hale
  William, 374
Halfway Swamp
  Skirmish at, 384
Halifax, 151, 163
Halifax County Militia, 262
Halifax District Militia, 44, 251,
  253, 259
Hall
  Clement, 38
  Josiah Carvel, 257
  North Carolina Lieutenant,
    104
Hambright

Frederick, 45, 323, 330, 334
Hamilton
   George, 277
   Jane, 374
   John, 57, 129, 225, 250, 265,
      327
Hamilton's North Carolina
   regiment. *See* Royal North
   Carolina Regiment
Hammond
   Samuel, 287, 325, 334, 365,
      373
   Sir Andrew Snape, 59
Hammond's Plantation
   Skirmish of, 122
Hammond's State Troops, 325
   Sumter's Partisans, 365
Hammond's Store
   Skirmish at, 393
Hampton
   Andrew, 45, 210, 243, 323
   Edward, 201, 202, 203
   Henry, 169, 203, 278, 284,
      365, 367, 370, 372
   John, 169, 217, 223, 265
   Noah, 202, 203
   Richard, 203
   Wade, 203
Hampton Plantation, 149
Hampton's Regiment of Light
   Dragoons
   Sumter's Partisans, 278, 365
Handly
   Samuel, 379
Hanger
   George, 229, 264, 272, 310,
      313, 314, 315, 316
Hanging Rock, 206, 213, 220,
   247
   Battle of, 221

Skirmish at, 216
Hannah
   Robert, 324
Hanover County Militia, 261
Hardin
   John, 181, 184, 185, 186
Hardman
   John, 257
Harmon
   Anthony, 182
Harney
   Selbey, 38
Harrington
   Henry William, 43, 80, 248
Harris
   William, 365
Harrison
   Charles, 258, 382
   John, 297, 308, 349, 351
   Robert, 349
Harrison's Corps. *See* South
   Carolina Rangers
Hart
   Joseph, 368, 369
Hartung
   Hessian Ensign, 118, 138
Hasting
   Charles, 58, 265
Hatfield
   John, 51
Hathorne
   John, 50
Hatton
   John, 382
Hawkins
   Militia captain, 379
Hawsey
   William, 288, 290
Hawthorne

Templeton
Andrew, 40, 104
Ternant
Jean-Baptiste, 131, 133
Ternay
French Admiral, 119
Theus
Simeon, 35
Thicketty Fort
Skirmish at, 209
Thomas
Jane, 197
John, Jr., 120, 165, 173, 197
John, Sr., 163, 173
Tristram, 208, 209, 384
Thompson
Adam, 223
Andrew, 218
James, 153, 319, 320, 360
John, 211, 222, 278, 325
Richard, 292
William, 167, 288
Thurman
Benjamin, 240
Timothy
Peter, 28
Tinsley
Golding, 291
Tipton
Jonathan, 286, 324, 379, 389
Torrence
Militia Captain, 180
Towles
Oliver, 37
Traille
Peter, 52, 104, 115
Trench
Eyre Power, 49
Treville
John Francis de, 40

Trice
Militia captain, 260
Trigg
Abraham, 347
Trimble
William, 287, 379
Trovin
Francois, 41
True Blue Company, 45
Tryon County Militia, 323
Tucker
Samuel, 31, 42, 46
Turnbull
George, 57, 172, 175, 176,
189, 191, 211, 213, 214,
216, 237, 244, 279, 353
Turner
Ball, 349
George, 35
Jacob, 44
Twiggs
John, 365, 367, 371, 372, 373
Twitty
Susan, 301
William, 301
Two Sisters, South Carolina
Skirmish at, 121
Tybee Lighthouse, 21
Tyger River
Murder at, 218
Tynes
Samuel, 350, 353, 378
Union District Militia, 211, 222,
287, 325
Upper District Loyalist Militia,
176
Upper Ninety-Six Militia, 135
Upper Richmond County Militia
Battalion, 356, 366, 382
Upshaw

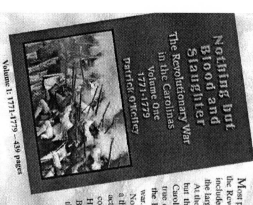

Endnotes

[1] Davies, *Documents, Volume XX*, p. 173; Smith, *Marines*, p. 246; *Pennsylvania Gazette, March 8, 1780; March 15, 1780*; Peckham, *Toll*, p. 124; John T. Hayes, *The Saddlebag Almanac, January 1998, Volume VI*, pp. 3-4

[2] Present-day Hilton Head

[3] Simmons Island is the present day Seabrook Island. The main landing took place on Wadmalaw Island near present day Rockville, about 20 miles south of Charlestown at that time

[4] The Patriot forces were most likely a detachment from Colonel Daniel Horry

[5] Smith, *Marines in the Revolution*, pp. 247-250, 355

[6] This is possibly Lieutenant Æneas McDonald of the 33rd Regiment. If it is, then the eight British Regulars would have been from the 33rd Regiment

[7] Joseph P. Tustin, *Diary of the American War, A Hessian Journal, Captain Johann Ewald, Field Jäger Corps*, (Yale University Press, 1979), pp. 197-198, 202-203; Bruce E. Burgoyne, *Diaries of Two Anspach Jaegers*, (Heritage Books, Inc. 1997), pp. 108, 113-114; Moultrie, *Memoirs, Vol. II*, p. 50; Wallace, *Orderly Book*, pp. 14-22; Bernard A. Uhlendorf, *The Siege of Charleston, With an Account of the Province of South Carolina: Diaries and Letters of Hessian Officers From the von Jungken Papers in the William L. Clements Library*, (University of Michigan, 1938), pp. 180-183; Carl Bauer, *The 1780 Siege of Charleston as Experienced by a Hessian Office, Part One, (Journal of the Hochfuerstlichen Grenadier Battalion Platte from 16 February 1776 to 24 May 1784 by the Regimental Quartermaster: Carl Bauer*, edited by George Fenwick Jones, (South Carolina Historical Magazine, Volume 88, Number 1, January 1987), pp. 26-27; Clinton, *American Rebellion*, p. 157; Hayes, *Saddlebag Almanac, Volume VI*, pp. 10-11, 15-16

[8] Captain Hinrichs wrote that the British lost six men wounded

[9] Tustin, *Diary*, pp. 197-198, 202-203; Burgoyne, *Diaries*, pp. 108, 113-114; Moultrie, *Memoirs, Vol. II*, p. 57; Wallace, *Orderly Book*, pp. 14-22; Uhlendorf, *Siege of Charleston*, pp. 194-195; Clinton, *American Rebellion*, p. 157; Hayes, *Saddlebag Almanac, Volume VI*, pp. 10-11, 15-16

[10] The 42nd Regiment of Foot was not officially known as the Black Watch until the Victorian age. The term Black Watch does date from the formation of the six independent companies of highlanders in 1725. They were from the loyal Clans of Campbell, Fraser, Munro, and Grant. The

term "watch" refers to the watch these companies kept in the highlands, while most histories state the "black" comes from their dark tartan

[11] "En barbette" was a carriage that was mounted on a very large heavy-duty pintle to allow it to traverse freely left or right over a wide area

[12] The *Boston* was described as having a broad pendant

[13] Another account states that the *L'Aventure* fired upon the fort, and not the *Boston*

[14] Smith, *Marines*, pp. 247-250, 355; Peckham, *Toll*, p. 67; Ira D. Gruber, *John Peebles' American War, The Diary of a Scottish Grenadier, 1776-1782*, (Stackpole Books, 1998), pp 343-344; Tustin, *Diary*, p. 203; Uhlendorf, *Siege of Charleston*, p. 195; Bauer, *1780 Siege, Part One,* pp. 28, 30; Moss, *Roster of the South Carolina Patriots*, p. 226

[15] Captain Johann Ewald entered the army at the age of 16 and had fought in the Seven Years' War. He lost his left eye during a duel in 1770. He published a book on military tactics in 1774 and was made a captain of the Liebjäger. He arrived in America as the commander of the 2nd Company of Jägers, on 22 October 1776. He went into battle the next day. He was a very adaptive commander and used tactics that would seem familiar to the modern day soldier

[16] Tustin, *Diary of the American War*, p. 204; Boatner, *Encyclopedia of the American Revolution*, pp. 356-357; Gruber, *John Peebles' American War*, p. 314; Uhlendorf, *The Siege of Charleston*, p. 197; Hayes, *The Saddlebag Almanac, January 1998, Volume VI*, pp. 20-21

[17] The 3rd Dragoons were also known as Baylor's Horse or Lady Washington's Horse. After Colonel George Baylor had been captured at Old Tappan in New Jersey, William Washington was given the job of reconstituting the 3rd Dragoon Regiment, and commanding it when they moved south to Charlestown. Regular dragoons were cavalrymen who fought on foot, with every fourth man holding the horses. Light Dragoons were never meant to fight on foot, and only did so in extreme conditions. The Light Dragoons carried carbines and were trained to fire from the saddle as skirmishers

[18] Gruber, *John Peebles*, p. 314; Hayes, *Saddlebag Almanac, Volume VI*, pp. 21-22; Sanchez-Saavedera, *Virginia Military Organizations*; PRO, *War Office, List of all the Officers of the Army*, p. 156

[19] South Carolina in the 18th century had the highest per capita income in the colonies, and could have been considered as one of richest countries in the world if it was independent. In 1780 Charlestown was described as

containing "about fifteen thousand inhabitants, and was one of the richest and gayest towns in North America. The large and handsome houses were not set close together as in other towns, but much free space was left for the circulation of air. They were well furnished with mahogany and silver-ware, and great attention was bestowed on keeping them clean. The streets were unpaved and sandy. On the sides of streets they have...laid narrow footpaths for the pedestrians, and these not everywhere. In the middle of the streets there is a single surface of sand, which is blown into the air by the strong wind and causes great discomfort for the eyes. Even the people in the front rooms of the houses are exposed to this evil because they must generally keep their windows open all the time because of the great heat. The inhabitants are the richest among the English colonies, as one can clearly see from their beautiful and splendid furniture and furnishings. We seldom enter a house in which we did not find almost all furniture of mahogany and also very much silverware. The inhabitants are very concerned about cleanliness; a number of Negroes were steadily occupied with washing, which contributes greatly to the coolness. All day and especially from nine in the morning until three in the afternoon the heat is extraordinarily penetrating. Most of the inhabitants arrange their business in such a way that they can remain home during all this time. Most of the rich families had fled at the approach of the British. There were many Germans and German Jews in the town, and many doctors, on account of the unhealthy climate. The place, of course, was full of negroes, who formed quite half of its population."

[20] The British campaign for Charlestown started on February 11th and went until the surrender on 12 May. The actual siege was opened in March. This was the longest siege of the war

[21] Benjamin Lincoln had been in the Third Suffolk Regiment of Massachusetts during the French and Indian War. He was appointed a Major General and commanded the Massachusetts militia in the New York campaign. When Burgoyne invaded down the Hudson River Valley, Lincoln commanded troops at the battles of Saratoga and was seriously wounded in the ankle. Splinters of bone were removed from his foot, but he walked with a limp for the rest of his life

[22] The South Carolina Continentals were brigaded under General Moultrie in the beginning of the siege. The losses from the siege of Savannah forced the South Carolina Continentals to consolidate into two regiments. After the consolidation they were placed under the command of Colonel

Richard Parker and the Virginia Brigade. There were four brigades in Charlestown by March of 1780. The North Carolina Brigade under Brigadier General Hogun; the Virginia Continental Brigade, consisting of the 1st Virginia Detachment, the 2nd Virginia Detachment and the 1st and 2nd South Carolina Continentals; the Brigade of Militia under Brigadier General Lillington; and the Brigade of Artillery under Colonel Beekman. On April 8th reinforcements arrived and one more Virginia brigade under Woodford was added to the force

[23] The 1st South Carolina Regiment was consolidated with the remnants of Pulaski's Infantry Legion, and the 6th South Carolina Regiment, after the failed assault on Savannah. Three companies were posted at Fort Moultrie at the beginning of the siege

[24] These rolls of each company were taken in May 1780, after 3 months of siege

[25] Also listed as Lavacher de St. Marie

[26] The rest were sick or on furlough. The 5th and 6th South Carolina Regiment was consolidated with the 2nd South Carolina after the regiments were decimated at Savannah. On February 27th the 2nd and 3rd South Carolina Regiments were attached to Colonel Parker's Virginia Continental Brigade. In March Lieutenant Colonel Francis Marion was ordered to form the 2nd South Carolina into a Light Infantry corps, to delay the British advance. Marion was able to choose men that he saw fit for this special duty. By April 8th the Regiment had detached 59 men to Lauren's Light Corps, had another 67 men "on command" and only had 92 men fit for duty. By May 2nd the regiment's command had almost ceased to exist. Marion had broken his ankle and had been sent out of town to recuperate, and Major Isaac Harleston was commanding the regiment in the place of Francis Marion. Captain Marion and Lieutenants Foissin and Legare were in the Hospital sick; Captain Roux was in Georgetown, recovering from wounds. Captains Mayzyck, Baker, Proveaux, Gray and Lieutenant Kolb were all commanding batteries on the defensive line

[27] In May 1780 the 2nd South Carolina Regiment mustered the following troops: Mazyck – 17; Shubrick – 19; Proveaux – 18; Warley – 20; Mason – 9; Gray – 19; Baker – 15; and Marion's company – 21

[28] This company was probably detached to Laurens's Light Corps. One of the captains of the regiment commanded the light infantry with Lauren, but I cannot determine which it was

[29] Henderson's father was born in Scotland, but his grandfather came from Wales. William Henderson was the lieutenant colonel of the 6th South Carolina Regiment in January 1780. When the South Carolina units consolidated due to losses suffered in Savannah, Henderson transferred to the 3rd South Carolina Rangers on 11 February 1780. Colonel Thomson had been "absent sick" from the regiment since the assault on the Spring Hill Redoubt at Savannah

[30] On April 28th the 3rd Regiment only had 132 fit for duty. There were 56 men attached to Lauren's Light Corps. Only three, out of seven captains, were present for duty. The rest of the regiment was sick or "on command". There were 2 officers and 60 men on command. The men on command were detached elsewhere. Ten were with Colonel Thomson as a guard; 3 were with the General Staff as a guard; 4 were at the General Hospital; 11 were at Haddrell's Point and 4 were artificers. Eight of the men who were fit for duty were officer's waiters. These were the Black servants, who had been given muskets and were put into the line.

[31] This company was probably attached to Laurens' Light Corps. Major Hyrne was listed as sick, but present for duty in May, and a captain was detached to the Light Corps, but I do not know which one

[32] These numbers were from a muster of troops in May 1780 after three months of siege

[33] Hogun would die in captivity on January 4th, 1781

[34] Hogun's North Carolina Continentals arrived in Charlestown on March 3rd and gave "great spirits to the Town and confidence to the Army." These men were battle seasoned veterans from Washington's Grand Army and had lived through the winter at Valley Forge, and fought in Brandywine, Germantown, Monmouth and Stony Point

[35] Colonel Clark may have commanded Lauren's Light Infantry upon his arrival. If he did, then Lieutenant Colonel Davidson would have commanded the regiment

[36] Lieutenant Colonel William Lee Davidson was not there during the siege of Charlestown because he was on furlough and stopped to visit his family on the march south

[37] Dixon was once described as "A dirty Buckskin, who would rather sit on his hams all day and play cards with his meanest private soldier, in his homespun dress, than wash or uniform himself and keep company with his fellow officers as a captain ought to do."

[38] Colonel John Patten's name is also written as Patton

[39] The day Finney was promoted to 1st Lieutenant he was also brevetted as a captain and placed in command of Thomas Armstrong's company

[40] The numbers of the men in the companies came from a muster roll taken on March 20th, 1780. The effective men in each company was: Harney – 18; Murfree – 14; Ingles – 12; Coleman – 16; Hall – 12; Armstrong – 14; Fenner – 11

[41] The Commandant was a commander of a regiment that did not have a colonel at that time

[42] The 3rd North Carolina Regiment had arrived in Charlestown in late December, earlier than the rest of the Continentals. There had not been a British threat on the horizon at that time and many of these men deserted to return home. On February 14th the men that remained had been organized into one brigade with the two Virginia Continental detachments under the command of Colonel Parker. They were placed under the command of General Hogun's North Carolina Brigade on March 6th after it arrived in Charlestown. The effective men in each company was: Campbell – 28; Ballard – 20; Bradley – 25

[43] On March 29th the Corps of Light Infantry was formed under Lieutenant Colonel John Laurens. This unit was made up of the light infantry companies from the 2nd and 3rd South Carolina Regiments and the North Carolina Continental Brigade. The 3rd South Carolina had 55 men and a captain detached to the Light Corps. The 2nd South Carolina had 57 men and two lieutenants detached to the corps. Colonel Thomas Clark is mentioned as having commanded the North Carolina Light Infantry Battalion, so Laurens may have had to step down from command upon the arrival of the North Carolina Brigade. For a short period of time at the beginning of the siege these Light Infantry acted as Marines on board the frigates

[44] Captain Montford was from the 3rd North Carolina and was wounded by a musket ball on May 1st, 1780. After the war he was commissioned as a Captain in the 1st US Infantry on June 3rd, 1790 and was killed by Indians near Fort Jefferson, OH on April 27th, 1792

[45] Hogg was carried on the rolls as a major in the 3rd North Carolina, but he commanded militia during siege of Charleston. He also served with the Light Infantry, but it is unknown if he did it with a militia detachment or a North Carolina Continental detachment

[46] Major Murfree was in the 2nd North Carolina Regiment and had commanded the North Carolina light infantry during the storming of Stony

Point. Some historians write that he was in the 1st North Carolina, but the 2nd North Carolina regimental returns have him listed during the siege of Charlestown

[47] After Colonel Parker was killed in April, the Detachment was commanded by Major Richard Anderson

[48] Also known as Brigadier General Charles Scott's Brigade of Virginia Continentals. After serving with Washington's army in the north the Virginia regiments had to be consolidated into other regiments. This Brigade was made up of the 1st, 2nd and 3rd Virginia Detachments. The 1st Virginia Detachment consisted of recruits still in Virginia. The 2nd Virginia Detachment consisted of soldiers and officers from the depleted Virginia Regiments. The 3rd Virginia Detachment consisted of men from the 7th Virginia Regiment and new levies from Virginia. Only the 1st and 2nd Virginia Detachments made it to Charlestown. The 3rd Virginia Detachment was under the command of Colonel Abraham Buford, and turned back to North Carolina once Charlestown fell

[49] Colonel Richard Parker commanded the 1st Virginia Detachment, but became the brigade commander in Charlestown. Lieutenant Colonel Hopkins was an officer of the 10th Virginia Regiment.

[50] On April 6th the regiment only had 179 men present for duty. There were 24 men "on command". There were 7 in Camden, 1 in Georgetown, 5 at the Laboratory (making cartridges), 2 with the artillery, 4 at the General Hospital, 1 at Head Quarters and 7 at "Places Unknown"

[51] Captain Parker was an officer of the 2nd Virginia Regiment. On April 6th he only had 45 men present for duty in his company

[52] Captain Taliaferro was an officer of the 2nd Virginia Regiment. On April 6th he only had 41 men present for duty in his company

[53] Captain Payne was an officer of the 1st Virginia Regiment. On April 6th he only had 32 men present for duty in his company

[54] Captain Stubblefield was an officer of the 2nd Virginia Regiment. On April 6th only had 36 men present for duty in his company

[55] On April 14th only 249 men were listed as present for duty. The rest were sick or "on command". The men on command were 16 men with Lieutenant Robert Higgins. With the regiment were 17 waiters (most likely Black servants with the regiment), 3 waggoners, 2 shoemakers, 4 barbers, 3 tailors, and 4 artificers

[56] Captain Buckner was an officer of the 5th Virginia Regiment. On April 14th he had 70 men present for duty in his company

[57] On April 14th Captain Butler had 59 men present for duty in his company. Lieutenant Colonel Wallace, Captains Butler and Malory were officers in the 11th Virginia Regiment. Captain Philip Malory was with Heth's Detachment, but he was not commanding any troops

[58] Captain Holt was an officer of the 1st Virginia Regiment. On April 14th he had 46 men present for duty in his company

[59] Captain Beale was an officer of the 3rd Virginia Regiment. On April 14th he had 59 men present for duty in his company

[60] His men referred to him as "Archie Ben" Lytle

[61] Lytle's Volunteers were assigned to Scott's Virginia Brigade, along with the South Carolina Continentals of Marion and Thomson. On April 15th the regiment had 156 men fit for duty. With the regiment were 10 waiters (most likely Black servants), 4 tailors, 1 waggoner, 1 shoemaker and 1 artificer

[62] On April 15th Pulliam only had 30 men fit for duty

[63] On April 15th Johnson had 55 men fit for duty

[64] On April 15th Hervey had 40 men fit for duty

[65] On April 15th Lowman had 30 men fit for duty

[66] The Legion was a concept introduced to the 18th century by Marshal Saxe of France in 1744 when he wrote a *Treatise Concerning Legions*. The Legion that he proposed was to include 64 companies of foot divided into 4 regiments each of 4 battalions, plus one company of horse, one company of grenadiers, and one company of light-armed foot per regiment. Saxe later wrote *Reveries, or Memoirs Concerning the Art of War* and renamed the battalion, calling it the Century. He also added artillery. Each regiment would have 4 centuries plus a half-century of horse and a half-century of light-armed foot. Each legion would have 4 regiments and two 12-pounders, and each century would have one amusette of half-pound caliber. In 1743, a Volontaires de Saxe was formed, containing a mix of lancers and dragoons. By the time of the Revolutionary War the tactic of having a mobile, combined arms army of cavalry, infantry (with rifles and muskets) and artillery, was being utilized by both sides.

[67] After Briar Creek and the siege of Savannah, the Georgia Continentals ceased to exist. These six Georgia officers were all that remained. They were known as the 2nd Georgia Battalion and included Major Philip Lowe, Captain Clement Nash and Captain Edward Cowan

[68] These cannons consisted of fifteen 24-pounders, thirty-one 18-pounders, forty-three 12-pounders, sixty-eight 9-pounders, three 13-inch brass mortars, four Howitzers and ten Coehorn mortars

[69] Colonel Grimkè manned all the artillery on the left of the line

[70] The batteries were numbered from left to right on the line. The Number 3 Battery was located on the left of the American line, and Captain de Treville and Captain Mitchell's company manned this battery.

[71] Captains Mazyck, Baker, Proveaux, Gray and Lieutenant Kolb were all from the 2nd South Carolina Regiment, but had been detached to command guns in batteries 3 and 4. The 2nd South Carolina Regiment had regularly trained on the artillery in Fort Moultrie

[72] Captain Wickly's company, the Laboratory, and the convalescent men manned this battery

[73] Captain John Gilbank assumed command of this company on February 20th. He then transferred and became a major in the militia

[74] Captain Mitchell and Roberts manned the eight gun battery located to the left of the Virginia encampment, in the Half Moon Battery

[75] Captain Templeton was an officer in the 4th Georgia Regiment

[76] The Number 7 battery was a redan, right of the Virginia Encampment at the Half Moon Battery. A redan was like a redoubt but it was open to the rear

[77] The Number 15 battery was the advanced redoubt

[78] Located to the right of the North Carolina Brigade, on the right of the line

[79] Cambray had arrived at Charlestown on 13 March 1779 and served as an engineer. He was a lieutenant colonel in the Continental army and a colonel in the militia

[80] Major Grimball's regiment manned all the artillery positions to the right of Grimkè

[81] After the Frigate *Queen of France* was sunk to block the channel, her Marines were placed at Gibbes Battery

[82] There were two mortar batteries, one at the east end of Tradd Street and one at Commodore Gillon's House

[83] After the Frigate *Boston* was sunk to block the channel, her sailors were placed at Broughton's Battery

[84] After the Sloop *Providence* was trapped in Charleston Harbor, her sailors were placed at the Exchange Battery

[85] These two companies of Berkeley County Militia were ordered to join the artillery brigade on February 28th and were instructed in "the Managem^t. & Exercise of Cannon"

[86] Captain Stiles manned the "heavy ordnance to the left of the Hornwork"

[87] Located behind Gibbe's house

[88] After the Continental Frigate *Boston* was sunk to block the channel, her Marines were placed at Cravens Battery and the Granville Bastion

[89] Located at the South end of East Bay

[90] The Congress rushed Duportail to Charlestown when it seemed that the city would no longer be able to hold out. He did not arrive until April 25th. Colonel de Laumoy commanded the Engineers before that time

[91] French Engineers in the American Army

[92] Luigi Cambray-Digny was an Italian lieutenant colonel of the American Corps of Engineers. His map of Charleston is in the South Carolina Historical Society collections

[93] Chief Engineer for South Carolina

[94] Also known as the Country Militia, and it was separate from the Charlestown Militia. Lincoln estimated that only 300 militia from the countryside participated in the siege

[95] Harrington assumed command of the North Carolina Brigade of Militia from Lillington in April 1780

[96] Only 156 out of the 302 were fit for duty. In each company the fit for duty was the following: Grenadier – 21; Forresters – 21; Light Infantry – 23; German Fusileers – 42; True Blue – 26; Volunteers – 23

[97] This Regiment was made up of non-English speaking French citizens of Charlestown. According to the General Orders of February 12th "Whereas there are many Frenchmen in Charleston who from their want of Knowledge in the English Language are incapable of rendering equal services by being incorporated with Americans – The Genl. desires that the Officers commanding Militia Companies in town will erase all such out of their Rolls, and directs that they do Duty in the Marquise de Bretangne's Corps – this to take place immediately. This unit may have also contained the guards to Monsieur Plombard, the French Consul to Charlestown

[98] Captain de la Morlière was an officer in the Grenadier Volontaires de Saint-Domingue (White Haitian Regiment)

[99] These were D'Estaing's French troops sent to Charlestown after Savannah that were too wounded to travel

[100] Unknown whether this company was Spanish sailors stuck in Charlestown, or if it was Spanish civilians of Charlestown

[101] The *Queen of France,* the *Notre Dame* and the *Boston* was sunk to block the channel

[102] These ships were sent to Charlestown by Admiral D'Estaing after the siege of Savannah

[103] The captain of the *L'Aventure* is also listed as Captain Sieur de Brulot

[104] The former captain of the ship, Lieutenant Du Rumain, had been killed at sea a couple of months after the siege of Savannah

[105] The *Truite* was originally built as a transport and not as a warship

[106] A Polacre was a ship with three masts that were generally furnished with square sails upon the mainmast, and lateen sails upon the foremast and mizenmast.

[107] This number of 1,000 men includes French and American Sailors from ships trapped in Charlestown Harbor

[108] The *Bricole* had the largest armament of all the ships on the Patriot side, but it was built as a transport ship and was not built to withstand naval warfare. She was an East India merchantman that in many accounts is listed as a French ship. She is a South Carolina frigate, but was commanded by a French captain during the siege of Savannah.

[109] Daniel Stevens wrote that the *Bricole* "though pierced for 44 guns, did not mount half of that number"

[110] These are volunteers from the 1st and 2nd Battalions that acted as marines

[111] There is another account that states Captain William Hall commanded the ship

[112] Sometimes listed as the *Marquis de Brittany*

[113] The captain had been Jacob Milligan in 1779, but he may have been wounded or hurt during the campaign for Savannah

[114] These Virginians were also veterans from Washington's Grand Army. They were at Valley Forge and fought in the battles of Brandywine, Germantown, Monmouth and Stony Point. Along with these reinforcements were 120 North Carolina militia under Lieutenant Colonel Harrington. Harrington was quickly selected as a Brigadier General and placed in command of the Salisbury Militia

[115] Also known as Woodford's Brigade of Virginia Continentals. Though Woodford had over 1,000 men assigned, only 737 men were considered effective when he arrived. Brigadier General Charles Scott arrived, but he

did not bring the rest of his brigade with him. He left them behind because "They are not yet clothed."

[116] Colonel Russell had been colonel of the 13th Virginia, and then the 5th Virginia Regiment

[117] Consolidation of 1st, 5th, 7th 10th and 11th Virginia Regiments

[118] Both Captains Minnis, along with Payne and Kendall, were officers in the 1st Virginia Regiment

[119] Captain Carrington, Moseley and Bentley were officers in the 5th Virginia Regiment

[120] Captain Johnston and Wright were officers in the 7th Virginia Regiment

[121] Captain Hunt was an officer in the 10th Virginia Regiment

[122] Consolidation of 2nd, 3rd and 4th Virginia Regiments

[123] Major Croghan was an officer in the 4th Virginia Regiment

[124] Captain Edwards and Blackwell were officers in the 3rd Virginia Regiment

[125] Captain Curry and Stith were officers in the 4th Virginia Regiment

[126] Consolidation of 6th and 8th Virginia Regiments and Gist's Additional Continental Regiment

[127] Captain Blackwell, Gillison and Shelton were officers in the 6th Virginia Regiment

[128] Captain Hite was an officer in the 8th Virginia Regiment

[129] Captain Breckenridge and Muir were officers in Gist's Additional Continental Regiment

[130] The surrender of Charleston was the worst defeat in United States history until the fall of the Philippines in 1942. Some historians dispute this, because casualties were light for the size of the action, and they state that St. Clair's Defeat in 1792 was the worst one. However Charlestown was the worst strategically. The United States lost the entire Continental army of the Southern Department, along with their equipment and artillery. They also lost the largest and richest port south of New York City. Like most battles in the Revolutionary War there are differing figures for the number of dead and wounded. The British figures of 5,500 captured included "the aged, the timid, the disaffected and the infirm, many of them who had never appeared during the whole siege." The Board of War reported the official total on 21 August 1781 as 2,571 captured. The killed included Colonels Armstrong and Parker, Major Gilbank, Captains Gadsden, Templeton and Moultrie. The wounded including Captains Elliot, Mitchell, Bowman, Montford and Kinlock

[131] Major General Leslie was in command of troops at Charlestown Neck

[132] An amusette was a light field cannon invented by Marshal Maurice de Saxe, but in this context it may have been a rampart, or wall gun. This was a very large musket, that fired a one inch ball, or bigger

[133] This included 7 Carpenters, 2 Collar-Makers, 1 Black Smith, 43 Labourers; 15 Small Pox; 12 Sick & Lame at the Artillery Park; 38 Labourers; 12 Small Pox; 8 Sick & Lame at Lenings Landing and 11 Labourers; 3 Small Pox; 2 Sick & Lame Transporting Stores in the Schooners

[134] This is Henry Clinton's Black Pioneers Provincial unit

[135] Referred to in several accounts as Brigadier Clarke

[136] This unit was assigned to Lieutenant General Charles Cornwallis, east of the Cooper River, once Monck's Corner was captured

[137] Referred to in several accounts as Brigadier Webster. Webster's Brigade was assigned to Lieutenant General Charles Cornwallis east of the Cooper River

[138] This unit was assigned to Lieutenant General Charles Cornwallis, east of the Cooper River

[139] This unit was assigned to Major General Leslie at the Charlestown Neck defenses

[140] Also listed as McIlraith

[141] This unit was assigned to Lieutenant General Cornwallis

[142] Also listed as von Huyn Regiment, or Vacant Von Huyn Regiment

[143] German regiments were named after their commander. This regiment became the Regiment von Knoblauch in February after the death of Lieutenant General Moritz von Wissenbach in November 1779

[144] The Hessian Grenadiers were formed with the grenadier companies of other regiments. They were assigned to Major General Leslie

[145] Also known as the Hesse-Kassel Grenadier Battalion von Linsingen. This battalion was formed from the Grenadier companies of other regiments. The 1st Company was the Grenadier Company of the Leib Regiment, the 2nd Company from the Regiment von Mirbach, the 3rd Company from the 2nd Guards Regiment and the 4th Company from the 3rd Guards Regiment

[146] Also known as the Hesse-Kassel Grenadier Battalion von Lengercke. This battalion was formed from the Grenadier companies of the musketeer regiments. The 1st Company was from the Musketeer Regiment von Wutgineau, 2nd Company from the Musketeer Regiment von Prinz Karl, 3rd

Company from the Musketeer Regiment von Donop and the 4th Company from the Musketeer Regiment von Trümbach

[147] Also known as the Hesse-Kassel Grenadier Vacant Battalion. This battalion was formed from the Grenadier companies of the Fusilier regiments. A German Regiment was called "Vacant" when no regular colonel or lieutenant colonel was in command. This was the old Grenadier Battalion von Minnigerode. The 1st Company was from the Grenadier Company of the Fusilier Regiment von Erbprinz, the 2nd Company from the Fusilier Regiment von Dittfurth, the 3rd Company from the Fusilier Regiment von Alt-Lossberg and the 4th Company from the Fusilier Regiment von Knyphausen

[148] Also known as the Hesse-Kassel Grenadier Battalion von Graff. This battalion was formed from the Grenadier companies of other Regiments. The 1st Company was the Grenadier Company of the Regiment von Rall, the 2nd Company was the Garrison Regiment von Wissenbach, the 3rd Company was the Garrison Regiment von Stein and the 4th Company was the Garrison Regiment von Bunau

[149] The 71st Highlanders did not have an official 2nd Battalion, but was tactically divided into three battalions and later into two battalions. The 2nd battalion did not become an official part of the regiment until 1782. This unit was assigned to Webster's Brigade upon arrival in Charlestown

[150] Twelve of the 243 were listed as being Black soldiers

[151] This is not the Provincial unit formed by Henry Clinton

[152] This unit was assigned to Lieutenant General Charles Cornwallis, east of the Cooper River

[153] Major Cochrane was the husband to Catherine Pitcairn, daughter of Major John Pitcairn of the Royal Marines. Cochrane was an ensign in the 25th Regiment then a lieutenant in the 7th Regiment. He purchased his captaincy in the 4th Regiment and was at Bunker Hill when his father in law was killed. He raised a body of infantry volunteers for the Legion in 1778 and was appointed Major of the Legion Infantry

[154] The British Legion infantry consisted of the Caledonian Volunteers, the West Jersey Volunteers, Emmerick's Chasseurs, the Royal American Reformees and the Roman Catholic Volunteers. There were even some Regulars in the Legion, two men from the 24th Regiment and two men from the 9th Regiment, who were part of Burgoyne's captured "Convention Army" and had escaped from American confinement

[155] The British Legion cavalry consisted of the two troops of Philadelphia Light Dragoons, the troop of Bucks County Light Dragoons, an independent troop raised by Captain Kinlock at New York, Emmerick's Chasseurs and the Prince of Wales American Regiment and at least eleven of the 16th Light Dragoons. Eleven of the 211 were listed as being Black troopers

[156] The American Volunteers was supposed to be a temporary unit, made up of men drawn from the 1st, 2nd & 4th Battalions of the New Jersey Volunteers; the 3rd Battalion of DeLancey's Brigade; the Loyal American Regiment; the King's American Regiment; the Prince of Wales American Regiment and the Nassau Blues. This unit was assigned to Lieutenant General Charles Cornwallis, east of the Cooper River. The men were supposed to be returned to their original units after Charlestown fell, but Ferguson was able to get them assigned in the South, much to the disgust of their original units. This unit is not Ferguson's rifle corps that had the famous breech-loading Ferguson rifle. The American Volunteers were a New York Provincial unit, armed with both muskets and rifles. Ferguson came up with the tactic of having the muskets in the front rank and the rifles in the rear rank. Their rifle was most likely the British Contract Rifle and not the famous "Ferguson rifle". The "Ferguson Rifle" was a breech-loading rifle was named after Major Ferguson and was turned into the army in 1777 after Ferguson was wounded at Brandywine. While Ferguson was recuperating General Howe disbanded his unit of riflemen. The Ferguson rifles with which they were armed were shipped to Nova Scotia. Many historians have claimed that if Ferguson had his rifle at such battles as King's Mountain, he could have changed the course of the war. However this is very wishful thinking. The Ferguson Rifle did adopt a new style of loading the cartridge, but the build up of powder residue in the breach made it not very reliable, and it had to be cleaned in the middle of the battle. Also having one regiment with one advanced piece of technology wouldn't help the logistic problems that eventually would lead to a British defeat in the United States

[157] Captain DePeyster was an officer in the King's American Regiment

[158] Captain McNeill was an officer in the Prince of Wales American Regiment

[159] Captain Dunlap was an officer in the Queen's Rangers

[160] Captain Ryerson was an officer in the 3rd Battalion, New Jersey Volunteers

[161] Captain-Lieutenant DePeyster was an officer in the Nassau Blues

[162] The South Carolina Royalists was assigned to Lieutenant General Charles Cornwallis, east of the Cooper River. The unit was unable to get their uniform yet in time for the siege, so Colonel Innes ordered "1,000 drab Russia Drill Jackets" until their uniforms arrived. Russia Drill was material made out of hemp, and drab would have been a grayish color. Innes thought that blue would be the material of the Provincial units, and had blue uniform made. He was mistaken, since red would be the color of the coats, but he still issued out the blue uniform to the Royalists, the South Carolina Rangers and the North Carolina Highlanders. They were given red uniforms as soon as they were made, and the blue coats were put into storage in Charleston

[163] This unit was assigned to Lieutenant General Cornwallis

[164] Daniel Manson was an acting Major in the Pioneers

[165] This unit was assigned to Lieutenant General Cornwallis

[166] This unit was assigned to Major General Leslie at the Charlestown Neck defenses

[167] This unit was assigned to Major General Huyn, west of the Ashley River

[168] Pattison had been a cornet in the 17th Light Dragoons, but was given the rank of lieutenant colonel in the Prince of Wales American Regiment

[169] This unit was assigned to Major General Huyn. The regiment was raised in 1776 in the Bahamas. It consisted of Connecticut Yankees. The commander of the regiment was Montfort Browne, Governor of the Island of New Providence (present day Nassau, Bahamas).

[170] This unit was assigned to Lieutenant General Cornwallis

[171] The Volunteers of Ireland was raised in the summer of 1778 by Colonel Francis Lord Rawdon, and was supposed to consist entirely of natives of Ireland. The Volunteers recruited mostly in New York City and some of the recruits were deserters from Washington's Army. They also had some Regulars in their ranks that had escaped from prisoner camps, were exchanged prisoners or were men who had been in hospitals but had recovered. They were 20 men from the 16th Light Dragoons, and one man each, drafted from the 27th, 28th, 35th, and 40th Regiments. This unit was assigned to Lieutenant General Cornwallis

[172] The total number of casualties, with both the British Army and the Royal Navy combined, was 99 killed and 217 wounded. The wounded included Major Ferguson, Captain Collins and McLeod

[173] The *Europe* was Admiral Arbuthnot's flagship prior to crossing over the Bar. This ship was too large to get over the Bar and Arbuthnot transferred his flag to the frigate *Roebuck*

[174] The Ship of the line *Russell*, *Robuste* and *Raisonable* were too large to come over the Bar, so they would remain outside to protect the rest of the Royal Navy from any attacking French fleets while they were crossing

[175] Captured Continental Navy frigate

[176] Captured Continental Navy frigate

[177] There were 47 transport ships, but these are the only ones that I could find the names for

[178] This was also known as the Jäger ship due to the troops it was transporting

[179] This is at the present day Albemarle Point

[180] A fireship was not just a ship that was set on fire and launched towards an enemy. To prepare an effective one took time. Troughs of combustible material were placed along the decks, so that the fire could burn from one level to the next. Barrels of incendiary material would be stacked at the end of these troughs. The decks would be "well paved with melted resin". Small portholes would be cut down the length of the ship and caulked shut. These would be blown open by an "iron chamber" once the ship was set on fire. This was needed so that the ship could be sailed to the target, and then set on fire quickly. The holes cut into the ship would let in air and also send out jets of flame into an enemy vessel. In military slang of the day a prostitute who had a venereal disease was also called a fireship.

[181] Elizabeth Ellet wrote in her book *Women of the American Revolution* "When the news reached Charleston that the British had encamped on Mr. Gibbes's plantation, the authorities in that city despatched two galleys to dislodge them. These vessels ascended the river in the night, and arriving opposite, opened a heavy fire upon the invaders' encampment. The men had received strict injunctions not to fire upon the house, for fear of injury to any of the family. It could not, however, be known to Mr. Gibbes that such a caution had been given; and as soon as the Americans began their fire, dreading some accident, he proposed to his wife that they should take the children and seek a place of greater safety. Their horses being in the enemy's hands, they had no means of conveyance; but Mrs. Gibbes, with energies roused to exertion by the danger, and anxious only to secure shelter for her helpless charge, set off to walk with the children to an adjoining plantation situated in the interior. A drizzling rain was falling,

and the weather was extremely chilly; the fire was incessant from the American guns, and sent-in order to avoid the house--in a direction which was in a range with the course of the fugitives. The shot, falling around them, cut the bushes, and struck the trees on every side. Exposed each moment to this imminent danger, they continued their flight with as much haste as possible, for about a mile, till beyond the reach of the shot. Having reached the houses occupied by the negro laborers on the plantation, they stopped for a few moments to rest. Mrs. Gibbes, wet, chilled, and exhausted by fatigue and mental anxiety, felt her strength utterly fail, and was obliged to wrap herself in a blanket and lie down upon one of the beds. It was at this time, when the party first drew breath freely-with thankfulness that the fears of death were over-that on reviewing the trembling group to ascertain if all had escaped uninjured, it was found that a little boy, John Fenwick, was missing. In the hurry and terror of their flight the child had been forgotten and left behind! What was now to be done? The servants refused to risk their lives by returning for him; and in common humanity, Mr. Gibbes could not insist that anyone should undertake the desperate adventure. The roar of the distant guns was still heard, breaking at short intervals the deep silence of the night. The chilly rain was falling, and the darkness was profound. Yet the thought of abandoning the helpless boy to destruction, was agony to the hearts of his relatives. In this extremity the self-devotion of a young girl interposed to save him. Mary Anna, the eldest daughter of Mrs. Gibbes-then only thirteen years of age, determined to venture back-in spite of the fearful peril-alone. The mother dared not oppose her noble resolution, which seemed indeed an inspiration of heaven; and she was permitted to go. Hastening along the path with all the speed of which she was capable, she reached the house, still in the undisturbed possession of the enemy; and entreated permission from the sentinel to enter; persisting, in spite of refusal, till by earnest importunity of supplication, she gained her object. Searching anxiously through the house, she found the child in a room in a third story, and lifting him joyfully in her arms, carried him down, and fled with him to the spot where her anxious parents were awaiting her return. The shot still flew thickly around her, frequently throwing up the earth in her way; but protected by the Providence that watches over innocence, she joined the rest of the family in safety"

[182] Hurdles were made of twigs interwoven close together and made in a rectangular shape. They were created to make the ground around gun

batteries firmer or to consolidate the passage over muddy ditches. They were also used to cover the trenches for the defense of the workmen against the enemy fire or the stones and other secondary projectiles that may be thrown against them

[183] Feu de joie is French for "fire of joy". When the army did a feu de joie each cannon, or musket would fire from left to right, or in a circle, one at a time

[184] Cainhoy was nine miles from Charlestown, and Lempriére's Point was a point of land on the Cooper River, beside the Wando

[185] Gabions were wicker tubes open at both ends, and filled with earth to strengthen the trench

[186] Fascines were bundles of sticks tied together, and resembled a wicker cylinder

[187] When a cannonball was fired en recochet, it bounced across the ground to its designated target, like a bowling ball gone beserk. Every time the cannonball struck the ground it would cause secondary projectiles to be flung at odd angles into the enemy

[188] Carronades were a short, large caliber cannon, named after the Carron Iron Works in Scotland. They were developed in the mid 1700's. It fired a large ball, but at a lower velocity and at a considerably shorter range than the traditional longer cannon generally in use aboard ships. The advantage of this gun was that at short range, due to the weight of the projectile and the low velocity, its fire would do terrific damage to wooden ships

[189] Captain Russell said that one officer was killed, and another wounded, while three rank and file were killed and fifteen wounded. Captain Peebles wrote that between twenty and thirty were killed and wounded. Ensign Hartung wrote that over 30 were killed and wounded.

[190] Captain Russell said that one officer was killed, and another wounded, while three rank and file were killed and fifteen wounded. Captain Peebles wrote that between twenty and thirty were killed and wounded. Ensign Hartung wrote that over 30 were killed and wounded.

[191] Captain Campbell was in the 2nd North Carolina Regiment. He is mentioned in accounts of Charlestown as Lieutenant Campaign, and he is also listed as Campen

[192] Edward Rutledge was one of the signers of the Declaration of Independence

[193] The powder magazine still exists in Charleston and is one of the points of interest for visitors to the city

[194] Of the muskets, 5,416 were "French and Portuguese manufacture."
[195] Stevens, *Autobiography*, pp. 9-10; Massey, *Hero's Life*, pp. 155-159, 370-372; Hanger, *Life, Opinions and Adventures*; Sir Henry Clinton Papers, Volume 95, (William L. Clements Library, University of Michigan); Volume 99; Davies, Documents, Volume XX, pp. 173-174; Tustin, *Diary*, pp. 190, 192, 199, 221-232; Gibbes, *Documentary History, Volume 2*, pp. 132-135; Burgoyne, *Diaries*, pp. 127-154; Boatner, *Encyclopedia*, pp. 21, 213, 404, 686, 952; *Regiment Book of Captain James Bentham*; Southern Studies Program, *Figures of the Revolution in South Carolina, An Anthology, Florence*, (University of South Carolina, 1976), p. 175; Louis-Antoine Magallon de la Morlière, *A French Account of the Siege of Charleston, 1780*, (The South Carolina Historical Magazine, Volume 67, Number 3, July 1966), pp. 140-154; Rosengarten, *German Allied Troops*, pp. 199, 289-320, 332-334; Edward J. Lowell, *The Hessians and the other German Auxiliaries of Great Britain in the Revolutionary War*, (Harper and Brothers Publishers, 1884); Oscar K. Weinmester, *The Hessian Grenadier Battalions in North America, 1776-1783*, (Military Collector & Historian, Winter 1975); Banastre Tarleton, *A History of the Campaigns of 1780 and 1781 in the Southern Provinces of North America*, (Ayer Company Publishers, 1999), pp. 52-57; Heitman, *Historical Register*, pp. 62-131, 498, 603; Duncan, *Royal Regiment of Artillery*; Robert Cannon, *Historical Record of the Seventeenth Regiment of Light Dragoons Lancers*, (John W. Parker, London, 1843), pp. 26-27; *Journal of the Siege of Charleston*, (The South Carolina Historical Magazine, Volume 66, Number 3, July 1965), pp. 149-182; Lamb, *Journal of Occurrences*, pp. 298-301; Gruber, *John Peebles*, pp. 314, 345-373; J.G. Simcoe, *A Journal of the Operations of the Queen's Rangers*, (The New York Times and Arno Press, 1968), pp. 217, 233; Draper, *Kings Mountain*, pp. 31, 33; Clark, *Loyalists in the Southern Campaign, Volume I*, pp. 1-48, 436, 453; Murtie June Clark, *Loyalists in the Southern Campaign of the Revolutionary War, Volume II*, (Genealogical Publishing Company, Inc., 1981), pp. 255-295, 311-630; *Volume III*, pp. 61-124, 177-213, 267-323, 353; Moultrie, *Memoirs, Vol. II*, pp. 50-114, 202; Smith, *Marines*, pp. 246-250; Uzal Johnson, *Memo of Occurrence During the Campaign of 1780*, (South Carolina Historical Society, Military Manuscripts); Wallace, *Orderly Book*, pp. 18-156; *Order Book of John Faucheraud Grimkè, August 1778 to May 1780*, (The South Carolina Historical and Genealogical Magazine, Volume XVII, Number 3, July 1916), p. 119;

(Volume XVIII, Number 2, April 1917), pp. 78-80, 82; (Volume XVIII, Number 3, July 1917), pp. 151-152; (Volume XVIII, Number 4, October 1917), pp. 175-176; (Volume XIX, Number 2, April 1918), pp. 101-103; (Volume XIX, Number 4, October 1918), pp. 181-182, 185, 187-188; *Pennsylvania Gazette, April 5, 1780; April 27, 1780; June 7, 1780*; Great Britain, Public Record Office, *Headquarters Papers of the British Army in America*, p. 2482; *Colonial Office*, Class 5, Volume 99, p. 493; *Cornwallis Papers*, Class 30, Volume 11, p. 2; *Chancery*, Class 106, Volume 90, Part 2, Bundle 13; John Buchanan, *The Road to Guilford Courthouse*, (John Wiley and Sons, Inc., 1997), pp. 26-72, 202; DAR, *Roster of Soldiers from North Carolina*, pp. 25-48, 50, 220; Salley, *Records of the Regiments*, pp. 9, 14-21, 39, 42-43; Moss, *Roster of the South Carolina Patriots*, pp. 48, 81, 101, 118, 226, 232, 290, 310, 339, 342, 440-441, 537-538, 673, 898, 940; Coggins, *Ships and Seaman*, pp. 102-103; Ervin, *South Carolinians*, pp. 63, 67-77; SCHS, *Troop Returns*; John T. Hayes, *Stephen Jarvis, The King's Loyal Horseman, His Narrative, 1775-1783*, (The Saddlebag Press, 1996), pp. 42-45; Uhlendorf, *Siege of Charleston*, pp. 87, 95, 109, 141, 209, 233, 243, 247, 251, 253, 263-287, 293, 373, 387-393, 405; Bauer, *1780 Siege, Part One*, pp. 24, 27, 31-33; Carl Bauer, *The 1780 Siege of Charleston as Experienced by a Hessian Officer, Part Two* (South Carolina Historical Magazine, Volume 88, Number 2, April 1987), pp. 63-69, 74-75; James, *Sketch of the Life*, p. 11; Walter Clark, *The State Records of North Carolina*, Volume XXII, Miscellaneous, (Nash Brothers, 1907), p. 1022; Clinton, *American Rebellion*, pp. 157-172; Crow, *Black Experience*, p. 74; Robert Scott Davis, *Thomas Pinckney and the Last Campaign of Horatio Gates*, (South Carolina Historical Magazine, Volume 86, Number 2, April 1985), pp. 83, 98; North Carolina Archives, *Troop Returns*, Box 4, Box 5, Box 7; Hayes, *Saddlebag Almanac*, Volume V, pp. 73-75; Volume VI, pp. 2-29, 53-54; Pancake, *This Destructive War*, pp. 56-69; *George Wray Papers*, Volume 6, (William L. Clements Library, University of Michigan); *Sir Henry Clinton Papers*, Volume 87, item 9; Volume 91, item 7; Volume 95, item 27; Volume 103, item 1, (William L. Clements Library, University of Michigan); McAllister, *Virginia Militia*, p. 16; Sanchez-Saavedra, *Virginia Military Organizations*, pp. 83-85, 124-125, 177-181; National Archives of Canada, *Ward Chipman Papers*, MG 23, D 1, Series 1, Volume 25, p. 23; PRO, War Office, *List of all the Officers of the Army*, pp. 93, 156, 311; Chesney, *Journal*; Carl P. Borick, *A Gallant*

Defense, The Siege of Charleston, 1780, (University of South Carolina Press, 2003); Draper, *Sumter Papers*, 1VV31-36, 39, 43, 49, 51, 10VV68

[196] Present-day Clyo, Georgia

[197] Clark, *Loyalists in the Southern Campaign, Volume I*, p. 453; Johnson, *Memo of Occurrence*, p. 4; Hayes, *Saddlebag Almanac, Volume V*, pp. 73-75; *Volume VI*, pp. 10-13; Allaire, Diary

[198] Also known as Savage's Plantation or St. Andrew's Church

[199] Tustin, *Diary*, pp. 208-209; Burgoyne, *Diaries*, pp. 127-135; Gruber, *John Peebles*, p. 314; PRO, *War Office, 30 List of all the Officers of the Army*, p. 156

[200] Tarleton, *History of the Campaigns,* pp. 7-8; Ruth Scott, *Loyalist Anthony Allaire*, (Officers Quarterly, Summer, 1997, York-Sunbury Historical Society of Fredericton, New Brunswick); Johnson, *Memo of Occurrence*, pp. 5-6; William Stryker, *The New Jersey Volunteers in the Revolutionary War*, (Trenton, 1887), pp. 9, 57; Hayes, *The Saddlebag Almanac, January 1998, Volume VI*, pp. 10-12, 28

[201] Jacksonborough consisted of "a village containing about sixty houses, situated on Pon Pon, or Edisto river. The most of the houses are very good; the people tolerable well to live; some large store houses for rice, from which they convey it by water to Charleston market. In short, it is a pleasant little place, and well situated for trade, but the inhabitants are all Rebels"

[202] Cannon, *Historical Record*, pp. 26-27; Hayes, *The Saddlebag Almanac, January 1998, Volume VI*, p. 28; Allaire, *Diary*

[203] This skirmish took place where US 17 crosses the Salkehatchie River near Yemassee. Salkehatchie River is also called Saltketcher River in other accounts

[204] In another account it says that Ladson lost 16 privates killed and a captain, while the British had four men wounded

[205] Johnson, *Memo of Occurrence*, pp. 8-9; Cannon, *Historical Record*, pp. 26-27; Hayes, *Saddlebag Almanac, Volume VI*, pp. 10-12, 28; James, *Sketch of the Life*, p. 56; Scott, *Loyalist Anthony Allaire*; Clark, *Loyalists in the Southern Campaign, Volume I*, p. 436; Lipscomb, *South Carolina Revolutionary Battles: Part II*, pp. 25-26

[206] Scott, *Loyalist Anthony Allaire*; Johnson, *Memo of Occurrence*, pp. 10-11; Peckham, *Toll of Independence*, p. 68; Allaire, *Diary*

[207] Tustin, *Diary of the American War,* pp. 210-211

---

[208] Tustin, Diary, pp. 211-212; Sir Henry Clinton Papers, Volume 83, item 38, (William L. Clements Library, University of Michigan), PRO, War Office, 30 June 1780, A List of all the Officers, p. 86

[209] Bee's Plantation was near the Edisto River, called Pon Pon River at the time. The plantation was on the east bank opposite Jacksonborough. Bee was the former Royal Lieutenant Governor of South Carolina

[210] Cannon, *Historical Record*, pp. 26-27; Scott, *Loyalist Anthony Allaire*; James, *Sketch of the Life*, p. 56; Johnson, *Memo of Occurrence*, p. 15; Hayes, *Saddlebag Almanac, Volume VI*, p. 13

[211] Tustin, *Diary of the American War*, p. 214

[212] Pickens' father was French, and had been driven out of France with the Edict of Nantz. He then lived in Scotland, then Ireland, and then came to Buck's Count, Pennsylvania. From there he moved to Augusta County, Virginia, then on to the Waxhaws in South Carolina

[213] Cashin, *King's Ranger*, pp. 87, 99-108; Lee, *Revolutionary War Memoirs*, p. 175; Moss, *Roster of the South Carolina Patriots*, pp. 20-21; Pancake, *This Destructive War*, p. 62; Peckham, *The Toll of Independence*, p. 68; Draper, *Sumter Papers*, 11VV536-540

[214] Rantowle's was what the locals called Kennedy's Tavern on Rantowle's Causeway. During the Yemassee War there had been Thomas Elliot's Fort in the same location, since it was on the approach to Charlestown. It is located on the present day US 17 bridge over Rantowles Creek

[215] Jameson was commanding the dragoons until Lieutenant Colonel Anthony White arrived in Charlestown

[216] Tustin, *Diary,* pp. 214-215; Burgoyne, *Diaries*, pp. 121-122; Tarleton, *History of the Campaigns,* pp. 8-9; Cannon, *Historical Record*, pp. 26-27; Scott, *Anthony Allaire*; James, *Sketch of the Life*, p. 56; Lee, *Revolutionary War Memoirs*, p. 146; *Pennsylvania Gazette, May 3, 1780*; *Pennsylvania Packet, April 25, 1780*; Thomas Farr, *Revolutionary Letters*, (South Carolina Historical and Genealogical Magazine, Volume XXXVIII, Number 1, January 1937), p.8; Peckham, *Toll*, p. 68-69; Hayes, *Saddlebag Almanac, Volume VI*, pp. 13, 30, 33; *Volume VII*, p. 58

[217] Pancake, *This Destructive War*, p. 62; Peckham, *The Toll of Independence*, p. 69

[218] Gibbe's farm was the plantation of Robert Gibbes and was also known as Peaceful Retreat Plantation, The Muck, or Gibbes Farm. Elizabeth Ellet described it as "A FEW hundred yards from a fine landing on Stono River, upon John's Island, about two hours' sail from Charleston, stands a large,

square, ancient-looking mansion, strongly built of brick, with a portico fronting the river. On the side towards the road, the wide piazza overlooks a lawn; and a venerable live oak, with aspen, sycamore, and other trees, shade it from the sun. On either side of the house, about twenty yards distant, stands a smaller two story building, connected with the main building by a neat open fence. In one of these is the kitchen and out-offices; the other was formerly the school-house and tutor's dwelling; Beyond are the barns, the overseer's house, and the negro huts appertaining to a plantation. The garden in old times was very large and well-cultivated, being laid out in wide walk, and extending from the mansion to the river. The "river walk," on the verge of a bluff eight or ten feet in height, followed the bending of the water, and was bordered with orange-trees. Tall hedges of the ever-green wild orange-tree divided the flower from the vegetable garden, and screened from view the family burial-ground. The beautifully laid out grounds, and shaded walks, gave this place a most inviting aspect, rendering it such an abode as its name of " Peaceful Retreat" indicated.

[219] The two Amusettes were manned by the Light Infantry

[220] John Barriedale was the eleventh Earl of Caithness. He was a lieutenant colonel in the 76th Regiment of Foot and a volunteer aide-de-camp of Henry Clinton. In another account it says that he was shot later in the fight

[221] Tustin, *Diary*, pp. 216-220; Massey, *Hero's Life*, pp. 370-372; Burgoyne, *Diaries*, pp. 123-125, 131; Gruber, *John Peebles*, pp. 314, 346, 352, 354; Morlière, *French Account*, pp. 142, 144; Rosengarten, *German Allied Troops*, pp. 189-220; Clinton, *Journal of the Siege*, p. 149; Scott, *Loyalist Anthony Allaire*; Moultrie, *Memoirs, Vol. II*, pp. 62-63, 65; Johnson, *Memo of Occurrence*, p. 19; Wallace, *Orderly Book*, pp. 23-24; *Pennsylvania Gazette, August 20, 1777*; Uhlendorf, *Siege of Charleston*, pp. 223-227, 381; Bauer, *1780 Siege, Part One*, p. 33; Clinton, *American Rebellion*, p. 163; PRO, War Office, *List of all the Officers of the Army*, pp. 93, 138, 156; Borick, *A Gallant Defense*; Elizabeth F. Ellet, *The Women of the American Revolution*, (New York, Baker and Scribner, 1849)

[222] *Pennsylvania Gazette, May 10, 1780*; Coggins, *Ships and Seaman of the American Revolution*, p. 203

[223] This action is also listed as occurring on 28 March, and on 4 April

[224] Brown, *Memoirs*; *Pennsylvania Gazette, May 24, 1780*; Great Britain, Public Record Office, *Headquarters Papers of the British Army in*

America, folio 2482; *Royal American Gazette, April 27, 1780*; Pancake, *This Destructive War*, p. 62; Peckham, *The Toll of Independence*, p. 69
[225] This shoal is the present day Fort Sumter
[226] Davies, *Documents, Volume XX*, pp. 173-174; Tustin, *Diary*, pp. 226-227; Boatner, *Encyclopedia*, p. 43; Morlière, *French Account*, pp. 144-145; Tarleton, *History of the Campaigns*, pp. 10-11, 50-51, 55-56; Scott, *Loyalist Anthony Allaire*; Moultrie, *Memoirs, Vol. II*, pp. 63-64, 67-68; Johnson, *Memo of Occurrence*, p. 22; *Pennsylvania Gazette, June 7, 1780*; Uhlendorf, *Siege of Charleston*, pp. 109, 241-243; Bauer, *1780 Siege, Part Two*, p. 4; Borick, *A Gallant Defense*; Allaire, *Diary*
[227] Also known as Biggin's Bridge
[228] Richard Vernon wrote in his pension that his company, under Bethel, was there, but Caswell and his brigade of militia were near Dupree's Ferry
[229] This is only an approximate number
[230] Major Vernier and Lieutenant Beaulieu were among the wounded that were captured. Major Vernier later died
[231] Captain David Kinlock had been an officer in the 71st Highlander Regiment
[232] Beaulieu had been wounded seven times before when General Prévost attacked Charlestown. Five of these wounds were in the face
[233] Though there were numerous propaganda stories about soldiers from one side, or the other raping women, this is the only case that I have been able to document in the entire eight year war in the Carolinas
[234] Tarleton, *History of the Campaigns*, pp. 15-17; Cannon, *Historical Record*, pp. 27-28; Scott, *Loyalist Anthony Allaire*; Moultrie, *Memoirs, Vol. II*, p. 72; Lee, *Revolutionary War Memoirs*, p. 154; Johnson, *Memo of Occurrence*, pp. 23-27; Buchanan, *Road to Guilford Courthouse*, pp. 59-64; Clinton, *American Rebellion*, pp. 165-166; Hayes, *Saddlebag Almanac, Volume VI*, pp. 34-54; Sanchez-Saavedera, *Virginia Military Organizations*; John T. Hayes, *A Gentleman of Fortune, The Diary of Baylor Hill, First Continental Light Dragoons, 1777-1781, Volume 3*, (The Saddlebag Press, 1995), pp. 70-77; Borick, *A Gallant Defense*; Draper, *Sumter Papers*, 10VV168
[235] Near present-day Remley's Point
[236] Scott, *Loyalist Anthony Allaire*; Clark, *Loyalists in the Southern Campaign, Volume III*, p. 289; Lee, *Revolutionary War Memoirs*, pp. 155-156; Johnson, *Memo of Occurrence*, pp. 34-36; Wallace, *Orderly Book*, p. 154; Moss, *Roster of the South Carolina Patriots*, p. 996; Uhlendorf, *Siege*

of *Charleston,* p. 283; PRO, *War Office, List of all the Officers of the Army,* p. 120; Borick, *A Gallant Defense;* Allaire, *Diary*

[237] Also known as Ball's Plantation or Hell Hole Swamp. Lenud's Ferry is pronounced as "Lund's Ferry." It is located where US 17-A crosses the Santee River

[238] This was Daniel Horry's plantation located at present-day Hampton Plantation State Park, near McClellansville

[239] Amazingly, two boys, Francis Deliesseline and Samuel Dupré, had the audacity to steal back fourteen of White's horses from the British, and return them to Major Jameson in Georgetown. They refused a reward.

[240] Hayes, *Gentleman of Fortune, Volume 3,* pp. 84-88; Alexander Garden, *Anecdotes of the Revolutionary War in America with Sketches of Character of Persons the Most Distinguished, in the Southern States, for Civil and Military Services,* (A.E. Miller, Charleston, 1822), pp. 384-385; Kennedy, *Historic Camden,* pp. 134-135; Tarleton, *History of the Campaigns,* pp. 19-20; Cannon, *Historical Record,* pp. 28-29; Scott, *Loyalist Anthony Allaire;* Lee, *Revolutionary War Memoirs,* p. 156; Johnson, *Memo of Occurrence,* p. 37; Uhlendorf, *Siege of Charleston,* p. 285; James, *Sketch of the Life,* p. 12; Clinton, *American Rebellion,* pp. 168-170; Hayes, *Saddlebag Almanac, Volume VI,* pp. 58-66; Sanchez-Saavedera, *Virginia Military Organizations;* Borick, *A Gallant Defense*

[241] These were North Carolina Continental soldiers detached as Artificers. Artificers were soldier mechanics who served with the artillery and engineers

[242] The phrase "Tol, lol, de rol" comes from the *Grub Street Opera,* and meant that the British could do whatever they wished to the fort, but it would only be an annoyance, and in the end the Patriots would be never give up

[243] Burgoyne, *Diaries,* p. 142; Morlière, *French Account,* p. 152; Tarleton, *History of the Campaigns,* pp. 20-21; Scott, *Loyalist Anthony Allaire;* Moultrie, *Memoirs, Vol. II,* pp. 84-85; Lee, *Revolutionary War Memoirs,* pp. 155-156; Johnson, *Memo of Occurrence,* pp. 36-38; *Pennsylvania Gazette, June 7, 1780;* Salley, *Records of the Regiments of the South Carolina Line,* p. 21; Borick, *A Gallant Defense*

[244] Morris's Ford is located near Barnwell. The grave of John Mumford is still there

[245] Clark, *Loyalists in the Southern Campaign, Volume I,* p. 537; Brown, *Memoirs;* Moss, *Roster of the South Carolina Patriots,* p. 710; Terry W.

Lipscomb, *South Carolina Revolutionary Battles Part Ten,* (Names in South Carolina, Volume XXX, Winter 1983, South Carolina Historical Society, 1983)

[246] Also known as Buford's Massacre

[247] Some historians mistakenly state that the men with Buford were the 3rd Virginia Regiment, or the 14th Virginia. The 3rd Virginia Regiment had been captured in Charlestown, and the only member of the 14th Virginia Regiment at the Waxhaws was Colonel Buford. His 350 recruits were the 3rd Virginia Detachment of Scott's 2nd Virginia Brigade. These men were Virginia recruits and recalled veterans intended for various regiments of the Virginia Line

[248] Captain Wallace was an officer in the 8th Virginia Regiment

[249] Captain Lawson was an officer in the 1st Virginia Regiment

[250] Captain Woodson and Wallace were officers in the 5th Virginia Regiment

[251] Captain Stokes and Catlett were officers in the 2nd Virginia Regiment

[252] There were 150 wounded among the captured. The killed included Captains Catlett and Wallace, the wounded included Captain Stokes

[253] Mounted for rapid movement

[254] Lieutenants McDonald and Campbell were among the killed. The wounded included Lieutenant Patteshall

[255] Stokes would later become a federal judge in North Carolina, marry and have children. He died in his eighties. Stokes County, north of Winston-Salem, is named after him

[256] The image of Tarleton as the butcher is carried on to this day. In the movie *"The Patriot"* starring Mel Gibson, the villain, Colonel Tavington, was loosely based upon Banastre Tarleton. However no British officer would have been able to do any of the atrocities that the Tavington character did in the movie without being relieved and placed under arrest

[257] *Clinton Papers, Volume 101, item 45*; Boatner, *Encyclopedia*, pp. 187, 1174; Kennedy, *Historic Camden*, pp. 134-139; Tarleton, *History of the Campaigns,* pp. 26-31; Cannon, *Historical Record*, pp. 29-31; Moultrie, *Memoirs, Vol. II*, pp. 203-207; Johnson, *Memo*, p. 52; Wallace, *Orderly Book,* p. 18; *Pennsylvania Gazette, July 19, 1780*; PRO, *Headquarters Papers of the British Army in America*, folios 2781, 2784; Buchanan, *Guilford Courthouse*, pp. 80-85; McAllister, *Virginia Militia*, p. 88; Pancake, *This Destructive War*, pp. 70-71; Hayes, *Saddlebag Almanac,*

Volume VI, p. 67; Sanchez-Saavedera, *Virginia Military*, pp. 37, 180-181; Draper, *Sumter Papers*, 11VV490-494, 11VV509-519

[258] Captain Christian Huck was a New York Loyalist who had been born in Germany in 1748. He had been commissioned a captain of infantry in Emmerick's Chasseurs in 1778. Emmerick's Chasseurs was disbanded due to discipline problems on 31 August 1779. Captain Huck was made captain of a troop of forty men drafted from Emmerick's Corps and given to the British Legion. This troop was not supposed to be incorporated into the Legion, but were when they embarked for the Siege of Charlestown in December of 1779

[259] Kennedy, *Historic Camden*, pp. 139-141; Simms, *The Life of Francis Marion*

[260] Kennedy, *Historic Camden*, pp. 140-144

[261] *The Pennsylvania Gazette, July 19, 1780*

[262] Ervin, *South Carolinians in the Revolution*, p. 48

[263] The camp was five miles south of the present day town of Union

[264] Like all partisan actions in the backcountry of Carolina, the date for this is in dispute. It is listed as either happening on 8th or 10th June

[265] Brandon was described as a "large portly man"

[266] Sometimes this is listed as the 1st and 2nd Battalions of the Spartan Regiment

[267] With Brandon was James McJunkin, who had commanded "Wood's or Thomson's Station till February 1779." In November 1779 McJunkin's company marched to defend Charlestown and remained until February 1780. McJunkin wrote "Once Charleston fell the powder for Brandon's regiment was hidden by Brandon, Captain Otterson, McJunkin, Lieutenant Benjamin Jolly, Joseph Hughes and William Sharp, in different places, in thickets, inaccessible woods, in hollowed logs." It was used when needed.

[268] Mrs. Charles Sims found him and nursed him back to health. He lived until 1852, in Pickens County

[269] One of the men killed was John or William Young

[270] Thomas Young, *Memoir of Major Thomas Young*, (Orion Magazine, October and November 1843); Terry W. Lipscomb, *South Carolina Revolutionary Battles Part Three,* (Names in South Carolina, Volume XXII, Winter 1975, South Carolina Historical Society, 1975), p. 35; Draper, *Sumter Papers*, 11VV316-321, 14VV77-79, 136

---

[271] Also known as Beckham's Old Field, or the Battle of Beckhamville. The skirmish happened near present-day Beckhamville. At the time of the battle there was no Beckhamville

[272] The date for this skirmish is in dispute. John Craig told Lyman Draper that it took place on May 24th, two days after Moberley's Meetinghouse. Daniel Stinson told him that it happened on May 28th, a few days before Moberley's. Draper wrote that both Beckhamville and Moberley's Meetinghouse happened between May 31st and June 11th. The most likely date for this incident was June 6th or 8th

[273] John Steele (also listed as James Stein, even though they were two different men) would be the only one of these men that would see the end of the war. Three would fall at Hanging Rock, and Alexander Gaston would die of small pox

[274] Daniel Stinson wrote, "Half of them were redcoats". He also wrote that "Several who had previously joined the British changed sides that day"

[275] This did not stop Joseph Gaston, and when he recovered he rejoined Sumter and was at the battle of Blackstocks. There are other accounts that state that Joseph Gaston and his brothers were wounded at Hanging Rock

[276] Lossing, *Pictorial Field-Book*; Lipscomb, *South Carolina Revolutionary Battles Part Three*, p. 33; Hayes, *The Saddlebag Almanac, January 1998, Volume VI*, pp. 83-84; Draper, *Sumter Papers*, 5VV150, 9VV159, 10VV235, 14VV436-443, 452-460

[277] The date for this incident is in dispute as is the location. It either happened on 29 May, 8 June or 10 June 1780. The location happened at Gibson's Meeting House near present-day Winnsboro. It is incorrectly listed as Mobley's Meeting House, but Richard Winn who was familiar with the area wrote that it occurred in "Gipson's Meeting House in Moberleys Settlement." Seventeen-year-old militiaman James Collins wrote in his autobiography that it happened after Huck's Defeat at the Waxhaws. One source says that Mobley's Meetinghouse was known as Monticello

[278] Present-day York County

[279] William Kennedy wrote in his pension that he "volunteered under Captain John Steele for the purpose of breaking up a body of Tories and was in the Battle at Maubly Meeting House." He also wrote that it was safer to be a volunteer with a partisan force, than to stay at home and be at the mercy of the Loyalists. This was an opinion shared by many pensioners.

[280] Collins went into detail describing how they made their dragoon's helmets. "We could go to a turner or wheelwright, and get head blocks turned, of various sizes, according to the heads that had to wear them, in shape resembling a sugar loaf; we would then get some strong upper, or light sole leather, cut it out in shape, close it on the block, then grease it well with tallow, and set it before a warm fire, still on the block, and keep turning it round before the fire, still rubbing on the tallow, until it became almost as hard as a sheet of iron; we then got two small straps or plates of steel, made by our own smiths, of good spring temper, and crossing in the centre above, one reaching from ear to ear, the other, in the contrary direction; the lining was made of strong cloth, padded with wool, and fixed so as to prevent the cap from pressing too hard on the ears; there was a small brim attached to the front, resembling the caps now worn, a piece of bear skin lined with strong cloth, padded with wool, passed over from the front to the back of the head; then a large bunch of hair taken from the tail of a horse, generally white, was attached to the back part and hung down the back; then, a bunch of white feathers, or deer's tail , was attached to the sides, which completed the cap."

[281] In October 1780 Governor Rutledge made Sumter's title of "General" official. John Taylor described Sumter as "small, but very active. He would place one hand on the saddle and vault into the saddle without every putting a foot in the stirrup." Alexander Smiley wrote that Sumter was "avaricious, indomitable, taciturn, sarcastic – exceedingly so – had a great contempt for Harry Lee, who was a great disciplinarian, while Sumter was simply a fighter, not much for discipline. His men were lawless and hard to control. Good soldiers and fighters." Thomas Sumter, Jr. wrote that his father's sword was 3 feet, 6 inches in length and made of a mill or whip saw." Martha Davis, his housekeeper, said "Sumter was particular in his diet, such as would not hurt anyone = soups, cornbread, not many vegetables, no bacon, but chickens and fresh meat food. Very prudent. Never intoxicated – always temperate. He was not communicative – never invited anything like familiarity, kept all at a distance, not haughty, yet somewhat proud and dignified."

[282] James Collins, *A Revolutionary Soldier*, (Felician Democrat, Print, 1859), pp. 35-38; *General Richard Winn's Notes – 1780*, (The South Carolina Historical and Genealogical Magazine, Volume XLIII, Number 4, October 1942), pp. 202-204; National Archives and Records Administration, *Samuel Walker Pension File #S3448*, (Washington, DC);

Lipscomb, *South Carolina Battles Part Three*, p. 33; Peckham, *Toll of Independence*, p. 71; Hayes, *The Saddlebag Almanac, January 1998, Volume VI*, p. 84; *Colonel William Hill's Memoirs*, Library of Congress, Washington, D.C.; Draper, *Sumter Papers*, 9VV159, 10VV41, 11VV509-519

[283] McDill said that there was a vulgar song written about he incident "Hawthorne and his men, their aim they did not miss. They caught old Phillips in their net, and scared him till he pissed"

[284] Draper, *Sumter Papers*, 4VV51-53, 56-58

[285] Draper, *Sumter Papers*

[286] In most accounts they list this incident as happening on 11 July, but Lyman Draper put the events into this timeline

[287] William Strong was described in one account as being simple minded. However he was a member of the Patriot militia. Robert Cooper told Lyman Draper that his father was Major Christopher Strong. This is not likely, since Christopher Strong was only a private. He was born in Ireland in 1760. Cooper wrote "Huyck came up Fishing Creek on Sunday morning, and finding a young man about 15 years of age at home about 3 miles below us took out and hanged him. The news spread and Major Strong had but one son about 16 years old who was very sick at home with fever but fearing the British & Tories would stop that way he got out of bed and attempted to conseal himself in a stock yard; but was discovered by them & shot & killed him as he crossed the fence."

[288] Southern Studies Program, *Figures of the Revolution in South Carolina, Spartanburg,* pp. 103-104, 208; Great Britain, Public Record Office, *Cornwallis Papers*, Class 30, Volume 11, 2, 158-9; Draper, *Sumter Papers*, 4VV16

[289] Benjamin Land was a Catholic, which was rare in the backcountry at that time

[290] Another Captain Benjamin Land was taken prisoner in March 1781, and died in captivity

[291] Elizabeth F. Ellet, *Domestic History of the American Revolution*, New York, Charles Scribner, 1859, pp 177-181; Moss, *South Carolina Patriots*, p. 551

[292] The Iron Works was located in present-day York County, where SC 274 crosses Allison Creek

[293] Draper wrote that the iron works were probably destroyed the same day as Reverend Simpson's house, on June 11th. He also wrote that another source said that it was burned on July 9th

[294] Andrew Neal's father, Andrew, had commanded the regiment before the fall of Charlestown

[295] Hill had been born in Belfast, Ireland in 1740. Draper wrote "Hill had come to York County very poor and started making sickles and scythes at Ellison Creek. Colonel Hayne was interested in the water power and entered into a partnership and sent up machinery and tools and a store of goods"

[296] Hill wrote that Huck had 500 men with him, but it was probably no more than 150. Hill did not mention the fight that happened at the Iron Works in his memoirs

[297] Collins, *Revolutionary Soldier*, p. 25; Lipscomb, *South Carolina Battles Part Three*, p. 33; Robert Stansbury Lambert, *South Carolina Loyalists in the American Revolution*, (University of South Carolina Press, 1987), pp. 119, 128; Hayes, *Saddlebag Almanac, January 1998, Volume VI*, pp. 87-88; Great Britain, Public Record Office, *Cornwallis Papers*, Class 30, Volume 11/2/158-159, 162-163, 171-172; Tarleton, *History of the Campaigns*, p. 117; *William Hill's Memoirs*; Saye, *McJunkin*; Draper, *Sumter Papers*, 11VV329-332, 17VV70-71

[298] Chesney, *Journal*, pp. 5-6; *William Hill's Memoirs*; Saye, *McJunkin*

[299] Draper, *Sumter Papers*, 14VV177-179, 9VV28-42

[300] Also spelled Ramsour's Mill, or Ramsaur's Mill. The first account of this battle was written forty years after it happened. No one knows exactly how many were killed on each side, nor the names of all the participants. Ramsour's Mill is located near present-day Lincolnton.

[301] Hugh Rankin wrote that Joshua Bowman was an officer in the 1st North Carolina Regiment, but that Joshua Bowman had been killed in Charleston during the siege

[302] Reid had been born in Ireland

[303] Otterson was described as 6 feet, 5 inches. A magnificent looking man, had a long face and very long and handsome nose. A very intelligent man

[304] Dan Alexander wrote in his pension statement that this unit was called Captain Fall's Company of Minutemen. He also refers to the commander as Gilly Falls

[305] William Armstrong was known as "pretty Billy" and was a captain in the 1st North Carolina Regiment

---

[306] Also listed as John Sloan

[307] Captain Armstrong was an officer in the 1st North Carolina Regiment, he was wounded in the engagement

[308] Martin's company arrived at the very end of the battle. Benjamin Newton wrote in his pension statement that he was under Captain Samuel Martin, Major William Chronicle and Colonel William Graham. He wrote, "General Rutherford ordered Conl. Graham and his men to be at Ramsours Mill at a certain time and we got there accordingly, but before we got there and before General Rutherford got there Major Falls and a company of men met and attacked Conl. Moore and the Tories at Ramsours Mill and defeated them and we got there as the battle was closing I shot at one of the Tories as he was running from the battle." There is a chance that this company was commanded by Benjamin Newton, because he wrote "A good part of this year I had command of our company as Capt. Samuel Martins family had the small pox and required him to be home."

[309] The killed included Captains Fall, Armstrong, Bowman, Smith, Dobson and Knox, the wounded included Captains McKissick, William Armstrong, Kennedy and Houston

[310] Captains Cumberland, Morrow and Warlick were among the killed, Captain Carpenter was one of the wounded

[311] In Benjamin Newton's pension he wrote, " We marched over to Green River in Rutherford where we met about eight hundred men under different colonels. Our object was to fight Col. Forgason and it was agreed that Conl. Charles McDowal should take the command, he being the oldest colonel. Colonel McDowal marched the whole eight hundred fighting men to the Big Shoal on the second Broad River in a direction off from Conl. Forgason and the other colonels all got made with Conl. McDowal and each took command of his men."

[312] About 125 feet

[313] Garden, *Anecdotes*, p. 378; William Graham, *The Battle of Ramsaur's Mill, June 20, 1780, Major on Staff of Adjutant General of North Carolina*, (North Carolina Archives, 1910); *List of Capt. James Houston's Company of North Carolina Rangers*, (North Carolina Archives, Microfilm Roll 79; Misc.) p.16; Boatner, *Encyclopedia*, p. 914; Winn, *Winn's Notes – 1780*, SCHGM Volume XLIII, Number 4, p. 203; Heitman, *Historical Register*, pp. 461, 491; White, *King's Mountain Men*, pp. 146, 196; DeMond, *Loyalists*, pp. 124-128; Clark, *Loyalists in the Southern Campaign, Volume I*, p. 410; Moultrie, *Memoirs, Vol. II*, pp. 217-219; Lee, *Revolutionary War*

Memoirs, pp. 167-168; David Schenck, *North Carolina 1780-'81, Being a History of the Invasion of the Carolinas by the British Army under Lord Cornwallis in 1780-'81*, (Edwards & Broughton, Publishers, 1889), pp. 51-63; *Pennsylvania Gazette, August 30, 1780*; Moss, *Roster of the South Carolina Patriots*, pp. 12, 31; Robinson, *Revolutionary War Sketches*, pp. 5-8; Clark, *State Records of North Carolina, Vol. XIX*, pp. 981-982; Morris, *Spirit of Seventy-Six*, pp. 1118-1120; Pancake, *This Destructive War*, pp. 95-96; Barefoot, *Touring*, pp. 237, 252; Draper, *Sumter Papers*, 10VV74-78

[314] Great Britain, Public Record Office, *Cornwallis Papers*, Class 30, Volume 11/2/250-251; Lyman Draper, *Thomas Sumter Papers, Draper Manuscript Collection*, State Historical Society of Wisconsin, 4VV120

[315] Winn, *Winn's Notes – 1780*, SCHGM Volume XLIII, Number 4, pp. 203-204; *William Hill's Memoirs*; Draper, *Sumter Papers*

[316] Also known as Cedar Springs

[317] Draper, *Kings Mountain*, pp. 85-86; Lipscomb, *South Carolina Revolutionary Battles Part Ten*, p. 14

[318] Also known as Huck's Defeat, or Williamson's Lane, since the battle took place in the road by Williamson's plantation

[319] The total number of men on both sides is in dispute. William Hill wrote that the total number of Patriots "was 133, and many of them were without arms." He also wrote that Huck had "100 horse & Col. Ferguson... had about 300 men"

[320] Lacey was described as "176 pounds, heavily formed"

[321] Nixon was described as having "the unhurried confidence of the Rocky Creek Irish"

[322] William Hill is described as "a strong, opinionated man, very decided and firm." Thomas Sumter said he was "5 feet, 9 inches, lean and spare"

[323] Lieutenant Jamieson had been born in Brandywine, Pennsylvania and moved to York District, South Carolina before the war began. When the war started he enlisted under Colonel Neal when he was 20 years old. He was in the ill-fated expedition to Georgia in 1776 and later went on an expedition against the Creek Indians in Georgia. He was in the battle of Briar Creek and after the fall of Charleston he was appointed a lieutenant under Colonel Bratton. When the Patriots were trying to decide what to do in South Carolina, Jamieson said that they didn't need a council of war, but instead needed a council of flight. When it was decided to dismantle the

regiments Jamieson took eleven men and went to join Sumter in North Carolina. He arrived in time for the battle of Ramseur's Mill

[324] Winn was described as having "blue eyes and light hair, about 5 feet 10 inches, very stout made, a powerful chest and shoulders". Another source described him as "6 feet tall and fine looking"

[325] James Saye said that Neil had 130 men, so Winn's "regiment" might have been 40 men

[326] Captain Summers was a Continental officer in the 1st North Carolina Regiment

[327] Colonel Bratton was wounded and Captain Summers was captured

[328] James Saye said that there was 100 "British" there, but this was like most backwoods battles. American versus American

[329] In some accounts his name is listed as Matthew Floyd

[330] Lieutenant Lisle had been a lieutenant colonel with the Patriot militia in 1775, and had been a lieutenant in the 3rd South Carolina Rangers. After Charlestown fell he joined the British

[331] Like most backwoods actions, the numbers of men killed and wounded are different with each account. One account lists twenty-one killed and twenty-nine wounded or taken prisoner

[332] The home is in present-day Rodman

[333] Hill wrote that the Loyalists "were encamped in a Lane a strong fence on each side, the Horse picketed in the inside of the field next to the land, with the furniture of the officers in a mansion house in the field, in which was a number of women, which the said Huck had brought there."

[334] There are several accounts, by men who were there, that says the attack happened in daylight, after the men were out of their beds and during the time that they were cooking breakfast. Draper wrote, "The Whigs were about to shoot Sam, Floyd's servant. Sam politely pulled off his hat, when it was light enough to see. Someone called "It's a Negro" and he was spared." Afterwards Sam joined the partisans. John Craig wrote that they were riding towards White's Mill, but "We found the enemy had left the mill and we immediately hurried on to attack them, and about daybreak came up to them at Williamson's lane."

[335] The "armour" would have been Huck's gorget. A gorget was a half-moon shaped piece of metal, usually silver, that was an indication of an officer's status.

[336] The home of William Bratton is located in present-day Historic Brattonsville, and was featured in the movie "The Patriot" starring Mel Gibson.

[337] In another version of this story a Loyalist named Campbell concealed a pistol and shot the man. He then escaped into the woods

[338] Many of the Loyalists had crawled off into the woods and died there. Hill wrote that the British had lost "considerable number of privates the number not known, as there were many of their carcasses found in the woods some days after."

[339] John Craig wrote, "We gathered up all the British and Tory spoils, and sold them. We then were disbanded for a short time to go home for clothing, &c."

[340] Huck and his men were buried on the battlefield. In the 19th century John H. Logan wrote, "Wm Bratton, when about 18, studying medicine, took up Hauk's body, made a skeleton of it as far as it remained -- this was taken by a member of the family to Alabama, where it is still."

[341] Collins, *Revolutionary Soldier*, pp. 25-27; Thomas, *The Dye is Cast*, p. 21; Southern Studies Program, *Figures of the Revolution, Spartanburg*, pp. 109-111; *Richard Winn's Notes*, SCHGM Volume XLIII, Number 4, pp. 204-206; Tarleton, *History of the Campaigns*, p. 93; Moss, *Roster of the South Carolina Patriots*, pp. 604, 806, 1006; Draper, *Kings Mountain*, p. 500; Moultrie, *Memoirs, Vol. II*, p. 217; Johnson, *Memo of Occurrence*, p. 53; *Pennsylvania Gazette, August 30, 1780*; DAR, *Roster of Soldiers from North Carolina*, p. 48; Heitman, *Historical Register*, pp. 113-123; Lambert, *South Carolina Loyalists*, pp. 119, 128; Pancake, *This Destructive War*, pp. 83-84, 96; Hayes, *The Saddlebag Almanac, January 1998, Volume VI*, pp. 87-89; *William Hill's Memoirs*; Draper, *Sumter Papers*, 4VV16-17, 5VV151

[342] The skirmish occurred at the site of the present day South Carolina School for the Deaf and Blind in Spartanburg

[343] This incident is also listed as having occurred on 13 July

[344] I am unable to determine why John Thomas, Sr. would have been arrested after he took parole. McJunkin wrote that Mrs. Thomas was visiting her sons, William and Abram, who were prisoners at Ninety-Six, and not her husband

[345] Anthony Allaire wrote that Ninety-Six consisted of "twelve dwelling houses, a court-house and a jail, in which are confined about forty Rebels, brought in prisoners by the friends to Government"

[346] Lipscomb, *South Carolina Battles Part Three*, p. 35; Hayes, *The Saddlebag Almanac, Volume VI*, pp. 90-91; *Volume V*, p. 92; Allaire, *Diary*; Draper, *Sumter Papers*

[347] Also known as Brandon's Camp, located four miles southeast of present-day York. It is also known as "Stallings"

[348] The date for this event is not known for sure. Other historians have the incident occurring after the raid on Reverend Simpson's house a month earlier

[349] Draper wrote that as Love's sister "opened the door he had fired at the doorknob and shot her dead."

[350] Draper wrote that Love dealt roughly with the Tories, hanging all he took. Only Stallion and his brother escaped." However Thomas Young wrote that "After the fight Love and Stallions met and shed bitter tears; Stallions was dismissed on parole to bury his wife and arrange his affairs." John Hollis wrote that in 1781 "John Stallions, a Tory Captain, came in & the twenty five or thirty men surrendered themselves prisoners of war. Stallions was shot by Wm. Goodwyn, on sudden quarrel & deponent recd. one of the balls through his left arm – Stallions on seeing Goodwyn's gun raised, seized hold of deponents arm & attempted to get behind deponent. One of the balls struck Stallion on the hand that held deponent's left arm, passing through his hand & deponent's arm, & the other ball lodged in his breast, entering at the left nipple, & proving mortal"

[351] Young, *Memoir*; Lipscomb, *South Carolina Battles Part Three*, p. 35; Saye, *McJunkin*; Draper, *Sumter Papers*, 11VV411

[352] Gowen's Old Fort was located near Gowen's Fort, in Spartanburg County, near present-day Landrum

[353] Draper wrote that this incident happened on July 14th

[354] Lyman Draper wrote that Jones did not go into a fort, but surprised a camp of Loyalists when they approached "the enemy with guns, swords and belt-pistols, they found them in a state of self-security and generally asleep. Closing quickly around them, they fired upon the camp, killing one and wounding three, when thirty-two, including the wounded, called for quarter, and surrendered."

[355] Davis, *Georgians in the Revolution*, p. 166; Lawrence, *Hogback Country*, pp. 20-21; Pancake, *This Destructive War*, p. 96; Hayes, *The Saddlebag Almanac, January 2000, Volume VIII*, pp. 92-93

[356] This incident is also known as McDowell's Camp. Earle's Ford was located a few hundred yards south of the North Carolina line, in present day Spartanburg County

[357] This incident is also listed as having been on 16 July

[358] Draper wrote that John Singleton was called "Major Jack" by friends

[359] McDowell was pronounced "McDole"

[360] Southern Studies Program, *Figures of the Revolution, Spartanburg,* pp. 174-175; Davis, *Georgians in the Revolution,* pp. 166-167; Lawrence, *Hogback Country,* pp. 20-25; Draper, *Kings Mountain and its Heroes,* p. 80; Johnson, *Memo of Occurrence,* pp. 54-56; Schenck, *North Carolina 1780-'81,* p. 123; Lipscomb, *South Carolina Battles Part Three,* p. 35; Pancake, *This Destructive War,* p. 96; Hayes, *Saddlebag Almanac, Volume VIII,* pp. 92-94; Chesney, *Journal*

[361] Also known as Criner's Fort. Prince's Fort was located approximately where Interstate 85 and SC 129 intersect

[362] Near the present day Shiloh Church

[363] Southern Studies Program, *Figures of the Revolution, Spartanburg,* pp. 174-175; Lawrence, *Hogback Country,* pp. 23-24; Schenck, *North Carolina 1780-'81,* p. 123; Lipscomb, *South Carolina Battles Part Three,* p. 35; Hayes, *The Saddlebag Almanac, Volume VIII,* p. 95

[364] Also known as Colson's Old Fields or Colson's Mill

[365] Mounted riflemen

[366] Some historians state that the commander was Colonel Samuel Bryan, but Bryan had rendezvoused with the 71st Highlanders and was not at Colson's on the day of the fight

[367] Colonel Davidson had been the commander of the 5th North Carolina Regiment, and was home on furlough when Charlestown was captured. After the fall of Charlestown Davidson became an officer without soldiers, and offered his skills to Rutherford. He was placed in command of 160 militiamen

[368] Kentucky Archives, *Kentucky Pension Accounts,* Frankfort, Kentucky; DeMond, *Loyalists,* pp. 61, 127; Clark, *Loyalists in the Southern Campaign, Volume I,* pp. 361-362; *Pennsylvania Gazette, August 30, 1780*; Pension Applications, *RG 15, Microcopy 804*; Clark, *State Records of North Carolina, Vol. XIX,* pp. 982- 985; Pancake, *This Destructive War,* pp. 95, 162

[369] Flat Rock is located five miles southwest of present day Kershaw

[370] Major Robert Crawford had been captured at Charleston and was just recently paroled

[371] Kennedy, *Historic Camden*, p. 263; Schenck, *North Carolina 1780- '81*, pp. 64-66; Lipscomb, *South Carolina Battles Part Three*, p. 35-36; Robinson, *Revolutionary War Sketches*, pp. 8-10, DeMond, *Loyalists in North Carolina*, p. 61

[372] The lieutenant that was killed was Thomas Elliot, who had been in Pulaski's Legion

[373] Kennedy, *Historic Camden*, p. 263; Schenck, *North Carolina 1780- '81*, pp. 64-66; Lipscomb, *South Carolina Battles Part Three*, p. 35-36; Robinson, *Revolutionary War Sketches*, pp. 8-10

[374] Also known as Hunt's Bluff. Hunt's Bluff is located on the Great Pee Dee River, five miles west of present day Blenheim in Marlboro County

[375] This incident is also listed as having happened on August 1st

[376] This later became known as Irby's Mills

[377] Many of the Loyalists were former Patriots, and they may have had a prior agreement with Major Thomas

[378] Southern Studies Program, *Figures of the Revolution in South Carolina, Spartanburg,* pp. 303-304; Tarleton, *A History of the Campaigns,* p. 98; *The Pennsylvania Gazette, August 30, 1780*; PRO, *Cornwallis Papers,* Class 30, Volume 11, p. 2; Lipscomb, *South Carolina Revolutionary Battles Part Three,* p. 37; Lambert, *South Carolina Loyalists,* pp. 116-117; Hayes, *The Saddlebag Almanac, January 1999, Volume VII,* pp. 4-6; PRO, *War Office, A List of all the Officers,* p. 145

[379] Also known as Fort Anderson. Thicketty Fort was located halfway between present-day Gaffney and Spartanburg, in a small community known as Thicketty

[380] This skirmish has also been documented as occurring on July 26

[381] Moore and his men aggressively raided the surrounding countryside, and on one occasion they stayed the night at Samuel McJunkin's home. McJunkin was a Patriot, but was too old to do military service. The morning after their stay, Moore's men took the family's "bed-clothes and wearing apparel." One Loyalist, Bill Haynesworth, grabbed a quilt and put it on his horse. McJunkin's daughter, Jane, snatched it back, and the two began to wrestle over the quilt. Moore told Jane that if she could take the quilt from Haynesworth, she could have it. The two wrestled until Haynesworth slipped on some mud, and fell. Jane quickly snatched up the quilt and placed her foot on the Loyalist's chest, winning back her quilt

[382] This is Sergeant Major Daniel Blue, also listed as Sergeant Major Blacksley

[383] Clarke had been in an engagement prior to this, but I don't know the location or the date. Matthew Nail was a militiaman with Clarke. He had been captured at Briar Creek and held five months on a prison ship before he escaped. He told Lyman Draper that he was "with Clarke at Enoree in Spring 1780" They were to attack "a band of British and Tories but were interrupted before daylight by spies." They charged them and took some prisoners. Clarke's men kept the field and remained under arms until morning. They were attacked the next day by "British and Tories from their Station." They "fought 4 to 1 odds." They "killed and took about a hundred of the British and Tories." They then "took the prisoners to the barracks." From the description of the fighting, Nail may have been describing the battle of Musgrove's Mill, that happened in August

[384] Near present day Gaffney

[385] Colonel Isaac Shelby had been in Kentucky securing lands that he had marked out five years before, but when he learned of the surrender of Charlestown he returned home to serve the Patriot cause

[386] Regular round ball and a handful of buckshot

[387] Lawrence, *Hogback Country,* p. 41; Draper, *Kings Mountain*, pp. 87-89, 423; White, *King's Mountain Men*, p. 178; Schenck, *North Carolina 1780-'81,* pp. 76-77; Johnson, *Memo of Occurrence During the Campaign of 1780,* p. 59; Hayes, *The Saddlebag Almanac, January 1999, Volume VII*, p. 4

[388] Located just south of present-day Great Falls

[389] This skirmish is also listed as occurring on August 1st

[390] Exact numbers were not known, but Sumter wrote that there were about 500 men there. There is a source that states there were some Catawba Indians there, under the command of Captain Thomas Drennan

[391] These were members of the Loyalist Rocky Mount Regiment that switched sides after Huck's defeat

[392] Stein is also listed as Steel, Steele or Steen. There is debate by many historians who as to whether James Steele and James Stein were two different people, or the same man. I am of the opinion that it is the same person. He is also confused with Captain John Steele, who is a different person. Stein was killed by a Loyalist after King's Mountain, but John Steele survived the war

[393] Referred to as the North Carolina Partisan Rangers in one account. The name *North Carolina Partisan Rangers* appears frequently in the fighting around the backwoods of North Carolina, and may not have been a specific unit, but just a description of the partisans in the area

[394] There are differing accounts as to the number of killed. Hill wrote that "Col. Neel was killed & 7 privates"

[395] There is another source that says there was a Colonel Black there, with 100 Broad River Loyalist Militia

[396] Joseph White wrote that the "Americans worried that the Catawbas would be offered liquor and presents and get them to engage on the side of the King. They alarmed their fears by saying since they aided the Americans, they would be destroyed. They did this to get them out of reach of the British. They enduced New River to abandon their town and retire awhile on the Yadkin, and camped on its banks above Salisbury. They stayed there till the fall of 1781. All of the Catawbas went except King Prow, who was nearly an imbecile." David Wallace told Draper that the Catawbas with Sumter would stretch out cowhides in between two trees to keep the cavalry away. He said, "They had a great fear of cavalry." Doctor Alexander Bradley wrote that they "fought most heroically when there was no cannon in the British line – they always ran from artillery." In other words, they were just like the typical militiaman from the Carolinas, by fearing Tarleton's cavalry and anyone's artillery. Reverend Samuel McCalla told him that Captain David Garrison and his son 1st Lieutenant Garrison were two white men who commanded a company of the Catawbas under Sumter

[397] Captain Robert Wilson wrote that they were organized into three companies. "The first company was under James Jamieson as Captain, Wm. Robinson, 1st Lieut. Wm. Hillhouse – Ensign. 2d Company: James Reed, Captain, Robt. Wilson (myself) Lieut., Hezekiah Lover, Ensign. 3d Company – John McClure, Captain, Hugh McClure, 1st Lieut. Hugh Knox, Ensign."

[398] Daniel Stinson wrote that "the Irish settlers of Fairfield, Chester and York formed the nucleus of Sumpter's Army at Heigler's and Clem's Branch". He also wrote that "a great many of those who formed Sumpters Camp at Clems Branch…were old soldiers, so that many of them was well acquainted with Sumter from 75 up to 80. This will account for their preference for Sumter over Col James Williams"

[399] Neal was shot in one shoulder, with the bullet exiting out the other side. Some accounts state that it was Andrew Neal who was killed at Rocky Mount, but Richard Winn wrote that it was his brother, Thomas Neal who was killed at Rocky Mount, and Andrew Neal killed a few days later near Rocky Mount

[400] Thomas Sumter, who was 15 years old, wrote "a Catawba indian, possibly New River, attempted to fire the fort." Reverend Samuel McCalla wrote that Hopping John Miller and Samuel Morrow "crawled up one side of the house and kindled a fire, but a heavy rain commenced and put it out."

[401] Thomas, *The Dye is Cast*, pp. 23-25; *General Richard Winn's Notes – 1780*, SCHGM Volume XLIII, Number 4, pp. 207-209; Tarleton, *A History of the Campaigns*, pp. 93-94; White, *The King's Mountain Men*, pp. 198, 226, 229; Clark, *Loyalists in the Southern Campaign, Volume III*, pp. 177-218; Moultrie, *Memoirs, Vol. II*, pp. 219-220; Lossing, *The Pictorial Field-Book*; Moss, *Roster of the South Carolina Patriots*, pp. 5, 427, 1006; Robinson, *The Revolutionary War Sketches*, pp. 11-12; *The State Records of North Carolina, Volumes XIV- 1779-'80*, pp. 540-543; Walter Clark, *The State Records of North Carolina, Vol. XIX – 1782 – '84. With Supplement – 1771 -'82*, (Nash Brothers, 1901), pp. 985-989; *William Hill's Memoirs*; Draper, *Sumter Papers*, 9VV62-63, 101, 11VV457-458, 14VV260-261, 436-443

[402] Also known as the battle of 1st Hanging Rock. Another battle was fought there seven days later that would become known as 2nd Hanging Rock. Hanging Rock was one of the British outposts detailed to protect the British at Camden. The name of the outpost came from a huge boulder, 30 feet in diameter, which sits on the 100-foot bank of a creek. The rock is still there to this day

[403] This skirmish is also listed as occurring on August 1st

[404] Surry County Loyalist Militia

[405] Davie wrote that they were known after this as "the bloody corps" by the British

[406] One of Davie's youngest soldiers in this battle was 13-year-old Andrew Jackson, who would one day be President of the United States. He was there with his brother, Robert. Jackson later spoke of his role in the war. "I was never regularly enlisted, being only fourteen when the war practically ended. Whenever I took to the field it was with Colonel Davie, who never put me in the ranks, but used me as a mounted orderly or

messenger, for which I was well fitted, being a good rider and knowing all the roads in that region. The only weapons I had were a pistol that Colonel Davie gave me and a small fowling-piece that my Uncle Crawford lent to me. This was a light gun and would kick like sixty when loaded with a three-quarter-ounce ball or with nine buckshot. But it was a smart little gun and would carry the ball almost as true as a rifle fifteen or twenty rods, and threw the buckshot spitefully at close quarters – which was the way I used it in defense of Captain Sand's house, where I was captured." Jackson also wrote "A lieutenant of Tarleton's Light Dragoons tried to make me clean his boots and cut my arm with his sabre when I refused. After that they kept me in jail at Camden about two months, starved me nearly to death and gave me the small pox. Finally my mother succeeded in persuading them to release Robert and me on account of our extreme youth and illness. It took me the rest of that year (1781) to recover my strength and get flesh enough to hide my bones."

[407] In the Royal American Gazette of September 21, 1780, it mentions that Captain Hewlett, of the New York Volunteers, died at Camden of wounds received at Hanging Rock on July 30th

[408] Clark, *Loyalists in the Southern Campaign, Volume I*, pp. 361-362; Moultrie, *Memoirs, Vol. II*, p. 220; Schenck, *North Carolina 1780-'81*, pp. 66-67; Robinson, *The Revolutionary War Sketches*, pp. 11-12; Morris, *The Spirit of Seventy-Six*, p. 1170; Hayes, *The Saddlebag Almanac, January 1999, Volume VII*, pp. 6-7; Draper, *Sumter Papers*, 5VV166-167, 7VV42

[409] There is no date for the death of Sam Brown, and is only referred to as taking place in the summer of 1780. I have placed it at the end of July due to the location of Josiah Culbertson at that time

[410] Near present day Statesville

[411] Culbertson called his .42 caliber rifle his "pocket piece"

[412] Present day Buncombe County

[413] Draper, *Kings Mountain and its Heroes*, pp. 135-138; Moss, *Roster of the South Carolina Patriots*, p. 223, Draper, Sumter Papers, 16VV402-405

[414] *The Pennsylvania Gazette, August 30, 1780*; Coggins, *Ships and Seaman of the American Revolution*, p. 73

[415] Dooly's home is located on present day Elijah Clarke State Park in Lincoln County, Georgia

[416] Corker is also listed as Captain Wilder. One source states that Colonel Dooly's family was also murdered, but this is unlikely

---

[417] The legend of Nancy Hart is associated with this incident. Elizabeth Ellet wrote "On the occasion of an excursion from the British camp at Augusta, a party of loyalists penetrated into the interior; and having savagely massacred Colonel Dooly in bed in his own house, proceeded up the country with the design of perpetrating further atrocities. On their way, a detachment of five from the party diverged to the east, and crossed Broad River to examine the neighborhood and pay a visit to their old acquaintance Nancy Hart. When they arrived at her cabin, they unceremoniously entered it, although receiving from her no welcome but a scowl, and informed her they had come to learn the truth of a story in circulation, that she had secreted a noted rebel from a company of "king's men" who were pursuing him, and who, but for her interference, would have caught. And hung him. Nancy undauntedly avowed her agency in the fugitive's escape. She had, she said, at first heard the tramp of a horse, and then saw a man on horseback approaching her cabin at his utmost speed. As soon as she recognized him to be a whig flying from pursuit, she let down the bars in front of her cabin, and motioned him to pass through both doors, front and rear, of her single-roomed house-to take to the swamp, and secure himself as well as he could. This he did without loss of time; and she then put up the bars, entered the cabin, closed the doors, and went about her usual employments. Presently, some tories rode up to the bars, calling vociferously for her. She muffled up her head and face, and opening the door, inquired why they disturbed a sick, lone woman. They said they had traced a man they wanted to catch near to her house, and asked if anyone on horseback had passed that way. She answered, no-but she saw some one on a sorrel horse turn out of the path into the woods, some two or three hundred yards back. "That must be the fellow!" said the tories; and asking her direction as to the way he took, they turned about and went off, "well fooled," concluded Nancy, "in an opposite course to that of my whig boy; when, if they had not been so lofty minded-but had looked on the ground inside the bars, they would have seen his horse's tracks up to that door, as plain as you can see the tracks on this here floor, and out of the other door down the path to the swamp." This bold story did not much please the tory party, but they would not wreak their revenge upon the woman who so unscrupulously avowed the cheat she had put upon the pursuers of a rebel. They contented themselves with ordering her to prepare them something to eat. She replied that she never fed traitors and king's men if she could help it-the villains having put it out of her

power to feed even her own family and friends, by stealing and killing all her poultry and pigs, "except that one old gobbler you see in the yard." " Well, and that you shall cook for us," said one who appeared to be a leader of the party; and raising his musket he shot down the turkey, which another of them brought into the house and handed to Mrs. Hart to be cleaned and cooked without delay. She stormed and swore awhile-for Nancy occasionally swore-but seeming at last disposed to make a merit of necessity, began with alacrity the arrangements for cooking, assisted by her daughter, a little girl ten or twelve years old, and sometimes by one of the party, with whom she seemed in a tolerably good humor-now and then exchanging rude jests with him. The tories, pleased with her freedom, invited her to partake of the liquor they had brought with them-an invitation which was accepted with jocose thanks. The spring-of which every settlement has one near by-was just at the edge of the swamp; and a short distance within the swamp was hid among the trees a high snag-topped stump, on which was placed a conch shell. This rude trumpet was used by the family to convey information, by variations in its notes, to Mr. Hart or his neighbors, who might be at work in a field, or "clearing," just beyond the swamp; to let them know that the" Britishers" or tories were about-that the master was wanted at the cabin-or that he was to keep close, or "make tracks" for another swamp. Pending the operation of cooking the turkey, Nancy had sent her daughter Sukey to the spring for water, with directions to blow the conch for her father in such a way as should inform him there were tories in the cabin; and that he was to "keep close" with his three neighbors who were with him, until he should again hear the conch. The party had become merry over their jug, and sat down to feast upon the slaughtered gobbler. They had cautiously stacked their arms where they were in view and within reach; and Mrs. Hart, assiduous in her attentions upon the table and to her guests, occasionally passed between the men and their muskets. Water was called for; and our heroine having contrived that there should be none in the cabin, Sukey was a second time despatched to the spring, with instructions to blow such a signal on the conch as should call up Mr. Hart and his neighbors immediately. Meanwhile Nancy had managed, by slipping out one of the pieces of pine which form a "chinking" between the logs of a cabin, to open a space through which she was able to pass to the outside two of the five guns. She was detected in the act of putting out the third. The whole party sprang to their feet; when quick as thought Nancy brought the piece she held, to her shoulder, declaring she would kill the first man who approached her. All were terror struck; for Nancy's obliquity of sight caused each to imagine himself her destined victim. At length one of them made a movement to advance upon her; and true to her threat, she fired and shot him dead! Seizing another musket, she levelled it instantly, keeping the others at bay. By this time Sukey had returned from the spring; and taking up the remaining gun, she carried it out of the house, saying to her mother-- "Daddy and them will soon be here." This information much increased the alarm of the tories, who perceived the importance of recovering their arms immediately; but each one hesitated, in the confident belief that Mrs. Hart had one eye at least on him for a mark. They proposed a general rush. No time was to be lost by the bold woman; -she fired again, and brought down another of the enemy. Sukey had another musket in readiness, which her mother took, and posting herself in the doorway, called upon the party to surrender" their d- - tory carcasses to a whig woman." They agreed to surrender, and proposed to "shake hands upon the strength of it." But the victor, unwilling to trust their word, kept them in their places for a few minutes, till her husband and his neighbors came up to the door. They were about to shoot down the tories, but Mrs. Hart stopped them, saying they had surrendered to her; and her spirit being up to boiling heat, she swore that "shooting was too good for them." This hint was enough; the dead man was dragged out of the house; and the wounded tory and the others were bound, taken out beyond the bars and hung! The tree upon which they were suspended was shown in 1828 by one who lived in those bloody times, and who also pointed out the spot once occupied by Mrs. Hart's cabin; accompanying the mention of her name with the emphatic remark-" Poor Nancy! she was a honey of a patriot but the devil of a wife!"

[418] Davis, *The Battle of Kettle Creek*, p. 97; Davis, *Georgia Citizens And Soldiers of the American Revolution,* pp. 163, 168; Heitman, *Historical Register of Officers,* p. 200

[419] Stroud had joined the British at Alexander's Old Field, but had switched sides after the attack there. Joe Wade had also switched sides that day, but he was not hanged and only received a thousand lashes"

[420] *Winn's Notes*, SCHGM Volume XLIII, Number 4, p. 209; Moss, *Roster of the South Carolina Patriots*, p. 427; Draper, *Sumter Papers*

[421] Also known as 2nd Hanging Rock or Cole's Old Field. The battle site is located in Lancaster County, east of the county line road which runs south of Heath Springs

[422] Sumter wrote in a letter to Pinckney that he had 600 men at Hanging Rock. Major Joseph McJunkin wrote, "The British had 278 and the Tory Militia had maybe 1,400, but more likely did not exceed 6 or 700. Sumter had 540, since a part was left to take care of the horses. Not more than 500 went into action"

[423] Captain John Miller was also in the battle. He was born in Ireland and came to America at the age of 15. I do not know which regiment John Miller was in. During the battle he was wounded in the ankle. He was taken to the hospital in Charlotte, but he refused to have his leg amputated. He died of his wounds.

[424] Jamieson was wounded in this battle and was sent to Charlotte to recover. He was captured enroute and brought before General Cornwallis. Cornwallis tried to convince him to switch sides, but he refused. He was carried to the hospital in Charlotte, and his wound broke open during the move. While in Charlotte he witnessed the panic of the British soldiers when they heard that Ferguson had been killed and his army captured. He was released on parole, but due to his wounds he never took the field again. He was only twenty-four.

[425] Lieutenant Hillhouse took command of Jamieson's company when he was wounded. John Hillhouse told Sumter that his grandfather, John Hillhouse, took the command and not William Hillhouse

[426] Also listed as Lisle, Lyles and Lile

[427] Crawford was born in Ireland and had been captured at the siege of Charlestown. After he was paroled he joined Sumter with the rank of major.

[428] Hugh McClure assumed command of the company when John McClure was mortally wounded

[429] Winn wrote to Hugh McCall after the war and told him that "you must understand our men was always mounted, their arms chiefly Rifles"

[430] Possibly Captain Daniel Coleman

[431] Sometimes mentioned as the refugees

[432] Also listed as Ervin

[433] Mecklenburg County Militia

[434] Davie wrote that after the first action at Hanging Rock his forces grew, "the North Carolina Militia under Col° Irwin and Major Davie numbered five hundred effective men Officers and privates, and about three hundred South Carolinians remained with Colonels Sumter, Hill, Lacy and others." Hill wrote that Davie had about eighty men who "behaved well."

[435] Draper wrote that "after the death of King Haigler the Catawbas only had a general a their head, first New River then General Scott

[436] McJunkin wrote that the Catawbas were "not more than 70 or 80 gunmen" in 1780. The actual commander of the Catawba militia is confusing. I believe it was based more upon tribal customs than any military organization. The commander of the Catawbas is listed as different men, depending on which account it is. Most agree that it is either New River or one of the Ayers brothers

[437] John Rosser told Draper that there were many Ayers brothers, General Jacob, Billy, John and Jesse. "They was very much alike... John Ayers was the greatest Indian of them all. Jesse was the greatest drunk of them all. I never knew the others as drinking men."

[438] The killed included Major McClure and Captain Reed. The wounded included Colonels Hill, Watson and Winn, Captains Flenniken, Otterson, Jamieson and Craighead, and Captain Bishop mortally wounded

[439] Samuel McCalla was born after the Revolutionary War, but he wrote Draper that Joseph Gaston told him "the regiment of British troops were Highlanders, dressed in Highland style kilts". This seems very unlikely, since there were no Highlanders there and none of the Loyalist units in the battle had kilts. By the time of the Carolina campaign the only unit that can be documented wearing kilts is the North Carolina Highland Regiment, who wore the cast off kilts of the 71st Regiment, so that they would have some clothing. Even this was temporary

[440] Captain McCulloch's company was originally raised as the English Volunteers. This company disbanded after August 1780 and its members distributed to other companies

[441] The British Legion uniform at this time was green jackets or coats

[442] William Dobein James wrote that the Prince of Wales American Regiment "had a detachment of the 63rd and 71st Regiments, amounting to about 400 infantry under Major Carden." Captain Thomas Hewlett, of the New York Volunteers was wounded in the battle, and later died in Camden

[443] Hill wrote that the British had "about 500 Regulars & about 800 Tories from N.Ca. commanded by Colonel Bryan." McJunkin said that there were 400 British Regulars and 1,400 Tories. The "regulars" that are mentioned would have been the Provincials

[444] William Dobein James wrote that Captain David Kinlock led the cavalry

[445] Captain McDonald was the son of Flora McDonald, the Scottish heroine who helped Bonnie Prince Charlie

[446] Captain McCulloch was mortally wounded, and died in Camden on August 16th. He was 45 years old

[447] Daniel Stinson wrote that the British were surprised because it had rained heavily the day before. They thought all of the rivers were impossible to cross, and therefore safe against any attack

[448] An army often constructed Bush huts when they did not have any tents. This was a construction made of limbs lashed together to form a frame, and then covered by pine or cedar branches, or some other type of material to create a roof. In the War Between the States this became known as a "shebang"

[449] In a later war the "Indian Halloo" would be known as a "Rebel Yell"

[450] The Prince of Wales Regiment was also called "Browne's Corps", after its commanding officer, General Montfort Browne, who had been captured in the raid on Nassau on 4 March 1776. Other historians have mistakenly placed Thomas Brown's King's Rangers at this battle, but they were never in that part of South Carolina. This confusion may be due to the mistaken identity of "Browne's Corps"

[451] Colonel Watson's son in law was killed during the battle. Stinson wrote that in another battle Watson was saved "by his Cartridge box stopping a musket ball- He always carried upturned a Large English Musket as he said for self defense"

[452] Daniel Stinson also wrote "McClure was badly wounded in the first fire, but plugging his thigh with wadding he rushed ahead of his command; and high above the din of the battle and the shrieks of the wounded, his shrill voice was heard urging them on. Just as the Tories fled he fell pierced by several wounds. Those near him ran up to his relief. He ordered them back into the fight, and as he lay bleeding his voice was still heard urging them forward. His command was dreadfully cut up, sustaining the largest share of the whole loss."

[453] Robert Mursh was also known as Marsh, or Mush. Doctor Alexander Bradley thought that Mursh was a Tuscarora, since his father had come from Virginia. However in his pension statement Mursh wrote that he was a Pamunkey Indian. This may be the same Pamunkey Indian who had enlisted in 1776 in the 15th Virginia Regiment. He fought at Brandywine and Germantown and was at Valley Forge. After serving two years he reenlisted in the "remnants of the 7th and 15th Regiment ... denominated

the 1st Virginia Regiment" and was at the siege of Charlestown." The only contradiction between the Robert Mursh of the 15th Virginia, and the one at Hanging Rock, is that in his pension the 15th Virginia Mursh wrote that he "was taken prisoner, but exchanged after 14 months." Interestingly both of the men ended up in York District, South Carolina, so it seems likely that it is the same person, and this may have been a bit of confusion from a 62 year old pensioner. Daniel Stinson heard him preach after the war at Hopewell Baptist Church. He said his hands "were cut all to pieces by Sabre wounds"

[454] After the war Winn would show people his uniform he wore at the battle. It was a "military coat" that was "shot through one arm, the ball entering the body, ranged around the ribs and out the other side, and through the other arm."

[455] The Earl of Cavan described street firing as "That absurd form of street fire;" and absurd I must beg leave to call it, and for the following reasons. In our present discipline we practise two methods of street firing; the one is, by making the division that has fired, to wheel afterwards by half ranks to the right and left outwards from the centre, and to march in that order by half-divisions down the flanks on each side of the Column, and to draw up in the rear, and there go on with their priming and loading. The other method is, to make the division, on having fired, to face to the right and left outwards from the centre, and one half rank to follow the other; and in that order to march in one entire file down on each side of the Column into the rear, and there draw up as before"

[456] British reports list the regiment as having lost 93 men killed, wounded or captured out of 181. Seventeen more would die within a month, due to disease

[457] This was Captain Kenneth McCulloch of the British Legion

[458] McCulloch was taken to Camden, where he died a month later

[459] "Irving" was Colonel Robert Irwin

[460] The McJunkin account leaves out any mention of Davie, or of the British forming square, or of Sumter's men getting drunk. He instead wrote that Sumter retreated because "some prisoners told Sumter that Colonel Turnbull was camped four miles away"

[461] Another sources says that the Legion lost 35 men killed and wounded

[462] Walkup told Draper that Craighead had been wounded at Guilford Courthouse, but that was not possible, since he wasn't there. She did say that the Indian visited Craighead once a year, after the war ended. J.C.

English wrote that the Indian saved him by carrying water to him during the battle, and dressing his wounds, until his friends arrived
[463] Captain James Jamieson, who was wounded in this battle, said that Sumter lost 65 men killed
[464] According to Webster's dictionary of 1828, "A stand of arms consists of a musket, bayonet, cartridge-box and belt, with a sword. But for common soldiers a sword is not necessary."
[465] Lorenzo Sabine, *Biographical Sketches of Loyalists of the American Revolution, Volume 2*, (Baltimore, 1994), p. 58; Davies, *Documents*, Volume XVIII Transcripts 1780, pp. 147-148; Thomas, *The Dye is Cast*, pp. 25-26; Robert D. Bass, *Green Dragoon*, (Columbia SC, 1973), p. 96; *Winn's Notes*, SCHGM Volume XLIII, Number 4, pp. 209-212; Tarleton, *History of the Campaigns*, pp. 95-96; White, *King's Mountain Men*, pp. 198, 229; DeMond, Loyalists, p. 61; Clark, *Loyalists in the Southern Campaign, Volume I*, pp. 147, 361-362; National Archives of Canada, RG 8, "C" Series, Volume 1883, pp. 16, 26; Schenck, *North Carolina 1780-'81*, pp. 69-74; Lossing, *Pictorial Field-Book*; DAR, *Roster of Soldiers from North Carolina*, p. 45; Moss, *Roster of the South Carolina Patriots*, pp. 5, 34, 70, 427, 604; Pension Applications, RG 15, Microcopy 804; Robinson, *Revolutionary War Sketches*, pp. 13-16; Lambert, *South Carolina Loyalists*, p. 117; Clark, *State Records of North Carolina, Volumes XIV- 1779-'80*, pp. 540-543; Clark, *The State Records of North Carolina, Vol. XIX - 1782 - '84*, pp. 972-973; Pancake, *This Destructive War*, pp. 97-98; *Royal Georgia Gazette, September 7, 1780*; George Hanger, *An Address to the Army in Reply to Strictures, by Roderick M'Kenzie on Tarleton's history of the Campaigns of 1780 and 1781* (London, 1789); *William Hill's Memoirs*; Saye, *McJunkin*; Draper, *Sumter Papers*, 4VV134-135, 5VV83, 7VV43, 9VV51, 167-168, 241-243, 275, 280-285, 10VV16, 11VV206-207, 329-332, 14VV254-257, 452-460; New York Commercial Advertiser, (Volume XXXI, No. 48, August 15, 1823)
[466] Also known as 2nd Cedar Springs, Berwick's Iron Works, Green Springs, Buffington's Iron Works or the Peach Orchard. This action has many different versions, depending on the source. One source states that Ferguson and Dunlap had 2,500 men, and lost a hundred men. Another source writes that Dunlap was not there, but Colonel Innes was. The location is different in each source. It happens in a peach orchard, or in an old iron works, or in a small town. The date is also different, depending on the source. Haywood wrote that it was on August 1st; McCall wrote it was

August 10th; McClaine says it was August 8th. Even the time of day is disputed in the different versions. Depending on the source it either happened at the dark of night, the early morning twilight, or in the afternoon. This confusion is typical of the backwoods encounters between the British and the frontiersmen

[467] McJunkin wrote that Clarke had 168 men

[468] The killed included Major Smith and Captain Potts. The wounded included Major Robertson and Captain Clark

[469] Mounted as cavalry

[470] Fair Forest Militia

[471] McJunkin wrote that the enemy consisted "of 150 volunteer mounted riflemen and sixty well equipped dragoons"

[472] Anthony Allaire wrote that they had 20-30 killed or wounded

[473] Draper wrote that Mrs. Dilliard is no doubt the one who gave Shelby and Clarke intelligence at Cedar Spring. Elizabeth Ellet agreed with Draper and wrote, "They inquired of Mrs. Dillard whether Clarke and his men had not been there; what time they had departed; and what were their numbers? She answered that they had been at the house; that she could not guess their numbers; and that they had been gone a long time. The officers then ordered her to prepare supper for them with all possible despatch. They took possession of the house, and took some bacon to be given to their men. Mrs. Dillard set about the preparations for supper. In going backwards and forwards from the kitchen, she overheard much of their conversation. It will be remembered that the kitchens at the South are usually separate from the dwelling-houses. The doors and windows of houses in the country being often slightly constructed, it is also likely that the loose partitions afforded facilities for hearing what might be said within. Besides, the officers probably apprehended no danger from disclosing their plans in the presence of a lonely woman. She ascertained that they had determined to surprise Clarke and his party; and were to pursue him as soon as they had taken their meal. She also heard one of the officers tell Ferguson he had just received the information that the rebels, with Clarke, were to encamp that night at the Great Spring. It was at once resolved to surprise and attack them before day. The feelings may be imagined with which Mrs. Dillard heard this resolution announced. She hurried the supper, and as soon as it was placed upon the table, and the officers had sat down, slipped out by a back way. Late and dark as it was, her determination was to go herself and apprize Clarke of his danger, in the

hope of being in time for him to make a. safe retreat; for she believed that the enemy were too numerous to justify a battle. She went to the stable, bridled a young horse, and without saddle, mounted and rode with all possible speed to the place described. It was about half an hour before day when she came in full gallop to one of the videttes, by whom she was immediately conducted to Colonel Clarke. She called to the colonel, breathless with eagerness and haste, "Be in readiness either to fight or run; the enemy will be upon you immediately, and they are strong!" In an instant every man was up, and no moments were lost in preparing for action."

[474] Joseph McJunkin said that Culbertson frequently commanded, but he did not hold a commission until the end of the war, when he was made a captain

[475] Ironically the Loyalist Alexander Chesney had used this same tactic against McDowell's militia in July. After Chesney had left McDowell's camp he "was taken at Grindal Shoals by a party of Rebels under Eusaw Smith and Desmond, who took from me a Rifle gun borrowed of John Heron my brother in law; but as soon as they set out for the rebel camp, I made my escape and joined Col. Ferguson at Culbered and received his thanks and friendship. On the 9th August I was appointed Capt. and assistant Adjutant General to the different battalions under Col. Ferguson."

[476] Davis, *Georgians*, p. 128; Heitman, *Historical Register*, p. 449; Draper, *Kings Mountain*, pp. 91-93, 423; White, *King's Mountain Men*, pp. 108-109, 158, 220-221; Cashin, *King's Ranger*, p. 113; Schenck, *North Carolina*, pp. 77-78; DAR, *Roster of Soldiers from North Carolina*, p. 45; Lambert, *South Carolina Loyalists*, pp. 110-111, 123; Saye, *McJunkin*; Chesney, *Journal*; Draper, *Sumter Papers*, 16VV402-405; Ellet, *Women of the American Revolution*

[477] Major General De Kalb was a fifty nine year old "giant" who had risen from Bavarian peasant to French officer, and the husband of a young heiress. He had been working for an American rebellion since 1768, when he was a French agent in America trying to gauge how much discontent there was. De Kalb had arrived in June 1777 with the Marquis De La Fayette at North Inlet in Georgetown, South Carolina

[478] Near present day Fort Bragg

[479] When Porterfield had left Virginia he had a detachment of Virginia State garrison troops, two troops of cavalry, and a large detachment of men from Col. Thomas Marshall's Virginia State Artillery Regiment. Many of

the men were taken from the garrisons in the harbor towns to form the detachment. They had been heading to Charlestown, but when they heard of the surrender and the defeat of Buford they moved towards the Continental army. Otho Williams wrote that Porterfield was "an officer of merit, who, after the disaster at Charleston, retired with a small detachment and found means of subsisting himself and his men in Carolina until the present time." One account mention that Porterfield's unit consisted of 420 infantry and 64 cavalry. Somewhere between Virginia and the rendezvous with Gates' army they had lost their artillery and their cavalry troops

[480] Davies, *Documents, Volume XVIII Transcripts 1780*, pp. 140-141; Kennedy, *Historic Camden*, pp. 143-159; Tarleton, *History of the Campaigns*, p. 99; Pension Applications, *RG 15, Microcopy 804*; James, *Sketch of the Life*, p. 17; Clark, *State Records of North Carolina, Volumes XIV- 1779-'80*, pp. 584-585; Richard John Batt, *The Maryland Continentals, 1780-1781*, (Tulane University Dissertation, 1974), pp. 24-25, 28-33; Davis, *Thomas Pinckney*, pp. 76-79; A.E. Miller, *Sketches of the Life, Volume I*, (Charleston, South Carolina), pp. 488, 493; William Johnson, *Sketches of the Life and Correspondence of Nathanael Greene, Major General of the Armies of the United States, In the War of the Revolution, Volume I*, (Charleston, 1822), pp. 488-489; A. Aspinall, Editor, *The Correspondence of George, Prince of Wales, 1770-1812, Volume 4*, (Oxford University Press 4:192-197), pp. 192-197

[481] Also known as Carey's Fort or Wateree Ferry

[482] Colonel Cary's first name is in dispute and some historians say it could have been either Matthew or James, however he signed a letter on November 15, 1780 with "James Cary"

[483] Captain John Taylor was the brother of Colonel Taylor

[484] James Harbison was one of Sumter's Irish militiamen. He wrote that there were 96 Highlanders captured. Doctor Alexander Bradley told Draper that Sumter had an artillery captain from Pennsylvania at Carey's Fort. The cannon was presented and the fort readily surrendered.

[485] White, *King's Mountain Men*, p. 198; Kennedy, *Historic Camden*, p. 153; Lawrence, *Hogback Country*, p. 105; Clark, *Loyalists in the Southern Campaign, Volume I*, p. 149; *Pennsylvania Gazette, September 13, 1780*; Moss, *Roster of the South Carolina Patriots*, pp. 5, 615-616; Clark, *State Records of North Carolina, Volumes XIV- 1779-'80*, pp. 540-543; Batt, *Maryland Continentals*, p. 41; Davis, *Thomas Pinckney* , p. 78; Johann

Christian Senf, *Extract from a Journal Concerning the Action of the 16th of August 1780 between Major General Gates and Gen. Lord Cornwallis,* (Manuscript Division, Library of Congress, Washington, D.C.); Hayes, *Saddlebag Almanac, Volume VII*, pp. 54-55; Miller, *Sketches of the Life,* pp. 494; John Austin Stevens, *The Southern Campaign, 1780, Gates At Camden,* (Magazine of American History, Volume V, No. 4, October 1880), pp. 265-266; Draper, *Sumter Papers,* 1VV189, 5VV262, 7VV27-28
[486] Chesney, *Journal*
[487] Also known as Gum Swamp, Saunder's Creek, Green Swamp and Sutton's Tavern
[488] Consisting of Porterfield's State Troops and 150 men from the General Stevens' Virginia Militia. The men were to be "the most experienced woodsmen, and men every way the fittest for the service" however Guilford Dudley wrote that the men joined right before the skirmish and they were "200 exhausted raw Virginia militia, and Col. Armand's corps of dragoons"
[489] Senf was an engineer who had been sent ahead to find the place for Gates's planned defensive works. He did not take part in the battle, but was detached to Sumter. Senf did arrive right at the end of the fight, and later made a map of the battle
[490] Sergeant Major William Seymour, of the Delaware Line, wrote that the action happened at Sutton's Tavern. The same engagement is also called Gum Swamp, or Green Swamp, but the ground was elevated beside these swamps. The first battle of Camden would happen eight miles north of the town of the same name. The battlefield has recently been purchased and the ground is being restored to what it looked like in 1780
[491] In that time Porterfield's men fired about five rounds
[492] Davies, *Documents, Volume XVIII Transcripts 1780,* pp. 149-150; Henry B. Carrington, *Battles of the American Revolution, 1775-1781, Historical and Military Criticism, with Topographic Illustration,* (A.S. Barnes & Company, 1876), p. 515; William Seymour, *A Journal of the Southern Expedition, 1780-1783,* (The Historical Society of Delaware, Wilmington, 1896), p. 5; Kennedy, *Historic Camden,* pp. 143-159; Tarleton, *History of the Campaigns,* pp. 99-110, 143; Great Britain, Public Record Office, *Cornwallis Papers,* Volume 103, folio 2; Pension Applications, RG 15, Microcopy 804; *Pennsylvania Gazette, September 13, 1780*; James, *Sketch of the Life,* p. 17; Clark, *State Records of North Carolina, Volumes XIV- 1779-'80,* pp. 584-585; H. L. Landers, *The Battle*

of Camden, South Carolina, August 16, 1780, (United States Government Printing Office, Washington, 1929), pp. 41-42; Batt, *Maryland Continentals*, pp. 24-25, 28-33; Davis, *Thomas Pinckney*, pp. 78-81, 86-88; Hayes, *Saddlebag Almanac*, Volume VII, pp. 43-53; PRO, War Office, 30 *June 1780, List of all the Officers of the Army*, p. 86; John Maas, *"That Unhappy Affair" Horatio Gates and the Battle of Camden, August 16, 1781*, (The Kershaw County Historical Society, 2000), p. 34; Guilford Dudley, *A Sketch of the Military Services Performed by Guilford Dudley, Then of the Town of Halifax, North Carolina, During the Revolutionary War*, (Literary Messenger, 1845), Part II, pp. 146-148, Part III pp. 231-235; Johnson, *Sketches of the Life*, p. 494; Charles Stedman, *The History of the Origin, Progress, and Termination of the American War, Volume II*, London 1794, pp. 205-207; Aspinall, *Correspondence of George*, pp. 192-197

[493] Also mentioned as "Gates Defeat"

[494] "Baron" DeKalb's royal title was fictitious. He was the son of a Bavarian peasant

[495] Captain Hoops may have been with the detachment with Woolford, and may have been captured at Fishing Creek, instead of Camden

[496] With remnants of Pulaski's Cavalry

[497] Captain Fierer is also known as Charles Friderich Fuehrer. He was born in 1756 in Felsberg, Germany and had been an ensign in a Hessian regiment, under the command of General Von Knyphausen. He was captured at Trenton on Christmas 1776 by Washington's army. He was sent to a prisoner camp at Dumfries, Virginia, and a year later he received pardon. He enlisted in the Virginia militia and by 1780 he had risen to the rank of captain. After the war Virginia awarded him 4,000 acres of land as a reward for his services. He founded the first newspaper in Georgetown and the first glass factory in Maryland. He was the first Mason in Washington and his lodge brother was George Washington. He fought for the founding of D.C. on the Potomac through his editorials. He died in 1794

[498] Also listed as the 11th Company of the Continental Artillery, or Dorsey's Maryland Artillery Company

[499] Also listed as the 12th Company of the Continental Artillery or Singleton's Virginia Artillery Company

[500] Shenandoah County Militia

[501] Northumberland County Militia

[502] Spotsylvania Militia

[503] Goochland County Militia

[504] Lockhart had been a Lieutenant Colonel in the 8th North Carolina Regiment, but he resigned after the battle of Germantown, "on account of his indisposition."

[505] There is a lot of confusion as to who was at this battle. Militiamen who were there stated that they were with a certain regiment or commander, but there is no way to know where they were on the field. I have placed many of the county militias in this order of battle based upon their geographic closeness to other counties back in their home States, but it is only a guess.

[506] It is not known where this regiment was assigned. I have placed it here in the geographic location to other counties

[507] In William Strong's pension application he states "That Rutherford's brigade and perhaps others were divided into platoons before the battle began and the Captains had command of their platoons instead of their companies; and that this applicant commanded a platoon on that memorable day, instead of his company". Davie wrote "the whole of the militia wanted arrangement and the ordinary preparation for a battle was intirely neglected among them, in Rutherfords Brigade there was scarce a cartridge made up, and their arms were generally in bad order; the consequence of continual marching & exposure"

[508] Also listed as John Armstrong

[509] After the fall of Charlestown there were North Carolina Continentals who had escaped capture by the British. This would have been officers who had retired on half pay, had been furloughed, were on recruiting duty, or were on leave when Charleston fell. There were North Carolina Continentals, who had been sent home on leave before Charlestown fell, that had contracted smallpox during the spring of 1780. At Camden there were twenty-five North Carolina Continentals in Dixon's Regiment, and these were in Captain Edward Yarborough's company. Yarborough would command some of these same North Carolina Continentals at Guilford Courthouse seven months later. There may have been another North Carolina Continental company there, under Captain William Lytle. There is a good chance that the reason that Colonel Dixon's militia did not run, but instead decided to stand and fight with the Maryland Continentals, is because of these Continentals, possibly two companies, who would not leave their Maryland comrades. Yarborough's men are also mentioned as protecting the artillery. Ten of those 25 North Carolina Continentals were

wounded in the battle. The names of the ten wounded men were Thomas Weeks, John Atkinson, Thomas Dobbin, Eli Crockett, William Wright, Zack Gallop, Thomas Clarke, Jardin and Kedar Harrel, William Powel, and James Wharton

[510] William Polk had been wounded in the left shoulder at the battle of the Cane Break in 1775. He was a major in the 9th North Carolina Regiment and was wounded in the cheek at the battle of Brandywine. Because of this wound he was "deprived of the power of speech" for a short period. Stinson wrote that it "rendered him a cripple", though he was commanding troops on the field afterwards

[511] Also listed as Aksom or Axum

[512] Also known as the 2nd Regiment of Virginia Militia

[513] It is not known what unit this company was assigned to. I have placed it here in the geographic location to other counties. There was another Colonel Elias Edmunds, but he was in the Virginia artillery. This may be the same person, and the unit was manning Virginia artillery

[514] Also listed as Richeson

[515] It is not known what unit this company was assigned to. I have placed it here in the geographic location to other counties

[516] Also listed as the 4th Regiment of Virginia Militia in the pension account of James Hopkins. The four regiments would have been the militias of Colonel George Stubblefield, Lieutenant Colonel Holt Richardson, Lieutenant Colonel Ralph Faulkner and Colonel James Lucas

[517] After their return to Amherst County these men were punished for fleeing the battlefield. They were ordered to serve eight months in Greene's Army, where they guarded the supply wagons as they delivered their goods. They were known as the "8 months men"

[518] Also listed as Dorman. Unable to find any information on this officer

[519] Major Conway was a Continental officer in the 3rd Virginia Regiment

[520] It is not known what unit this company was assigned to. I have placed it here in the geographic location to other counties

[521] Captain Waller was a Continental officer in the 3rd Virginia Regiment

[522] Most likely less than thirty men

[523] John Barkley told Draper that Cathey was "captured at Camden, was only a 1st Lieutenant, but commanded a company. He was 6 feet, 6 inches tall and 220 pounds. He died later in Charleston of yellow fever"

[524] After the night march only 3,052 were fit for duty

[525] Patriot losses have never been accurately determined. Boatner's *Encyclopedia of the American Revolution* estimated that 188 were killed, the rest were wounded and captured. The killed included Major General de Kalb, Captains William, Starns, Roach and Duvall. Among the wounded were Captains Somervell, Gibson, Morris, Gaffaway, Harman, and Roun. The captured included Lieutenant Colonels Adam, Forrest and Vaughan, Majors Winder, Pinckney and Patton, Captains Brice, Hoops, Lynch, Hamilton, Smith, Dorsey, de Bellecour, Rhoads and Lamont, Captain-Lieutenant Waters. Marion's Partisans rescued 147 Continentals who had been captured when they were en route to Charleston. The rest of the prisoners were placed in prison ships in Charleston where many of them died. Some of the prisoners won release by joining the British forces in Jamaica.

[526] One source lists that the Fusiliers only had three companies in the battle, however the muster rolls of the dead and wounded from the 23rd Regiment lists eight companies of the regiment (one of these companies was Lieutenant Colonel Balfour's). The 23rd had six rank and file killed, Captain James Drury and seventeen rank & file were wounded

[527] The 33rd Regiment only had five companies in the battle. Mentioned in accounts are some wounded officers at the battle, such as Captain Richard Cotton, who must not have had a command

[528] There were a total of five companies from the two battalions in the battle; this included the two light infantry companies under Captain Charles Campbell. These companies formed a composite battalion. Lieutenant Archibald Campbell and eight soldiers were killed. Captain Hugh Campbell, Lieutenant John Grant, two sergeants and thirty privates were wounded. There is a bit of a debate among historians as to whether any Highlander Regiment wore kilts in the South during 1780-1781. The Camden battlefield has recently been purchased and is being turned into a historic park. There are the remains of many soldiers on the battlefield, who were buried where they lay after the battle. A grave of a Highlander was found that had brass or britania metal one-piece flat buttons in it, indicating that they were wearing trousers and not kilts in this battle

[529] This is the remnants of the light infantry that had been under the command of Colin Graham in Charlestown

[530] This was a composite company made up of the two companies from the two battalions of the 71st Regiment. Some historians mistakenly claim that the light infantry of the 71st returned to New York with General Clinton

[531] Additionals were men from the Regular regiments who helped man the cannons

[532] Major Hanger came to America in 1776 as a Captain in the Hessian Jäger Corps. The Jäger Corps were part of the Hessian forces recruited by Great Britain to help put down the rebellion in America. Hanger participated in the siege of Charlestown, and after the fall of the city he was appointed a Brevet Major of Militia, with the duty of raising local militia to assist the British Army. He and Tarleton had become friends during the campaign and Tarleton wrote to Clinton requesting that he be reassigned to him, as a Major of Legion Cavalry. This was granted on August 6, 1780

[533] This unit was largely made up of Irish deserters from the American army

[534] 154 of the 202 were without arms

[535] The killed included Captain Malcolm and Lieutenant Archibald Campbell. The wounded included Lieutenant Colonels Webster and Hamilton, Captains Cotton, Drury and Hugh Campbell

[536] This may have been the morning gun from the Camden garrison, or the opening shots of the battle of Camden

[537] After Porterfield was taken prisoner he wrote that he was "without any surgeon to attend me." A surgeon visited him once from the Maryland line that was also a prisoner. Porterfield wrote to Gates "The British officers at Rugley's have treated me with the utmost attention and politeness, and have furnished me with such necessaries as in their power. I have to pray a surgeon will be sent to attend me for some time." Several days later, Porterfield died of his wounds

[538] Camden was not a battle fought in an open field, as many have imagined, but was a battle in the woods. The trees were long leaf pine, and there was not much underbrush underneath the trees. It is easy to see for hundreds of yards through woods such as these, since the trees are spaced apart. Woods of this sort can still be seen on the numerous Military Reservations in the Carolinas, where the long leaf pine forests thrive in a natural state

[539] When the two armies clashed in the initial fight at Gum Swamp, many of Gates's baggage wagons were still at the start point at Rugeley's Mill, and had not even moved forward yet. Even when the battle happened the next day, many of the wagons were still Rugeley's

[540] The battlefield of Camden is being restored to its original condition. This is a slow painstaking process, so that any artifacts can be cataloged. George Fields is one of the experts working at the site and he believes that no rifles were used at Camden due to the artifacts that have been found. Only one account in Draper mentions a rifle, and that was written in the 19th century

[541] Hundreds of soldiers were captured, including twelve Black soldiers. One of these Black soldiers was named Levi. In 1835 Levi advertised to sell his musket in the "Camden Journal and Southern Whig". It stated, "The musket belonging to Levi, a French negro, who was brought over by Lafayette and fought during the entire Revolution, was found bedded in the mud in Gum Swamp, where Levi had hidden it, being wounded at Gates's defeat. The barrel is badly eaten with rust, the bayonet eaten and broken. The powder flashed on being fired."

[542] Garden, *Anecdotes*, p. 208; Brooklyn Historical Society, *Mss Book* 42, folio 27; Johnston and Guertin, *Collections of the Connecticut Historical Society Revolution Rolls and Lists*, p. 429; Davies, *Documents, Volume XVIII Transcripts 1780*, pp. 149-152; Boatner, *Encyclopedia*, pp. 168-169; Balch, *French in America*, pp. 147-148; Kennedy, *Historic Camden*, pp. 146-198; Tarleton, *History of the Campaigns*, pp. 99-110, 136-140, 143, 150-153, 170; Heitman, *Historical Register*, pp. 63, 74-89, 97-113, 121, 124-131, 201, 209, 244, 247, 262, 270, 273, 300, 314, 343, 361, 383, 402, 454, 464, 509, 559, 575, 596, 600, 635; Duncan, *Royal Regiment of Artillery*; Cannon, *Historical Record*, pp. 31-32, Johnson, *Memo of Occurrence*, pp. 302-304; Clark, *Loyalists in the Southern Campaign, Volume I*, pp. 95-96, 147-148, 361-362; *Volume II*, p. 256; *Volume III*, pp. 267-323; Moultrie, *Memoirs, Vol. II*, pp. 231-237; William H. Sparks, *The Memories of Fifty Years*, (J.W. Burke & Co. 1870); National Archives and Records Administration, *William Armstrong Pension File, #S30831, William Beasley Pension File, #W9352, James Hopkins Pension File, #W3553, Willoughby Blackard # S29638, Dan Alexander Pension File #S2905, William Kelly Pension File #W25993*, (Washington, DC); Schenck, *North Carolina 1780-'81*, pp. 92-94; Robert Kirkwood, *The Journal and Order Book of Captain Robert Kirkwood of the Delaware Regiment of the Continental Line, Part I, "A Journal of the Southern Campaign" 1780-1782*, (edited by Rev. Joseph Brown Tucker, Kennikat Press, 1970), p. 11; *Pennsylvania Gazette, September 13, 1780*; PRO, *Headquarters Papers of the British Army in America*, p. 2482; PRO,

Cornwallis Papers, Volume 103, p. 2; PRO, *War Office*, Class 65, Volumes 30, p. 113; PRO, *Cornwallis Papers*, Class 30, Volume 11, folio 3; DAR, *Roster of Soldiers from North Carolina*, pp. 25-37; Dann, *Revolution Remembered*, pp. 214-216; Pension Applications, *RG 15, Microcopy 804*; Robinson, *Revolutionary War Sketches*, pp. 16-18, 34-35; Lambert, *South Carolina Loyalists*, pp. 115, 117, 119; Roderick Mackenzie, *Strictures on Lieut. Colonel Tarleton's History of the Southern Campaigns of 1780 & 1781*, (London, 1787), pp. 110-113; James, *Sketch of the Life*, pp. 16-17; Clark, *State Records of North Carolina, Volume XXII*, pp. 523-524; Stevens, *Southern Campaign*, pp. 248, 254, 273, 277; Clinton, *American Rebellion*, pp. 452-454; Landers, *Battle of Camden*, pp. 42-50; Christopher Ward, *The Delaware Continentals*, (Historical Society of Delaware, 1941), p. 486; Pancake, *This Destructive War*, pp. 91-92, 101-106; Batt, *Maryland Continentals*, pp. 12, 17, 19, 24-25, 33, 35-41; Davis, *Thomas Pinckney*, pp. 87, 92-93; Hayes, *Saddlebag Almanac, Volume VII*, pp. 8-16, 43-53; *Volume VIII*, pp. 12, 40; Dudley, *Sketch, Part III*, pp. 234-235, *Part IV*, p. 284; McAllister, *Virginia Militia*, pp. 16, 23, 26-27, 35, 37, 122, 139, 158, 168; Sanchez-Saavedera, *Virginia Military Organizations*, pp. 94, 123-127, 142-143; PRO, *War Office, List of all the Officers of the Army*, pp. 86, 93; Albert Lee, *History of the Thirty-Third Foot*, (Jarrold & Sons Ltd, The Empire Press, Norwich. 1922); National Archives of Canada, *RG 8, "C" Series, Volume 1887*; Richard Cannon, *History of the Twenty-Third Regiment, or Royal Welsh Fusiliers, 1689-1850*, (Parker, Furnival & Parker, London 1847), pp. 104-106; PRO, *War Office, Class 12*, Volume 3960; Johnson, *Sketches of the Life*, p. 495; Stedman, *History*, p. 208; Draper, *Sumter Papers*, 4VV213-215

[543] Also known as Catawba Ford, Leonard's Old Fields, Sumter's Defeat or Sumter's Surprise. Daniel Stinson wrote that Sumter was insulted if anyone called it a defeat, and he always called it a surprise. The battle site is located in Chester County, on US 21, two miles north of Great Falls, but its exact location is in dispute

[544] Samuel Martin was with Sumter at Fishing Creek and wrote that Sumter had ten companies there

[545] Samuel McCalla wrote that "no stand worth the name was made, but among them that did try was Capt. Archibald Gill...his exertions on that occasion ever afterwards gave him the name of Mad Archy"

[546] James Pagan had been born in Antrim County, Ireland in 1746

[547] Taylor was described as "six feet, one inch high and finely proportioned wit an eagle eye and ruddy countenance"

[548] Smith wrote in his pension that his company was in Colonel Exum's Regiment, and was detached right before the Battle of Camden

[549] Captain Pagan was one of the killed. Colonel Woolford was among the wounded

[550] Captain Charles Campbell was among the killed

[551] Reverend McCalla wrote, "You never can get a true reliable account of it. Men, even officers, in the same battle, differ greatly in their statements. You heard of Sumter sleeping in a marquee. I don't believe there was a tent of any kind in the army. As soon as the army halted he lay down in the rear of his baggage wagon on a blanket, and from excessive fatigue, loss of sleep and anxiety, was asleep in three minutes... There were a few long bushes out and leaned against the waggon to keep the sun off." John Wheeler also wrote that Sumter was asleep under a wagon. Daniel Stinson wrote, "Sumpter captured 44 wagons loaded with munitions of war, probably a number of tents, if not wagon covers. This was the 18th of August in an open field. I have no doubt but Sumpter had a tent. If the men had not tents, they would make arbours of bushes. White men do not generally sleep in the sun."

[552] Draper said that Lacey also believed this. He wrote, "Just before the attack Sally Featherstone, a rather loose Tory woman, rode through camp, just as they stopped. He always believed she went to the Cowford and told Tarleton."

[553] Robert Walker was one of the men shooting beeves. He was able to escape

[554] Joseph White wrote that Major Robert Crawford "was blamed by his men in neglecting to put out proper guard. He was thirsty... he found a bottle of whiskey, which was taken down to a spring, where the major imbibed until he forgot Genl Sumter was waiting his return."

[555] This rum was part of the shipment that was captured at Cary's Fort

[556] Davie wrote "Col° Tarlton had the merit of audacity and good fortune but the glory of the enterprise was stained by the unfeeling barbarity of the legion who continued to hack and maim the militia long after they had surrendered, scarce a man was wounded until he considered himself a prisoner, and had deprived himself of the means of defence. Numbers of these were old gray headed-men, who had turned out to encourage &

animate the younger citizens." Ironically Davie's men did the same thing when they attacked the Loyalists at the first Hanging Rock

[557] She said that Tarleton had six boys who were his trumpeters

[558] The British buried Pagan before his friends were able to identify the body. It was never found

[559] Reverend McCalla wrote "At the first alarm Captain Steel, always on the alert, threw off his back to his horse, helped him to mount and he went off to try rally the men"

[560] Draper wrote that James Cary afterwards "never appeared in arms. He was evacuated with the British in 1782". However Cary was promoted to Colonel and placed back in command of his fort. Many of the British command, such as Cornwallis and Rawdon, did not find him a very effective officer. Patriot bands were constantly raiding him, and had his supplies, horses and slaves taken, or killed. When Camden was evacuated in 1781, Cary and his wife withdrew with the British Army.

[561] Another account states that George Peay did not die there, but "served till peace was declared"

[562] After she crossed the Yadkin, Tories stole her horse. She returned to South Carolina, and eventually married John Nickle (or Nichole). She was supposedly at the battle of Guilford Courthouse in March 1781, and three days after the battle she gave birth to a child "among strangers who treated her kindly". She lived to be 83 years old and died in 1836

[563] Taylor told Draper that Tarleton could have been defeated if Sumter had put the artillery in the road to drive back any enemy cavalry

[564] Collins, *Revolutionary Soldier*, pp. 41-43; Boatner, *Encyclopedia*, pp. 189, 368-369; Kennedy, *Historic Camden*, pp. 199-201; Tarleton, *History of the Campaigns,* pp. 111-116, 140; Cannon, *Historical Record*, pp. 30-31; White, *King's Mountain Men*, p. 458; Draper, *Kings Mountain*, pp. 198, 229; Moultrie, *Memoirs, Vol. II*, p. 235; Lee, *Revolutionary War Memoirs*, pp. 179-180, 189; Great Britain, Public Record Office, *Cornwallis Papers*, Class 30, Volume 11, folio 25; Moss, *Roster of the South Carolina Patriots*, pp. 4-5, 12; Robinson, *Revolutionary War Sketches*, pp. 18-21; Ervin, *South Carolinians*, pp. 80-87; Mackenzie, *Strictures*, pp. 110-113; Batt, *Maryland Continentals*, pp. 41-42; Hayes, *Saddlebag Almanac, January 1999, Volume VII*, pp. 54-57; Saye, *McJunkin*; Draper, *Sumter Papers*, 4VV213-215, 5VV267, 9VV9, 46-47, 10VV225, 227, 11VV336, 15VV90, 132

[565] Reports of this battle conflict, as do most fights in the backcountry of the Carolinas. The date is either August 18th or 19th

[566] David Hamilton wrote that after the surrender of Charlestown Hammond "collected a small force of 73 – some time afterwards dispersed themselves in the swamps & were taken by the British, but that he Hammond & the balance of succeeded getting away from. Rejoined Col. LeRoy Hammonds & retreated northward to join any troops that might find opposing the British invaders."

[567] Among the killed was Captain Inman. Captain Barry was one of the wounded

[568] The wounded included Colonel Innes, Major Fraser and Captains Hawsey and Campbell

[569] William Hill writes of a controversy with James Williams. When Williams first joined Sumter's force he was made the commissary. He was given 25 men and Horses, along with four wagons and teams. After the battle of Hanging Rock he and "Col. Brannon had eloped & taken a great number of the public horses, a considerable quantity of provisions with the camp equipage, & a number of men." Sumter sent Colonel Lacey after Williams and when the found them on the Catawba River Lacey was outnumbered. Lacey "presented a pistol to his breast & informed him that if he made any noise to call for assistance he was then a dead man." Williams gave his word that he would bring the items back. After Lacey went back, Williams took the supplies to Major McDowell in North Carolina and joined him right before the battle of Musgrove's Mill. There is a different version of the story by McJunkin that says Williams joined Sumter after Hanging Rock, and when Sumter was moving on Camden, Williams took men and moved on Ninety-Six

[570] Another account says that they withheld their fire until the Loyalists were 40 yards away

[571] Hairr, *Colonel David Fanning*, pp. 64-67; Lawrence E. Babits, *A Devil of a Whipping, The Battle of Cowpens*, (University of North Carolina Press, 1998), pp. 14-15; Heitman, *Historical Register,* p. 89; White, *King's Mountain Men*, pp. 103, 423; Draper, *Kings Mountain*, pp. 105-113, 146, 166, 181-182, 192, 204, 220-221; Clark, *Loyalists in the Southern Campaign, Volume I*, pp. 197-341; Moultrie, *Memoirs, Vol. II*, p. 220; Fanning, *Narrative*, pp. 32-33; Johnson, *Memo of Occurrence*, p. 66; Schenck, *North Carolina*, pp. 78-81; Caruthers, *Old North State*, pp. 35-36; Pension Applications, *RG 15, Microcopy 804*; Robinson,

Revolutionary War Sketches, p. 35; Lambert, *South Carolina Loyalists*, pp. 110-111, 133; Mackenzie, *Strictures*, pp. 25-26; *William Hill's Memoirs*; William T. Graves, *James Williams: An American Patriot in the Carolina Backcountry*, Writers Club Press, 2002, pp. 29, 32-33; Saye, *McJunkin*; Draper, *Sumter Papers*, 11VV361, 16VV210-212

[572] Chesney, *Journal*, p. 7

[573] The site of Great Savannah is currently under Lake Marion

[574] Another source lists this action happening on August 20th

[575] After the fall of Charlestown the remaining South Carolina Continentals were placed into two battalions, and designated as the 1st South Carolina Regiment. The 1st Battalion was under the command of Colonel Charles Pinckney, and was imprisoned in Charlestown. The 2nd Battalion was with Francis Marion and became part of his partisans

[576] In his account Marion said that one man, Josiah Cockfield, was killed. However William Dobein James wrote that Cockfield was shot through the breast but lived to fight and get wounded at another time

[577] Garden, *Anecdotes*, p. 441; Southern Studies Program, *Figures of the Revolution, Spartanburg*, pp. 282, 323-324; Simms, *Life of Francis Marion*, pp. 67-71; Moultrie, *Memoirs, Vol. II*, pp. 223-224; Robert D. Bass, *Swamp Fox, The life and campaigns of General Francis Marion*, (Sandlapper Publishing Company, 1974), pp. 40-45; James, *Sketch of the Life*, pp. 14-18; Ward, *Delaware Continentals*, p. 354

[578] Local deer hunters knew of the two artillery pieces for years afterwards.

[579] This was Amy's or Amis Mill, near the Lumber River. It was located near present day Fair Bluff, North Carolina

[580] Simms, *Life of Francis Marion*, p. 18; James, *Sketch of the Life*, pp. 74-76; Clark, *Loyalists in the Southern Campaign, Volume I*, pp. 98-100; PRO, *Cornwallis Papers*, Class 30, Volume 11, p. 79; Lambert, *South Carolina Loyalists*, p. 115; Bass, *Swamp Fox*, pp. 37-38

[581] Kell, *North Carolina's Coastal Carteret County*, p. 69

[582] Also known as Port's Ferry or Little Pee Dee River. Blue Savannah is currently located a short distance southeast of Ariel Crossroads at the intersection of US 501 and SC 41. This is near Gallivant's Ferry

[583] Mounted as cavalry

[584] Simms, *Francis Marion*, pp. 69-71; Clark, *Loyalists in the Southern Campaign, Volume I*, pp. 187-188; Moultrie, *Memoirs, Vol. II*, p. 225; Bass, *Swamp Fox*, pp. 49-52; Hayes, *Saddlebag Almanac, Volume VII*, pp. 105-106; Draper, *Sumter Papers*

[585] Susan Twitty later married a soldier named John Miller. After her husband died she married the widowed William Graham

[586] Southern Studies Program, *Figures of the Revolution, Spartanburg,* p. 128; White, *The King's Mountain Men,* pp. 145-146; Barefoot, *Touring North Carolina's,* pp. 252-253

[587] Witherspoon's family all gave distinguished service in the Revolutionary War. His sons John and Gavin were captains. His other sons Robert and William were privates. His daughters married both the Ervins, who were Colonels in Marion's Brigade

[588] Southern Studies Program, *Figures of the Revolution, Spartanburg,* p. 347; Simms, *Francis Marion,* pp. 77-78

[589] Peckham, *The Toll of Independence,* p. 75

[590] Peckham, *The Toll of Independence,* p. 75

[591] Also known as Bickerstaff's or Cowan's Ford. Cane Creek is located in Burke County, near McDowell

[592] I don't know who Burwell or Grimes was in this statement, and most likely is bad information on the part of Chesney

[593] Due to this wound Dunlap was not in the action at King's Mountain

[594] Present-day Rutherfordton

[595] Boatner, *Encyclopedia,* pp. 180-181; Chesney, *Journal,* p. 7; Draper, *Kings Mountain,* pp. 147-149; White, *The King's Mountain Men,* p. 196; Johnson, *Memo of Occurrence;* Schenck, *North Carolina,* p. 126; Dennis Conrad, *The Papers of General Nathanael Greene,* (Model Editions Partnership, 1996), pp. 242-243; Allaire, *Diary*

[596] Also known as the White House or Garden Hill

[597] Captain Bugg was an officer in the 1st Georgia Regiment

[598] Captain Martin was one of the killed and Captain Bugg was one of the captured. Thirteen of the captured, including Captains Ashby and McCoy, were hanged by Brown after the battle

[599] Captain Johnston was among the killed

[600] The King's Rangers had originally been named the East Florida Rangers, but when they became a Provincial unit they changed their name. They are sometimes referred to as the King's Carolina Rangers, so as not to be confused by the northern Loyalist unit by the same name. The East Florida Rangers were initially organized as a rifle regiment. The King's Rangers had been issued cut down French and British muskets that were captured at Charlestown

---

[601] These New Jersey Volunteers were the sick and wounded men from the battle of Musgrove's Mill, who had been left behind to recuperate when the rest of the battalion marched on to Ninety-Six

[602] Davies, *Documents, Volume XVIII Transcripts 1780*, pp. 167-169; Olson, *Dr. David Ramsay*, pp. 260-261; Davis, *Georgia Citizens And Soldiers*, pp. 168-169; Tarleton, *History of the Campaigns*, pp. 161-163; Heitman, *Historical Register*, pp. 74-89, 131; White, *King's Mountain Men*, p. 156; Cashin, *King's Ranger*, p. 126; Clark, *Loyalists in the Southern Campaign, Volume I*, pp. 1-60; Moultrie, *Memoirs, Vol. II*, p. 238; Lee, *Revolutionary War Memoirs*, pp. 199-200; Johnson, *Memo of Occurrence*, p. 73; PRO, *Cornwallis Papers*, Volume 103, p. 4; PRO, *Audit Office*, Class 13, Volume 34, folio 357; Class 30, Volume 11, p. 103 folio 4; O'Donnell, *Southern Indians*, pp. 102-104; *Royal Georgia Gazette, September 28th, 1780*; William L. Clements Library, *George Wray Papers*, Volume 7, (University of Michigan); Davis, *Georgians in the Revolution*, p. 128

[603] Simms, *Francis Marion*, p. 78; PRO, *Cornwallis Papers*, Class 30, Volume 11, p. 3; Lambert, *South Carolina Loyalists*, p. 115; Bass, *Swamp Fox*, pp. 55-58; James, *Sketch* , p. 18

[604] Mounted riflemen

[605] Wauchope is pronounced "Walkup", but is known more commonly as Wahab in the accounts of the time. James Wauchope had been born in Belfast, Ireland in 1727, and after the war became the governor of North Carolina.

[606] Riflemen divided into two companies

[607] This is Davie's method of dealing with the enemy throughout his time as a partisan

[608] One of Davie's partisans was future President Andrew Jackson. Susannah Smart told Lyman Draper that when Jackson came by her house she asked how was the fight going. He told her that Davie was "popping them occasionally."

[609] Barnett was taken to his home in Charlotte to recover. While he was there the British occupied the town and wanted his house for their wounded. He was moved from his bedroom to the kitchen to make room for the British wounded. When the British doctor saw him lying on the table he asked him what was the matter. Barnett said that he was sick. The doctor examined him and told him that he wasn't sick, he was wounded. He replied, "What if I am?" The doctor let Barnett stay where he was, but

when the British left they took 100 head of cattle and pigs. While Barnett lay on the table he heard the British musicians "play a mournful air, and then took up their line of march with a lively tune and a quick step." He learned that they played the music when they had hanged one of their own soldiers for trying to desert to Davie. The British had also tried to plunder the home of a Mrs. Barrett. When they bridled her horse, she ran over and took it off. The British threatened to kill her; she merely told them that it was in their power to do so, but they would surely die afterwards. She saw that they were going to take a crock of milk, and she kicked it over. The British rushed upon her and threatened to cut her to pieces. She told them, "If you dare you will be shot at from every bush in the country." They knew that what she said was true, and left without the milk or the horse

[610] Thomas, *Dye is Cast*, pp. 31-32; Lee, *Revolutionary War Memoirs*, pp. 195-196; Schenck, *North Carolina*, p. 104; Robinson, *Revolutionary War Sketches*, pp. 21-23; Pancake, *This Destructive War*, pp. 84, 115-116; Hayes, *Saddlebag Almanac, January 2000, Volume VIII*, pp. 13-17; Draper, *Sumter Papers*

[611] Present-day Charlotte, also listed as Charlotteburgh in some accounts

[612] All of these units were mounted, like most western Carolina militia

[613] Major Hanger, Captains Campbell and McDonald were among the wounded

[614] The Legion infantry followed behind the cavalry, and was not with the other infantry units in the column

[615] Hanger, *The Life, Opinions and Adventures*; Thomas, *Dye is Cast*, pp. 33-34; Tarleton, *History of the Campaigns, pp.* 158-159; Kentucky Archives, *Kentucky Pension Accounts*; Lee, *Revolutionary War Memoirs*, pp. 196-197; Schenck, *North Carolina*, pp. 106-112; PRO, *Cornwallis Papers*, Class 30, Volume 11, p. 3; Robinson, *Revolutionary War Sketches*, pp. 24-26; Clark, *State Records of North Carolina, Vol. XIX - 1782 - '84,* pp. 958-959; Batt, *Maryland Continentals*, pp. 45-46; Hayes, *Saddlebag Almanac, January 1998, Volume VI*, pp. 93-94

[616] Colonel John Peasley is sometimes listed as Paisley

[617] Draper, *Sumter Papers*, 10VV169

[618] Shepherd's Ferry is currently located where US 41-51 crosses Black Mingo Creek on the Georgetown-Williamsburg county line

[619] Dollard's Tavern was also known as Red Tavern

[620] Simms, *The Life of Francis Marion*, pp. 78-80; Bass, *Swamp Fox*, pp. 59-67; Moss, *Roster of the South Carolina Patriots*, p. 577; James, *A Sketch of the Life*, p. 19

[621] Near Morganton

[622] The sheriff's name was Hedgspeth

[623] D. M. Furches, *A Leaf of History - A Reminiscence of the Revolutionary Battle of Shallow Ford*, (The Landmark, Statesville, NC, February 17, 1887); Walter Clark, *The State Records of North Carolina, Volumes XV - 1780*, (Winston, 1896), pp. 123-125; Clark, *The State Records of North Carolina, Volumes XIV- 1779-'80*, pp. 421, 429, 580-581, 667, 669, 675-676, 698-699, 692-693, 790; Clark, *The State Records of North Carolina, Volume XXII*, pp. 113-114

[624] Also known as McIntyre's Farm or Bradley's Farm. There are differing accounts on this action, that states it happened at Bradley's Farm, and not at McIntyre's Farm

[625] This may have been the Volunteer's of Ireland, since this was Doyle's Regiment

[626] In an 1820 letter Joseph Graham claims there were 450 British infantry, 60 cavalry, and 40 wagons, opposed by 14 locals

[627] Bradley was known as the strongest man in the county and was famous for his skill with a rifle

[628] Thomas, *Dye is Cast*, p. 35; Clark, *Loyalists in the Southern Campaign, Volume III*, p. 296; *Pennsylvania Packet, January 9, 1781*; Clark, *State Records of North Carolina, Vol. XIX - 1782 - '84*, pp. 968-969, 990; Barefoot, *Touring*, pp. 177, 179-180

[629] The nickname "Pet Tory" was given to Loyalists who were not a threat to the Patriot cause, and were easily coerced to inform on other Loyalists

[630] Saye, *McJunkin*

[631] Like most backwoods battles there was no over-all commander. William Campbell co-commanded the battle of King's Mountain, along with Benjamin Cleveland, Isaac Shelby and John Sevier

[632] It may seem that the officers almost number as many as the rank and file. An officer may have the title of colonel, but only have ten men with him. Aaron Guyton wrote "Sometimes we had four or five colonels, with from 50 to 150 men. Each of them had command of a regiment at home, sometimes not more than five of his men would be with him."

[633] Also listed as McColloch

[634] Also called Cleveland's Bulldogs, Cleveland's Devils and Cleveland's Heroes

[635] Robert Cleveland was the brother of Benjamin Cleveland. His company appears to have not been in the battle, but was left behind as "footmen" to follow the mounted troops as quick as they could

[636] All of this company, except six men, stayed behind at Green River

[637] Samuel Johnson's company was left behind as footmen. He went on without them and served as a lieutenant in Joel Lewis's company. During the battle he told his men to "Aim at the waistbands of their breeches, boys!"

[638] Cousin of Colonel McDowell

[639] Also known as the South Fork Boys

[640] Hambright was described as "a red headed, big faced, fair skinned, bow legged Dutchman"

[641] In reserves

[642] Brandon was described as a "rough knock down sort of man"

[643] Sometime after the battle of King's Mountain Stein "was stabbed to death while attempting to arrest a Tory" in Rowan County, North Carolina

[644] Colonel Hill had been "unable to ride without my arm in a sling, not being recovered from the wound I recd at the Hanging Rock." Lieutenant Colonel Hawthorne commanded his men in his absence

[645] Captain Anderson lost his leg in this battle

[646] Captain Williams was the 17 year old son of James Williams

[647] There was only a handful of Georgians in the battle, and these men were most likely Clarke's militia that had come north after the failed siege of McKay's Trading Post. Besides the officers mentioned in the order of battle, the Georgians were at King's Mountain were John Black, Henry Candler (son of William Candler), John Crawford, Timothy Duick, Ebenezer Fain, William Hammet, Richard Heard, James Patterson. John Rainey, John Torrence, Peter Strozier and Peter and Denis Tramel. John Rainey died of wounds on the farm of Jacob Randolph, where Colonel James Williams was buried

[648] John Clark was Elijah Clark's son

[649] William Hill wrote that the army consisted of 933 men mounted on the fleetest horses

[650] The killed included Colonel James Williams, Captains Robert Sevier and Mattocks, and all three Captain Edmondsons. The wounded included

Majors Porter, Anderson, and Gordon, Captains Minor Smith, Espey, Shelby, Lenoir and all three Lewis brothers, Micajah, Joel and James

[651] Ferguson was an officer in the 71st Regiment of Foot

[652] Also known as the Fair Forest Militia

[653] Also known as the Long Cane Militia. These men all had rifles

[654] Also known as the Stevens Creek Regiment

[655] Also known as the Spartan Militia

[656] Also known as the Little River Militia

[657] Also known as the Dutch Fork Militia

[658] Also known as the Stevens Creek Militia

[659] The killed included Majors Ferguson and Plummer. The wounded included Captains Biggerstaff and Larimore. All were captured. Nine men, including Colonel Mills and Captains Gilkey, Chitwood, and Wilson, were tried and hanged at Gilbert Town

[660] Present-day Elizabethtown, Tennessee

[661] There are many accounts as to what Ferguson was wearing and they describe him as wearing a light hunting shirt, a checked duster, or checked hunting shirt.

[662] Many romantic notions are made of the individualistic frontiersmen at this battle. In reality the backwoodsmen moved up the mountain in a common formation known as "open order." The men were commanded by their officers and moved according to the tactics of the day. The other misconception is that the Patriots all had rifles and the Loyalists were all carrying muskets. There were quite a few rifle carrying Loyalist militia in the ranks of Ferguson's force. These men were as good as the Patriot force, since they all came from the same Carolina settlements

[663] Plug bayonets are different than the standard socket bayonet used by the British army. A socket bayonet fits around the musket and allows the soldier to fire with the bayonet on the weapon. The plug bayonet fits into the barrel and does not allow the soldier to fire while it is in the barrel. Hill wrote that the men that could not get a bayonet were "contrived a substitute by getting the blacksmiths to make long knives to answer the purpose with a tang put in a piece of wood to fit the caliber of the gun & a button to rest on the muzzle of the piece"

[664] There were no British Regulars at King's Mountain, except Major Ferguson. These "Regulars" were the American Volunteers

[665] Loyalist Colonel Robert Gray wrote that the North Carolina Loyalists were not as disciplined as the South Carolina Loyalists, and they broke. "While they were communicating this disorder, Ferguson fell"

[666] This was either John Moore, or Patrick Moore

[667] William Hill wrote extensively on the cowardly and treacherous character of James Williams. In Hill's memoirs he devotes ten pages on how Williams tried to steal all their supplies, and how he attempted to get his men to go to South Carolina to plunder the Loyalists, while the rest of the army went to fight Ferguson. He also writes that Williams knew where Ferguson was, but he tried to lead the army away from fight. Hill states that Williams was probably killed "by some of the Americans, as many of them had been heard to promise on oath that they would do it when they had an opportunity." No other source mentions any of this and it seems to be fabricated, possibly due to some unresolved personal conflict between Hill and Williams

[668] Both of these stories are local legend, and most likely did not happen at all. There are no accounts of women roaming the battlefield by any of the participants at the time of the battle. When Draper did his interviews in the 19th century, stories of the British women were being "remembered". Ben Rowan told Draper he was "grazed on his temple, stunned and knocked down, but soon recovered. Said Ferguson's woman was greatly lamenting his fall, and relating how neatly she had dressed him that morning and Rowan did not console her by saying "Madam – we gave him the holy pocus"

[669] Loyalist descendants would eventually murder Carr in 1802

[670] Collins, *Revolutionary Soldier*, pp. 51-54; Heitman, *Historical Register,* pp. 89, 281; Chesney, *Journal,* pp. 8-10; White, *King's Mountain Men*, pp. 215, 237, 245, 249-255, 262, 266-267, 271, 273, 275, 277, 283-285, 288-289, 292, 340, 406, 416-424, 456-461, 464-465, 467, 470, 473-474-476, 481-483, Draper, *Kings Mountain*, pp. 139-245; Kentucky Archives, *Kentucky Pension Accounts*; Clark, *Loyalists in the Southern Campaign, Volume I*, pp. 221-341; Moultrie, *Memoirs, Vol. II*, pp. 242-245; Young, *Memoir*; Johnson, *Memo of Occurrence*, pp. 79-100; National Archives and Records Administration, *Mathew Sparks Pension File, #S31385,* (Washington, DC); Schenck, *North Carolina*, pp. 130-177; New York Historical Society, *Gates Papers*, Reel 12, (New York), p. 829; *The Pennsylvania Gazette, November 15, 1780; October 25, 1780;* DAR, *Roster of Soldiers*, pp. 28-50; Moss, *Roster of the South Carolina Patriots,*

pp. 54, 827, 850; Pension Applications, *RG 15, Microcopy 804*; Robinson, *Revolutionary War Sketches*, p. 35; PRO, *Cornwallis Papers*, Class 30, Volume 11, p. 3 folio 261-262; ; Lambert, *South Carolina Loyalists*, pp. 110-111, 144-147, 218-222; Ervin, *South Carolinians*, pp. 80-87; Mackenzie, *Strictures*, pp. 66-67; Morris, *Spirit of Seventy-Six*, pp. 1142-1143; Pancake, *This Destructive War*, pp. 116-121; Barefoot, *Touring* , pp. 217, 242, 245, 252-261, 268-269, 335; *Royal Gazette, February 24, 1781*; Sanchez-Saavedera, *Virginia Military Organizations*, pp. 143-144; *William Hill's Memoirs*; Graves, *James Williams*, p. 54; Draper, *Sumter Papers*, 4VV213-215, 9VV28-42, 14VV177-179

[671] *The Pennsylvania Gazette, November 1, 1780*; Coggins, *Ships and Seaman of the American Revolution*, pp. 72-73

[672] Furches, *A Leaf of History*; Clark, *State Records of North Carolina, Volumes XIV- 1779-'80*, pp. 421, 429, 580-581, 667, 669, 675-676, 698-699, 692-693, 790; *Volumes XV – 1780*, pp. 123-125; *Volume XXII*, pp. 113-114; Barefoot, *Touring*, pp. 334

[673] There was another skirmish around this time, but I have not been able to document where, or when. Benjamin Newton wrote in his pension "I was in an engagement against Colonel Tarleton in the Haw Fields, Orange County, No. Car. at Colonel Mebanes Lane, where Major Harris of Rocky River and No. Carolina had his hand cut off. I was a volunteer and went with my friend Major Harris to that engagement and the returned. I was in a small engagement with the British at Polks Mill when the enemy lay in Charlotte. I was under Captain John Clark and was wounded in the thigh by a British ball at the same Mills."

[674] Thomas, *Dye is Cast*, p. 35; Tarleton, *History of the Campaigns,* p. 160; Schenck, *North Carolina*, p. 114; Cary and McCance, *Regimental Records of the Royal Welch Fusiliers, Volume 1 & 2*, (Forster Groom and Company, LTD, 1921); *Pennsylvania Gazette, October 25, 1780*; Mackenzie, *Strictures*, pp. 54-55

[675] Jack Barnett told Lyman Draper there was only four Tories in all of Mecklenburg County.

[676] There are no contemporary accounts that have Cornwallis making this statement, and it first appears many years after the war. Most likely Cornwallis never actually said this.

[677] Blythe, *Hornet's Nest*, pp. 7, 8; Tarleton, *History of the Campaigns,* pp. 166-168; Draper, *Kings Mountain*, pp. 370-371; Moultrie, *Memoirs, Vol.*

II, pp. 246-247; Schenck, *North Carolina*, pp. 180-181; Robinson, *Revolutionary War Sketches*, pp. 26-27; Draper, *Sumter Papers*

[678] Schenck, *North Carolina*, pp. 128-129

[679] Captain Parris was one of the wounded

[680] Captain Burke and Bryan were killed, and Captain Lakey was wounded

[681] Furches, *Leaf of History*; *Pennsylvania Gazette, November 8, 1780*; Clark, *State Records of North Carolina, Volumes XIV- 1779-'80*, pp. 421, 429, 580-581, 667-676, 692-693, 698-790; *Volumes XV – 1780*, pp. 123-125; *Volume XXII*, pp. 113-114; Barefoot, *Touring*, pp. 323-324; Draper, *Sumter Papers*, 10VV169

[682] Clark, *Loyalists, Volume I*, p. 101; Lambert, *Loyalists*, p. 115; Bass, *Swamp Fox*, p. 105

[683] Also known as Tarcote, Turncoat Swamp, or Pee Dee Swamp

[684] All of the officers here did not have a company, but they were in the skirmish. There is not enough information to determine exactly how the men were organized

[685] Possibly James Bonneau, sometimes pronounced Bone

[686] Possibly Thomas Mitchell, aide de camp and nephew to Francis Marion

[687] Simms, *Life of Francis Marion*, pp. 80-82; Clark, *Loyalists in the Southern Campaign, Volume I*, p. 151; Bass, *Swamp Fox*, pp. 75-77; James, *Sketch of the Life*, p. 19

[688] This action is listed as having happened in either the fall of 1779 or 1780. I placed it in October 1780 due to the time of Cornwallis's expedition into North Carolina, but there is no definite date of when it occurred

[689] William Dickson, *Duplin County History to 1810*, (The North Carolina Historical Review, 1928)

[690] Moss, *Roster of the South Carolina Patriots*, p. 854; Peckham, *The Toll of Independence*, p. 76

[691] Kell, *North Carolina's Coastal Carteret County*, p. 69

[692] Supposedly Tarleton said that he dug up Richardson to look upon the face of a brave man. Richardson's wife was Dorothy Sinkler

[693] According to some historians, Marion received his nickname "The Swamp Fox" at this time from Tarleton. When Tarleton was given a new mission of finding Sumter's force, Tarleton supposedly stated, "Let us go back and we will find the Gamecock, but as for this damned old fox, the devil himself could not catch him!" However this is not mentioned in Tarleton's book or letters. The name "Swamp Fox" does not appear in any

writings of the time, and first appears in 1821 in William Dobein James's book "A Sketch of the Life of BRIG. GEN. FRANCIS MARION". James is also the first one to mention that Sumter's nickname was "The Gamecock"

[694] Lorenzo Sabine, *Biographical Sketches of Loyalists of the American Revolution, Volume 1*, (Baltimore, 1994), p. 569; Sabine, *Biographical Sketches, Volume 2*, p. 58; Tarleton, *History of the Campaigns,* pp. 171-173; Simms, *Life of Francis Marion*, pp. 84-85; Clark, *Loyalists in the Southern Campaign, Volume I*, pp. 101-102; *Volume II*, pp. 197-246; Bass, *Swamp Fox*, pp. 78-84; James, *Sketch of the Life*, pp. 19-20

[695] A piggin is "a small pail, especially a wooden one with one stave longer than the rest serving as a handle"

[696] Draper, *Sumter Papers*

[697] Fishdam Ford is currently located where SC 72-121 crosses the Broad River. The old Indian fish dam that it is named for still exists a short distance north of the highway bridge

[698] John Winn had been the lieutenant colonel of the Fairfield Regiment in 1779, but he had been reduced in rank for some unknown reason

[699] Captain Stephen Carr was among the wounded. Winn wrote that Carr was the only casualty when he was wounded, then he crossed the river and died of exposure on the riverbank. Sumter gave a higher number of casualties

[700] Also listed as Stirke

[701] Mounted as cavalry

[702] S. Hopkins said that there was "seven killed on the ground & four died of their wounds that evening." Major Wemyss and Lieutenant Hovenden were among the wounded. The South Carolina Royal Gazette wrote, "Our loss upon this occasion was 1 Sergeant and 5 rank & file killed, and besides the Major, 1 Sergeant and 15 rank & file wounded.

[703] Sumter said that he lost his cocked hat and five feathers at Fishdam Ford, but he picked up an old hat, torn in the rim

[704] Colonel Taylor always thought that the British surgeon had done this on purpose, so that he could kill Captain Taylor and infect all of Sumter's men.

[705] Samuel C. Williams, *General Richard Winn's Notes – 1780*, (The South Carolina Historical and Genealogical Magazine, Volume XLIV, Number 1, January 1943), pp. 2-4; Tarleton, *History of the Campaigns,* pp. 200-201; White, *King's Mountain Men*, p. 185; Moultrie, *Memoirs, Vol. II*, pp. 248-

249; Lee, *Revolutionary War Memoirs*, pp. 204-205; PRO, *Cornwallis Papers*, Class 30, Volume 11, p. 82 folio 15-16, 28; Moss, *Roster*, pp. 4, 12, 149, 1005; Robinson, *Revolutionary War Sketches*, pp. 28-30; Ervin, *South Carolinians*, pp. 80-87; Hayes, *Saddlebag Almanac, Volume VIII*, pp. 21-24; PRO, *War Office, List of Officers*, p. 137; *William Hill's Memoirs*; Saye, *McJunkin*; Draper, *Sumter Papers*, 12VV276-278

[706] Barefoot, *Touring*, pp. 177-178

[707] Chesney, *Journal*

[708] Ashton's Plantation was also known as The Pens

[709] In South Carolina inland swamps are called "bays"

[710] Southern Studies Program, *Figures of the Revolution, Spartanburg*, p. 272; Simms, *Life of Francis Marion*, pp. 90-93; Bass, *Swamp Fox*, pp. 87-92; James, *A Sketch of the Life*, p. 21

[711] Also known as Shirar's Ferry

[712] William Blackstock was about 80 years old when the battle happened on his farm. He was "a large, stout Irishman" who sided with the King during the war. L. Miles wrote "When the British and Torys camped at his house or nearby, he used to pilot them to my father's to rob & plunder. I have heard my mother say the only way she could keep anything to eat was to put it in a jar in the jamb of the house, & cover it with ashes." Both of Blackstock's sons were in the Patriot militia. One of his sons, Captain William Blackstock, was not at the battle, but was with Roebuck's militia

[713] Williams, *Winn's Notes*, (January 1943), pp. 4-5; Tarleton, *History of the Campaigns*, pp. 174-176; Clark, *Loyalists in the Southern Campaign, Volume II*, pp. 197-246; Hayes, *Saddlebag Almanac, Volume VIII*, pp. 25-26; Draper, *Sumter Papers*, 5VV91-94, 16VV210-212

[714] Also known as Blackstock's Ford or Tyger River. The battlefield at Blackstocks is located on the south bank of the Tyger River in Union County, a half a mile from the Spartanburg County line

[715] Colonel William Hill wrote the "Americans did not exceed 600 and many of that number very indifferently armed." He thought Tarleton had "1,200 horse and infantry together with a field piece" but his numbers are high. Charles Jones said that Sumter had 420 militia in the battle and Thomas Charlton agrees, and said that a return of Major Jackson listed 420 militia

[716] Hill wrote that there were only two killed, and Sumter was severely wounded. Hill was also wounded. Captain John Nixon was described as being "killed in a skirmish against the Tories in Newberry District" on

November 20th, 1780. Though no one mentions Nixon being killed at Blackstocks, it is most likely the location of his death

[717] The 71st had two companies of mounted soldiers that were in the battle with the mounted soldiers of the 63rd Regiment. The rest of the 71st Highlanders, about 250 men and an artillery piece, arrived at the end of the battle and did not get into the action.

[718] Captain Hovenden had been the commander of the Philadelphia Light Dragoons in January 1778. His troops were later absorbed into the British Legion

[719] Captain Jacob James was a resident of Goshon Township, Chester County, Pennsylvania. He joined the British as a guide the day after the Battle of Brandywine on September 13, 1777. He commanded an independent troop of cavalry, the Chester County Light Dragoons, in February 1778. His troops were later absorbed into the British Legion. He was captured by the *Columbia* of South Carolina while on board one of the troop transports that sailed to Savannah, Georgia in 1779. He was a prisoner in North Carolina in April 1780

[720] Lieutenant Skinner was attached from the 16th Regiment's light infantry company

[721] William White, one of Sumter's men, wrote, "God, we put 200 of them out of their saddles." Charles Jones wrote, "The British lost in killed 92 and upwards of 100 wounded. Nehemiah Blackstock, who was a boy at the time, wrote that he had nine plots on the Blackstock property, "containing 81 dead British". Myddleton wrote, within days of the battle, that the British "left 92 dead and 100 wounded upon the field"

[722] This is one of many different versions of how Sumter was warned. Draper wrote, "General Sumter and Negro Tom spoke of a woman arriving and giving information – thinks it was Mrs. Dillon". Nehemiah Blackstock said that Sumter had several female scouts; they were "Mrs. Martindale, the wife of Genl Martindale...Miss Mary Musgrove... and Miss Sally Blackstock". Elizabeth Ellet wrote "Sergeant Rowan and Mr. Hannah of York were sent back by Sumter to reconnoiter Tarleton's movements. They were under the inspiration of a good draught of whisky and waylaid a couple of British officers in advance, killing them – Rowan returning and getting the sword from one of them, then returning to Sumter."

[723] Alexander Bradley told Draper that Sealy was killed at Fishdam Ford "by the British in the melee, mistaken for Sumter's men"

[724] Though Farr was a colonel, he did not command, and acted as a volunteer rifleman. He did the same thing at the Battle of the Cowpens a few months later

[725] Golding Tinsley was the man who shot Money. Joseph Hart said that Tinsley told him "Several of the boys had shot at him. At length I told them to give me a crack. He was on an Excellently trained horse, which kept moving backwards and forwards across an opening in the woods in front of us. As he passed this time, I fired, and he fell from his horse." The grandson of Tinsley was told that Money remained on the battlefield. "When they went down to where he lay one of them pulled out pulled out of his pocket a fine gold watch and presented it to my father and said he was entitled to it and his reply was he had no use for it."

[726] Samuel Morrow wrote that when Sumter was wounded Lacey took command. Sumter's son, Thomas, wrote that Dr. Robert Brownfield cut out the bullet with a case knife

[727] Samuel Walker was in Colonel Bratton's regiment during the battle, and wrote in his pension application "Gen. Sumpter was wounded in the shoulder and had it not been for Col. Hill, we would have taken every person there. He behaved so cowardly that he had his side arms taken from him and a wooden stick placed in the scabbard." However Walker does not give any details on Colonel Hill's actions, and it seems that Winn's actions might have carried the battle. Charles Jones, a Georgian, said that the battle was won due to the efforts of Twiggs and Jackson

[728] Morrow told Draper that he left behind a hat, shirt, overalls, shot bag and rifle, and he was barefoot during the battle

[729] Nettles was an officer of the Catawba Indians, and an interpreter for Sumter's partisans

[730] Davies, *Documents, Volume XVIII Transcripts 1780*, pp. 246-247; Boatner, *Encyclopedia*, pp. 78-80; Williams, *Winn's Notes*, (January 1943), pp. 4-8; Tarleton, *History of the Campaigns*, pp. 176-179, 205; Johnson, *Memo of Occurrence*, pp. 309-310; White, *King's Mountain Men*, pp. 181-182, 185, 188; Clark, *Loyalists in the Southern Campaign, Volume II*, pp. 197-246; Moultrie, *Memoirs, Vol. II*, p. 249; Lee, *Revolutionary War Memoirs*, pp. 205-207; NARA, *Samuel Walker Pension File #S3448*; *Pennsylvania Gazette, January 3, 1781*; PRO, *Cornwallis Papers*, Class 30, Volume 11, p. 4 folio 366; Moss, *Roster of the South Carolina Patriots*, pp. 4-5, 11-12, 408, 447; Ervin, *South Carolinians*, pp. 80-87; Mackenzie, *Strictures*, p. 74; Hayes, *Saddlebag Almanac, January 2000*,

Volume VIII, pp. 25-29; PRO, *War Office, A List of all the Officers of the Army*, pp. 86, 137; *William Hill's Memoirs*; Saye, *McJunkin*; Draper, *Sumter Papers*, 5VV75-76, 91-96, 115-117, 125, 141-143, 9VV28-42, 11VV316-321, 509-519, 526-529, 15VV91, 16VV214-216, 337

[731] Also known as Hoil's Old Place

[732] In the Sumter Papers Samuel Morrow writes that after the battle at Blackstocks he was with a detachment that defeated a small party of Tories. It may have been this skirmish. Morrow also wrote that on another occasion they were able to get into the rear of the British columns while they were marching, and capture "Two Regular Captains and a Lieutenant" along with a detachment of infantry. I do not know where or when this incident happened

[733] Moss, *Roster of the South Carolina Patriots*, pp. 408, 594; Lipscomb, *Revolutionary Battles Part Ten*, p. 12; Hayes, *The Saddlebag Almanac, January 2000, Volume VIII*, p. 35

[734] Draper, *Sumter Papers*, 4VV12-13

[735] Captain Robert Wilson wrote that this skirmish happened before the battle at Blackstock's

[736] Captain John McCool, of Brandon's regiment

[737] I don't know which Fanning this is. It may be Edmund Fanning, since David Fanning was only a captain at the time

[738] Daniel McJunkin was the brother of Major Joseph McJunkin, who had been wounded through the chest with a bayonet at Brandon's defeat

[739] Draper, *Sumter Papers*, 7VV135, 11VV459; Moss, *Roster of the South Carolina Patriots*, pp. 606, 630

[740] Rugeley's Fort was located at the present day fork of Grannies Quarter and Flat Rock Creek in Kershaw County, west of S-28-58 and north of S-28-40

[741] Captain Kirkwood's Orderly Book has this action taking place on November 28th

[742] Their uniform was a blue coat with red facings, and may have been the French Lottery coats of 1778

[743] Tarleton, *History of the Campaigns,* p. 182; Simms, *Life of Francis Marion*, p. 109; Clark, *Loyalists in the Southern Campaign, Volume I*, p. 147; Moultrie, *Memoirs, Vol. II*, pp. 247-248; Lee, *Revolutionary War Memoirs*, pp. 221-222; Kirkwood, *Journal*, pp. 12-13; *The Pennsylvania Gazette, January 3, 1781*; Lambert, *South Carolina Loyalists*, p. 117;

Hayes, *Saddlebag Almanac, Volume VIII*, pp. 30-33; Johnson, *Sketches of the Life*, pp. 508-509; Draper, *Sumter Papers*

[744] After the war Tynes and Sumter became partners in merchandizing near Land's Ford. Tynes died of a fever in 1795. Draper wrote "The people thought well of him."

[745] *Marion's Orderly Book*; Simms, *The Life of Francis Marion*, pp. 100-101; Bass, *Swamp Fox*, pp. 105-107

[746] Draper wrote that Blue Parties in the German Wars were those men who would go out without orders of proper officers and they were hanged whenever they were found

[747] Simms, *Life of Francis Marion*, pp. 94-95; James, *A Sketch of the Life*, p. 22; Draper, *Sumter Papers*, 3VV58-63

[748] Also known as Boyd Creek

[749] Colonel Campbell lists this action as happening on December 16th

[750] White, *King's Mountain Men*, pp. 176, 182, 189, 206, 224; *Pennsylvania Gazette, February 28, 1781*; Dann, *Revolution Remembered*, pp. 307-309; O'Donnell, *Southern Indians*, pp. 107-108

[751] Reverend J. D. Bailey, *History of Grindal Shoals and Some Early Adjacent Families*, 1900, pp. 75-83

[752] Another source states that the battle happened on December 4th. Draper wrote that it happened on December 11th

[753] Captain Carr was mortally wounded

[754] James Dunlap may have not been there, due to his wounds received at Cane Creek

[755] Lindsay recovered from this wound and was "compensated for the loss of his right hand by covering it with an ornamental silver bandage. From this Lindsay became known as "Old Silver Fist"

[756] Davis, *Georgians*, p. 128; Tarleton, *History of the Campaigns,* p. 183; Clark, *Loyalists in the Southern Campaign, Volume III*, pp. 125-175; PRO, *Cornwallis Papers*, Class 30, Volume 103, pp. 335-336; *Ruddiman's Weekly Mercury, 28 February 1781*; Hayes, *Saddlebag Almanac, Volume VIII*, pp. 36-37

[757] Halfway Swamp is currently in Clarendon County where the Poinsett State Park is located

[758] Captain Kelly was among the wounded

[759] Joseph Gaston thought that the smallpox that spread through the Carolinas was a British plot to use the virus in biological warfare. He

wrote "The Tories brought the small pox from the British camp and scattered it among the people."

[760] One account states that the British army cashiered McLeroth because he did not burn down the area, however this is not true since he was promoted to lieutenant colonel of the 57th Regiment

[761] *Francis Marion's Orderly Book*; Simms, *Life of Francis Marion*, pp. 120-124; Ervin, *South Carolinians*, pp. 67-77; Bass, *Swamp Fox*, pp. 95-99, 107-111; James, *Sketch of the Life,* pp. 30-31; Draper, *Sumter Papers*

[762] Present-day Newberry County

[763] Clark, *Loyalists in the Southern Campaign, Volume I*, pp. 233, 296, 491; Moss, *Roster of the South Carolina Patriots*, pp. 77, 156, 300, 421; Lipscomb, *South Carolina Revolutionary Battles, Part Ten*, p. 13

[764] Draper, *Sumter Papers*

[765] *Pennsylvania Gazette, February 28, 1781*; Dann, *Revolution Remembered*, pp. 308-309; O'Donnell, *Southern Indians*, pp. 107-108

[766] Simcoe, *Journal*, pp. 241-242; Clark, *Loyalists in the Southern Campaign, Volume II*, p. 510; *Volume III*, pp. 61-124; PRO, *Cornwallis Papers*, Class 30, Volume 11, p. 83 folio 63-64; Bass, *Swamp Fox*, pp. 132, 135-137; James, *Sketch of the Life,* p. 29

[767] Clark, *Loyalists in the Southern Campaign, Volume III*, p. 131

[768] There is a version of this story has been distorted due to the fabrications of Weems and his fictional account of Marion's life in "The Life of General Francis Marion". Weems wrote that Horry's horsemen chased the outnumbered British cavalry into Georgetown, where there was a large British garrison. Major Ganey's Loyalists dashed out to meet Horry's dragoons, who did not slow down their pursuit. Horry found himself alone in a section of woods, when he came across Captain Lewis, one of Ganey's men. Horry was only armed with a small sword, but Lewis had a musket. Lewis fired, hitting Horry's horse and knocking Horry from the saddle. As Lewis fired his musket at Horry, a shot from the woods knocked him from his horse. A boy named Gwin, who had been watching the fight from the woods, had killed Lewis. Weems used the incident that happened on 15 November, at White's Plantation, where "Otterskin" Lewis was wounded, as the basis for this story. Weems continued by telling how Ganey suspected an ambush and had his men turn and run back to the safety of Georgetown. With Horry was Sergeant McDonald, who chased Major Ganey for two miles on his horse Fox, until McDonald had almost caught up to him. McDonald was one of the Maryland Continentals that Marion

rescued from the British. Instead of going back to the Maryland Line, he stayed with Marion. Weems wrote that a rich Tory gave McDonald a horse called *Selim*, when McDonald fooled the Tory into thinking that he was British. This is another incorrect statement from Weems. Peter Horry wrote, "This Horses Name was Fox. McDonald was a private man. A Scotch Man." Weems continued with the Georgetown story, when he wrote that one of Ganey's men threw himself in the way, but McDonald fired his carbine at the man. Realizing that the carbine was unloaded, and he couldn't reach him with his sword, he took his musket and speared Ganey in the back and out through the chest with his bayonet. When McDonald attempted to free the weapon, the bayonet remained in Ganey. Ganey rode up to the redoubts, blood streaming from his wounds, screaming and clawing at his side. Ganey amazingly recovered from his wounds. Horry wrote that Weems had it wrong again, and in this action it was Sergeant Cryer and not McDonald, who was on this raid. He also wrote that no British were killed, and sixteen were captured. Only Cornet Merrit and a sergeant escaped. Unfortunately most of Marion's history has been obscured by the sensational fiction of Weems, and even today there are historical highway markers in Georgetown, South Carolina, that repeat this fantasy of Weems

[769] Salley, *Horry's Notes*, p. 121; Simcoe, *Journal*, pp. 243-244; Simms, *Life of Francis Marion*, pp. 90-92, 119-120; Clark, *Loyalists in the Southern Campaign, Volume I*, p. 187; *Volume II*, p. 510; Bass, *Swamp Fox*, pp. 120-123; James, *Sketch of the Life*, pp. 29-30

[770] *Pennsylvania Gazette, February 28, 1781*; Dann, *Revolution Remembered*, pp. 308-309; O'Donnell, *Southern Indians*, pp. 107-108

[771] The present location for Hammond's Store is three miles southwest of Clinton, very close to Oakland Mill

[772] This may have been Captain Joseph McJunkin. He told Draper that he "conducted Colonel Washington to Hammond's Old Store and defeated the Tories"

[773] Thomas Waters had been quartermaster in 1767 with the Georgia Provincial Rangers. In 1773 Governor Wright again raised the Georgia Rangers until 1774 to enforce land sale in the Ceded Lands of Wilkes County. Waters was a Lieutenant in this unit. He loaned money to families that settled in Wilkes County, and he had one of the first plantations that contained a fort, a blacksmith shop and a mill. McJunkin disagrees with most historians and wrote that Waters was not the

commander, but the Loyalists "were commanded by a Col. Pearson and Major Ben Wofford"

[774] Edwin C. Bearss, *Battle of Cowpens*, (The Overmountain Press, 1996), pp. 3-4; Seymour, *Journal*, p. 11; White, *King's Mountain Men*, p. 185; Moultrie, *Memoirs, Vol. II*, pp. 252-253; Young, *Memoir*; Pension Applications, *RG 15, Microcopy 804*; Batt, *Maryland Continentals*, p. 72; Saye, *McJunkin*

[775] Also known as Mud Lick, Mount Pleasant or Williams' Plantation.

[776] McJunkin wrote that Cornet Simmons had 11 men and the militia had 25 men

[777] Also known as the Little River Militia

[778] Captain William Cunningham was not related to General Cunningham. When he escaped this fight, he stayed in the backcountry and would become known as "Bloody Bill" Cunningham

[779] Garden, *Anecdotes*, pp. 441-442; Boatner, *Encyclopedia*, pp. 481-482; Clark, *Loyalists, Volume I*, pp. 221-341; Pension Applications, *RG 15, Microcopy 804*; Lambert, *South Carolina Loyalists*, p. 207; Ward, *Delaware Continentals*, p. 371; Hayes, *Saddlebag Almanac, Volume VIII*, pp. 39-40; Graves, *James Williams*, p. 55; Draper, *Sumter Papers*

[780] Lookout Town was located near present-day Tiftonia, Tennessee. Crow Town was near Stevenson, Alabama. Long Island was near Bridgeport, Alabama. Runningwater was near Haletown, Tennessee, and Nickajack was near present-day Shellmound, Tennessee

[781] *Pennsylvania Gazette, February 28, 1781*; Dann, *Revolution Remembered*, pp. 308-309; O'Donnell, *Southern Indians*, pp. 107-108

Lightning Source UK Ltd.
Milton Keynes UK
UKOW03f0640280317
297682UK00001B/17/P